Logics of Organization Theory

Logics of Organization Theory

Audiences, Codes, and Ecologies

Michael T. Hannan
László Pólos
Glenn R. Carroll

PRINCETON UNIVERSITY PRESS
PRINCETON AND OXFORD

Published by Princeton University Press
41 William Street, Princeton, New Jersey 08540

In the United Kingdom: Princeton University Press
3 Market Place, Woodstock, Oxfordshire OX20 1SY

Library of Congress Cataloging-in-Publication Data

Hannan, Michael T.
Logics of organization theory : audiences, codes, and ecologies / Michael T. Hannan, László Pólos, Glenn R. Carroll.
p. cm.
Includes bibliographical references and index.
ISBN-13: 978-0-691-13106-1 (alk. paper)
ISBN-13: 978-0-691-13450-5 (pbk.: alk. paper)
1. Organizational sociology–Methodology. 2. Nonmonotonic reasoning. 3. Categories (Philosophy) I. Pólos, László. II. Carroll, Glenn. III. Title.

HM711.H36 2007
302.3′501–dc22 2006052862

British Library Cataloging-in-Publication Data is available

This book has been composed in Times-Roman in LaTeX

The publisher would like to acknowledge the authors of this volume for providing the camera-ready copy from which this book was printed.

Printed on acid-free paper. ∞

press.princeton.edu

Printed in the United States of America

10 9 8 7 6 5 4 3 2 1

To

Stephanie Olzak Hannan

Márton Kristóf, Bálint László,
Áron Gergely, and Dorottya Ilona Pólos

Lishan Nan Carroll

Contents

Preface

In Molière's *Le Bourgeois Gentilhomme,* Monsieur Jourdan, on learning from the philosophy teacher the distinction between prose and poetry and that all speech is one or the other, reacts: "Good Heavens! For more than forty years I have been speaking prose without knowing it."

Sociologists and other social scientists might react similarly to the main message of this book. Like Moliere's teacher, we point out that sociological theorists rely almost exclusively on a particular kind of logic—classical predicate (or first-order) logic—and its foundational set theory. This logic and set theory, usually operating in the background, comprise the standards that we almost all learned in high school. But we claim that, given current conceptual and empirical practice, first-order logic and its associated set theory seldom serve as good cornerstones for sociological theory. In reaction, we expect that many social scientists will be surprised even to learn that there is more than one kind of logic, and perhaps, that there is more than one kind of set theory.[1]

Yet, in this book, we (a pair of sociologists and a logician, turned at least half-sociologist) propose that the standard language of theory needs to be rethought to meet the challenges posed by sociological analysis. First-order logic imposes the formidable constraint that premises in arguments be stated as universal truths; and the associated set theory requires that all relevant objects be either (fully) in or (fully) out of sets, with no shades of membership allowed between these extremes. We argue that these constraints can be loosened and the language of theory can be linked more tightly to actual sociological practice if we adopt an alternative approach based on a nonmonotonic logic and fuzzy-set theory.

This book reports an extended application that we undertook to explore the potential value of this approach. Precisely, we attempted to reconstruct and integrate "fragments" of one well-developed line of sociological theory: organizational ecology. Despite what some might regard as its narrow focus, this effort raises general issues about strategies for building sociological theories. We think that the lessons from this work might illuminate some of the difficulties of building and integrating sociological theories; we further suggest the exercise demonstrates the value of making changes to the standard theory-building strategies.

To wit, we argue below that formalizing sociological arguments typically faces three complications: (1) available knowledge about the relevant causal processes is partial; (2) the processes involved are inherently stochastic; and (3) the boundaries

[1]Even the grammar-checking tools of popular word-processing software object to the plural use of the word logic.

around the social units are fuzzy. While these issues arise in our substantive application, we believe that they occur frequently—perhaps generally—in the social sciences.

Because we found that the standard formal languages do not deal adequately with the challenges presented by these three complications, we set out to construct a more appropriate language. This new language is designed to deal with systematic reasoning about arguments that contain properties of partiality and fuzziness.

Partiality implies that some of the causal claims of the argument are given as rules with exceptions. (In this context, "exception" does not refer to stochastic variation; exceptions involve deviations from general patterns in the underlying probability distributions, as we explain below.)

Vagueness implies that some basic concepts in arguments lack sharp boundaries and should thus be regarded as fuzzy. We suggest that social codes, including those that specify organizational categories such as "labor union," "organic farm," and "hedge fund," arise when audience members come to partial agreement about the memberships of various individual objects (organizations or products) in these categories. Audience members can differ in the extent to which they participate in a consensus (memberships in audiences can be partial); and organizations can differ in their degree of membership in categories (memberships in categories can be partial).

We realize that making changes so deep in the theoretical core of a discipline is not a step to be taken lightly. We also fully recognize that new complications will likely arise if multiple logics—some with perhaps unsettling properties—are deployed. Nevertheless, we argue that the basic approach requires rethinking for two important reasons. First, research has shown that some important sociological concepts (such as identity, legitimation, and authority) lack sharp boundaries. Representing such sociological concepts as crisp, unambiguous sets glosses over an interesting and important property. Second, bridging theory and evidence in sociology proves problematic because, for most areas of intensive study, coexistence of conflicting arguments and empirical findings appears to be the norm. Resolving such conflicts in the standard (classical first-order) logic requires that some arguments and bodies of evidence be ignored or discounted. But which, and on what basis?

The approach that we propose offers a systematic way to reason about sociological arguments that contain rules with exceptions and apply to agents whose concepts lack sharp boundaries. That is, it points to a different mode of theory construction. Using this approach in the book, we believe that we have succeeded in rebuilding key fragments in organizational ecology. Moreover, we think that we were able to do so in a unified way whereby certain core concepts and arguments build on each other in modular fashion.

Although we are mainly concerned with developing sociological theory, we draw on concepts and techniques from a diverse array of disciplines, including cognitive anthropology, cognitive psychology, linguistics, logic, mathematics, and philosophy. We hope that these strategic moves will encourage other sociologists to pursue these openings and will also serve as an invitation to scholars in these other disciplines to contribute to the development of sociological theory.

ACKNOWLEDGMENTS

We are grateful to the Stanford Graduate School of Business, the Durham Business School, and the Netherlands Institute for Advanced Study for providing financial support for this work.

We have benefited from the advice, criticism, and encouragement of a large number of colleagues. Greta Hsu collaborated in our work on organizational identity (and is a coauthor of Chapter 5) and provided valuable comments on the rest of the book. The extremely detailed and incisive criticism of Ezra Zuckerman convinced us to reorient and reorganize the book. Very helpful detailed reactions resulting from careful readings of the entire manuscript were offered by Elizabeth Pontikes, Balazs Kovacs, Martin Ruef, Olav Sorenson, and Jarrett Spiro. We also received valuable suggestions from Bill Barnett, Jerker Denrell, Stanislav Dobrev, Peter Hedstrom, Özgecan Koçak, Gaël Le Mens, Susan Olzak, Salih Ozdemir, Huggy Rao, Jesper Sørensen, and Deborah Yue.

We thank the publishers for permission to reproduce and adapt portions of the following copyrighted articles: Michael T. Hannan "Rethinking age dependence in organizational mortality: Logical formalizations." *American Journal of Sociology* (1998) 104:85–123; László Pólos and Michael T. Hannan. "Reasoning with partial knowledge." *Sociological Methodology* (2002) 32:133–81; László Pólos, Michael T. Hannan, and Glenn R. Carroll. "Foundations of a theory of social forms." *Industrial and Corporate Change* (2002) 11:85–115; Michael T. Hannan, Glenn R. Carroll, and László Pólos. "The organizational niche." *Sociological Theory* (2003) 21:309–40; Michael T. Hannan, László Pólos, and Glenn R. Carroll. "Cascading organizational change." *Organization Science* (2003) 14:463–82; Michael T. Hannan, László Pólos, and Glenn R. Carroll. "The fog of change: Opacity and asperity in organizations." *Administrative Science Quarterly* (2003) 48:399–432; László Pólos and Michael T. Hannan. "A logic for theories in flux: A model-theoretic approach." *Logique et Analyse* (2004) 47:85–121; and Greta Hsu and Michael T. Hannan. "Identities, genres, and organizational forms." *Organization Science* (2005) 16:474–90.

Logics of Organization Theory

Chapter One

Language Matters

Sociological theorists rarely give explicit attention to the language used in formulating arguments and drawing conclusions. We argue that attention ought to be paid to the choice of a theoretical language. This chapter discusses such language matters; and it also argues that choice of a language matters for what a theory can express and whether (and how) it can unify fragmentary knowledge.

1.1 LANGUAGES FOR THEORY BUILDING

Sociological theories can be built and arguments can be unified without any special tools or methodologies. However, we believe that attempts in this direction face daunting challenges. The essential problem lies with language, with the natural language used in most sociological theory.

Natural languages such as English and Hungarian are less-than-perfect tools for eliminating ambiguity in the claims that one might wish to make. In fact, ambiguity normally comes in two varieties.

Lexical ambiguity. Although technical terms might be defined formally, the choice of words used in expressing their meanings brings about associations that soon generate deviations from the initial definitions. Such deviations lead, in turn, to ambiguities. We describe such ambiguity in detail in analyzing the concept of niche in Chapter 8.

Structural ambiguity. Even when a language is freed from lexical ambiguities, and it "sounds" like the language of first-order logic, there is still room for structural ambiguity. For example, the sentence "There is a period of endowment for all organizations" can be interpreted in two ways. According to one reading, the endowment period is the same for all organizations; a second, more liberal, reading allows for different periods of endowments for the different organizations. In Chapter 7, we make clear that the choice between these readings matters for the explanatory power of the theory, so that it should be settled prior to implementing a formal approach.

As a result of such ambiguities, theoretical arguments in natural language admit multiple interpretations. Historians of classical sociological theory have written hundreds of papers on what Weber, Durkheim, or Marx really meant in certain passages. Such very close study of the passages does not appear to yield agreement on the interpretations of the sociological classics. The situation does not appear to differ for contemporary theories, which suggests that the natural-language statements are not getting any clearer.

Such unavoidable ambiguity makes it very hard to analyze complicated arguments in a natural language. Questions inevitably arise about whether some combination of premises does or does not warrant a given claim (or yield some inconsistency). It is notoriously hard to reason about the implications of complex structures stated in natural language. The chances of success in building coherent theories run higher if the arguments are stated in some kind of formal language. This is the strategy that we follow.

Success in efforts at formalization depends critically on issues of interpretation and translation. Translation from natural languages to constructed (artificial) languages is far from automatic. Introductory courses and texts in logic seek to train students in making consistent translations of indicative sentences, sentences that state facts (e.g., "Durham University is an organization"). Once students have learned the rules of this game, they are confronted with more complicated indicative sentences, e.g., "Every organization faces a competitor," whose translation requires learning the mysteries of quantification. But even the initiation into these mysteries leaves some problems unsolved. Translating indicative natural-language sentences to a logical language has to clear the hurdles posed by lexical and structural ambiguities. In other words, the sentences have to be interpreted. Formal languages are designed to rule out lexical and structural ambiguities; but the evolution of natural languages did not follow such guidelines.

Sometimes the logical structure of claims in a natural language appears on the surface; but often it is hidden. "Every person has a mother" indicates a quantificational structure on the surface. But "Men are mortal" does not. Both sentences have a conditional nature; but the conditionality is not always given on the linguistic surface by typical expressions such as "if . . . , then . . . " Although a course in (first-order) logic might provide some guidance for identifying the logical structures of natural-language statements, one has to analyze the *use* of a sentence in scientific argumentation in order to excavate its logical structure. Finding the "intended" logical structure of a sentence requires interpretation. Sometimes it is sufficient to analyze the sentence to find such an interpretation. In other cases, attention to the theoretical context and examination of how a certain sentence is used in argumentation is needed to find the intended interpretation.

To this point, our examples share a tacit assumption of most introductory textbooks in logic, that the intended interpretation is available in logic (typically first-order logic). That is, the standard texts assume that the expressive power of the formal language is sufficient to distinguish among sentences with inferentially different behavior. But this need not be the case in real problems. For example, "Men are mortal" and "All men are mortal" might appear to be similar from one point of view. But in conjunction with "Socrates is a man," the second sentence leads to the conclusion that "Socrates is mortal," whereas the first sentence does not. "Men are mortal" might be sufficient to support the conclusion "Socrates is presumably mortal" in an appropriately chosen logic. Classical first-order logic does not have sufficient expressive power to account for this difference. Nonetheless there are logics with sufficiently fine-grained semantics to deal with this challenge.[1]

Given an infinite variety of logics,[2] no formalization can avoid the fundamental problem of choosing a formal language with adequate expressive power. Some typical problems in this respect can be analyzed with reference to the notion of extensionality.

Extensionality means that the replacement of names by other names with identical denotations (or predicates by other predicates with the same extension) yields logically indistinguishable expressions, that is logically equivalent formulas. Extensionality simplifies the logic, but it makes its notion of meaning rougher. In other words, the notion of logical consequence in first-order logic is less sensitive to nuance than are intensional logics (logics that relax the restriction to extensionality). Classical first-order logic, for example, cannot model the inferential impact of modalities such as perception or default, nor can it express the quantificational structures of rules with (unknown) exceptions, such as "Men are mortal."

Our study of relevant sociological theories suggests that considerations of genericity and modality arise regularly. Linguists refer to bare plural sentences such as "Organizations seek to seal off their technical cores from environmental uncertainty" as generic sentences, because they are general but not universal. These sentences typically express generality with (possible) exceptions. Modalities are expressed by sentential operators such as "possibly," "necessarily," and "allegedly." These modalities (or attitudes) do not fit into an extensional framework. Because genericity and modality appear to be ubiquitous in sociological theorizing, attempted translations of these theories into standard mathematics (whose underlying logic is the classical first-order logic) might not capture some key intuitions. Indeed, this problem might explain why formalizations in sociology so often seem to sterilize arguments, washing away the insights that made them appealing in the first place (Hannan 1997a).

A central challenge in formalizing and integrating sociological theories is to retain the core insights in making the translation from natural to formal languages. This task can be especially hard if the formal language is some kind of classical mathematics, such as algebra, calculus, or probability theory, as just noted. Fortunately, modern logic offers some appealing alternatives. The syntax and semantics can remain reasonably close to the natural-language argument; issues of genericity and modality can be handled systematically; and one can still "calculate," that is, derive implications, prove soundness, check for consistency, and so forth. For these reasons, we base our theory-building strategy on the use of modern logic(s).

In addition to choosing a language, a formalizer must adopt a strategy. A common misconception about strategy in formalizing theories comes from the mode of presenting formal work. The usual published report of a formal analysis begins by laying out definitions and assumptions and then uses them to derive lemmas and theorems. This mode of presentation suggests a mechanical process whereby deep insights follow from innocuous assumptions. Although this picture perhaps reflects

[1] We sketch such a logic in Chapter 6.

[2] The use of "infinite" in this context is not hyperbole. Modal logic alone contains an infinity of defined logics.

a common belief about scientific activity, it seems hard to find cases of insightful theories that were actually generated in this way. In particular, insight seems to have no role in this view, and there is certainly no guarantee that anything derived in this manner will be insightful.

Because they more closely resemble scientific work as we know it, we prefer two alternative views of theory construction. We attribute both views to Imre Lakatos (1976, 1994). Both hold that insights occur first (in any imaginable manner) and then formalization is undertaken as a way to preserve, strengthen, and possibly amplify the impact of the insight.

Lakatos' first alternative sees the central insights of an argument as stemming from its conceptual definitions and the explanatory principles (causal stories) that link them. Here the formalization effort seeks to clarify how and when the explanatory principles operate by recasting them in a sharper language. As a result, the explanatory principles inherent in the insight might be discovered to be more or less consequential than originally thought; they also can be more readily compared to accounts based on other rival principles that attempt to explain the same phenomena. We illustrate this approach thoroughly in chapters on age dependence (Chapter 7) and the niche (Chapters 8 and 9).

The alternative view holds that the deep insights reside in the key theorems. Given a theorem containing such an insight, the formalization enterprise attempts to identify assumptions that might be used to derive it. In other words, the formalization effort works to create a formal argument that yields this "target" theorem as an implication. In the process, some assumptions might be found to be more plausible than others, just as some sets of assumptions might be more parsimonious than others. The chapters that analyze density dependence (Chapter 4), resource partitioning (Chapter 9), and structural inertia (Chapters 10 and 11) follow this strategy. Other chapters typically use a combination of the two approaches.

As these two views suggest, formalization does not automatically generate insight. Rather, it allows us to understand and sharpen insights already in mind by tracing ideas and concepts through chains of reasoning that might be hard (or even impossible) to follow precisely in natural language. For instance, one possible result of the target-theorem approach is that the formal analysis might show that a theorem does not follow from commonly accepted or empirically verified premises. On the other hand, if the target theorem can be shown to be implied by sensible premises, then the process of building the formal model might lead to unexpected insights as well. For example, fewer or different assumptions might be needed than was initially believed. Or the formalization might produce additional, previously unconsidered derivations that could be subjected to empirical scrutiny.

An important related point is that formal tools—including logics—can often be used to show inconsistencies or deficiencies in verbal theories that contain nontrivial chains of reasoning. This kind of demonstration makes little contribution, in our opinion. After all, a main reason for using logic and mathematics in science is to avoid the ambiguity of natural language. So no one should be surprised to learn that a "rational reconstruction" and analysis using mathematics and logic can uncover the deficiencies of natural language as an analytical tool. The greater challenge in using logic and other formal languages—the one that top modelers take on—is to deploy the formal tools to deepen the insights contained in a verbal theory, even if this takes considerable reconstruction. As the theory building in this book illustrates, reconstructing a verbal theory in a formal language is rarely a trivial, or even an easy, task.

1.2 USING DYNAMIC LOGIC

In the sociological context, an unusual feature of our work is its explicit use of modern logics. We now explain why we make this strategic choice.

The main role of logic in scientific applications is to clarify the notion of "logical inference" or that of a "sound argument." Many logics have been proposed over the last 2500 years. Most of them share a core idea: an argument is sound if and only if it is impossible that all of the premises are true and the conclusion is false. In other words, an argument is sound if the truth of the premises guarantees the truth of the conclusion. Given that various well-studied logics share this view, how can they differ? These differences arise from many sources. For instance, some logics construct and use different formal languages, others use somewhat different conceptions of truth, or different interpretation of what "impossible" means.

The first (more-or-less) formal system of logic, Aristotle's syllogistic logic, focused on reasoning about premises that express some kind of quantification. That is, it analyzed logical implication for sets of sentences that contain expressions such as "all," "some," and "none." (Recall the paradigmatic syllogism: "All men are mortal"; "Socrates is a man"; therefore, "Socrates is mortal.") Another Greek tradition of logic, that of the Stoics, dealt with sentential connectives such as "not," "and," and "if . . . then."

Today logics similar to the Aristotelian and Stoic logics are called propositional logics, because they do not deal with the internal structure of the propositions. Modern logics, beginning with predicate logic (also called first-order logic) deal with quantification and sentential connectives and also analyze the internal structure of propositions. In a sense, predicate logic incorporates (modern) propositional logic as well the (modern) logic of quantification. Modern first-order logic, developed by the German philosopher Gottlob Frege, assigns interpretation to some components of the language somewhat differently than does the Aristotelian tradition.[3]

Frege's first-order (predicate) logic provides a fairly general account of correct argumentation in mathematical reasoning. Because the reasoning in mathematics is possibly more accurate and better scrutinized than any other kind of reasoning, its formal model—first-order logic—became *the* logic for most scientists who pay attention to the formal details of argumentation. Because mathematics works with sharp definitions and its predicates are perfectly well characterized by their extensions, Frege constructed his logic (first-order logic) to be strictly extensional, even

[3] Aristotle thought that if "all men are mortal," then "some man is mortal" follows. For Frege, a universal sentence like "all men are mortal" is vacuously true if there are no men. The sentence would only be false if there was an immortal man.

though it was Frege (1892) himself who noted the limitations of extensionality.[4] In modern science and mathematics, first-order logic is the default; and it usually sits in the background. In other words, unless an analyst announces reliance on some other logic, we can safely assume that the logic to be used in analyzing the arguments is first-order logic. Moreover, our experience in the discipline leads us to think that first-order logic is the default in sociology as much as in any other science.

However it is also our experience that sociologists resist the suggestion that the patterns of reasoning in sociological theories are based on any particular logic (such as predicate logic). Our discussions with leading theorists suggest to us that they do not think that one or more logics belong in the toolkit of the discipline. Nonetheless, when questions arise about what conclusions follow from certain premises, these same analysts routinely appeal to the rules of "logic" (considerations of contradiction among premises, invalid inference, mistaken reasoning, etc.). Interestingly, appeals to logic enter the picture especially when someone contends the validity of a chain of argument, as in "Comments" and "Replies" sometimes published in the sociological journals.[5]

We conclude that theory building and reasoning in sociology do indeed depend on a logic but that this dependence is typically left implicit (until someone claims to find a gap or a contradiction in an argument). Because the explicit use of logic is episodic and informal, analysts have not generally made clear what kind of logics they deploy in analyzing the reasoning that underlies sociological theories. Perhaps the reason for this state of affairs is that analysts are tacitly assuming that there is only one kind of logic. Indeed, discussions in the social sciences about inference in arguments—what follows from what—generally make this tacit assumption. This is understandable because we generally learned logic in the context of studying mathematics, whose standard branches use only classical first-order logic.[6] This logic provides a formal characterization of the sound reasoning patterns typically found in mathematical analysis. Given that general education does not go beyond this logic, this is the end of the story for most social scientists.

But, in the discipline of logic, the story does not end here. Patterns of what seems to be sound argumentation can be found beyond the realm of mathematics, and some of these patterns do not fit into classical logics such as predicate logic. During most of the twentieth century, logicians were busy offering formal renderings for these other kinds of inference patterns. In the process, they created a very large number of logics.

A century of research in logic yields an important insight: what a set of premises implies can differ, depending upon what logic is chosen. As the leading logician Johan van Benthem (1996: 22) put it,

[4]Interestingly, there are still numerous applications for which only a fragment of this logic, such as the modern propositional logic, is needed.

[5]Not surprisingly, (predicate) logic plays a more central role in explicit treatments of theory construction, e.g., Coleman (1964), Stinchcombe (1968, 2005).

[6]Some parts of mathematics use other logics such as intuitionist logic and second-order logic. However, these are not the parts of mathematics that have been applied in sociology.

> Observed inferential patterns which seem "wrong" according to one notion of inference might just as well signal that the speaker is engaged in correct execution of patterns of another style of reasoning.

This book takes the implications of this view seriously. Indeed, van Benthem's claim could serve well as a motto for our effort to design a formal language for sociological theory.

The received wisdom of late-twentieth century logic indicates that *the choice of a logic* is a key step in building and integrating theories. Predicate logic initially seems to be an attractive choice. It is standard and familiar as one of the best-studied logics; and it also has many desirable properties.[7] This logic might provide the most appropriate tools for formal renderings of argumentation within established theories (but see below).

Unfortunately, using first-order logic requires more than sociology and other social sciences can usually deliver. Claims in sociological theories are generally *partial.* Instead of supplying the strict (universal) rules required for analysis in predicate logic, sociological arguments typically offer rules that admit exceptions. Such rules provide incomplete or partial accounts of the sociological regularities. Considerations of partial knowledge suggest that classical logics, such as predicate logic, might not suit the challenges of theory building in sociology.

In particular, predicate logic does not offer promise for the theory building and unification project that we undertake. We provide examples in the following chapters of the coexistence in organization theory of seemingly inconsistent theories. Making sense of the state of knowledge in such cases requires efforts to learn what claims can be unified and how the unification might best be attempted. Unfortunately, first-order logic offers only the following unsatisfying recipe for unification: collect all of the relevant premises and consider the consistency of the set. In the best case, the complete set of premises is consistent (in the sense that some state of the world could possibly satisfy all of the assumptions). In this happy case, the unification is complete. With less luck, we end up with an inconsistent set of premises, a failed unified theory.[8] Under these circumstances, it becomes obvious that some of the premises have to be dropped in the interest of consistency.

Unfortunately, predicate logic does not offer advice about what premises should be dropped. In other words, a set of partial theories (which we call *theory fragments*) stated as universal rules and formalized in predicate logic can rarely, if ever, be integrated. The key problems arise from the fact that this standard logic does not provide any way to isolate or control the different premises so as to avoid clashes among the universal rules from the different fragments.

A more useful strategy would be to choose a logic that provides some specific clues about how to deal with premises that lead to opposing predictions (inconsistencies). More generally, it would be better to choose (or define) a formal language that more accurately expresses how sociological theorists actually argue. We are

[7] These advantages include such properties as finite axiomatizability and compactness.

[8] Even if the unification does not yield inconsistency, it might be the case that the full set of premises imply unwanted theorems, theorems that run counter to the intuitions that motivate the theories, as we noted above.

convinced that theory building and theoretical argumentation in sociology do not adhere closely to the strictures of classical logics such as predicate logic (or the propositional fragment of predicate logic).

Sociologists typically do not often want to claim complete generality (universality) for propositions. They build theory fragments. As we use the term, a theory fragment consists of a set of interrelated assumptions, concepts, and propositions focused on one or several closely related explananda. Theory fragments typically arise from some core insight or intuition about these phenomena.

Upon scrutiny, sociology's theory fragments appear to be inconsistent, if the premises in each fragment are considered to hold universally. And they often rely (implicitly) on the specificity of arguments to control possible contradictions. We contend that casting arguments and patterns of reasoning in a dynamic logic provides a way to formalize sociological practice.

Moreover, premises in sociological arguments are not restricted to deal with facts. They often treat the "attitudes" of agents to some factual state of affairs, where attitude can mean perception, belief, valuation, and so forth. Such claims resist consistent translation into predicate logic (and other classical logics).

Perhaps the reason for sociologists' reluctance to admit that their theoretical argumentation relies on a logic is an implicit recognition that the language of classical logics does not fit the patterns of sociological argumentation. We agree about the mismatch. We think that the situation calls for examining the patterns of argumentation and the search for systematic methods for judging the soundness of arguments that do not fit classical patterns. This kind of effort might yield languages that allow sociologists and other social scientists to represent formally the actual structure of their arguments.

We try to show (without presenting all of the technical details) that dynamic logics hold promise for this task. (Chapters 6 and 7 introduce the particular dynamic logic that we use.) As we noted above, the generally used notion of logical inference holds that an inference is valid if the truth of the premises guarantees the truth of the conclusion. A "sound" logic satisfies this principle. First-order logic, along with most formal logics, builds on this principle.

An alternative way to provide a foundation to the idea of sound inference takes account of the *information content* of the premises and the conclusion. According to this view, if learning the premises (in a precise abstract sense) brings about the knowledge of the conclusion, then inferring the conclusion from the premises is logically valid. This dynamic notion of logical inference extends the usual static approach. When applied to the language of classical predicate logic, the static and dynamic approaches turn out to be equivalent. However, there is a broad class of situations in which the dynamic notion of inference applies but the classical static one does not.

In formalizing the theory-building process in dynamic logic, we refer to stages of a theory to characterize the information content of the theory (given the premises available at that stage). Claims of a stage of a theory tell how the world is expected to be according to the theory stage. Such claims need not be classical (universal) propositions; and inference based on these claims is best described by the dynamic approach to inference. These considerations motivated us to design a logic in line with the dynamic approach.[9]

The variant of dynamic inference that we develop is a nonmonotonic logic. In a theory built on such a logic, claims can be stated as generic rules, that is, as rules-with-exceptions. (As we explain below, exceptions can be patterned, more than simply stochastic variation.) Specificity is used to control arguments, to decide which of a set of possibly applicable arguments should be used. Arguments are built of conditional sentences, sentences with an antecedent and a consequent, e.g., "If ϕ is the case, then ψ is the case." Now suppose we have two arguments that begin as follows: (1) "If an object is an organization, then . . . ;" and (2) "If an object is a young organization, then. . . . " Now consider the class of young organizations. It is clear that the antecedent in the second argument better approximates the class than does the antecedent in the first argument. In this case, we say that the second argument has greater specificity and is more relevant to the class of young organizations.

Establishing a specificity ordering is sometimes a straightforward matter unlikely to engender discussion, as in the foregoing example. In other cases, however, determining specificity orderings can be difficult and subject to varying interpretations. Indeed, it often takes considerable empirical knowledge of a subject to be able to settle matters of specificity.

The basic principle of nonmonotonic logic is that the most specific applicable argument prevails in the case of clashing implications. Our substantive applications seek to show that use of this nonmonotonic logic eases the task of integrating partly conflicting fragments while still allowing the theorist to derive the implications of an argument and to test the soundness of such inferences.

We supplement the nonmonotonic logic with a modal logic. Modern modal logics were developed to analyze arguments that use premises that express the attitudes (modalities) of agents. The issue of modality plays a central role in our theory of the interaction of producers and audiences in creating categories and forms.

Clearly, these logics are nonstandard tools. We justify their use by noting that they allow a formal treatment of sociological theories that expresses the actual patterns of argument used by leading theorists and researchers—not some disembodied notion about how theory should be constructed in an idealized world. Readers can judge for themselves whether this is the case for the class of organizational theories that we propose.

Stochastic Variations

When empirical researchers first confront the idea of rules-with-exceptions, they naturally think that this term refers to stochastic variations. Any stochastic process allows for exceptional events, events that occur with low probability given the structure of the process. There is no need for a new kind of logic to deal with such events—this is the business of probability theory.

Many processes of interest to social scientists are inherently stochastic. The formalizations presented in this book address stochastic variations explicitly. The key

[9]Translating this notion back to a standard truth-conditional approach is possible if truth is relativized to information states.

premises and conclusions hold for functions of probability distributions (usually expectations or hazards). For instance, a key outcome of interest is the hazard of organizational mortality, a function of the distribution of the lengths of lifetimes in a population of organizations.

What, then, do we mean by rules-with-exceptions in such cases? The exceptions refer to unusual probability distributions, those that might arise under specific circumstances. So, for instance, a theory might lead to the conclusion that the general case is such that the hazard of mortality of large organizations is lower than that of small ones. This is the relationship that we expect to find in normal circumstances, those in which more specific arguments do not come into play. Note that we do not expect that all large organizations will outlive all small ones. The usual stochastic variation in mortality processes makes it very unlikely that this will be the case. The exceptional cases that we have in mind are those in which specific considerations lead to a reversal of the general rule, cases in which small organizations persistently display a lower hazard.

Scope Restrictions

Science has long dealt with issues of partiality and possible contradictions among premises by restricting the scope of explanatory principles and causal claims.This is the only solution offered by classical logics, such as first-order logic, for dealing with clashing premises. If research identifies systematic exceptions to an argument, then theorists incorporate (strict) limits on the scope of applicability of premises. That is, they define precise bounds on processes such that the original argument holds within the bounds but not outside of them.

Reliance on scope restrictions to fix apparent inconsistencies dominates scientific practice in sociology and most social science. Arthur Stinchcombe (2005: 117) reflects the prevailing theoretical wisdom in sociology:

> Sociology is pervaded by boundary conditions on its causal processes . . . Contextual variations directly determine values of some causal or effect variables. They also determine the impact of variations in some causes on effects, and so produce different relations of causes to effects in one context than in another.

Under the strategy of relying on explicit restrictions on scope, the price to be paid for consistency is a limitation of explanatory power. Although we recognize the value of paying such a price, we insist that restricting the scope of premises is justified only if the restrictions can be well motivated substantively. Otherwise the cure is ad hoc, and it does not contribute to understanding.

Indeed, it takes a highly developed theoretical and empirical understanding to be able to state precise restrictions on the scope of arguments. One might well question whether sociologists and other social scientists can supply such precise information. Stinchcombe (2005: 121) clearly believes that they can; but he laments the current lack of attention paid to the problem: "we ordinarily want to spend as little time as possible on the theory of the context so as to spend as much as possible on the main subject of the research." He also recognizes the great difficulty of the task of determining scope or boundary conditions:

> As a practical matter, many aspects of context vary a great deal from time to time and from place to place. Often these aspects are crucial for socially constructed boundaries, meanings and the various determinants of how sparse acts are. Our "second order units of analysis," on which we observe distances between contexts, frequently are times and places. The relations between times and places and social action are crucial to investigating distance between contexts. (Stinchcombe 2005: 1)

How should such boundary (or scope) conditions be expressed? So long as sociological arguments rely (often implicitly) on classical logic, there is no way to avoid stating these conditions as universals—at least implicitly. In other words, the implicit language of theorizing is such that scope conditions in the standard strategy do not admit any exceptions. In our experience, this is not what sociologists intend when they express limits on the scope of an argument. Knowledge about the limits on the scope of an argument is generally partial. This means that proposed scope conditions also generally come with not-yet-explained exceptions. Therefore, we conclude that the strategy of restricting scope does not really solve the problem of partiality if the pattern of reasoning is restricted to classical logic. We suggest that the use of a dynamic logic provides a way to handle limitations on scope formally in a way that better fits actual sociological practice.

To illustrate these points, consider an early contribution to organization theory. James Thompson, in his classic book, *Organizations in Action,* advanced many insightful propositions. One that influenced theory for many years states: "Under norms of rationality, organizations seek to buffer environmental influences by surrounding their technical cores with input and output components" (Thompson 1967: 20). Obviously, with this proposition (and many others in the book) Thompson explicitly stakes out a universal scope condition with the clause "under norms of rationality." This is admirable. Nonetheless, Thompson does not really do much with this scope restriction, either in terms of justification or implication in subsequent arguments. Instead, given its level of abstraction, the clause might be seen as a way to finesse around problematic empirical cases: should one encounter an organization that does not engage in buffering environmental influences with input and output components, then it can be said to operate under norms other than rationality. We think that similar usage surrounds much current practice where scope conditions are specified in sociological theory.

But now let us assume that the interpretation of the antecedent clause is not problematic and consider the rest of the proposition. It gives a "rule" for a structural process that organizations are expected to follow without exception. Research has shown clearly that very many organizations do follow this rule and exhibit the expected empirical implications. This was especially true in the 1970s and 1980s. However, with the advent of total quality management programs, just-in-time manufacturing practices, and other supply-chain management techniques driven by advances in information technology, it became clear in the 1990s that organizations did not need to buffer their technical cores with bureaucratic input and output structures to be effective. Instead, a number of leading organizations showed that such structures were sometimes unnecessary and costly to maintain, that there were other, better ways to reduce uncertainty in the core by managing directly environmental agents. So, the rule does not appear to be universal—there seems to be good reason to think that some organizations might operate differently than it predicts, even when norms of rationality prevail. Unfortunately, the exact conditions under which certain organizations operate differently have yet to be clearly identified (at least to our knowledge).

What can a theorist do when facing this type of situation, assuming she wants to retain a degree of formalism and generality? Under the principles of first-order logic, the options are limited: either declare the proposition false or specify additional new scope conditions (stated as universals) knowing full well that these might be ad hoc and likely to need revision as soon as evidence appears. Both options are unattractive—the first because the original proposition does contain some insight and does explain many situations, the second because it misrepresents the state of theoretical knowledge.

Our impression is that sociologists and other social scientists typically respond to such situations by adopting the second option, while making it clear in their accompanying text that the formulation is tentative. In other words, they let it be known that the bounds of the argument are still unclear and that there are likely to be exceptions, which perhaps might be systematically delineated in the future. While perhaps sensible, this approach is easily subject to misinterpretation. In our opinion, the nonmonotonic logic that we put forward in this book does a similar job of specifying the state of theoretical knowledge but in a clearer, more systematic, and more parsimonious way.[10] As we explain below, this logic specifies propositions as rules with exceptions and uses differences in the specificities of arguments to determine which of several possible interpretations should apply. The textual markers that indicate we are employing nonmonotonic quantification in the equations consist of the words "normally" and "presumably." (The distinctions are also marked in the formal syntax, which uses the quantifiers $\mathfrak{N}$ and $\mathfrak{P}$ to express these kinds of quantification and also uses a third quantifier, $\mathfrak{A}$, to express nonmontonic quantification for auxiliary assumptions.)

1.3 PARTIAL MEMBERSHIPS: FUZZINESS

Classical logics such as the predicate (or first-order) logic—and, by extension, nearly all of mathematics—impose two important requirements. The first, discussed above, is that the theoretical statements must be universal, admitting no exceptions. The second requirement characterizes the concepts used. The concepts of a theory must satisfy what are typically called classical rules.

Frege developed logic in its modern form by (among many other things) making explicit the connections between logic and set theory, by linking concepts and sets.

[10] For a detailed and more complex illustration that parallels the Thompson example, see Chapter 10 on resource partitioning.

For Frege, the meaning of a concept is given by its extension, the set of objects for which the concept holds (in the sense that the statement that the object is an instance of the concept is true). For example, the meaning of the concept "red," according to this view, is given by the set of all those objects (in some specified universe of discourse) for which it is the case that they are red, that the statement "this object is red" is true. Knowing the membership of this set, the extension on the concept, is tantamount to understanding the concept. For this reason, the logics that build on the Fregian structure, such as modern predicate logic, are said to be *extensional.*

Frege sought to retain the classical principle that truth functions can take only two values: "true" and "false." Logicians refer to this principle as the *law of the excluded middle* (no truth value is allowed between false and true). Classical set theory fits this requirement, because a set is defined as a collection of objects for which a given property is true. Partial memberships in sets are excluded by definition. Frege (1893/1903, Vol. 2: 139) formulated his position on concepts as follows:

> The concept must have a sharp boundary. If we represent concepts in extension by areas on a plane, this is admittedly a picture that may be used only with caution, but here it can do us good service. To a concept without sharp boundary there would correspond an area that had not a sharp boundary-line all round, but in places just vaguely faded away into the background. This would not really be an area at all; and likewise a concept that is not sharply defined is wrongly termed a concept. Such quasi-conceptual constructions cannot be recognised as concepts by logic; it is impossible to lay down precise laws for them. The law of excluded middle is really just another form of the requirement that the concept should have a sharp boundary. Any object that you choose either falls under the concept or does not fall under it; *tertium non datur.* E.g., would the sentence "any square root of 9 is odd" have a comprehensible sense at all if *square root of 9* were not a concept with a sharp boundary? Has the question "Are we still Christians?" really got a sense, if it is indeterminate whom the predicate "Christian" can truly be ascribed to, and who must be refused it?

Frege's approach retains what E. E. Smith and D. L. Medin (1981) call the classical theory of concepts. Gregory Murphy (2002: 15) summarizes this perspective as follows:

> First, concepts are mentally represented as definitions. A definition provides characteristics that are (a) necessary and (b) jointly sufficient for membership in the category. Second, the classical theory argues that every object is either in or not-in the category, with no in-between cases . . . Third, the classical view does not make any distinction between category members. Anything that meets the definition is just as good a category member as anything else. (Aristotle emphasized this aspect of categories in particular.)

The classical theory has come under sustained attack in philosophy and cognitive science over the past half century. The leading figure on the philosophy side was Ludwig Wittgenstein. In his *Philosophical Investigations,* Wittgenstein (1953) repudiated his own influential work in logic (his *Tractatus*) and that of Frege and Bertrand Russell by abandoning the classical notion of the concept. His analysis of the social use of natural language led him to question whether our ordinary concepts satisfy the classical requirements and whether these requirements matter for human communication. Consider, for instance, his famous analysis of the concept "game."

> Consider for example the proceedings that we call "games." I mean board-games, card-games, ball-games, Olympic games, and so on. What is common to them all?—Don't say: "There *must* be something common, or they would not be called 'games'"—but *look and see* whether there is anything common to all.—For if you look at them you will not see something that is common to *all,* but similarities, relationships, and a whole series of them at that . . . And we can go through the many, many other groups of games in the same way; can see how similarities crop up and disappear . . .
>
> And the result of this examination is: we see a complicated network of similarities overlapping and criss-crossing: sometimes overall similarities, sometimes similarities of detail.
>
> I can think of no better expression to characterize these similarities than "family resemblances"; for the various resemblances between members of a family: build, features, colour of eyes, gait, temperament, etc. etc. overlap and criss-cross in the same way.—And I shall say: "games" form a family. . . .
>
> One might say that the concept "game" is a concept with blurred edges. —"But is a blurred concept a concept at all?"—Is an indistinct photograph a picture of a person at all? Is it even always an advantage to replace an indistinct picture by a sharp one? Isn't the indistinct one often exactly what we need? (Wittgenstein 1953)

Subsequent psychological research found broad and general support for the view that cultural concepts, coded in natural language, point to family resemblances rather than to something like classical concepts. The modern research tradition on the psychology of concepts began with Eleanor Rosch's (1973, 1975) examination of subjects' perceptions of the relationships of subconcepts to concepts. She asked subjects to tell how typical were certain fruits, e.g., apples, oranges, melons, olives, of the category "fruit." The subjects reported great differences in typicality among the specific kinds of fruit, and they agreed strongly on the typicality judgments. Apples, it was agreed, are very typical, and olives are very atypical. This pattern was replicated for "furniture" (tables and chairs are very typical items of furniture, and mirrors and carpets are atypical) and for "birds" (robins and sparrows are typical birds, and chickens and penguins are atypical). The robust finding that ordinary concepts have an internal structure (of graded typicality) runs against the classical theory, which holds that all instances of a concept are alike.

Eleanor Rosch and C. B. Mervis (1975) claimed that these patterns reveal that concepts such as fruit and furniture constitute Wittgensteinian family resemblances. Several major lines of work in cognitive psychology and cognitive science have sought to explain the ubiquity of graded typicality for both natural concepts (such as those mentioned above) and artificial ones constructed for laboratory experiments. Although they disagree about the structure of categories, these strands of research agree broadly that concepts do not fit the classical story.[11]

One way to adapt to these empirical findings is by changing the foundational set theory. Standard set theory defines sets as the collections of objects in a universe of discourse that satisfy a given predicate, as noted above. The main alternative, fuzzy set theory, describes situations in which set membership can be partial, a matter of degree (Zadeh 1965). It defines a *grade-of-membership,* a function that maps from elements of the universe of discourse to the [0,1] interval. This function tells the degree to which the entity belongs to the set. Consider the grade-of-membership score for a single agent with regard to a particular concept. An agent's assigning an object a grade of membership of one indicates that the agent sees the object as clearly or unambiguously fitting the concept—there is no doubt about it. Conversely, a grade of membership of zero signifies that the agent has no doubt that the object does not fit the concept. For grades of membership between zero and one, the values tell the degree to which the agent categorizes the object in the concept.

It seems natural to link the structure of typicality found by Rosch and many others to vagueness of concept boundaries of the sort that worried Frege. Indeed, Rosch and other researchers made this connection in the 1970s. They suggested the general experimental finding that instances ("exemplars") of a category differ in typicality indicates that categories lack sharp boundaries. They proposed that fuzzy-set theory provided a language for analyzing this feature of concepts. In technical terms, this early research claimed a monotonic relationship between a grade of membership in typicality and a grade of membership as an instance of the concept (or category).

The initial enthusiasm for building a psychology of concepts on fuzzy-set theory was deflated by a series of papers that argued that concepts with fuzzy boundaries yield patterns that do not fit what we expect of a language. A basic property of a language is productivity, the idea that a speaker of a language can construct a new (not-yet-uttered) sentence that can be understood by the competent speakers of the language.

Productivity arises from *compositionality,* the idea, first formalized by Frege, that the meaning of a sentence ought to depend only on the meanings of the components and on the structure of the composition. The fuzzy representation of concepts can fail to conform to the principle of compositionality. In an influential pairs of papers, D. N. Osherson and E. E. Smith (1981, 1982) analyzed situations like the following. Suppose that we know what is a typical "pet" (a dog or cat) and what is a typical "fish" (a trout or salmon). What then do we expect of the concept "pet fish"? We

[11] Murphy (2002) gives an admirably lucid overview of these developments.

lack good grounds for providing an answer. Moreover, the typical "pet fish" (a guppy or goldfish) is a very atypical pet and also a very atypical fish. And here we have a potential problem with the use of fuzzy-set theory to represent typicality. In this set theory, the rule for constructing the intersection of two sets is that an entity's grade of membership in the intersection is the minimum of its grades of memberships in the two sets. The guppy or goldfish is problematic because it has a high grade of membership as a "pet fish" (the intersection) and low grade of membership in each of the component sets.[12]

The commentaries sparked by the Osherson-Smith critique made evident that a useful analytical distinction can be drawn between the two grades of membership (in typicality and in membership in the concept), between the internal structure of a concept (variations in typicality) and fuzzy boundaries (variations in membership)—see Laurence and Margolin (1999) and Hampton (1998). In other words, the existence of an internal structure to a concept does not imply the absence of a sharp boundary.

Cognitive psychologists responded to the critique that the use of fuzzy-set theory might sharply limit compositionality by drawing a sharp distinction between the notions of graded typicality (and the associated idea of an internal structure of concepts) and vagueness of category boundaries (Osherson and Smith 1997). Psychological research now downplays the idea of graded membership in concepts (vague concept boundaries)—but see James Hampton (2006) for an interesting exception. We think that this reaction went too far, at least as concerns socially constructed categories (as distinct from "natural kinds"). We discuss these issues in more detail in Chapter 2.

We follow the path blazed by Wittgenstein and followed by Rosch and her associates. We think that the social categories constructed by local audiences involve *both* typicality judgments and vagueness (or fuzziness) in category boundaries (Hampton 2006). Our reading of the evidence suggests that agents often detect shades of difference and decide that some producers fit comfortably in a category, some do not fit at all, and others fit to a greater or lesser degree. For example, consider the socially constructed organizational category "university" and some specific organizations that use—or at least sometimes lay claim to—the label. Everyone likely agrees that some obvious cases belong in the category: University of Bologna, Oxford University, Harvard University, and so forth. Then there are others which almost every audience member would say do not belong: the Hamburger University of McDonald's Corporation (an employee training center) is such a case, as is the Dreyer's Leadership University of the previous Dreyer's Grand Ice Cream Company.

Consider some more interesting cases. Rockefeller University is a great basic-

[12]Noun-noun combinations, such as "pet fish," allow wide scope for creativity in interpretation (Costello and Keane 2000). Some linguists argue that convergence in interpretations depends upon pragmatics, how the expressions are used. Moreover, it is worth noting that members of societies that lack the practice of keeping pet fish would not be expected to know that a guppy is a prototypical pet fish. Likewise, those unfamiliar with instance of various forms of financial institutions would likely have difficulty coming up with interpretations of such forms as "venture capital," "hedge fund," and "building society." See Werning, Machery, and Schurz (2005a, 2005b) for a variety of perspectives on the philosophical and empirical status of compositionality.

research organization but has few post-graduate students, no undergraduate students, and a tiny formal curriculum. The University of Phoenix calls itself the largest "university" in the United States in terms of student enrollment, has many online courses, has few regular or permanent faculty,and is part of a for-profit corporation. Bob Jones University has students and faculty, but also has a code of conduct subscribing to fundamental Baptist religion, including restraints on speech and research. The Maharishi University of Management has curricula in business and the humanities; and it emphasizes transcendental meditation by students and faculty as a central part of its academic mission. The National Defense University, which includes the National War College, trains top military and some State Department staff, gives masters degrees, and offers faculty appointments (that do not allow the possibility of tenure), and has a web page declaring that it subscribes fully to the AAUP guidelines on academic freedom. Britain's Open University enrolls 150,000 part-time long-distance students and does not require any qualifications for admission (other than a lower age limit). We suspect that much disagreement exists over the inclusion of these organizations in the university category. [13] Some might argue that one or another fits the category and others do not. More likely, they will claim that these organizations are universities "in some respects," are "technically" universities, or are "unusual" or "atypical" universities. The use of such hedge words is the classic linguistic sign of partiality—that is, fuzziness.

Even if social processes were to eliminate fuzziness for mature categories (contrary to what we see for "university"), it strikes us as implausible that fuzziness could be avoided at all stages of the emergence of a category as a cultural object. We try to account for the processes of emergence, beginning with efforts at clustering similar producers and products in social domains. We doubt that the conception of the emergence of graded typicality within a sharp concept (or category, as we call it) can serve as a credible story about emergence.

The theoretical research we report in this book treats the consequences of the categories created by audiences for various kinds of collective social action. The research in cognitive psychology that we have just sketched leads us to claim that these audiences create categories that lack classical properties. Fuzziness in category boundaries seems inescapable. Therefore, we seek to deal systematically with its implications head on.

This means that we confront two kinds of partiality: (1) incomplete knowledge about the causal processes at work; and (2) partial applicability of concepts and categories. As we see it, the first kind of partiality characterizes the situation facing the theorist, and the second kind characterizes the situation facing the agents whose actions the theory treats (and possibly also the theorist). We think the two kinds of partiality have different impacts on arguments, and we want to distinguish them clearly. Therefore, we mark the two kinds of partiality in our formal language. We represent the first kind of partiality as *genericity* (and we develop quantifiers that can deal with genericity). We represent the second kind of partiality by *graded membership* in categories. This means that the fuzziness is restricted to the lan-

[13] Interestingly, the Open University's Web site has a section entitled "Is the Open University a 'real university'?"

guage of the agents; our theoretical language is classical in this respect.[14]

1.4 ORGANIZATIONAL ECOLOGY

We next introduce the main subject of our theory building: the program of organizational ecology. This body of theory and research examines interactions within and between populations of organizations. The approach differs from other sociological research on organizations by focusing on the population level, relying on selection mechanisms, and studying the life histories of all organizations in populations over their full histories. Organizational ecology initially borrowed ideas from neoclassical population bioecology, which analyzes numerical aspects of population interactions from an evolutionary perspective. In paraphrasing the bioecologist G. Evelyn Hutchinson (1959), Michael Hannan and John Freeman (1977) posed the orienting question: Why are there so many kinds of organizations? They suggested that social science at the time lacked good answers to this question and that seeking answers would clarify the dynamics of the organizational world. Three decades of subsequent research shows clearly that organizational diversity exerts important consequences for individuals and social structures (Carroll and Hannan 2000).

Organizational ecology sought initially to resolve a theoretical tension about what sociologist Amos Hawley (1968: 334) termed the principle of isomorphism: "Units subjected to the same environmental conditions or to environmental conditions as mediated through a given key unit, acquire a similar form of organization." Hannan and Freeman (1977) argued that Hawley's principle, like other adaptationist premises, does not apply straightforwardly in uncertain, heterogeneous environments. Extending the received wisdom about adaptation requires specification of the underlying dynamic processes and attention to selection. In the organizational world, selection occurs through the emergence and demise of organizational forms, which depend on the fates of individual organizations. Accordingly, theory and research in this tradition focuses on the demographic vital rates of organizations and organizational populations: rates of founding, growth, and mortality.

The ecological research program progressed by fostering empirical research in a variety of distinct theory fragments. Among other topics, the major theory fragments of organizational ecology address questions about:

Organizational forms and populations. This fragment addresses questions about how to define forms and populations and how to classify them meaningfully into higher-order forms. Early ideas focused heavily on patterns of exchange among organizations and other environmental actors; however, recent theory and research centers on ideas about social identities and social codes. (See Hannan and Freeman 1986; Zuckerman 1999; McKendrick and Carroll 2001; Rao, Monin, and Durand 2003, 2005; Ruef 2000, 2004a; and Baron 2004.)

[14]This division of assignment contrasts markedly with that of some other applications of logic in sociological theory where the analytical problems faced by the theorist are characterized by fuzzy concepts (see Montgomery 2000; Ragin 2000).

Structural inertia and change. The inertia fragment develops arguments about the rigidity of organizational structures and argues that strong inertia makes selection an important motor of change in the world of organizations. It addresses the main possible mechanisms behind such phenomena, including the predilection in modern society to value accountability and reliability, as well as inertia's evolutionary implications. (See Hannan and Freeman 1984; Haveman 1992; Amburgey, Kelly, and Barnett 1993; Barnett and Carroll 1995; Baron, Hannan, and Burton 2001; Hannan, Pólos, and Carroll 2003a, 2003b, 2004; and Phillips and Owens 2004.)

Age dependence. Theory and research on age dependence asks how and why the age of organizations matters for their structures and life chances. The proposed answers to the problem, which involve issues such as knowledge, capabilities, bureaucratization, and obsolescence, transcend the seemingly narrow question. Yet theoretical progress in the fragment has been clouded by conflicting empirical evidence. (See Carroll 1983; Freeman, Carroll, and Hannan 1983; Levinthal 1991; Barron, West, and Hannan 1994; and Sørensen and Stuart 2000.)

Dynamics of social movements. Social movement research in organizational ecology emphasizes the organizational basis of collective action, especially that related to the competition and mutualism of movement organizations. It also ties movements to the rise of new organization forms. Social movement theorists naturally focus on the possibility that institutions can sometimes be changed, and they stress the importance of attending to movement audiences and their dynamics. (Relevant publications include Hannan and Freeman 1987; Minkoff 1999; Ingram and Simons 2000; Olzak and Uhrig 2001; Swaminathan and Wade 2001; Sandell 2001; Koopmans and Olzak 2004; and Greve, Posner, and Rao 2006.)

Density dependence. This theory fragment comprises what is perhaps ecology's most sustained research program on population dynamics, the model of density dependence in legitimation and competition. The core theory posits relationships between density, the number of organizations in a population, and legitimation of the form of organization and competition among the population's members. Its main empirical implications are nonmonotonic relationships between density, on the one hand, and population vital rates on the other hand. Extensions to the theory attempt (1) to extend the model to explain late-stage declines in population density, an observed empirical regularity, and (2) to treat legitimation as "sticky" or not easily reversible. (See Hannan and Freeman 1989; Carroll and Hannan 1989; Hannan and Carroll 1992; Barron 1999; and Ruef 2004b.)

Niche structure. An organization's niche summarizes its adaptive capacity over the various possible states of its environment. Theories in this fragment build on the concept of niche width, the span of environmental states in which an organization can thrive. These theories claim that a broad niche comes at the expense of viability in a stable, competitive environment, but that environmental uncertainty and variability affect the tradeoff between niche width and viability. (See Hannan and Freeman 1977; McPherson 1983; Freeman and Hannan 1983; Baum and Singh 1994; Podolny, Stuart, and Hannan 1996, Dobrev, Kim, and Hannan 2001; Sørensen 2000; Dobrev, Kim, and Carroll 2003; and Barnett and Woywode 2004.)

Resource partitioning. This fragment can be seen as a variant of general niche theory, one based on different assumptions and scope conditions. This fragment explains the endogenous partitioning of markets (environments) as an outcome of competition between populations of generalists and specialists. (See Carroll 1985; Swaminathan 1995; Carroll and Swaminathan 2000; Péli and Nooteboom 1999; Park and Podolny 2000; and Boone, Carroll, and van Witteloostuijn 2002.)

Diversity of organizations. Research in this fragment deals with the social and economic consequences of the level of diversity among the types of organizations in a community or sector. An initial stream deals with the interplay of careers of individuals and the organizational ecologies within which careers play out. (See Hannan 1988; Carroll, Haveman, and Swaminathan 1990; Greve 1994; Haveman and Cohen 1994; Fujiwara-Greve and Greve 2000; Phillips 2001; and Sørensen and Sorenson 2007. Recent research addresses religiosity (Koçak and Carroll 2006) and election turnout (Carroll, Xu, and Koçak 2005).)

As these brief summaries illustrate, organizational ecology contains diverse theory fragments and associated lines of empirical inquiry. Moreover, these fragments can sensibly be regarded as parts of a larger research program—they build on a common conception of the organizational world as shaped by processes of selection operating on organizational forms and also share methodological presumptions and practices (Carroll and Hannan 2000). Nonetheless, the relationships of the fragments to each other remain ambiguous. Key points of apparent conceptual intersection sit unexplored and require clarification. The preponderance of effort over the last three decades has focused on empirical testing, with less attention paid to issues of theoretical integration. This empirical emphasis, though highly successful for producing new knowledge, limits further progress. Because empirical research has not been balanced by theoretical efforts to examine the relations among the fragments, we lack a clear vision of what empirical projects would move the larger program forward substantially.

An effort to integrate the fragments provides an opportunity to rethink foundational issues in the light of the successful record of research. Initial theoretical formulations did not have a strong empirical base. Some aspects of these formulations bore fruit; others did not. Naturally, many processes turned out to be more complicated than anticipated in the early phases of theoretical work. Accordingly, we do not think it worthwhile to try to fit all of the fragments into a single whole or to insist on the priority of the initial theoretical claims. Instead, we try to retain what we see is a core set of apparently related insights that proved to be useful in the various facets of the research program.

This theory-building strategy leads us to place social codes at the forefront of ecological analysis. As we use the concept here, a social code denotes and connotes both cognitive recognition and imperative standing. A social code can be understood (1) as a set of interpretative signals, as in the "genetic code," and (2) as a set of rules of conduct, as in the "penal code." Some of the most interesting and important processes are those that convert interpretative schemata into imperative codes.

Our theoretical strategy of rebuilding foundations so as to enable integration stands in sharp contrast to one that animated an earlier vigorous phase of formalization of fragments of organizational ecology. In this earlier phase, initial formulations of various fragments were subjected to rational reconstruction and logical analysis designed to test the soundness of the arguments. Fragments analyzed in this manner include (1) structural inertia and change (Péli et al. 1994; Péli, Pólos, and Hannan 2000); (2) niche width (Péli 1997); (3) life-history strategies (Péli and Masuch 1997); and (4) age dependence (Hannan 1998; Pólos and Hannan 2002). These efforts took seriously the "frozen" published texts. They translated the natural-language renderings of the arguments into a formal language (and sought to tune translations to the intuitions that animated the original arguments) and checked the proofs of the claims in that language. This work has been valuable in establishing the soundness of the main arguments and in filling gaps in arguments. However, the approach takes a largely passive role with respect to moving the theories forward. In particular, because these efforts considered each fragment in isolation from the others, they could not clarify the relationships among the fragments.

We take a much more active stance in this book. We seek to rebuild, formalize, and integrate the fragments while still trying to preserve the main substantive insights. As the Table of Contents indicates, our efforts mainly encompass the fragments about age dependence, forms and populations, niche structure and resource partitioning, and structural inertia and change.

1.5 UNIFICATION PROJECTS

Fragmentation in a discipline or a theory program (as just sketched for organizational ecology) seems to be endemic in sociology. If this assessment is accurate, then developing strategies for unification ought to be high on the agenda of sociological methodology (in the broad sense).

Fragmentation clearly is an outgrowth of the common mode of tying empirical investigation to the development of the type of middle-range theory advocated by Robert K. Merton. In responding to the grand sociological theories of Talcott Parsons and others, Merton (1968) proposed that greater scientific progress could be achieved if sociological theory focused on problems in the middle range. He described middle-range theories as those

> . . . that lie between the minor but necessary working hypotheses that

> evolve in abundance during the day-to-day research and the all-inclusive systematic efforts to develop a unified theory that will explain all the observed uniformities of social behavior, social organization and social change. (Merton 1968: 39)

Merton argued that despite their specific foci, middle-range theories also possess a "general character" that allows them to be applied in new contexts and elaborated conceptually. Yet

> . . . it is equally clear that such middle-range theories have not been logically *derived* from a single all-embracing theory of social systems, though once developed they may be consistent with one. Furthermore, each theory is more than a mere empirical generalization—an isolated proposition summarizing observed uniformities of two or more variables. A theory comprises a set of assumptions from which empirical generalizations have themselves been derived. (Merton 1968: 41)

Although social scientists do not commonly use the term, what we call a theory fragment bears a close resemblance to the Mertonian notion of a middle-range theory.

In our view, the strategy of working at the middle range mitigates some serious obstacles to conceptual innovation. It eases the tasks of formulating and communicating new assumptions, propositions, and the like. In particular, new fragments of middle-range theory do not face the possibly formidable challenge of integrating tightly with existing theory. Accordingly, the strategy of constructing middle-range theory allows new insights to develop rapidly and diffuse through the scientific community—spurring a healthy development of scientific knowledge through the flowering of ideas.

Yet, a bouquet of theoretical blossoms yields a certain theoretical fragmentation that limits the broader development and use of a body of scientific knowledge. These issues come into sharp focus when we consider prediction and empirical testing, cornerstones of any scientific knowledge base. Fragmentation raises a serious problem for prediction: different theory fragments might yield different predictions for a not-yet-seen case. What, then, is the predictive power of the larger body of knowledge in which the fragments sit? A similar problem arises in empirical testing. With fragmentation, the relation of a given empirical finding to a set of theory fragments is generally indeterminate (so long as the interrelations of the fragments are problematic); therefore, empirical implication has smaller scope under fragmentation.

A profusion of theories of the middle range can be likened to the consequences of fertilizing a garden. Initially, new and old vegetation of a wide variety sprouts and blossoms; the garden looks very lush because of all the new growth. After a period of time, however, it needs pruning to remain healthy. Some plants grow too big and block the sun. Dead and diseased plants need to be removed, and vibrant ones need to have some space cleared for further growth.

In similar fashion, a new burst of middle-range theory construction in a substantive area eventually needs to have some order restored through integration. An integration project might cause some fragments to be discarded (or subsumed by others), while other fragments are straightened out and given more attention. To be more specific, the challenge of dealing with fragmentation involves learning (1) if and how the various fragments fit together, and (2) what changes must be made to some fragments to make them fit (and whether these changes retain the basic insights). In fact, some changes usually must be made, because fragments are typically tuned to particular applications for which specialized assumptions might be warranted. However, theoretical integration should embrace the goal of preserving the core insights whenever possible (especially when the fragments have survived empirical testing) while making the fragments fit together so that their interrelations can be stated precisely.

Theory fragments come with different sets of concepts and assumptions. Attempting to unify disjoint conceptual vocabularies is uninteresting, because nothing can be done. However, if the sets of concepts overlap, then it becomes interesting to investigate the compatibility of the assumptions of the different fragments.

We do not propose that all social science theory would currently benefit from attempts at unification. If serious doubts arise about the arguments in some available fragments, unification can produce disastrous results. Consider, for instance, a unification of a pair of hypothetical theory fragments A and B, where B happens to be very misguided (in hindsight), possibly based on flimsy or incorrect empirical evidence. The problem, of course, is that the unified theory is also necessarily flawed and, in the worst-case scenario, so too are the remains of fragment A, which have now become intertwined with B as it developed.

Theories often emerge as the results of efforts more or less coordinated by research programs conducted by many individual scientists. This kind of origin does not guarantee that different fragments of a theory use concepts in a coordinated manner. What does it take to develop a coordinated conceptual inventory? First comes the task of eliminating ambiguities and inconsistencies of different usages of concepts. As long as the concepts sit close to the surface of the theory, i.e., the key concepts are explained informally but not defined in terms of other primitive terms, then concepts can be changed easily, and the changes remain (relatively) local. For this reason, it makes sense to use locally defined (close-to-the-surface) conceptual inventories in the early phases of the development of a theory. The absence of deep, intricate connections between different concepts carries a less desirable side effect, though. It limits the explanatory and predictive power of the theory. If, on the other hand, the undefined, atomic concepts of a theory lie further from the surface (i.e., the important theoretical concepts are defined via sequences of definitions), then the modular nature of the conceptual inventory leads to more insightful explanations and more informative predictions. All these benefits become increasingly important as the theory matures.

Building deeper definitional structures requires an exploration process. Analysis of the "intended content" of the surface concepts leads to the deeper definitions and meaning postulates. Generally such an exercise can be carried out in different ways. One might go deeper, while another might try to stay closer to the surface. Some disassemble a complex notion in one way, and someone else does it differently. (A square can be seen as a rectangular rhombus or as an equilateral rectangle.)

Even though there is no single best way to execute these theoretical excavations, a number of indicators signal whether a process is running on a good track. If the number of atomic (undefined) concepts stops growing, (i.e., new definitions reuse the already excavated atomic concepts), then the network of definitional relationships gets denser. This is a good sign! If, as a result of such explorative work, previously unrelated theory fragments now jointly imply new consequences, then the conceptual excavation starts to reveal treasures. On the other hand, if deeper definitional structures do not bring unforeseen new connections, and if the new theorems derivable as a consequence of adding the new definitions show the signs of triviality, then one might seriously consider stopping the dig.

Attempts at unification presuppose a certain level of confidence in the component fragments. Such confidence will always reflect judgment; but it seems safe to say that attempting to integrate new fragments, or those without much empirical basis, typically involves greater risk. Such fragments might be better left isolated or unintegrated, at least until they mature as fragments with strong empirical foundations.[15]

As long as analysts restrict themselves to the rules of classical (first-order) logic as the way to test the soundness of arguments, the dangers of integration are still greater if two or more fragments offer incompatible explanations of a phenomenon. Suppose, for instance, that fragment A explains a set of facts from one set of premises and fragment B explains the same facts from incompatible[16] premises. The incompatibility means that the unification of these fragments will be logically inconsistent. Inconsistency is a theoretical disaster. The standard approach to testing the soundness of an argument is to analyze the set of premises together with the *negation* of the purported conclusion. If this set can be shown to be unsatisfiable (in the sense that there is no set of circumstances that make all of the premises and the negation of the conclusion true), then the theorem is proven, the conclusion follows as a logical implication of the set of premises (see Appendix C). This leads to a surprising conclusion: an inconsistent theory would explain all the facts that any fragment explained, and it would also explain a lot more, even the negations of all of these facts. Indeed, every possible theorem can be shown to follow as an implication of an inconsistent premise set.

The parallel to inconsistency in a classical logic shows up in the dynamic logic that we propose as the presence of arguments of equal or incomparable specificity lead to opposing conclusions. Any theory that contains such arguments is not much more useful in our (nonclassical) framework than it is in the classical framework. Instead of implying everything, opposing arguments with equal or incomparable specificity block any conclusion (see Chapter 6).

Given what seems to be the common interpretation of the strategy of building middle-range theory, it might come as a surprise to learn that the type of unification that we advocate does not contradict Merton, his views on middle-range theory

[15]In this book, we sometimes end chapters (and treatments of various fragments) by making speculative theoretical claims that seem to be natural extensions of developed arguments but for which we have no empirical evidence. Although these extensions might be readily made formal and integrated into the developed body of theory, we usually refrain from doing so for this reason.

[16]Incompatibility means that it is impossible for both sets of premises to be true simultaneously.

notwithstanding. In describing his full views about how theoretical activity should proceed, Merton wrote:

> Sociological theory, if it is to advance significantly, must proceed on these interconnected planes: (1) by developing special theories from which to derive hypotheses that can be empirically investigated [that is, with middle range theories] and (2) by evolving, not suddenly revealing, a progressively more general consolidated group of special theories. To concentrate entirely on special theories is to risk emerging with specific hypotheses that account for limited aspects of social behavior, organization and change that remain mutually inconsistent. (Merton 1968: 51)

So, although it seems to have been forgotten or disregarded by many,[17] there is no question that Merton saw middle-range theory and research as only an initial step in a larger process that eventually produces a more unified theory. This book deals with the subsequent step: integration.

Given the potential benefits of theoretical integration, why does scientific activity of this kind play such a limited role in sociology and other social sciences? One answer is that many researchers value integration but regard this activity as little more than collecting disparate fragments together into an available portfolio of theories (rather than pruning, trimming, and discarding some of them).[18]

Another answer points to social processes: theory groups, collections of analysts who support a theory, form around fragments. These groups commonly see themselves as advocates of the theory, and they commonly resist attempts to weaken its identity and prominence, as integration might possibly do. Interestingly, the view of integration as appending fragments with minimal alteration dovetails nicely with the interests of theory groups because, in this approach, the fragments retain their original coherence.

A third answer to the question about the rarity of integration projects recognizes that, even if a social scientist believes in deep integration and acts dispassionately towards the theory fragments of interest, it would often be hard to make progress. This is because good tools for theoretical integration are largely absent from the social-science toolkit for theory building, leaving the impression that integration relies more on genius and deep insights rather than on systematic procedures. We hope that our efforts to use a formal logic as a method for theoretical integration in rebuilding and extending a line of sociological theory will demonstrate that systematic procedures can be developed (and, to some extent, already exist implicitly in the best practice of contemporary social scientists).

Finally, we also suspect that the uncertainty of knowing where and how to start an integration project plays a role. If various fragments appear to be connected to others but in unclear ways, it is hard to pick the place where foundational concepts and arguments should be developed a priori. We have no good solution to this

[17]For example, Stephen Cole (2001), a student of Merton, laments the use of abstract general theory in sociology, suggesting (or so it seems) that only middle-range theory building makes sense.

[18]Some claimed integrations amount to little more than including indicators associated with causal processes featured in different theories as covariates in some kind of lengthy regression equation.

dilemma; we can only suggest that trial-and-error makes it possible to discover eventually an integration that proves useful.

In fact, our own efforts experienced considerable backtracking and rethinking as we attempted to integrate fragments. As our record of previous journal publication illustrates, we began by addressing what we saw as foundational issues concerning organizational forms and structural inertia. We rebuilt theories of each, using what we saw as the core concepts: audiences, social codes, and identity. We then proceeded to redraw theories of ecological niches and resource partitioning using this framework. As we then attempted to prepare a fuller treatment in this book, we realized that it was important to develop a theory of form emergence. After great deliberation, our work on form emergence eventually caused us to make the agents more explicit, attend to their perceptions, and emphasize the degree of agreement among the agents. This approach then led us to introduce vagueness in perception and grades of membership in clusters, categories, and forms—developments that begged us to deploy fuzzy-set theory and perception and default modalities. However, after doing all this, we realized that much of our previously reconstructed fragments were obsolete: they did not incorporate the very basic notion of vagueness in perception but instead something that denied this key insight. So we then reconstructed the reconstructions, building these ideas into the various fragments, sometimes with great pain but also at other times with interesting new insights. We report the results of this iterative effort in this book.

PART 1

Audiences, Producers, and Codes

Chapter Two

Clusters and Labels

Sociologists routinely invoke the concept of form. For example, in analyzing French collective action across four centuries, Charles Tilly (1986) describes the "forms of contention" that arose and spread through the provinces. These include seizures of grain; collective invasions of forbidden fields, forests, and streams; attacks on machines; serenades; tendentious holiday parades; forced illuminations; turnouts; strikes; demonstrations; petition marches; planned insurrections, and electoral campaigns. Likewise, in developing a sociology of art, Howard S. Becker (1982) characterizes various activities involving works of music, literature, film, television, sculpture, painting, and photography as "art forms." And, in organizational sociology, all major theorists occupy themselves in one way or another with "organizational forms," often used to describe established ways of producing most specific goods and services.

What exactly is a form? What roles do forms play in sociological theories? Despite the centrality of the concept in the research literatures on organizations, collective action, art, and culture, surprisingly little attention has been paid to clarifying these questions. Although ambiguity about the meaning of such a key concept might have been useful at earlier, exploratory stages of inquiry, it now hampers efforts to sharpen theoretical research programs; it also likely thwarts attempts at theoretical unification across disparate areas of the discipline.

Persons and corporate actors routinely identify social forms in the process of social discourse. Indeed, most treatments of forms emphasize their socially constructed nature. So, in defining forms of organizations (or forms of protests, genres, and so forth), the conceptual apparatus should build toward theories that would provide empirically testable answers to the question: What do social agents recognize when they "see" a form? How do they identify forms? That is, the conceptual apparatus should be capable of supporting theories that treat how social agents construct and distinguish forms.

Given the focus of the book, we pay attention mainly to forms in the organizational world, although we intend our approach to be general, to apply broadly to sociological analysis. The standard approach to defining organizational forms regards a form as a particular pattern of feature values. The example par excellence is Max Weber's (1968/1924) specification of the form of rational-legal bureaucracy in terms of the nature of authority (professional expertise in evaluating abstract rationalized codes), procedures (the impersonal exercise of authority and reliance on written rules and files), and the employment relation of the official (bureaucratic employment as a career of full-time work, office separated from the private sphere, and compensation by salary). Weber introduced his concept of rational-legal bureaucracy as what he called an ideal type, meaning (among other things) that he had abstracted from the historical details in identifying the properties that define the form. He sought to capture the essential properties of the bureaucratic organizations of the late-nineteenth-century Prussian state. Yet he noted that the form was not limited to its Prussian instance, arguing that the civil-service bureaus created by the Progressive reform movements in the United States in the first decades of the twentieth century, for example, also fit the form. In the language of contemporary theory, the Prussian and American instances were organizational populations based on the form of rational-legal bureaucracy.

Subsequent developments of the feature-based conception of forms recognize some features as more important than others in distinguishing forms. In this vein, analysts utilize the distinction between core and periphery and have identified forms with a pattern of values of a set of core features. That is, organizations that display a common pattern are treated as belonging to a form. Various analysts' ideas about forms differ mainly in envisioning different sets of features in the core.

Feature-based approaches treat distinctions among forms as reflecting only structural arrangements, suggesting that forms can be assessed in purely objective terms. A second, less developed, line of work defines forms in terms of the clarity and strength of *social boundaries*. Hannan and Freeman (1986) argued that the processes that create and reproduce the boundaries—social network ties, closed flows of personnel among a set of organizations, technological discontinuities, social movements articulating the interests of a set of organizations, and so forth—are the key to understanding the emergence and disappearance of forms. When segregating processes operate more powerfully than blending processes (those that blur distinctions among forms), then the world of organizations gets structured by form distinctions.

Paul DiMaggio (1986) proposed a similar approach: locating sets of structurally equivalent organizations in networks of important ties. Structural equivalence partitions a set of entities into equivalence classes that might be argued to represent forms. This proposal would actually define a population in the ecological framework, because it pertains to a localized set of interacting entities. Forms, as ecologists typically construe them, are more abstract entities; they potentially extend over space and time. Bringing network ideas into the picture is a very valuable step; so we follow this lead. That is, we use the term "feature value" to refer both to internal arrangements and to external arrangements (network ties or other kinds of relational properties, such as positions in distributions of size or status).

Organizational ecology pays more attention to form distinctions than do other strands of organization theory and, indeed, other lines of sociological inquiry. This emphasis causes some to conclude that the theoretical status of the concept matters mainly for theory and research in the ecological vein. We find this view mistaken. Current research practice in organizational sociology makes these issues central to all kinds of work. This is because researchers of all theoretical persuasions now design their research around organizational populations, adopting the conventional view that an organizational population is a spatial-temporal instantiation of a form.

Although some sociologists argue that studies ought to collect data on random samples from the (whole) world of organizations, as in the National Organizations

Study (Kalleberg, Knoke, Marsden, and Spaeth 1996), most researchers now argue that detailed institutional knowledge is needed to interpret empirical patterns. Gaining and using such knowledge is most feasible when research considers one or a few populations of organizations. And the bulk of published studies now use this approach (Carroll and Hannan 2000). Examples of recent research on populations of organizations include studies of populations as art museums (Blau 1995), audit firms (Boone, Bröcheler, and Carroll 2000), banks and life insurance companies (Ranger-Moore, Banaszak-Holl, and Hannan 1991), baseball teams (Land, Davis, and Blau 1994), brewers (Carroll and Swaminathan 1991; 2000), Broadway musical productions (Uzzi and Spiro 2005), credit unions (Barron 1999), ethnic and women's social-movement organizations (Minkoff 1999), investment banks (Park and Podolny 2000; Kuilman and Li 2006), law firms (Phillips 2001), micro radio stations (Greve, Posner, and Rao 2006) newspapers (Carroll 1987; Olzak and West 1991; Dobrev 2001), restaurants (Freeman and Hannan 1983; Rao et al. 2003), semiconductor manufacturers (Hannan and Freeman 1989; Podolny, Stuart, and Hannan 1996), symphony orchestras (Allmendinger and Hackman 1995), television stations (Sørensen 2000), wineries (Swaminathan 1995), and worker cooperatives (Russell 1995). The value of such research depends heavily on the populations studied representing instances of sociologically meaningful forms.

In this chapter and the next three (Chapters 3–5), we attempt to develop a fresh perspective on forms and populations. This approach retains a focus on features (defined broadly to include relations, as noted above). However, it also emphasizes the social construction of categories, forms, and populations. In this respect, it follows the institutionalist tradition started by Max Weber and reinvigorated by Philip Selznick, which strongly suggested that normative matters needed to be incorporated in any attempt to understand organizations. That is, organizations should not just be analyzed objectively in terms of their patterned activities, functions, and external ties—they must also be considered in terms of their social meanings and interpretation given to them by contemporaneous actors.

We think that use of a well-constructed formal language for expressing ideas about forms is crucial for disambiguating sociological claims about them. The language that we use allows for partial memberships in forms and what we see as their precursors— clusters, categories, and the like. It also uses a multimodal logic for analyzing statements about what audience members perceive about organizations' feature values and about what defaults they apply when feature values are only partially perceived. We suggest that stating the formalization in a language that allows partial memberships and modalities sharpens and refines the classical sociological ideas about forms and their usage in identities.

Our previous work (Pólos, Hannan, and Carroll 2002) defined forms as constructions built on certain kinds of *social codes*. We posited that certain codes exist, that code violations generate devaluation by relevant actors, and that identities build on such codes. Yet we did not identify the agents who do the codification. This kind of "passive-voice" construction, which characterizes much institutional sociology, makes it very difficult to explain change in institutional arrangements, including social codes, except by reference to exogenous shocks.

Social movement theorists, who naturally focus on the possibility that collections of agents can sometimes change institutions, stress the importance of attending to audiences and their dynamics. In the spirit of their work, we now propose that more theoretical traction can be gained by couching arguments about forms (and, subsequently, identities) in the active voice, by identifying the *agents* who create and use the codes. In essence, we shifted to analyzing codification as a process. This shift prompts us to consider a related series of processes that might yield a form. These subprocesses are (1) constructing similarity clusters, (2) labeling them, (3) creating schemata to explain their understandings, (4) creating categories by coming to social agreement about the meanings of labels, and finally (5) constructing forms by taking for granted that members of a category satisfy the relevant schemata.

We analyze these processes from the point of view of individual members of an audience as well as from that of the audience as a whole. This shift in the argument allows us to build on the work of cognitive anthropologists, especially Frederik Barth (1987, 1993), Roy D'Andrade (1995), and Claudia Strauss and Naomi Quinn (1997), who have moved from considering cultures as unitary objects to characterizing the distributions of semantic objects (interpretations) within and between communities. It also provides strong connections with contemporary research by organizational theorists such as Ezra Zuckerman (1999; Phillips and Zuckerman 2001; Zuckerman, Kim, Ukanwa, and von Rittman 2003) and Hayagreeva Rao (Rao et al. 2003, 2005), who have been pioneers in analyzing how audiences and audience structures affect organizations.

Accordingly, we modify our earlier formulation in several ways. The most important is that, by building on the perspective of contemporaneous agents whose views might be partial and lack consensus, we treat membership in clusters, categories and forms as potentially *partial.* This view leads us to define clusters, categories, forms, and populations as fuzzy sets. Although we did not realize it at first, it turns out that our efforts in this direction essentially reinvented the wheel. A major line of work in cognitive psychology and cognitive science begun by Rosch (1973, 1975; Rosch and Mervis 1975) shows that natural categories tend to lack sharp boundaries and clear definitions, that the members of such categories share what Wittgenstein (1953) called a family resemblance. We now build explicitly on this line of work. We show that this shift in focus, from considering classical categories to fuzzy ones, clarifies some core issues concerning organizational categories, forms, and populations.

2.1 SEEDS FOR CATEGORIES AND FORMS

Where do organizational categories and forms come from? As noted above, this complex but important question has only recently started to attract serious attention among organizational theorists. Clearly, many individuals learn about "new" categories from the words and actions of experts, authorities, social-movement activists, or journalists. Likewise, new categories also often build on existing categories, cultural rules, and languages. Although a theory of forms might rely on any of these contextual conditions to make predictions, we think that grasping the dynamics of form emergence requires attending to the initial establishment of the codes that define categories and forms in a less information-rich context. Only through such consideration can we develop an adequate explanation of how experts, enthusiasts, and authorities (among others) create the seeds of new categories and forms.

Accordingly, our theoretical account of form emergence begins with a conceptual rendering of what we consider to be a minimally structured situation, a kind of "primal soup" of forms. We focus on an audience segment, a differentiated set of all those agents with an intense interest in the organizations, their activities, and their products, and we follow a constructionist approach. That is, instead of treating categories as analytic, as products of researchers' distinctions, we assume that the members of audience segments create categories and forms. Members of audiences observe producers and products, notice similarities, try to make sense of them by clustering similar producers/products, and possibly assign labels to clusters. These activities comprise the first steps in the audience's creation of what might turn into a category or even a form.

We faced two big challenges in modeling the emergence of categories and forms in such a bottom-up way. In our initial attempts at formalization, we found ourselves slipping unnoticed into a realist—as opposed to a constructionist—stance. This tendency manifested itself in two ways. First, we repeatedly found ourselves assuming that "real" clusters exist and that the task of the audience is to recognize them.[1] Second, we found it hard to avoid the tacit assumption that the dimensions that audience members use to compare organizations and their products are given. In the end, we decided that progress in understanding bottom-up categorization requires a more thorough constructionism, as we explain in detail in the chapters in this part of the book.

We also make another radical strategic move. Our earlier efforts to define categories and forms of organizations, like all of the others that we know, treated memberships in clusters (or categories or forms) as *classical* set memberships. That is, we assumed that each member of an audience either regards an organization as a member of a cluster or does not. In other words, we represented memberships in clusters (and categories and forms) with classical set-theoretical models. We eventually decided that this approach asks too much of the audience.

As we explained in Chapter 1, we know of many situations where some organization neither clearly belongs to a set (cluster, category, or form) nor clearly does not belong. An organization can be a member of a set in some respects but not in others. Representing this possibility demands that we modify the underlying set theory. Therefore, we use a nonclassical approach: fuzzy-(sub)set theory. Allowing memberships to be fuzzy complicates the analysis considerably; but we think that it increases its realism and sociological value. Moreover, we argue (in Chapter 4) that building a fuzzy machinery solves several long-standing problems in analyzing organizational populations.

Making these two important shifts in basic theory requires conceptual preparation. This chapter reports that work, which includes quite a few definitions and

[1] We do not claim that the features of producers and products are not real—only that the clusters do not have some real existence absent a clusterer.

conceptual clarifications. Subsequent chapters build directly on this work, where we (re)generate central fragments of ecological theory from these core concepts and derive implications.

As will become clear below and in the chapters that follow, many of the ideas that we use come from diverse literatures (including anthropology, cognitive science, linguistics, philosophy, and sociology). Our goals include pulling together these theoretical ideas in a new way, building a more tightly unified framework, and sharpening their representations and usage through formalization. The resulting theory is, we believe, not only a solid foundation for rebuilding other theory fragments in organizational ecology, but also a more elaborate and comprehensive account of the form emergence process. Detailed specification of the possible form emergence process should encourage and facilitate empirical research, which we believe has been hindered by a lack of detailed conceptualization.

2.2 DOMAINS

We concentrate on what we call domains: culturally bounded slices of the social world, such as agriculture, art, finance, medicine, and sport. This construction faces an obvious problem of infinite regress, because a domain is itself a cultural category, whose emergence and persistence need explaining. We do not try to go back to the organizational "big bang" here. Instead, we take domains (and possible subdomains) as given.[2] Domains may, of course, overlap: for example some fraction of the art world overlaps with the world of commerce. At this point in the development of the theory, we see little to be gained by attempting to treat the full set of domains and their overlaps. So, in the interest of analytical tractability, we analyze an isolated domain.

For us, a minimal structure for a domain consists of a pair of roles and a language for telling what the roles mean. As a domain develops, these roles get elaborated and the language gets filled with content that articulates what it means to occupy the roles. We define these concepts formally as follows.

Definition 2.1 (Domain). *A domain is a triplet $\mathcal{D} = \{\mathcal{A}, \mathcal{O}, \mathcal{L}\}$, where*

1. $\mathcal{A} = \{\mathbf{a}_1, \mathbf{a}_2, \ldots\}$ *is a collection of the* audience segments *in the domain. Each audience segment consists of an interacting set of agents that inspect, evaluate, and consume the output of the producers. We use the term audience segment to emphasize that we refer to a component of a domainwide audience that is relatively closed with respect to communication and interaction.*

2. $\mathcal{O} = \{\mathbf{o}_1, \mathbf{o}_2, \ldots\}$ *is a collection of sets of either (1) the agents that occupy the role of* producer *in the domain (producers create goods and services for inspection, evaluation, and consumption within a bounded region of social*

[2] The framework we propose ought to be able to serve as a basis for explaining the emergence of domains. Indeed, the emergence of a form might result in a new domain, which itself might become populated with subforms. We do treat these issues in this book.

space) or (2) products, the outputs of the producers. There is a correspondence between the elements in $\mathcal{A}$ and $\mathcal{O}$ such that each audience segment is paired with a producer/product segment. We think of this correspondence as one of visibility: *for each* $\mathbf{a} \in \mathcal{A}$, $\mathbf{o}$ *is the set of producers/products that fall in the purview of the members of* $\mathbf{a}$.[3]

3. $\mathcal{L} = \{\mathbf{l}_1, \mathbf{l}_2, \ldots\}$ *is a set of functions that map from time points and audience segments to a language that contains a set of proper names (individual constants) and labels for sets. The characteristic (atomic) sentences of these languages tell that an entity in some subset associated with the label possesses or does not possess a certain feature value at a point in time.*

The concept of domain differs from other well-known characterizations of macro environments in sociological studies of organizations and economic action. For instance, an organizational set (the organizational analog to a role set) consists of the cluster of relations that an organization engages in (Scott 1981). An organizational field consists of "those organizations that, in the aggregate, constitute a recognized area of institutional life: key suppliers, resource and produce consumers, regulatory agencies, and other organizations that produce similar services and products" (DiMaggio and Powell 1983: 148). A societal sector is "a collection of organizations operating in the same domain, as identified by the similarity of their services, products or functions, together with those organizations that critically influence the performance of the focal organizations: for example, major suppliers and customers, owners and regulators, funding sources and competitors" (Scott and Meyer 1991: 117). Notice that each of these concepts bounds its relevant unit by organizations, not role sets and languages, as does our concept of domain.

We use the terms "producer" and "product" abstractly. We mean the terms to apply to the most obvious reference of the terms: organizations or individuals who produce material products, including such pairs as

automobile manufacturer/sports utility vehicle,

organic dairy farm/organic milk,

potter/ceramic bowl.

Moreover, the pairs can also be providers of services (defined very broadly), e.g.,

architect/design for a building,

orchestra/symphonic performance,

political party/electoral campaign,

school/instruction,

social movement/collective protest.

[3]Note that we define $\mathbf{a}$ and $\mathbf{o}$ as "crisp sets," which rules out ambiguity about the boundaries of the audience and the set of producers/products. This treatment is an analytical simplification and could be relaxed, which would mean considering broader sets. We justify the use of the assumption of crispness on the grounds that the distinctions among segments are largely an analytical distinction, as contrasted with a distinction made by the members of a domain.

We consider audience segments as the units (sets of agents) within which categories and forms emerge. Therefore, we treat segment boundaries as barriers to the easy flow of communication and to achieving consensus about classifications. When we speak of an audience segment, we mean that a portion of a domain-wide audience that is bounded in this manner.

Relevant audience segments generally include what are usually called "insiders"—the actual and potential members or employees of producer organizations—as well as various kinds of outsiders: buyers and suppliers, investors, critics, regulators. Moreover, the producers themselves are audience to each other. These diverse sets of agents possess an interest in the products/services and in the producers. In addition, audience members control essential material resources such as capital, labor, purchasing power, and symbolic resources such as approval or endorsement. Gaining access to resources is *not* incidental or epiphenomenal in our theory—it matters decisively for the success and failure of the products and their producers. Because the members of the audience segment control the critical resources for producers, the perceptions and cultural understandings of the audience members affect the resources available to a producer. Put simply, the audience controls the resources that matter to the producers.

A critical basic resource is the attention of the agents in the audience. Producers/products that fail to get noticed do not fare well; and gaining positive valuations requires first gaining attention. Attracting attention generally requires the expenditure of time and effort and the commitment of other resources. In other words, producers must make an effort to engage the members of an audience in order to gain their attention and, subsequently, other resources that the audience controls.

There are, of course, often many distinct audiences present in a domain, however, for purposes of analytical clarity, we typically consider only a single focal audience segment in constructing theory. We leave to future work the task of modeling the implications of the coexistence of multiple segments. In formal terms, we pick a particular audience segment for analysis; we refer to the chosen segment as $\mathbf{a}$. All definitions, postulates, auxiliary assumptions, and theorems should be interpreted as applying to this chosen audience segment. Therefore, we will *not* constantly refer to the segment in formal definitions and propositions, unless we need to refer to the size of the segment, in which case we refer to the *cardinality* of $\mathbf{a}$ (in notation, $|\mathbf{a}|$).[4]

Once we have fixed the focal audience segment, we have also fixed the producer/product segment. Therefore, we do *not* refer to the relevant set $\mathbf{o}$ explicitly in the formulas unless we need to refer to the number of producers, in which case we refer to the cardinality of this set: $|\mathbf{o}|$. All of the formulas that refer to a producer or product should be read as pertaining to an element of the relevant set, $\mathbf{o}$. The same convention applies to the language.[5]

[4]The cardinality of a (finite) set is the number of unique items that it contains.

[5]In developing a formal rendering of these processes, we start by describing the language of an audience segment in two stages. In this chapter, we consider an extensional, factual stage. The language of facts can be regarded as a part of the language of first-order logic, as sketched in Appendix C. The next chapter considers an intensional stage in the development of the language of a domain, as described in Chapter 6 and Appendix E.

We posit that the two main roles in the domain—audience and producer or product—coevolve. A domain develops a structure when an audience segment develops a common language. For our initial purposes in this part of the book, an important aspect of an audience segment is its degree of consensus about the categories and forms of producers/products (Rosa et al. 1999).

The decision to treat audience and producer roles symmetrically makes the theory more complicated than would be the case if we followed the convention of treating the properties of the audience as given. Nonetheless, we think that the increased power of the theory more than compensates for the added complexity.

An agent's announced goals or purposes associate it with the role of producer. Organizations and individuals generally announce their claims to competence for membership in a domain. For instance, a newly founded organization typically announces through both direct and indirect claims that it intends to be, say, a biotechnology drug-discovery firm, or a restaurant, a political party, a protest movement, and so forth. Alternatively, an existing commercial bank might announce that it plans to enter into investment banking, or an art museum might announce that it wants to become a university. An individual might claim to be an actor or an artist, and so forth.

The important connection for us is that a claim to membership in some set (or label or concept) exposes an agent to scrutiny and evaluation by the audience that follows the action in the domain and controls relevant resources. At the same time, the producers are audiences to each other, as Harrison White (2001) has stressed. Artists and scientists criticize and evaluate each other's work; organizations pay close attention to their peers and competitors. This is why we refer to audience and producer *roles* and assume that the same agent can play both roles simultaneously. Agents (individuals or organizations) often occupy both roles. For instance, in the system of peer evaluation in science, many scientists play both producer and evaluator roles.

The way that we model the audience changes according to the stage of the domain's evolution. When (as in Part I) we consider processes of emergence, we envision the audience segment as limited to a well-defined, socially circumscribed group, within which sociodemographic position does not matter much (at least by our theory). When a category emerges, its name occasionally enters the common language and the audience expands. In this phase, even the schemata associated with the category might drift throughout the audience—along social networks lines delineated by sociodemographic characteristics of audience members, according to much research. In Part III of the book, we reconceptualize the audience as ordered by positions defined by sociodemographic characteristics where position affects tastes. (We leave the details of the process of the internal structuring of the audience to future research.)

2.3 SIMILARITY

We noted above that many categories and forms might have originated in fairly structured situations, those in which the audience has a well-developed language (including schemata for categories). In these kinds of situations, new categories can be formed by analogy to existing ones (by making slight modifications in schemata), by merging a pair of categories, and so forth. Nonetheless, we find it insightful to consider the unstructured case—how some actors with only a minimal language initially perceive and learn about the entities that eventually might cohere into a category. To this end, we focus on similarity clustering as a possible seed for the crystallization of a category. In analyzing classifications of artworks into genres, DiMaggio (1997: 441) emphasized such a process: "I use *genre* to refer to sets of artworks classified together on the basis of perceived similarities. The challenge to the sociology of art is to understand the processes by which similarities are perceived and genres enacted." We think that this is exactly the challenge for organizational sociology.

How does an audience come to think of some collection of organizations as being alike? In our view, the first step involves identifying the distinct mechanisms that create the "seeds" around which grouping and categorization might occur. Someone must take action to create such seeds.

Engaging in efforts at clustering demands a considerable effort from the members of the audience. It seems likely that some members of the audience must be in a high-energy state for these processes to be completed. Some members of the audience segment must gather information, compare producers and products, and propose and defend different ways of understanding distinctions among them. These activities involve much more effort and engagement than is required when arrangements and distinctions are settled. To highlight this difference, we refer to the subset of the audience that produces clusterings as *activists* or *enthusiasts.*

In the least structured case, categorization begins with some individuals (enthusiasts) judging the producers/products in terms of what they perceive as similarities of feature values. We found it surprisingly difficult to develop a coherent account of this process. The problem, as we now see it, is that we were blinded by our previous work in which we recognized that social codes (which we now render as schemata) shape judgments and valuations. Having argued that a language of codes is appropriate for expressing properties of identities and forms, we found it natural to envision that evaluators might use such codes in establishing similarities and differences. Eventually, we realized that there is no reason for assuming that the interested parties agree on the relevant features (much less on the appropriate values on these features) at the outset. We have shifted to the view that the enthusiasts discern clusters of producers/products in the domain based on similarity judged in an *unconstrained* manner.

As we noted above, audiences maintain an interest in the activities within domains. Such an interest causes them to compare the entities operating, or claiming to be operating, in a domain (rather than some arbitrarily chosen entities in a society). The relevance criterion also means that audiences typically do not pick up arbitrary similarities; instead they consider those that are relevant for sorting potential members of the domain given by their interest. Thus we allow for the presence of what cognitive scientists often call domain-specific background knowledge. Psychological research reveals that such background knowledge facilitates recognition of patterns of similarity by directing attention to what are generally the relevant dimensions in the domain (Murphy 2002: Chapter 6). Use of background knowledge eases the task of gaining agreement among the members of an audience segment, because that knowledge will direct their attention to more or less the same features. Nonetheless, we do not need to rely on the existence of background knowledge for the story that we develop; and we do not refer explicitly to background knowledge in our formulation.

Diverse aspects of a domain might spark the attention of the enthusiasts, especially when they change (Hannan and Freeman 1986). These aspects include:

Patterns of resource utilization: producers/products that rely on the same sources of capital, material, and personnel might be evaluated simultaneously in domain publications, at domain events (venture capital events, job fairs), and as they present their offerings to individual consumers, potential employees, and so forth.

Patterns of audience attention: producers/products that engage socially similar audience members often come to be seen as similar. Pierre Bourdieu (1984) emphasized this kind of process in cultural consumption.

Agglomeration: producers/products in close geographical proximity often come to be seen as similar. For example, if a customer visits one of them, she finds it hard not to learn about others near by. Certain kinds of producers display strong agglomeration tendencies. Classic examples include: the diamond-merchant districts of Manhattan and Antwerp, the Hollywood film industry, Silicon Valley, and the financial centers of the City of London and Wall Street. For instance, Richard Peterson (1997) links the development of the "country music" form to its recurrence in four different kinds of local venues: community dances, fiddling contests, street corners in cities, and events (social, political, and commercial). Colocation can also foster imitation and cause practices to converge, making it easier for an audience to perceive clusters of similarity.

Network ties: social ties among producers might provide common pointers. Learning about an organization often leads one to understand which producers its members see as its competitors, labor sources, suppliers, alliance partners, and the like. The social network of an organization provides a natural path for identifying other similar producers in a domain.

Technology: producers that use similar technologies (regardless of what they produce) might come into the focus of attention at once (e.g., companies using biotechnology for drug discovery and/or horticultural research, organic farms that produce diverse products such as meat, vegetables, or wine).

Social institutions: formal and informal social institutions structure how agents experience and perceive the world. Whether by design or not, these institutions often order and group producers in particular ways and these groups affect perception of similarities.

A Formal Approach

We model agents' perceptions of similarity in clustering by building on Amos Tversky's (1977) well-known contrast model. Tversky (and others) found experimental evidence that the formal properties of geometrical similarity fail in human perception. Geometrical similarity is a binary function: two figures are either similar or different, *tertium non datur.* However, human perception admits degrees of similarity. An entity can appear as more or less similar to another. Human subjects often report that an object, say, a, is more similar to another b than b is to a (see Tversky 1977 for details). For example, most subjects judge the letter F to be more similar to the letter E than E is to F. Likewise, people judge portraits as more similar to their subjects than the subjects are similar to their portraits. Why? In the eyes of most observers, the subject of the painting possesses many more observable features than the portrait (and E has one more stroke than F). Thus, the human subject matches most of the portrait's feature values; the portrait does not match many of the subject's feature values. The difference in the number of features observed for the members of a comparison pair gives rise to the possibility of asymmetry.

The precategory stage might exhibit little conceptual order. Enthusiasts have not yet even settled on the features that will be used to specify a (not-yet-defined) category. How do they make sense of things? We conjecture that observers look at the producers/products in simple paired comparisons and focus on the features that they see as present, rather than on those that they might consider to be missing.[6] They might indeed see many more features for one object than for another, as when two producers differ in prominence. Similarity judgments will exhibit asymmetry in such cases.

In defining the similarity of a pair of objects from an observer's perspective, we use Tversky's ratio measure.

Definition 2.2 (Similarity). *Tversky's ratio measure of degree of similarity (as perceived by an unspecified agent) of the entities x and x' at time t is*

$$sim(x, x', t) = \frac{f(\mathbf{x}_t \cap \mathbf{x}'_t)}{f(\mathbf{x}_t \cap \mathbf{x}'_t) + af(\mathbf{x}'_t \setminus \mathbf{x}_t) + bf(\mathbf{x}_t \setminus \mathbf{x}'_t)}, \qquad a, b \geq 0; x \neq x',$$

where $\mathbf{x}_t$ and $\mathbf{x}'_t$ denote the sets of features that the agent perceives as characterizing the producers/products x and x' at time t, $\setminus$ denotes set subtraction, and f is a monotonic function.

(We impose the restriction that similarity is defined only if $x = x'$ as a way of requiring that the sets of objects that are perceived as similar cannot be singletons.)

In other words, the perceived similarity of a pair of entities grows with number of overlaps of (perceived) features and declines with the number of nonoverlaps in (perceived) features. In most applications f is a counting function, one that gives the cardinality of the set.

Obviously, similarity judgments depend on perceptions, rather than on objective facts. The dependence on perception ought to be represented in the formal lan-

[6]We argue in the next chapter that the observation that an entity lacks a feature depends on a schema that specifies the relevant features.

guage. We do so by defining a modal operator for perception in Chapter 4 and Appendix E.

2.4 SIMILARITY CLUSTERS

When the attention of the enthusiasts in an audience segment gets drawn to some part of a domain, they generally try to sort out what they see. The sensemaking begins with similarity judgments and efforts to identify sets of similar producers/products. As we mentioned above, similarity clustering can attend to features of products, of producers, or both. Cases in which products/services apparently got clustered directly, and their producers indirectly, include newspapers (Carroll 1985), semiconductors (Hannan and Freeman 1989), art genres (DiMaggio 1987), and life insurance (Zelizer 1978). This kind of similarity clustering seems likely to occur when audience members can experience the products/services without direct contact with their producers. Thus, an individual can subscribe to a newspaper without ever having seen a newsroom, appreciate artworks in books, and so forth.

Clustering (and codification) of the characteristics of the individuals and organizations behind the products likely occurs when consuming the product (or service) requires direct interaction with the producer. Typical cases in which such clustering takes place include hospitals, museums, schools, labor unions, and brewpubs.

At least two potential audiences—members of producer organizations and the producers themselves—always engage in interaction with producers and can, therefore, see their characteristics. When members of these insider audiences delineate clusters, they frequently attend to features of the producers, which might be hard for other audiences to see. The category "bulge-bracket" investment bank (Podolny 1993), which distinguishes those banks that engage in a distinctive, high-status pattern of association (in syndicates), seems to have developed this way, as did the category "white shoe" law firm. Efforts at clustering and codification by producers generate what DiMaggio (1987) calls professional classification.

Enthusiasts often cluster both producers and their products on the basis of similarity. In the case of restaurants, features of the restaurant organization and of product/service sometimes get captured in clustering (and codification). The distinction between classical and *nouvelle* French cuisine presents a nice example (Rao et al. 2003, 2005). The features used in making the distinction include the role of the chef in the management of the organization, the organization of the menu, the rhetoric used in naming dishes, the prototypical ingredients, and the rules of cooking.

Enthusiasts might form clusters using characteristics of the producer or product, e.g., the ingredients used in brewing beer, the processes used in brewing lagers versus ales, or the kind of barrel used in aging wine. They might also form clusters based on relational properties, such as network ties (as in the case of bulge-bracket investment banks), blessing from some authority or critic (e.g., museums certify art objects as high art), membership in a guild, location, and so forth. We design our account of clustering and labeling so that it can accommodate both cases.

In a world represented by the rules of standard (classical) set theory, clusters would be regarded as crisp sets, sets with the property that each producer (or product) is either a (full-fledged) member or not a member at all. Such a picture does not seem realistic. Observers often detect shades of difference and decide that some producers fit comfortably in the cluster, some do not fit at all, and others fit to a greater or lesser degree. Indeed, several major lines of research in cognitive psychology and cognitive science have documented the ubiquity of graded membership for both "natural categories" (such as fruits, animal species, and types of furniture) and artificial categories constructed for laboratory experiments. (Murphy (2002) gives an admirably clear overview of these developments.) Research in marketing has applied this work to consumer products (Loken and Ward 1987; Viswanathan and Childers 1999). Much less attention has been paid to applying this work to the producers.[7]

In Chapter 1, we considered the category "university" and some specific organizations that lay claim to this label. We proposed that some organizations that call themselves universities clearly belong to the category (e.g., Oxford University), some clearly do not (e.g., McDonald's Hamburger University), and some others belong to some degree (e.g., Rockefeller University, University of Phoenix, the National Defense University, Bob Jones University, Maharishi University of Management, and Open University). These claims correspond to long-noted sociological observations about the permeability of social boundaries surrounding roles and categories (Goffman 1963; Phillips and Zuckerman 2001). Our approach differs in placing these distinctions at the center of the theory and representing these differences using the machinery of fuzzy-set theory.

A Fuzzy-Set Construction

Standard set theory defines sets as collections of objects in a specified universe of discourse that satisfy a given predicate. Let the universe of discourse (the world of interest) be denoted by U. For example, the (crisp) set of universities is the collection of all those objects in U that satisfy the predicate "is a university":

$$\mathbf{A} = \{x \mid (x \in \mathrm{U}) \wedge \textsc{university}(x)\}.$$

This set is the collection of ordered pairs whose first element is an object in the universe of discourse and whose second element is either zero or one. (Here and elsewhere, we use the pair of braces $\{\}$ to denote a set.)

A set can be characterized fully in terms of its characteristic function. The characteristic function of a set, say **A**, maps from elements of the universe to either zero or one, that is, it maps to the set that contains 0 and 1, $\{0, 1\}$:

$$\mathbf{A} : \mathrm{U} \longrightarrow \{0, 1\},$$

where the long right arrow $\longrightarrow$ denotes a mapping or function (we use a short arrow $\rightarrow$ to denote the (logical) material implication relation).

The membership of the set **A** in the standard theory consists of those objects for which the mapping equals (exactly) 1. In other words, the set-membership relationship is binary: an element is either a member of a set or it is not. Truth values of statements about set membership, therefore, have only two values: $\{true, false\}$.

[7]For an interesting exception, see Porac et al. (1995).

Fuzzy sets provide descriptions of situations in which membership can be partial, a matter of degree (Zadeh 1965; Klir and Folger 1988). The parallel to the characteristic function for a standard ("crisp") set is the *grade-of-membership function,* which maps from elements of the universe to the [0,1] interval.[8] The GoM function for the fuzzy set **A** is

$$\mu_{\mathbf{A}} : \mathrm{U} \longrightarrow [0,1].$$

If $\mu_{\mathbf{A}}(x) = 0$, then the object x clearly does not belong to the set **A**; if $\mu_{\mathbf{A}}(x) = 1$, then it is a full-fledged member. Values falling between 0 and 1 refer to different grades (or degrees) of membership. The membership function provides a complete characterization of a fuzzy set. That is, a fuzzy set is defined as the set of ordered pairs such that the first element is a member of the universe of discourse and the second element is the membership function for that element:

$$\mathbf{A} = \{x, \mu_{\mathbf{A}}(x)\}, \quad x \in \mathrm{U}.$$

It is common to refer to a fuzzy set simply in terms of its membership function; and we use $\{x, \mu_{\mathbf{A}}(x)\}$ and $\{\mu_{\mathbf{A}}\}$ interchangeably.

Of course, a grade of membership between zero and one might result from any of a number of sources, including (1) a lack of full information about the object (not enough relevant features are observed); (2) a lack of full observation on the other potential members of the set; (3) incomplete cognition about the nature of the set (the agent has not yet figured out how to define it); or (4) genuine ambiguity about the relationship between the object and the set, given full information. Cases (3) and (4) might be closely related. We find them much more interesting than the partial information cases, and we will focus on them throughout our discussion.

Returning briefly to our problematic "university" examples (that is, Rockefeller, Phoenix, Bob Jones, National Defense, Maharishi, and Open), we have little doubt that most observers would classify each of these organizations as having grades of membership as "university" between 0 and 1.0. But there might be some disagreement about how well each fits the label "university" and even about their rank ordering in terms of fit. For instance, someone whose notion of university places more weight on the presence of a research faculty than on enrolled students might assign Rockefeller a high grade of membership and place it above Phoenix and the others. If another's conception places more weight on academic freedom, then Bob Jones would likely have a low—possibly zero—grade of membership.

In addition to the grade of membership, we will make frequent reference to the *support* of a fuzzy set: the classical (crisp) set that consists of those elements in U with a positive grade of membership in the set:

$$\mathrm{supp}\{\mu_{\mathbf{A}}\} \equiv \{x \mid \mu_{\mathbf{A}}(x) > 0\}, \qquad x \in \mathbf{o}.$$

We will also make reference to the cardinality of a fuzzy set (Zadeh 1983). In the case of classical (crisp) sets, the cardinality of a set refers to the number of distinct elements in the set. We denote the cardinality of the crisp set **A** as $|\mathbf{A}|$. In the

[8]Throughout, we use the standard mathematical notation for open and closed intervals. The closed interval, denoted $[a, b]$, includes its end points a and b; the open interval, denoted by (a, b) does not include a and b.

fuzzy case, objects can have partial memberships. Therefore, the generalization of cardinality to this case, for a finite universe, sums the grades of memberships in the set over the universe of discourse:[9]

$$\text{card}\{\mu_{\mathbf{A}}\} \equiv \textstyle\sum_{x \in U} \mu_{\mathbf{A}}(x).$$

We also want to characterize the degree to which a fuzzy set stands out from its background, what we call its contrast (reflecting its sharpness against the background). Because we did not find any treatment of this issue in the literature on fuzzy sets, we devised our own. We want a measure that equals one when a set is crisp and otherwise tells how much the fuzzy set resembles a crisp set. We propose that the contrast of a fuzzy set be considered as the average grade of membership in the set among those with positive grade of membership:

$$c(\{\mu_{\mathbf{A}}\}) \equiv \frac{\text{card}\{\mu_{\mathbf{A}}\}}{|\text{supp}\{\mu_{\mathbf{A}}\}|},$$

if $\{\mu_{\mathbf{A}}\} \neq \emptyset$, and it is undefined otherwise. Obviously, the contrast of a crisp, nonempty set equals one. The greater the departure of the contrast of a set from one, the less clearly the fuzzy set stands out from its background (the domain).

Experienced researchers who learn about this fuzzy conception of forms and associated grades of membership worry about the exacting demands that it makes on empirical research. Obviously, researchers embracing this view must do more than identify organizations and record their features, as previous work did. And, while it might seem immediately feasible to consider measuring grades of membership of organizations in laboratory experiments or with survey instruments, collecting average grades of membership by audience segment over long periods of a population's history might appear daunting. Clearly, some innovative measurement techniques will need to be advanced and evaluated positively for this approach to blossom. Along these lines, we are encouraged that already two potentially promising but very different efforts seem well underway. Sandy Bogaert, Christophe Boone and Glenn Carroll (2006) use the distribution of professional association memberships in auditing to calculate the fuzziness of various schema used for the emergent auditor form in nineteenth-century Netherlands, and Balazs Kovacs (2006) characterizes fuzziness using similarities calculated from links generated by Web pages on the Internet.

With this background in hand, we now use the fuzzy-set machinery to define a similarity cluster.

Definition 2.3 (Similarity cluster). *A (fuzzy) set k is a similarity cluster, in notation* $\text{CLUS}(k, y, t)$*, if k's grade of membership function, $\mu_k(x, y, t)$, satisfies the following properties:*

1. $\mu_k : \mathbf{x}, \mathbf{y}, \mathbf{t} \longrightarrow [0, 1]$ *(μ maps triplets of producers/products, audience members, and time points to the [0,1] interval);*

2. $\mu_k(x, y, t) = 0$ *for at least one producer or product (some producers or products must be excluded); and*

[9]This function is generally called the *scalar* cardinality of the set (Klir and Folger 1988). The restriction to finite universes fits our intended scope of application.

3. *$\mu_k(x, y, t)$ increases with the average similarity of x to other producers or products with $\mu_k(x, y, t) > 0$ and decreases with average similarity with nonmembers of the cluster (those with $\mu_k(x, y, t) = 0$).*

Efforts at similarity clustering involve a considerable cognitive load because they require making many pairwise similarity judgments, each involving multiple features, and keeping them in mind when constructing grades of membership in the cluster. The high cognitive load entailed requires that the agent doing the clustering be in what might be called a *high-energy state.* In such a state, the actors devote an unusually high fraction of attention to the objects in the domain, and they likely expend considerable time and resources in collecting information about them. This is why we refer to those active in this stage as enthusiasts or activists.

For example, we know that the American craft-brew movement, which eventually spawned the microbrewery and brewpub categories, began among home brewers in the 1970s. No relevant producer organizations existed at the time; in fact, what would become brewpubs were still illegal in all states. There were, however, home-brewer clubs and informal associations of enthusiasts who were interested in making their own beers. So, the enthusiasts were the home brewers and the focus was on the products, beers in this case. Although we lack data on these people for this period, it would be consistent with our story to imagine that, when these enthusiasts got together, they examined and sampled each other's beers and perhaps compared them with European products. Furthermore, we think it is reasonable to imagine that these interactions led to product-based similarity clusters from comparisons of these beers to each other and to others on the commercial market.

The dependence of clustering on pairwise similarity judgments has an important implication about stability. An observer will generally have great difficulty in extending clusters when new observations become available. Two problems arise. First, the cognitive load grows exponentially as the number of entities considered for the cluster rises linearly. Second, the appearance of not-yet-considered objects can activate new dimensions and require that all similarity judgments be reconsidered. Reconsideration raises the possibility that the cluster will collapse in the sense that the objects cohere in some way gets lost. (In the next chapter, we consider schemata as more stable representations of similarity.)

The definition of a similarity cluster does not preclude the formation of a cluster with very low average μ_k, that is, a cluster whose members are quite dissimilar. In a purely volitional process of perception and cognition, it is doubtful that a sensible person would bother to do this; she would likely direct attention only to those clusters with average μ_k above some threshold. Yet some social institutions sometimes present organizations in bundles of a sort, thereby encouraging onlookers to regard the bundles as clusters, even if some of the pairs of organizations are somewhat dissimilar. For instance, professional committees charged with reviewing particular organizations, practices, or individuals often assign the objects to be reviewed on a basis other than similarity (say, geographic location, alphabetical order, or size). Similarly, despite a focal-industry orientation, the portfolios assigned to stock-market analysts for observation and evaluation often group together firms with (some) activities in disparate industries, implying that the degree to which the analyst includes them in the focal category of the portfolio might be low (Zuckerman 1999). These cases exemplify what DiMaggio (1987) calls administrative classification.

Rather than specify some threshold that the average similarities must meet for a set to be considered a cluster, we leave the definition open on this point. This does not do any damage. Below we argue that clusters with low average similarity are very unlikely to serve as the seeds for codification. We develop substantive arguments that enthusiasts are unlikely to go to the trouble of labeling clusters with low average similarity, which, in turn, means that they are also unlikely to go to the trouble of creating schemata for them. In other words, clustering generally implies enduring significance only when the resulting clusters possess high average similarity.

It will be useful to have a notation for the density of a cluster.

Definition 2.4 (Cluster density). *Let k be a cluster for y at time t. We call the cardinality of this set cluster density.*

$$n_k(y,t) \equiv \text{card}\{\mu_k(y,t)\} = \textstyle\sum_{x \in \mathbf{o}} \mu_k(x,y,t).$$

It might seem odd that the summation in the foregoing formula ranges over *all* of the producers/products in the domain. We use this kind of construction because we do not want to presume that the agents know the precise boundaries and, therefore, can isolate some subset of the producers/products in the domain. This treatment remains faithful to our assumption about the information sets available to the agents. It has no substantive effect, because many—perhaps most—producers/products in a domain might have a zero grade of membership in a cluster and therefore would not contribute to its density.

Clusters can reach the same density by many different configurations. For instance, a cluster density of 10 can result when 100 producers have $\mu_k = 0.1$ and $\mu_k = 0$ for the rest, when 20 have $\mu_k = 0.5$ and the rest have $\mu_k = 0$, or when 10 have $\mu_k = 1.0$ and the rest have $\mu_k = 0$. As the average μ_k among those with nonzero membership increases, a cluster stands out with greater contrast from its background (the set of all producers/products in the domain). In the foregoing example, the third case has higher contrast than the second, which has higher contrast than the first. Because clusters are (fuzzy) sets, the notion of contrast is defined for (nonempty) clusters as well.

Definition 2.5 (Cluster contrast). *Let k be a cluster for y at time t.*

$$c_k(y,t) \equiv \frac{\text{card}\{\mu_k(y,t)\}}{|\text{supp}\{\mu_k(y,t)\}|},$$

if supp$\{\mu_k(y,t)\} \neq \emptyset$; *and it is undefined otherwise.*

Figures 2.1 and 2.2 illustrate differences in contrast for clusters. In figure 2.1, the distances between points tell dissimilarity and the shading of points tells the grade of membership in the cluster. Clearly the cluster on the left has much higher contrast than the one on the right: the average similarity is higher and there are

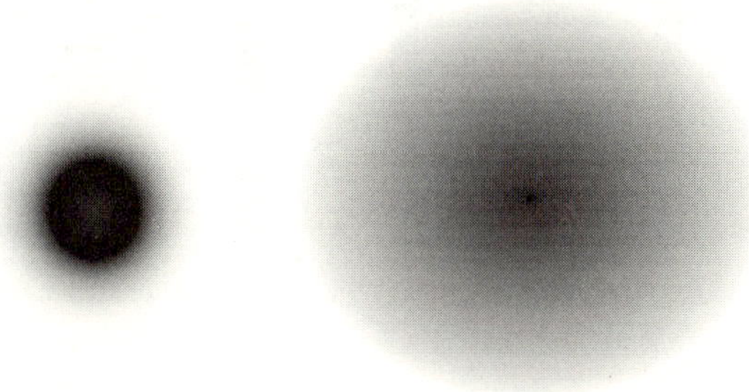

Figure 2.1 Clusters with different levels of contrast

many fewer objects with a low grade of membership. Figure 2.2 provides a more detailed account. It illustrates clusters with the same density but varying levels of contrast. The upper-left panel illustrates a crisp set: all 100 objects in the universe of discourse are either fully in the set or fully out and the contrast equals one. As we move to from left to right in the upper row of panels and then from left to right in the bottom row, the contrast falls.

2.5 LABELS

When enthusiasts delineate clusters, they sometimes crystallize the sense that they have identified a commonality by attaching labels to the clusters. For example, many food enthusiasts and critics in the United States now refer to a set of restaurants as purveyors of "new American cuisine;" and wine enthusiasts have begun talking and writing about "traditional" and "modern" (or "international style") wines. Consider, for instance, this account of a major change in labeling in the music domain of the United States in the middle of the twentieth century:

> In 1923 millions of people in rural areas and towns all across North America sang and played the fiddle and the guitar, but "country music" was not recognized as a form of music distinct from others, and this became obvious when record company executives tried to merchandise the music. They didn't know what music to include and what to exclude, and a number of appellations were applied by the early merchandisers, ranging from "Old-time," "Old Time Tunes," "Old Familiar Tunes," "Hearth and Home," and "Hillbilly and Western" . . .
>
> Just thirty years later, ironically, the situation was reversed. The look, sound and lyric of country music was instantly recognizable, and the music that had been entirely home-made was largely store-bought. What had been the music of non-city regions across the continent be-

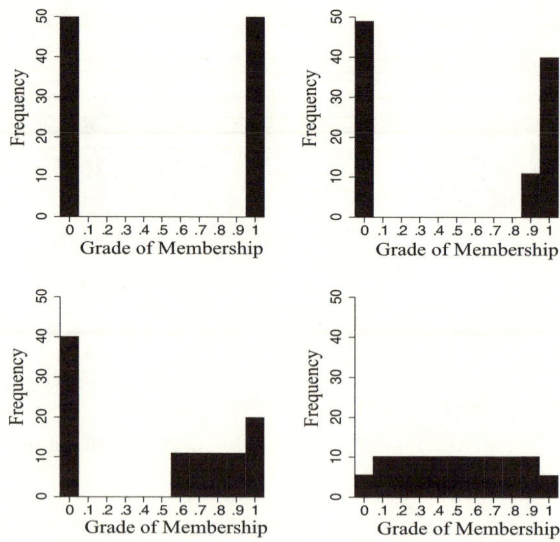

Figure 2.2 Examples of distributions of grades of membership in clusters with (approximately) the same level of density and different levels of contrast

> came symbolically centered in the South and the Southwest. In 1953 a few hundred largely southern professionals played and sang for a living, while millions of people attended country music concerts, listened to it on the radio, and played it—on the phonograph. (Peterson 1997: 4)

For a number of reasons, we regard labeling as an important step in abstracting from similarity judgments (Hsu and Hannan 2005). A label emphasizes the homogeneity of a set of objects by inducing people to focus on similarities among them and to connect them in their minds (Zerubavel 1997). For example, experimental studies reveal that assigning a common label increases the degree to which subjects perceive objects as behaving in the same way or possessing similar properties (Sloutsky, Lo, and Fisher 2001) and that subjects perceive a set of objects as less variable when they receive a label for it before learning about its members rather than after (Park and Hastie 1987). Entities that fall under a common lexical type tend to be perceived as possessing similar features. This tendency is an instance of the tendency for labels to heighten the psychological availability of the cluster.

Psychological research also finds that available mental representations facilitate automatic cognition (Fiske and Taylor 1991). This argument presumably carries over to the organizational domain: availability of a label for a cluster heightens the strength (and psychological availability) of perceived similarity.

Labels also facilitate communication about clusters. Individuals learn about clusters and share their knowledge about them through interaction with others.

In formalizing the labeling process, we first define a function that attaches tags to sets.[10] Let $\mathbf{l}$ be a collection of tags (labels) and proper names used in the domain (at an unspecified time point). A label function associates labels and names with objects (individuals or sets). In defining this function, we want to take account of the possibility that an agent might apply more than one label to an object, e.g., a proper name and one or more cluster/category labels. Therefore, we want the label function to pick out a set of labels. One way to define the label function in this manner uses the powerset of the set of labels. The powerset of a set, denoted formally as $\mathcal{P}(\cdot)$, is the set of all subsets of the set.

Definition 2.6 (Label function). *A label function maps triplets of sets of producers/products, audience-segment members, and time points to the powerset of the tags (labels and proper names) used in the audience segment.*

$$\mathbf{lab} : \mathcal{O} \times \mathbf{a} \times \mathbf{t} \longrightarrow \mathcal{P}(\mathbf{l}),$$

where $\mathcal{P}$ denotes the powerset of a set: the set of all of its subsets.

Of course, an agent might not apply a label to some set, in which case the label function equals the emptyset.[11] Also, a label might be applied to a set consisting of a singleton, e.g., a particular producer or product (e.g., a brand name).

We express the fact that an agent labels a cluster with a formalism: $l \in \mathbf{lab}(k, y, t)$ given $\text{CLUS}(k, y, t)$. This notation makes clear that we treat the set of labels as a crisp set. We do so because the more interesting fuzziness arises in considering the degree to which individual members of a cluster deserve a label.

Chapter 1 introduced Frege's notion of the extension of a classical concept as the set of objects that satisfy the concept. We generalize the idea by considering the extension of a fuzzy concept. In particular, we consider an audience member's extension of a label. This turns out to be useful for expressing the implications of the labeling. Because the producers/products might vary in their GoMs in a labeled cluster, they might bear its label to varying degrees.

One way of expressing this idea is by defining a grade of membership in a label. In formal terms, we define the function $\mu_{e(l)}(x, y, t)$, which tells x's grade of membership in y's extension of the label l at time t. Although GoMs cannot generally be given a probabilistic interpretation (because they do not satisfy the requirement of a probability measure that the sum of values over a set of disjoint and mutually exclusive events equals unity), we do think that a probabilistic interpretation is warranted in this case. Consider the set of situations that demand that an audience member apply a label to a particular producer, e.g., a conversation with other audience members. If an agent assigns a very high GoM in the label to that producer, then she will likely include it in a list of the bearers of the label. On the other hand,

[10] The field of formal semantics distinguishes between grammatical types and the names of the types. Linguists define both the grammatical types and their names (the so-called types) in a recursive manner, so that the grammatical content of a type makes visible the name of the type. Because sets of producers/products are defined socially by enthusiasts rather than formally by analysts, they do not get defined recursively; and it makes no sense for us to propose such a definition either.

[11] The label function tells simply that the focal actor applies a set of labels and names to a set, not that she invented the labels. In most cases, members of audience segments merely adopt labels and names proposed by others (below we discuss further some issues related to borrowing).

if she assigns a low GoM to the producer, she will be unlikely to include it. James Hampton (2006) provides a broad motivation, based partly on arguments by Max Black (1937), for this view:

> What people may be estimating when giving a judgment of degree of membership M is how comfortable they would feel using the term in a certain way or context, and this sense of easiness will be more or less directly related to the proportion of language users who would agree to the use of the word in that context (Black 1937). It is in this sense that it might be reasonable to treat the probability of categorization as a measure of graded membership M.

Notation. We want to define this idea formally as the first step in a nonmonotonic argument, as sketched in Chapter 1. We have not yet prepared the groundwork for this kind of construction; we address these issues in Chapter 6. Nonetheless, we make the notation consistent with what will appear in the rest of the book. Therefore, we use a quantifier, denoted by $\mathfrak{N}$, that is nonmonotonic parallel of the usual universal quantifier $\forall$. The new quantifier tells what is *generally* the case (but it admits exceptions). In other words, application of this quantifier to a formula signals that the formula states a rule-with-exceptions.

A second quantifier, $\mathfrak{P}$, tells that a formula is an implication of an argument based (at least partly) on rules with exceptions. As we explain in Chapter 6, this quantifier does not have a direct parallel in the first-order logic.

Now we come to grades of membership in the extension of a label. Standard definitions have an if-and-only-if form. The argument that we are building does not quite fit the standard form. Instead, we define the concept indirectly by stating a postulate that relates it to an already defined concept. Such a postulate is usually called a meaning postulate.

Meaning postulate 2.1 (Grade of membership in the extension of a label). *A producer's or product's grade of membership in an agent's extension for a label normally equals the probability that the agent applies the label to the producer or product.*

$$\mathfrak{N}\, l, t, x, y\, [\mu_{e(l)}(x, y, t) = \Pr\{l \in \mathbf{lab}(x, y, t)\}].$$

[Read: with l, t, x, y taken arbitrarily from appropriate sets, it is normally the case that an object x's grade of membership in y's extension of the label l at time point t equals the probability that y assigns the label l to x at time t.]

An example that supports this interpretation comes from interviews with wine makers, enologists, agronomists, and wine journalists about the social codes and organizational forms in the production of Barolo and Barbaresco wines in Italy's Piedmont region and of Brunello in Montalchino, Tuscany by Giacomo Negro and collaborators (2006). Much of the interest in these sites stems from reports of twenty years of contention between two different visions: tradition and modernity (sometimes called internationalism). In discussions with leaders of both camps and with local experts, the researchers asked informants to tell the difference between these views and to identify the producers aligned with each camp. Some names came up in all lists and some in only a few. In the latter case, informants often reported that the producer was hard to label because it was traditional in some respects and modern in others. In terms of the present theory, these interviews suggest considerable variation in grades of membership in these labels; and they point to the utility of thinking about these GoMs as reflecting the probability that an audience-segment member will list a producer as a member of the extension of a label.

When will an enthusiast attempt to label a cluster of producers/products? We argue that, because the enthusiasts are trying to make sense of the domain and seek to capture and retain what they view as pockets of similarity, either the density or the contrast of the cluster must be high (relative to those of the agent's other clusters) to induce the agent to go to the trouble of coming up with a label.

Representing this kind of dual dependence requires a choice. One is to state a pair of postulates, one relating density to the probability and the other relating contrast to the probability. In other words, we could tell two simple causal stories (that density increases the probability and that contrast also increases the probability) and leave it to the nonmonotonic logic to control their effects, as we explain in Chapter 6. So, for instance, if one cluster has higher density and lower contrast than another, then two arguments that do not differ in specificity point in opposite directions and no conclusion would be warranted in the nonmonotonic logic. The other strategy combines the two arguments into one postulate and "controls" for each in considering the effect of the other. This kind of postulate states that a higher level of either condition yields a higher probability of labeling so long as the comparison on the other condition does not run in the other direction.

Both approaches possess some merit. However, we think that the "partialing" approach better fits the state of knowledge. If all that we know about the situation is that larger density implies a higher probability of labeling, then this should be the claim. Study of many relevant empirical situations leads us to think that we know more than this. We surmise that higher density does not imply a higher probability when the contrast is lower. In other words, we try to tune the formulas in the postulate(s) to the current state of knowledge. In this case, this leads us to propose a single combined postulate.

Postulate 2.1. *The probability that an agent labels a similarity cluster normally increases with the density and the contrast of the cluster.*

$$\begin{aligned}\mathfrak{N}\, k, k', t, t', y, y' \,[&\textsc{clus}(k, y, t) \wedge \textsc{clus}(k', y', t') \\ &\wedge ((n_k(y,t) > n_{k'}(y',t')) \wedge (c_k(y,t) \geq c_{k'}(y',t')) \\ &\vee ((n_k(y,t) \geq n_{k'}(y',t')) \wedge (c_k(y,t) > c_{k'}(y',t'))) \\ &\quad \rightarrow (\Pr(\exists l[l \in \mathbf{lab}(k,y,t)]) > \Pr(\exists l'[l' \in \mathbf{lab}(k',y',t')]))].\end{aligned}$$

(The symbol $\rightarrow$ denotes the material implication relation—see Appendix C.)

Among other things, this postulate provides some expectations about the order in which members of an audience segment will assign labels. Those with high-density and high-contrast clusters should be the quickest to come up with labels. Social conditions likely produce great variations in density and contrast, thereby implying that social conditions also affect labeling. An interesting additional sociological issue, which we consider below, concerns whether the slower adopters of the labels use the labels applied by the early labelers, or wait and develop their own.

2.6 EXTENSIONAL CONSENSUS

To this point, we have considered the cognitions of an arbitrary member of an audience segment. Clustering and labeling gain social significance only if consensus emerges within an audience segment about clustering and labeling. That is, semantic consensus about a label constitutes a critical step in constructing a category (and a form) and in building the language of the domain.

Semantic consensus in an audience segment might develop along several dimensions. Here we focus on extensional consensus, agreement about the application of a label. Extensional consensus occurs within an audience segment when its members use a common label and also agree on the extension of this common label—the objects to which the label applies in varying degrees. To define extensional consensus formally, we first introduce a function that tells the degree of (pairwise) consensus in an audience segment regarding the extension of a label. In other words, we consider a label, say "charter school" (King, Clemens, and Fry 2004), and we consider the degree to which the members of the segment agree about which entities qualify as "charter schools."

We define extensional consensus with the function, denoted by $\nu_{e(l)}(y, t)$, which maps from pairs of members of the audience-segment and time points to the [0,1] interval. We refer to this function as the audience member's grade of membership in an extensional consensus about the label l.

$$\nu_{e(l)} : \mathbf{a} \times \mathbf{t} \longrightarrow [0, 1].$$

We make explicit the dependence of these grades of membership in a consensus on the pattern of agreements about how well each object fits the label. The first step is to define a function that tells the degree of agreement of y's extension for the label l with that of y at t. In this definition, we make use of the (symmetric) set difference.

Notation. Suppose that **A** and **B** are fuzzy sets defined over the same universe. Then the symmetric set difference is defined as

$$\mathrm{d}(\mathbf{A}, \mathbf{B}) \equiv \textstyle\sum_{x \in \mathrm{U}} \mathrm{abs}(\mu_{\mathbf{A}}(x) - \mu_{\mathbf{B}}(x)),$$

where abs$(\cdot)$ denotes absolute value.

We use this set difference to construct a symmetric measure of extensional agreement as follows. Given that there are $|\mathbf{o}|$ producers/products, the agents can compare $|\mathbf{o}|$ entities. Therefore, the maximum set difference for a pair of labelers is $|\mathbf{o}|$. We set the measure of agreement to zero if the set difference for a pair of labeled clusters equals the maximum. We set the agreement to one if the set difference is zero. These constraints suggest the following definition.

Definition 2.7 (Extensional agreement). *The extensional agreement between two agents, y and y', about the label l at time t:*

$$ex(l, y, y', t) \equiv \frac{|\mathbf{o}| - \mathrm{d}(\{\mu_{e(l)}(y,t)\}, \{\mu_{e(l)}(y',t)\})}{|\mathbf{o}|},$$

if y and y' both use the label l; and it equals 0 otherwise. ($|\mathbf{o}|$ denotes the number of producers in the domain.)

Study of the patterns of agreement reveals how much each audience-segment member shares in an extensional consensus. Therefore, we define a grade of membership on the audience side as well.

Definition 2.8 (Grade of membership in an extensional semantic agreement). *An agent's grade of membership in an extensional semantic consensus about a label is the degree to which his extension agrees with those of other audience members who employ the label.*

$$\nu_{e(l)}(y, t) \equiv \frac{\sum_{y' \in \mathbf{a}} ex(l, y, y', t)}{|\mathbf{a}| - 1},$$

where $|\mathbf{a}|$ denotes the number of members of the audience segment.

This definition of extensional consensus allows for the possibility that some members of an audience segment have zero GoM in the consensus. How strong is a consensus? We propose that the strength of an extensional semantic consensus is the average grade of membership in the audience segment.[12] Let $ec(l, t)$ be a nonnegative, real-valued function whose range is the [0,1] interval and that gives the strength of the consensus about the extension of the label l in the audience segment.

Definition 2.9 (Strength of extensional consensus). *The strength of the consensus about the extension of a label is the average among the members of the audience segment of their grades of membership in the extensional semantic consensus about the label.*

$$ec(l, t) \equiv \overline{\nu}_{e(l)}(t) = \frac{\mathrm{card}\{\nu_{e(l)}\}}{|\mathbf{a}|}.$$

We mark those situations in which an audience segment comes to agree on the extension of a label with the concept of a *class.* The predicate $\textsc{class}(l, t)$ reads as "the audience segment has reached a high level of agreement on the extension of the label l at time t."

Definition 2.10 (Class). *A class (for an audience segment) is a label for which the level of extensional semantic consensus exceeds a threshold $\mathfrak{c}$.*

$$\textsc{class}(l, t) \leftrightarrow (ec(l, t) \geq \mathfrak{c}).$$

(The symbol $\leftrightarrow$ means "if and only if." See Appendix C.)

[12]Note the asymmetry in the treatments of fuzziness for producers and agents.

We use a threshold construction in the preceding definition (and in some other definitions that follow). We do this because we regard the concepts as analytic (that is, as our constructs), rather than social constructions by the audience (see Chapter 1). We want the concepts of the analytic language to be crisp so that the theoretical language can be compositional. It is, of course, a challenge for future empirical research to come up with practical guidelines for discerning the value of this threshold.

Choice Among Labels

The ability of the members of an audience segment to reach agreement about the extension of a label is potentially problematic. In many instances, social connections will influence the willingness to agree and conform to a common label. For instance, some might be members of the same social movement and might try to cooperate to achieve a collective goal. Or they could be ordered in some hierarchical fashion by either formal or informal social arrangements, thus prompting a set of deference actions. Alternatively, some could be in open competition with others, and conflict and strategic behavior designed might preclude agreement. How might this admittedly complex process unfold? What happens when an agent who has not yet developed her own label instead adopts the same label already announced by a faster labeler?

As we see it, the agreement problem has at least two dimensions. One involves differences in what the audience-segment members perceive, and the other concerns their willingness to call the (partially) similar something by the same label. The first condition will be satisfied when a late-to-label agent's cluster overlaps with the labeled clusters of one or more early labelers. In fact, we think the degree of overlap of clusters will boost the likelihood of agreement. In the extreme , the clusters overlap completely, but one is labeled and the other is not.

For the second dimension, if the slow labeler's cluster has low contrast, then she likely will be more willing to conform to an early labeler. This is because low contrast likely represents a situation of high ambiguity and low conviction—adopting another's label helps resolve the ambiguity and does not require a lot of cognition, adjustment, or dissembling. We think that the probability that an agent adopts a label that another agent applies to a cluster rises with the overlap of the former's cluster with those of other audience members and falls with the contrast of the former's own cluster. By similar reasoning, agreement should be hardest to reach when the clusters do not overlap and when the late-to-label agent's cluster has high contrast.

The combined effect of overlap and contrast on the probability of adopting an existing label is worth thinking about. Consider a case in which an agent with a higher-contrast cluster attaches a label to it and the one with the lower-contrast cluster does not. We think that the probability that the latter agent adopts the label of the former increases with the overlap of the clusters. Overlaps can be asymmetric. Because a GoM of an entity in the intersection of a pair of fuzzy sets is the minimum of its GoM in each set, the overlap of the two sets under consideration will be low if the overlap is confined to the periphery of the low-contrast cluster.

Substantial overlap in such cases requires that the center of the low-contrast cluster intersect with the high-contrast cluster. Hence, our reasoning that the agent with the low-contrast cluster will be influenced by the label of the other agent stems from the recognition that the cores of the clusters will overlap, that any label applied to the two clusters will point most strongly to the same objects.

Choice among a set of labels can become contentious at the level of groups of audience members for at least two reasons. First, although different social groups (or social movements) might initially agree on different labels for more or less the same cluster, the subsequent choice of label in the larger audience can turn into a political contest among these groups or movements. In such cases, the content of the label is inconsequential; what matters is which group/movement succeeds in having its preferred label adopted in the broader community. An instance of such contention arose in the early automobile industry. The industry first gained a foothold in and around Paris. The French enthusiasts adopted the label "automobile" for the new product. Enthusiasts in the English-speaking world strongly resisted adopting a French label for their own versions of the product. For instance, the editor of America's leading periodical on this product, *The Horseless Age,* argued vociferously for the adoption of an "Anglo-Saxon" term and favored "motor vehicle." (The vestige of this contention can be seen in the title used routinely in American states for the beloved bureaucracies that register these products and their users: Department of Motor Vehicles.)

The second reason for contention over labels comes when social groups rely on existing terms in a natural language to name the new class (as contrasted with the use of a neologism like "automobile"). Terms in the natural language can have connotations that impede agreement. Gary Fine (2004) provides a compelling example in an ethnographic study of an art world peopled by self-taught artists from the margins of society—the rural poor, the homeless, prison inmates, etc. Three labels for this cluster of artists have broad currency: "self-taught artists," "outsider artists," and "folk artists."

> A label must be simultaneously descriptive, political, and aesthetic . . . The label should make sense in light of the body of objects that the participants "know" belong together. The meaningful character of the word should correspond to the content of the object and the position of the creators . . . Terms such as "primitive" or "naive" art, once acceptable to define those who are unsophisticated in light of the cultural capital of art-world participants, are now inappropriate . . . A poorly chosen term can marginalize artists . . . The label should [also] be "good to think" and "good to say" . . . Art brut—raw or brutal art—served the French well as the label for a type of untaught art by those outside the social system of art. Perhaps because of its foreignness or perhaps because art brut suggests that the artists were "brutal," the term has not been widely accepted among English speakers. (Fine 2004: 24–5)

The theme of foreignness recapitulates the debate about the labeling of the automobile/motor vehicle/motor car. Moreover, the connotations of the words figure prominently in what Fine refers to as "term warfare." Here the issues go far beyond mere labeling. The different familiar terms evoke different meanings or schemata (which we discuss in the next chapter). In this sense, agreement about extensions and intensions (meanings) of labels get invoked in the kind of contention seen in this art world.

2.7 COMPLEX LABELS

As we have defined the label function in D2.6, it is possible that an agent can apply several different tags to a producer. If this actually happens, then the tag is a complex label, a composition of simple labels. We need to consider this scenario in the chapters that follow, which requires that we specify how labels combine. To build a formal model of the construction of such complex labels, we define a label composition function, denoted by $\oplus$.

Definition 2.11 (The label composition operator). *Let $\oplus$ map pairs of labels to labels, and let l_1, l_2, and l_3 be labels. $\oplus$ satisfies the following properties:*

1. *Commutativity:* $\forall\, l_1, l_2\, [l_1 \oplus l_2 = l_2 \oplus l_1]$.
2. *Associativity:* $\forall l_1, l_2, l_3\, [l_1 \oplus (l_2 \oplus l_3) = (l_1 \oplus l_2) \oplus l_3]$.
3. *Idempotence:* $\forall l_1\, [l_1 \oplus l_1 = l_1]$.

(The symbol $=$ stands for an equivalence relation on the set of labels.)

The foregoing definition reflects the view that the agents do not distinguish between equivalent labels. It also reflects the assumption that the agents do not have "preference orderings" over the set of labels. In other words, we assume that the sequence of labels and their association does not have any significance. The only issue is whether or not each label applies to the producer. Although this assumption is a simplification, it yields interesting results.

Lemma 2.1 (Simplifiability of complex labels). *For any complex label, there exists an equivalent label in which all simple labels occur at most once.*

Proof. Suppose we start with a complex label where some components have multiple occurrences. With the help of associativity and commutativity, we can find an equivalent complex label where the multiple occurrences of the components are next to each other. Idempotence allows all but one of the multiple occurrences to be eliminated. □

The foregoing lemma shows that complex labels operate like (crisp) sets: only the presence or absence of a label matters. To make sure that the label function works appropriately, we offer the following postulate

Postulate 2.2. *The label function is closed under equality and composition).*

Suppose that $x \in \mathbf{o}$, $y \in \mathbf{a}$, and $t \in \mathbf{t}$.

Then, if $l_1 \in \mathbf{lab}(x,y,t)$ *and* $l_1 = l_2$*, then* $l_2 \in \mathbf{lab}(x,y,t)$*; and if* $l_1 \in \mathbf{lab}(x,y,t) \wedge l_2 \in \mathbf{lab}(x,y,t)$*, then* $(l_1 \oplus l_2) \in \mathbf{lab}(x,y,t)$*.*

These formal definitions pave the way for defining the identity of an object that bears multiple labels (in Chapter 5).

DISCUSSION

Given their grounding in cognitive psychology, the clustering and labeling processes we describe might, at first glance, seem far removed from the macrosociological concept of organizational form. We believe that such a perception likely arises largely because, following John Meyer and collaborators (Meyer and Rowan 1977; Meyer and Scott 1992), much sociological theory on organizations takes forms as given and concentrates on demonstrating the powerful effects of form status for organizations and society.

Once the focus shifts to form emergence, we must take account of the perceptions and cognitions of members of the relevant audience(s) and of the social processes entailed in gaining agreement on a language. In an earlier effort (Pólos, Hannan, and Carroll 2002), we initiated a move in this direction by defining form in terms of social identities. Here we developed it more fully by depicting explicitly the partial (fuzzy) perceptions of audience-segment members and by specifying a particular cognitive process: similarity clustering. We envision similarity clustering as the primitive origin of a category emergence process that—many times and for many members of an audience segment—appears to begin at a much later stage, as when someone adopts an available schema without having experienced any prior clustering.

We think that this approach builds on and clarifies the insights of prior research. For example, David McKendrick and collaborators (2003) developed ideas about how two observable aspects of organizations in a market might generate perceptually focused identities: (1) firms that began as participants in this market (called de-novo entries) and (2) agglomeration in a place with a related identity. These analysts argued that de-novo entry matters because the entry of firms that derive their primary identities from activities in other markets (something typically true of lateral or de-alio entrants) causes the activities of the producers in the focal market to appear less coherent. Spatial agglomeration also exerts an effect on perception because it intensifies social interaction with possibly similar organizations, thereby increasing prospects for recognition as a common identity.

The current theory helps to sort out and relate these two processes. Agglomeration facilitates clustering and labels; and any two de-novo entrants are likely to be judged as more similar than is an arbitrary pair of de-alio entrants. This suggests that a similarity cluster that includes a high proportion of de-novo organizations will exhibit high contrast (a condition with important additional implications, as we shall see in Chapter 4).

In the next chapter, we take up the next step in structuring the domain, the creation of schemata and the formation of types and categories. In this stage, enthusiasts try to create dimensions for the labeled clusters—to elucidate the distinctions that govern which producers clearly belong to a label, which belong partly, and which do not belong at all.

Despite the sequential nature of our rendition of this theoretical story, we do not intend to suggest that the sequence gives the natural path of organizational evolution, or even a common one. In our view, form emergence might start at a later stage (described in the following chapters) and based on elements of an existing form; certainly this is the way most individual audience-segment members learn about and experience "new" categories, as we noted at the start of the chapter. Moreover, clusters, as we define them, are extremely fragile and commonly ephemeral. In fact, the vast majority of clusters that might be regarded as potential categories (and perhaps even forms) fail to make it to the next stage.

Indeed, the "successful" clusters might quickly advance to the next stage, thus explaining the inherent difficulty in identifying vivid examples at this stage and in demarcating an unambiguous start or origin of an activity, industry, or population. Consider, for instance, the following statement we wrote some years ago with collaborators in describing our attempts to date the origins of the automobile industry (Hannan et al. 1995: 515):

> Dating the exact start of the automobile manufacturing industry is difficult. Experimental use of mechanical energy (steam during the early period) to propel vehicles began sometime in the late eighteenth century. Most of these experiments were attempts to produce farm machinery or commercial transport vehicles. In some sense, then, the motor vehicle as a technical product has existed for 200 years. However, this early experimentation did not produce an industry. Only in the closing years of the nineteenth industry did a recognizable industry emerge, with firms declaring intentions to manufacture automobiles for the market. Most historians of the industry place the industry's birth between 1885 and 1895.

A major source of this difficulty occurs, we think, because we lack the analytical framework to identify and describe the early steps in industry or form emergence. However, once we can visualize the full process theoretically, it should be easier to envision conducting research on how selection occurs among audiences and cultural objects like clusters (and categories). At the current state, we hear only anecdotal stories about these stages. As a next step, ethnographic and other qualitative research might prove extremely useful in simply identifying and describing interesting relevant cases. Where do clusters come from, and how do they develop? How do agents perceive and interpret clusters? Where does the label come from? How do agents come to a consensus, if and when they do? How frequently does consensus occur?

Chapter Three

Types and Categories

Clustering and labeling create seeds for the development of categories. An emergent extensional consensus, which converts a cluster into a class, strengthens the durability of a labeled cluster. However, extensional consensus on a label, by itself, generally does not tell us how to think about a not-yet-seen object (producer) that might, or might not, deserve a label to one degree or another. This uncertainty creates a source of instability. It makes it likely that many—perhaps most—classes disappear before they gain much recognition or undergo much development. On occasion, a class might prove robust and resist getting overrun by larger social forces. This chapter argues that schematization provides a basis of stability.

Schematization entails the development of a set of abstract rules or codes to provide an interpretation of a label. If an observer can invoke such an abstract representation (a schema) telling what criteria determine degrees of membership in a label, then making judgments about the grade of membership of a not-yet-seen object becomes much simpler. The observer can decide a producer/product's grade of membership by assessing the degree to which its feature values fit the defining schema straightaway. This means that there is no need to compute all of the pairwise similarity scores. In terms of a common distinction made in cognitive science, this chapter treats the shift from *similarity-based* to *rule-based* classification (Smith and Sloman 1994).

In the processes depicted in this stage of the story, the audience-segment members try to dimensionalize classes, to elucidate the distinctions that they use implicitly in deciding which producers or products belong to a label (and to what degree) and which do not. This activity, like clustering and labeling, involves a kind of sensemaking. A cluster has been formed provisionally and labeled, and consensus has been reached about the degrees of membership of products/producers in the label. In other words, after the audience segment has defined a class, the enthusiasts (and possibly other agents) try to abstract from extensional descriptions to some abstract code that makes sense of the class and can be used to decide not-yet-considered cases.

We describe this activity as the creation of a schema that specifies the feature values that convey full membership. An agent's coupling of a label and a schema creates what we call a type.

Category construction involves a process similar to type formation but at the collective level: gaining agreement within the audience about what it means to carry a label. In this stage, the interested members of the audience segment try to sort out what it means to be a "university," "organic farm," "anarchist movement," or "hedge fund."

Although we describe theoretically the emergence of categories and forms from a similarity clustering as a sequence, it is important to recognize that many forms actually start with one of the later stages, such as those that we now describe. This might be the case, for instance, if an existing schema serves as the basis for the construction of a new schema or category. Of course, many possible potential forms disappear before proceeding to a subsequent stage.

3.1 SCHEMATA

Typification means codifying the basis of membership in a label. In other words, typification means generating an abstract rendering of the assignment of grades of membership in a label. (Sometimes the "generation" consists in modifying an existing schema.) We define a type as a coupling of a label and a schema that articulates a view about what pattern of feature values determines the applicability of the label.

In forming schemata, agents abstract from the observed patterns of covariation of the feature values. The abstraction might be considerably simpler and cleaner than the observed joint distribution of feature values. That is, a schema will generally simplify a complex reality. Indeed, a schema has little value for information processing and communication unless it makes a considerable simplification of reality. The fact that some bird species do not fly or that some universities do not have students does not gainsay the utility of the common schemata for "bird" and "university"; complicating these schemata to take account of the few persistent exceptions would likely not be worth the cost of an increased cognitive load of multiplying schemata and making them more complicated.

A natural step in seeking to comprehend the bases of membership in a label involves relating the feature values of the producers/products to their grades of membership in a label. Certain configurations of feature values might be associated with full-fledged membership, others with moderate standing as a member, others with low but nonzero standing, and still others with zero grade of membership. A mental representation of such a pattern is generally called a schema. A schema for a label is a kind of model that explains who is in, who is out, and who lies at various positions between these extremes.

The various fields in cognitive science have used the term schema in several ways. Gregory Murphy (2002: 47) provides a nice summary of what seems to be the common core notion.

> A schema is a structured representation that divides up the properties of an item into dimensions (usually called *slots*) and values on those dimensions (*fillers* of the slots) . . . The slots have restrictions on them that say what kinds of fillers than can have. For example, the head-color slot of a bird can only be filled by colors . . . Furthermore, the slot may place constraints on the specific value allowed for that type. For example, a bird could have one, two or no eyes (presumably through some accident), but could not have more than two eyes. The slot for

> number of eyes would include this restriction. The fillers of the slots are understood to be competitors. For example, if the head color of birds included colors such as blue, black, and red, this would indicate that the head would be blue OR black OR red . . . Finally, the slots themselves may be connected by relations that restrict their values. For example, if a bird does not fly, then it does not migrate south in the winter. This could be represented as a connection between the locomotion slot (which indicates how the bird moves itself around) and the slot that includes information on migration.

Consider three sociological examples. First, Charles Tilly (1986: 394) characterizes the French "turnout" as a protest that obeys the following script (a schema for the production of some outcome):

> Workers in a given craft who had a grievance against the employers of their locality went from shop to shop within the locality, calling out the workers to join them in a march around the town, ended the circuit with a meeting at the edge of town, voted to make a certain set of demands, sent a delegation to the employers, declared a work stoppage, and enforced it as best they could throughout the town until they reached an agreement with the employers.

Richard Peterson (1997: 218) describes what it takes for a performer to be perceived as an authentic producer of the American country-music form:

> Music and performance are vital to the audience, but signifiers are also vital. The boots, the hat, the outfit, a soft rural Southern accent, as well as the sound and subjects of the songs, all help. Finally, being able to show a family heritage in country music is perhaps the strongest asset among authenticity claims. Many artists recall learning first from their mothers or playing in a family band.

Hayagreeva Rao, Philippe Monin, and Rudolphe Durand (2003) consider a pair of oppositional schemata from the world of elite French gastronomy. The classical schema includes:

> Culinary rhetoric: Names of dishes refer to *Rhetoric, Memory, and Legitimacy.* Rules of cooking: *Conformation,* or staying in conformity with Escoffier's principles . . . *Sublimation,* or sublimating the ingredients . . . Archetypical ingredients: High game, shellfish, cream, poultry, river fish . . . Role of the chef: The restauranteur, rarely the owner, and never the cook, has the power in the rooms of luxury hotels and palaces. The classical service is organized through the saucepan. The waiters cut and serve the dishes . . . The rituals are outside the plate. (Rao et al. 2003: 801, Table 1)

The *nouvelle cuisine* schema runs opposite:

> Culinary rhetoric: Names of dishes refer to *Poetry, Imagination and Evocation* . . . Rules of cooking: *Transgression.* or using old cooking

> techniques with new ingredients, or using old cooking techniques with old ingredients, yet for which these cooking techniques were not legitimate . . . Archetypal ingredients: Fruits, vegetables, potatoes, aromatic herbs, exotic ingredients, sea fish. Role of the chef: The chef is at the center of the operations . . . waiters no longer intervene in the process. (Rao et al. 2003: 807, table 2)

Schemata need not provide explicit definitions. Many powerful schemata apparently operate largely implicitly, as Supreme Court Justice Potter Stewart famously acknowledged in considering how to define "hard core pornography." His decision on *Jacobellis v. Ohio* stated "I shall not today attempt further to define the kinds of material I understand to be embraced ... [b]ut I know it when I see it." In studying artists, Becker (1982: 199) observes similarly that "artists find it difficult to verbalize the general principles on which they make their choices. They often resort to such noncommunicative statements as 'it sounds better that way,' 'it looked good to me,' or 'it works.'" Despite their informal character, schemata such as the examples from French political contention, American country music, and forms of French cuisine have been given linguistic expression and have become widely shared.

We represent schemata for a label as sets of formulas that pick out a set of relevant features and distinguish the values of those features that are consistent with membership in the label from those that are not. Schemata for organizations can be based on any number of organizational features or relations. The "university" examples introduced in Chapter 1 rely primarily on structural characteristics or employment features of the organizations to define membership in the cluster. Although we are not aware of systematic research on these topics, we suspect that these kinds of features dominate the schemata of many members of the mass audience. Of course, enthusiasts, activists, and critics often develop subtler, fine-grained distinctions and might even develop more analytical schemata.

Upon schematization, an agent's view of a labeled cluster of organizations undergoes a very important change. In the preschema stage of checking similarities, agents do not face constraints in the choice of features to be used in any pairwise comparison. Instead, comparisons might consider only the readily observable and salient features of each pair of producers/products considered. It is especially important to note that those making similarity judgments do not necessarily take note of all of the features that an object does *not* possess. (As we noted above, the possibility that agents perceive different numbers of feature values for a pair of objects gives rise to the possibility of asymmetry in similarity judgments.)

In the schema formation phase, ambiguity about the relevance of dimensions gets reduced considerably, if not eliminated. As the audience members sweep away this form of ambiguity, they assign values to producers/products for *all* of the relevant features. For instance, imagine that many enthusiasts in an audience note high similarity among organizations that call themselves "charter schools." Suppose further that some of these organizations maintain libraries while others do not. In the preschema stage, a comparison of two organizations lacking libraries does not consider them to be similar in lacking libraries—the feature value "does not maintain a library" does not appear in the comparison. But comparisons of organizations with and without a library makes this feature relevant. If typification occurs and the feature value "maintains a library" becomes an element of the schema, then the charter schools that lack libraries now get a value of "does not maintain a library" on this dimension; it becomes relevant for all organizations in the type.

In defining schemata formally, we make explicit the dependence on the set of features considered. We do so by identifying the relevant features and their schema-conforming values.

Should we regard the patterns of feature values that define schemata as crisp sets or as fuzzy ones? If we follow the implications of Wittgenstein's argument about concepts—as in his analysis of the concept of "game," which we discussed in Chapter 1—then we should use the fuzzy version. If we took this route, then we would define a schema as a set of family resemblances with no pattern serving as the standard. Instead, we made the opposite choice, because we think that this fuzzy image does not represent how agents actually use schemata. The literature on cognitive science makes clear that people use schemata to simplify, to clarify a complex reality for ease of cognitive processing. Murphy's (2002) characterization of schemata, quoted above, reflects this view. Fuzzy schemata do not fit this goal well.

Therefore, we define schemata as *crisp* sets of feature values. We posit that the actors make judgments about the degrees to which particular instances (objects) fit a schema. So, for instance, we think that the common schema for "bird" includes the feature "flies." As we noted above, someone who encounters objects that fit the rest of the "bird" schema but do not fly (e.g., penguins, ostriches, emus) does not usually complicate the schema; instead he or she likely regards these instances as atypical of the "bird" category. Similarly, knowledge of a number of atypical universities, such as those listed in Chapter 1, does not seem to undercut the common schemata for "university."

Notation. We need some additional notation to define schemata formally. The ordering of elements in a listing of the membership of a set is generally taken to be arbitrary. Now we fix the ordering of elements by expressing the relevant sets of features and of their values as indexed sets.[1] Let $\mathbf{f}_i = \{f_1, f_2, \ldots f_i\}$ be the set of i features that are relevant for a schema. Each feature in the set has a range of possible values. We denote the set of possible values of feature f_j by $\mathbf{r}_j$.

Schemata point to certain patterns of values of the full set of features, that is, to elements of the Cartesian product of the ranges of the features.

Definition 3.1 (Schema). *An agent's schema for a label maps pairs of audience-segment members and time points to a nonempty subset of the set of the ordered n-tuples of the values of the relevant features; this subset contains the schema-conforming patterns (n-tuples) of feature values.*

$$\sigma_l : \mathbf{a} \times \mathbf{t} \longrightarrow \mathbf{s}_i^l \subseteq \mathbf{r}_1 \times \cdots \times \mathbf{r}_i, \quad \mathbf{s}_i^l \neq \emptyset,$$

where $\sigma(l, y, t)$ is defined provided that $\exists\, k\, [\textsc{clus}(k, y, t) \wedge (l \in \mathbf{lab}(k, y, t))]$.

[1] Suppose we have a set $\mathbf{x} = \{x_1, x_2, \ldots x_n\}$ and a set I containing the first i natural numbers: $\mathbf{i} = \{0, 1, 2, \ldots i\}$. We can express the indexed set $\mathbf{x}_n = \{x_i \mid i \in \mathbf{n}\}$.

We express instances of schemata with expressions of the form $\sigma(l, y, t) = \mathbf{s}_i^l$, which reads as "the (indexed) set of ordered n-tuples of the values of the i features, $\mathbf{s}_i$, conforms to the schema for the label l from y's perspective at time t." The subscript i tells the number of features addressed by the schema, the maximum index. (When the dimensionality of the schema, the number of features that it constrains, is not relevant, we drop the subscript that tells the maximum index.)

In the previous chapter, we noted that the labels applied to some producers or products might be complex. Therefore, we must specify how the schema for a complex label can be calculated from the schemata for simple labels. To keep our approach as compositional as possible, we offer the following postulate.

Postulate 3.1. *Schemata for complex labels are formed compositionally from the schemata for simple labels.*

Let $\sigma(l, y, t) = \mathbf{s}_i^l$ *and* $\sigma(l', y, t) = \mathbf{s}_i^{l'}$.

$$\sigma(l \oplus l', y, t) = \mathbf{s}_i^{l \oplus l'} = \mathbf{s}_i^l \cap \mathbf{s}_i^{l'}.$$

This postulate guarantees that the schematization of a complex label is simply the schemata attached to the simple labels applied in "conjunction."[2]

Because we define a schema as a function, we indirectly impose the restriction that a schema for a label is *unique.* We think that this restriction accords well with the view that schemata serve to promote comprehension of a complex reality: an agent's possession of multiple schemata for a label will only create confusion. However, we do not impose the restriction that different agents have the same schemata for a common label, as we explain below.

It might be helpful to consider a more concrete example of the abstract definition. Consider an example. Suppose, for simplicity, that an audience member's schemata for a pair of labels pertain to (the same) two features, f_1 and f_2. For instance, this might be a simplified version of the schemata for paired opposites such as "industrial brewer" and "microbrewer" or "classical" and "nouvelle" French cuisine, as discussed above. Suppose further that the (socially expected) range (possible values) of the first feature, f_1, is $\{a, b, c\}$ and the range of f_2 is $\{d, e\}$. Then each schema can be represented as a set of feature values that conform to the schema. For instance, the schema for l_1 might be the pairs of feature values: $\mathbf{s}^{l_1} = \{\langle a, d\rangle, \langle b, d\rangle\}$, and the schema for l_2 might consist of the pairs: $\mathbf{s}^{l_2} = \{\langle b, e\rangle, \langle c, e\rangle\}$.[3] The fact that the schemata are disjoint is expressed by the fact that the intersection of the sets of schema-conforming pairs is empty, $\mathbf{s}^{l_1} \cap \mathbf{s}^{l_2} = \emptyset$.

[2]Had there been a preference ordering over the labels, we would need a more complicated nonmonotonic logic to calculate the effects of schematization. The schemata associated with the more preferred labels would be able to override the schemata associated with the less preferred ones. This is particularly relevant in cases there the feature values admissible by the different schemata conflict with one another. Although our present formulation assumes away this possibility, the use of nonmonotonic reasoning would allow this possibility to be incorporated into our framework.

[3]Here and elsewhere we use a pair of angle brackets to denote an ordered n-tuple, in this case ordered pairs.

Fit to Schemata

Because memberships in clusters and labels can be partial, as expressed by a grade of membership, it also makes sense to treat an object's fit to an agent's schema as potentially partial. Therefore, we define a grade of membership function for an object's fit to schema. This function, denoted by $\mu_{\sigma}(x, y, t)$, tells the degree to which the feature values of producer x at time point t fit y's schema σ. For example, $\mu_{\sigma}(x, y, t)$ might be defined as one minus the proportion of the relevant feature values that would have to be changed for the object to fit the schema. In the example in given in the previous paragraph, the $\langle c, d\rangle$ pair does not fit either schema. However, changing the value of the first feature from c to either a or b would make an object fit the first schema. Likewise, changing the value of the second feature from d to e would make it fit the second schema. If someone used the rule suggested above for deciding partial memberships, then $\mu_{\sigma(l_1)} = 0.5$ and $\mu_{\sigma(l_2)} = 0.5$, because changing the value of half of the relevant features changes the value of the schema function from zero to one. (Exactly how the audience members make these judgments is a subject for future research.)

3.2 TYPES

In order to present a full picture of the form emergence process, we tie schematization to clustering. We use labels to make the link. That is, we consider cases in which an audience-segment member identifies a cluster, applies a label, and develops a schema for the label. We know that a schema connects to a cluster if the same label applies to each.

For all of the reasons discussed in arguing that enthusiasts (and ordinary members of an audience segment) might attach labels to salient clusters, we think it is also likely that they will carry out a parallel operation by attaching schemata to labels. In our formulation, the meaning of a label is given formally by its *intension.* The intension of a predicate is defined as the function that tells the extension of the predicate in every possible world. The intension of an expression provides an abstract characterization of its meaning.

We think that agents typically refer to labels rather than to schemata. Therefore, we represent an entity's GoM in an agent's type as a function of the intension of the label. In formal terms, we define the function $\mu_{i(l)}(x, y, t)$ that tells x's GoM in y's meaning for the label l at time t. Because the meaning of a label is given by its associated schema, we define $\mu_{i(l)}(x, y, t)$ indirectly in the following meaning postulate.

Meaning postulate 3.1 (Grade of membership in the meaning of a label). *A producer's grade of membership in an agent's meaning for a label, in notation $\mu_{i(l)}(x, y, t)$, is given by the producer's grade of membership in the schema associated with the label, $\mu_{\sigma(l)}(x, y, t)$.*

$$\mathfrak{N}\, l, t, x, y\, [\mu_{i(l)}(x, y, t) = \mu_{\sigma(l)}(x, y, t)].$$

When a member of an audience segment associates a schema to a label, we say that she has a type for that label.

Definition 3.2 (Type). *A type is a function that maps from pairs of audience-segment members and time points to the powerset of the Cartesian product of the set of available labels and the set of available schemata:*

$$\mathbf{ty} : \mathbf{a} \times \mathbf{t} \longrightarrow \mathcal{P}(\mathbf{l} \times \mathbf{s}),$$

such that

$$\langle l, \mathbf{s}^l \rangle \in \mathbf{ty}(y,t) \leftrightarrow \sigma(l,y,t) = \mathbf{s}^l,$$

where $\mathbf{s} = \{\mathbf{s}^l | l \in \mathbf{l}\}$.

From the definition of a schema as a function that maps to a pattern of feature values, it follows that at most one schema can be paired with a label. Therefore, types for labels are unique.

In the previous chapter, we argued that the probability that a cluster gets labeled increases with its density and its contrast. We think that contrast and density also affect the probability that an agent associates a schema to a label.

Postulate 3.2. *The probability that an agent creates a type (schematizes a labeled similarity cluster) normally increases with the density and contrast of the cluster.*

$$\begin{aligned}&\mathfrak{N}\, k, k', l, l', t, t', y, y' \,[\text{CLUS}(k,y,t) \wedge \text{CLUS}(k',y',t')\\ &\quad \wedge (l \in \mathbf{lab}(k,y,t)) \wedge (l' \in \mathbf{lab}(k',y',t')) \wedge ((n_k(y,t) > n_{k'}(y',t'))\\ &\wedge (c_k(y,t) \geq c_{k'}(y',t')) \vee ((n_k(y,t) \geq n_{k'}(y',t')) \wedge (c_k(y,t) > c_{k'}(y',t'))\\ &\qquad \rightarrow (\Pr(\exists\, \mathbf{s}_i^l\, [\sigma(l,y,t) = \mathbf{s}_i^l]) > \Pr(\exists\, \mathbf{s}_{i'}^{l'}\, [\sigma(l',y',t') = \mathbf{s}_{i'}^{l'}]))].\end{aligned}$$

The membership in a type consists of the set of pairs of producers/products and grades of membership in the meanings assigned to the label. In other words, we have a parallel to a cluster, but one defined in terms of fit to the meaning of a label rather than fit to a pattern of perceived similarities.

Definition 3.3 (Type density). *The density of an agent's type is the sum of the grades of membership in the type for this label that the agent assigns to the producers/products in the domain.*

Let $\langle l, \mathbf{s}_i^l \rangle$ *be a type for* y *at time* t*:* $\langle l, \mathbf{s}_i^l \rangle \in \mathbf{ty}(y,t)$*. The density of the type is*

$$n_{i(l)}(y,t) \equiv \text{card}\{\mu_{i(l)}(y,t)\}.$$

Definition 3.4 (Type contrast). *The contrast of a type for an agent, in notation* $c(\{\mu_{i(l)}(y,t)\})$*, is the average of the nonzero grades of membership that the agent assigns to the objects in the cluster (the cluster density divided by the cardinality of the support for the cluster):*

$$c_{i(l)}(y,t) \equiv \frac{\text{card}\{\mu_{i(l)}(y,t)\}}{|\text{supp}\{\mu_{i(l)}(y,t)\}|},$$

if $\text{supp}\{\mu_{i(l)}(y,t)\} \neq \emptyset$*; and it is undefined otherwise.*

3.3 INTENSIONAL SEMANTIC CONSENSUS

Because they can be idiosyncratic, types do not usually have broad social implications.[4] How can we mark the distinction between such types and pairings of labels and schemata that gain currency in an audience segment? We do so by considering intensional consensus, that is, consensus on the meaning of a label.

Again we use a fuzzy-set construction on *both* sides of the role relation. We say that an audience member has a high grade of membership in an intensional consensus when she agrees with other members of the audience segment about the meaning of the label, about what patterns of feature values convey a high degree of membership in the label.[5] We define this idea formally with the function $\nu_{i(l)}(y, t)$, which gives the grade-of-membership of the audience member y in the prevailing intensional semantics in the audience segment with respect to the label l at time t.

We find value in expressing agreement about meanings in terms of the patterns of feature values admitted by the relevant schemata. There are two issues here: (1) agreement about the features that matter and (2) agreement about the ranges of values of those features that fit a schema. Achieving consensus on each is potentially problematic. In the cases that we have studied, the debate more commonly focused on the acceptable values of a set of agreed-upon features. For instance, in the emergence of the (American) "labor union" form, debate among enthusiasts generally centered on choices of values of a few features including:

goals: {utopian reform, radical political change, (improvement of) working conditions},

basis of membership: {craft/occupation, industry, community, racial-ethnic group},

tactics: {strike, boycott, collective violence, cooperative ownership}.

So, for instance, the classic craft form was defined by the following combination of values of the features listed above:

goal: {working conditions},

membership: {craft/occupation, racial-ethnic group},

tactics: {strike, boycott}.

Because schemata are patterns (n-tuples of feature values), the schema for the classic craft form contains the following four patterns (ordered triplets of feature values):

1. ⟨working conditions, craft/occupation, strike⟩,

[4] In Chapter 5 we treat an important exception involving authority: an authority's type can have broad consequences.

[5] Again, we recognize that getting agents to agree and reach a consensus might be problematic; but, for brevity, we refrain from reiterating here the arguments made above with respect to labels and cluster conditions. Also, there is an obvious favorable precondition of agreement on the label for semantic consensus.

2. $\langle$working conditions, racial-ethnic group, strike$\rangle$,

3. $\langle$working conditions, craft/occupation, boycott$\rangle$,

4. $\langle$working conditions, racial-ethnic group, boycott$\rangle$.

These considerations suggest the following specification of intensional agreement. Consider the set of feature values that (some fraction of) the agents in the audience segment regard as possible alternatives, as in the list above for American labor unions. An agent with a restrictive schema for the label might consider only one option on each feature as consistent with full membership in the schema For instance, a restrictive schema for a labor union might include only the first triplet of feature values in the example above. Another with a loose schema might consider all of the options as consistent with full membership (all four triplets). In this case, the two agents would not have a high level of intensional agreement about the meaning of the label. We can express quantitatively the level of agreement with a generalization of Tversky's contrast measure of similarity to apply to the sets of ordered n-tuples of schema-conforming feature values for a pair of agents in the audience segment.[6]

Definition 3.5 (Agreement of schemata). *The level of agreement of one schema with another, $is(\sigma, \sigma')$, is the similarity of the patterns of feature values that they admit as fitting the schemata.*

Consider a pair of schemata that the agents y and y' associate with the (same) label l at time t: $\sigma(l, y, t) = \mathbf{s}_i$ and $\sigma(l, y', t) = \mathbf{s}'_i$. Their level of intensional agreement about the label is

$$is(\sigma(l, y, t), \sigma(l, y', t)) \equiv sim(\mathbf{s}_i, \mathbf{s}'_i),$$

where sim is Tversky's contrast measure of similarity, as defined in D2.2.

In the example of restrictive and loose schemata for a labor union given above, $sim(restrictive, loose) = 1/(1 + 3b)$, because there are no patterns included in the restrictive schema that are excluded from the loose one (giving $a \cdot 0$) and there are three patterns in the loose schema that do not appear in the restrictive one. As we mentioned in Chapter 2, most applications of the contrast model of similarity set $a = 1 = b$. With this restriction, the level of similarity of the pair of schemata is 0.25.

With these definitions in hand, we can characterize the degree of intensional agreement about a label within the audience segment. We assume that as long as a high fraction of pairs of members of the audience segment agree, then the segment can function as a linguistic community with respect to the meaning of the label. So we rely on the following definition of such consensus.

[6]If an agent's schema does not consider a feature to be relevant to the meaning of the label, we propose to fill in as schema-conforming all of the feature values that the plurality of other audience members consider as the relevant alternatives for the feature.

Definition 3.6 (Grade of membership in an intensional semantic consensus). *An agent's grade of membership in an intensional semantic consensus about a label, in notation $\nu_{i(l)}(y,t)$, is the degree to which his or her meaning of the label agrees with those of other members of the audience segment who employ the label.*

$$\nu_{i(l)}(y,t) \equiv \frac{\sum_{y' \in \mathbf{a}} is(\sigma(l,y,t), \sigma(l,y',t))}{|\mathbf{a}| - 1}.$$

As we discussed in considering the extensions of labels in Chapter 2, some members of the audience segment might have zero grade of membership in a semantic consensus. Again, we propose that the strength of a consensus—intensional, now—equals the average grade of membership in the consensus. Let $ic(l,t)$ be a nonnegative, real-valued function with range [0,1] that gives the strength of the intensional consensus about l in the audience segment at time t.

Definition 3.7 (Strength of intensional consensus). *The strength of the intensional consensus among the users of a label, $ic(l,t)$, is the average (among the members of the audience segment) of the grades of membership in the intensional consensus for that label.*

$$ic(l,t) \equiv \overline{\nu}_{i(l)} = \frac{\sum_{y \in \mathbf{a}} \nu_{i(l)}(y,t)}{|\mathbf{a}|}.$$

3.4 CATEGORIES

We can now define a category as a type for which an audience segment achieves a high level of extensional and intensional consensus. The predicate $\textsc{cat}(l,t)$ indicates that l is the label of a category for the audience segment at time t.

Definition 3.8 (Category). *A category is a class about whose meaning an audience segment has reached a high level of intensional semantic consensus.*

$$\textsc{cat}(l,t) \leftrightarrow \textsc{class}(l,t) \wedge (ic(l,t) \geq \mathfrak{c}).$$

An obvious corollary holds that

$$\textsc{cat}(l,t) \leftrightarrow \textsc{class}(l,t) \wedge (ec(l,t) \geq \mathfrak{d}) \wedge (ic(l,t) \geq \mathfrak{k}).$$

It bears noting that the definition of category does not make direct reference to the meanings of the label. In other words, it leaves open the details of the set of schemata that the members of the audience segment associate with the label. A high degree of intensional consensus means that the members use very similar schemata. But following the lead of cognitive anthropologists (especially Frederik Barth), we designed the definition so that it does not require agreement on any single schema. This means that we do not refer to *the* schema for a category in an audience segment.

A key task of empirical research on categories is to learn the details of the schemata used in an audience. In particular cases, we might learn that nearly all members of the audience segment share a single schema. In others, we might learn that the enthusiasts hold more highly elaborated schemata than those with a more casual interest in the producers/products to which the category pertains. And so forth.

For instance, consider the disk-array industry (McKendrick et al. 2003). Disk-array producers typically offer large-capacity storage systems composed of arrays of hard-disk drives bundled together with a controller and/or associated software. The software, technology, and applications vary widely. The common features of hard-disk-drive arrays include high accessibility, security, and compactness. These arrays form the backbone of the Internet; they also are widely used by consumer-product companies whose millions of records need to be accurate and secure, but also available on an instant's notice. Among the bigger producers are EMC and Network Appliance; but there are scores of other smaller companies too.

Due to the newness of the technology, the wide variations in which it is offered, the obscurity of the technical differences, and differing applications and functionalities of various products, we venture that its audience was characterized by a high level of extensional semantic consensus but not so for intensional semantic consensus over a recent period in the population's history. That is, if audience members were asked to name or list the "disk-array producers," they might well have largely agreed about the lists. However, we also suspect that they would have had great trouble reaching agreement on the meaning of "disk-array producer" or even on the meaning of "disk array." (In fact, the company Network Appliance went so far as to develop and publish a glossary of terms to help consumers and others sort out the language used in referring to this population and its products.) A similar situation might currently prevail for "outsider art" (Fine 2004). By contrast, the emergence of the minivan category of automobiles appears to have been a situation in which intensional agreement reached a high level (Rosa et al. 1999).

We think that an audience segment reaches a high level of intensional agreement most commonly when the producers/products in a class stand out sharply from the background for most audience members. When the average contrast of the class is high, it contains few marginal members, for whom disagreement about grades of membership is likely. Moreover, the members of a class will tend to have very similar feature values, ones that differ from those of the nonmembers of the class. So not only will there be few marginal members when contrast is high, but the members will generally share feature values. Both conditions make it likely that the members of an audience segment will attend to the same features and pick out the same feature value ranges as relevant.

We next implement this line of reasoning as a postulate. However, we first introduce some notation designed to simplify the formal representation of monotonic relationships.

Notation. Many of the assumptions and theorems in the theory presented in this and subsequent chapters involve functional monotonicity statements. We simplify presentation of formulas stating such relations by adopting a notational shorthand. Suppose that f and g are functions defined for a label, an organization, an audience member, and a time point. We can denote such a function in the following format: $f(l, x, y, t)$, where l is the label that identifies a population, x refers to a producer, y

is an audience member, and t is a time point. We use the expression $(f \uparrow g)\,(\mathbf{q},\mathbf{q}')$ to indicate a monotonic positive relationship between the two functions evaluated for the variables in $\mathbf{q},\mathbf{q}'$, and $(f \downarrow g)\,(\mathbf{q},\mathbf{q}')$ to indicate a monotonic negative relationship. And, as Appendix D explains, we drop the variables in predicates and functions that fall within the scope of quantification over $\mathbf{q},\mathbf{q}'$ unless doing so causes confusion.

Postulate 3.3. *The expected level of intensional consensus about a label in an audience segment,* $\mathrm{E}\{ic\}$, *normally increases with the average (over the audience segment) of the average contrast of members of the class defined by the label* $\bar{c}$.

$$\mathfrak{N}\,\mathbf{q},\mathbf{q}'\,[\textsc{class}(l,t) \wedge \textsc{class}(l',t') \rightarrow (\bar{c} \uparrow \mathrm{E}(ic))\,(\mathbf{q},\mathbf{q}')\,],$$

where $\bar{c}_{i(l)}(t) = \sum_{y\in\mathbf{a}} c_{i(l)}(y,t)/|\mathbf{a}|$, $\mathbf{q} = \langle l,t\rangle$, *and* $\mathbf{q}' = \langle l',t'\rangle$.[7]

3.5 INTRINSIC APPEAL AND CATEGORY VALENCE

In many societies, some categories of producers receive a general positive evaluation from most audience segments, while others receive a negative evaluation, e.g., "sweatshop," "loan shark," "diploma mill," "ambulance chaser," "Frankenfood," and so forth.[8] This difference matters for how we represent the consequences of fitting or not fitting schemata, which we discuss in the next chapter.

We define valuation in terms of the concept of the intrinsic appeal of a producer (or product) to an agent. The degree to which an agent finds an offering appealing depends on the perceived fit between the offering's attributes and the agent's taste. We use the qualifier "intrinsic appeal" to allow a distinction with the actual appeal of an offering. As we explain in Part III, intrinsically appealing offers do not generate actual appeal if they are not made available or are presented in a manner that conflicts with the agent's tastes.

Depending on the type of audience under consideration, the product/service being offered differs, as we noted in the previous chapter. For firms, salient audiences include consumers (on the product-market side), employees (on the labor-market side), and investors (on the capital-market side). In applications to nonprofit organizations such as political parties, voluntary associations, and social-movement organizations, the audience might variously include donors, members, volunteers, voters, and so forth, depending upon the domain and the organizational category under consideration. The nature of what we call the offer obviously also differs across these contexts. For instance, firms make product offers to consumers, job offers to potential employees, and debt and equity offerings to potential investors.

---

[7] The full "official" statement of this premise is

$$\mathfrak{N}\,l,l',t,t'\,[\textsc{class}(l,t) \wedge \textsc{class}(l',t') \rightarrow (\bar{c}_{i(l)}(t) > \bar{c}_{i(l')}(t')) \rightarrow (\mathrm{E}(ic(l,t)) > \mathrm{E}(ic(l',t')))].$$

[8] See, for example, the Website http/!/www.sweatshopwatch.org for a definition (schema) for a "sweatshop."

As we see it, intrinsic appeal is based on a complex assessment of the "offer," including the feature values of the product/service being offered and the feature values of the producer. For instance, in the case of a job offer, a prospective employee generally attends both to the details of the offer (salary, job assignment, hours, benefits) as well as to the features of the firm making the offer (e.g., status and reputation).

We harness the fuzzy-set machinery to represent this idea as well. The intrinsic appeal function of an offering to a member of the audience segment exhibits the form of a grade of membership.

Definition 3.9 (Intrinsic appeal). *The intrinsic appeal of a producer's offering as an instance of a label to an agent at a time point, in notation* $\widehat{ap}(l, x, y, t)$*, is a function that maps triples of producers, audience-segment members, and time points to the* $[0, 1]$ *interval. It tells the level of intrinsic appeal of the offering to the agent at that time.*

$$\widehat{ap}(l) : \mathbf{o} \times \mathbf{a} \times \mathbf{t} \longrightarrow [0, 1].$$

In this (official) notation, we express instances of the function as $\widehat{ap}(l)(x, y, t)$. Whenever it does not cause confusion, we use a shorthand: $\widehat{ap}(l, x, y, t)$, which is easier on the eyes.[9]

A level of intrinsic appeal of one means that the offer displays the maximal possible appeal; a value of zero means that it lacks any appeal. We elaborate the theoretical import of the intrinsic appeal function by tying it to grades of membership in the meaning of the relevant category in two steps. First, we tie a zero GoM in a label to the absence of appeal in a meaning postulate; then we define valenced categories as those in which expected intrinsic appeal is a monotonic function of grade of membership in the intension of the relevant label.

Meaning postulate 3.2. *A producer's or product's offering associated with a type has zero expected intrinsic appeal to an agent who does not regard the producer or product as having a positive grade of membership in the meaning of the label.*

$$\mathfrak{N}\, l, x, y, t[(\mu_{i(l)}(x, y, t) = 0) \rightarrow (\mathrm{E}(\widehat{ap}(l, x, y, t)) = 0)].$$

Definition 3.10 (Positively valued class and category). *In a class (category) with positive valence, the agents with higher GoM in the extensional (intensional) consensus supporting the class (category) normally prefer (find intrinsically more appealing) the offerings of more clear-cut members of the class (category), those with higher GoM.*

$$\begin{aligned}\mathrm{PCLASS}(l, t) \leftrightarrow \mathrm{CLASS}(l, t) \wedge \mathfrak{N}\, \mathbf{q}, \mathbf{q}'\, [(\nu_{e(l)}(y, t) \geq \nu_{e(l)}(y', t')) \\ \rightarrow (\mu_{e(l)} \uparrow \mathrm{E}(\widehat{ap}(l)))(\mathbf{q}, \mathbf{q}')];\end{aligned}$$

[9]The formal languages used in this book contain only two nonlogical functor categories, predicates and functions. It is important that everything we want to express can be expressed in such languages. However it is convenient to borrow some expressions from a type-theoretical language. For example, we could rewrite a two place predicate $f(.,.)$ as a one place functor $f(.)$ that takes a name and gives a one place predicate $f(a)(.)$. According to this approach, a two-place functor $f(a, b)$ can be seen as a one-place functor f that takes a and produces a one-place functor $f(a)$ that, in turn, takes b and produces $\mathrm{f}(a)(b)$. But, as we note in the text, we generally write $f(a, b)$ for the sake of simplicity.

$$\text{PCAT}(l,t) \leftrightarrow \text{CAT}(l,t) \wedge \mathfrak{N}\,\mathbf{q},\mathbf{q}'\,[(\nu_{i(l)}(y,t) \geq \nu_{i(l)}(y',t')) \rightarrow (\mu_{i(l)} \uparrow \mathrm{E}(\widehat{ap}(l)))\,(\mathbf{q},\mathbf{q}')\,],$$

where $\mathbf{q} = \langle t, x, y \rangle$ *and* $\mathbf{q}' = \langle t', x', y' \rangle$.

[Read: a label marks a positively valued class (category) for an audience segment at a time point if and only if the label marks a class/category for that audience segment and time point and it is normally the case for every pair of agents and pair of producers/products that so long as one of the agent's GoM in the consensus about the extension/intension of the class/category is at least as high as that of the other agent and that same agent assigns higher GoM to one producer than the other agent does the other producer, then the expected intrinsic appeal of the higher GoM producer to the higher GoM audience member is greater than that for the other audience member–producer pair.]

Note that letting $y' = y$ in the foregoing definition tells that a member of the audience finds more intrinsically appealing a producer with higher grade of membership for a positively valued category.

Definition 3.11 (Negatively valued class and category). *In a class (category) with negative valence, the agents with higher GoM in the extensional (intensional) consensus supporting the category normally find intrinsically less appealing the offerings of more clear-cut members of the class (category), those with higher GoM.*

What difference does it make if an audience assigns an organization one social category or another? Joseph Porac and colleagues (Porac and Thomas 1990; Porac et al. 1995; Rosa, Judson, and Porac 2005) have stressed the competitive implications of same-category classification. According to them, firms simplify the competitive environment by using abstract classifications; and those classified similarly tend to be viewed as rivals or competitors. For instance, in studying Scottish knitwear producers, Porac et al. (1995: 222) conclude that

> Managers encounter existing organizational configurations . . .
> A model that describes tangible and informative features of these configurations provides the necessary guideposts for managers to locate their firms within a competitive milieu. From the standpoint of today's knitwear managers, a common-sense model organized around size, technology, location and product styles cogently summarizes the industry. It provides a straightforward inference system such that knowing a firm's position on any one of the model's dimensions allows a manager to infer its position on the other four and on related noncentral attributes. The cognitive economy that the model provides seems a major reason why rivalry coheres around it. Moreover, to the extent that managers use the model to formulate and enact strategic moves, the model becomes self-reinforcing within the limits imposed by the material conditions of knitwear production.

As the research program conducted by institutionalists shows clearly, classification, while institutionally specific, implies pervasive and often profound consequences. The effects transcend competitive issues in importance for the success and failure of producers and their products. To name a few obvious instances and their implications, in contemporary America those organizations classified by societal members as churches or religions receive a large proportion of the total charitable donations given annually because of the meaning of this classification; likewise, universities receive much largesse because of the social interpretation of their classification. More generally, classification as a nonprofit or charitable organization entitles an entity to such considerations as well as favorable treatment from other organizations as well as authorities. Yet these organizations might perform the same activities and functions as other organizations that do not qualify for a high GoM in these classifications. For instance, for-profit colleges and universities in the United States, e.g., the University of Phoenix (the major subsidiary of the Apollo Group), enroll about 1.7 million students, roughly 9 percent of total enrollments in higher education (Hechinger 2005).

At the organizational level, the implications of category membership often affect viability and even life chances. Time Inc., the parent company (of the weekly publication *Sports Illustrated,*) for instance, recently found itself the subject to an appeals court order (emanating from a libel suit) requiring it to identify the source used for a contentious story even though the state in which the relevant events took place has a shield law that protects news reporters from divulging the identities of anonymous sources. The problem? The court ruled that *Sports Illustrated* is a magazine and that the shield law covered only "newspaper, radio and television reporters," not magazine reporters (Fatsis 2005).

McKendrick and Carroll (2001) cite the example of Reuters, a venerable old-media company that ventured into many new areas during the Internet and "e-commerce" boom. This created an institutional problem of sorts, in that analysts and investors could not decide on how to evaluate the company:

> . . . even the most seasoned media-sector investors concede that they are less than secure when evaluating Reuters. "We built a huge [earnings] model" said Mark Beilby, an analyst in London with Germany's Deutsche Bank. "We're confident in it" for many media companies, "but we don't know whether it works or not for Reuters." Other firms express similar uncertainty. (Goldsmith 1999)

The consequence of the difficulty of classifying Reuters apparently contributed to the high volatility of its stock price at the time. The firm incurred huge losses that appear to be attributable to nothing other than the classificatory uncertainty.

DISCUSSION

This chapter provides a conceptual framework and a formal language for expressing how agents come to label a cluster of perceived similar organizations, and then how the cluster is used inductively to develop an abstract code or schemata. In our depiction, there is both an individual and a collective process of labeling and coding. In the collective process, the members of the audience segment come to

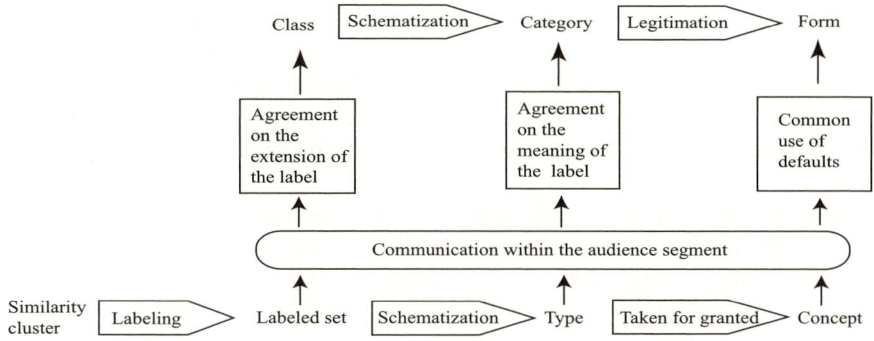

Figure 3.1 Summary of the form emergence process

a shared understanding about the labels and schemata that have been developed individually.

Figure 3.1 provides a graphical summary of the stages in the theorized process of form emergence. The lower level of the diagram depicts what happens at the individual level; the upper two levels depict the level of the audience segment, assuming agreement and consensus. This chapter and the previous one describe the first several stages of the process, depicted on the left of the figure, up to and including the box for emergence of a category. The next chapter addresses the processes depicted on the right-hand side of the figure, how taken-for-grantedness creates concepts and how legitimation processes create forms. It is worth noting again that, in our view, most emergence processes will not make it past the first or second stages of the process, moving neither to the right nor upwards in the diagram. It surely is not inevitable that a class becomes a category, that extensional consensus gets converted to intensional consensus.

In the stage we analyzed here, the enthusiasts *construct* the coded feature space. Empirical research can often identify the period within which the emergence process unfolds and the nature of the debates that arose. For instance, David Strang (1995) analyzed the construction of the category of health maintenance organization; and David Barron (1998) gives a similar type of account of credit unions. Indeed, this is generally a time-honored method of conducting institutional analysis in sociology. However, we suspect it would be even more informative for empirical researchers to identify and study cases at this earlier stage, before the outcome has been determined, as McKendrick and collaborators (2003) did for disk-array producers. In the contemporary world, we think that the "new American cuisine" case is currently at this stage. For example, some critics want to construct an associated schema based on reliance on indigenous ingredients, others want to base it on historical invention, yet others want to define it on the basis of types of ingredients or techniques, or combinations thereof.

Where do such schemata come from? Enthusiasts debate the merits of alternative schemata for clusters. In many cases, the actions of *social movement* were decisive in constructing schemata and gaining consensus about them. For instance, the Association of Brewers, the craft brewers' industry association, begun in the late 1970s, engaged in lively debates about what constituted a craft brewer and what did not, including whether the distinction should hinge on the features of the products and their method of production or on the organizational characteristics of the producers. The eventual agreement held that both matter for membership in the type.

In other cases, the seeds for schemata come from *actions of authorities*, such as a law or regulation that defines a formal type and associates rights and responsibilities to its members. Such actions have been subject to much research in the neo-institutionalist tradition. In many cases, it seems that authorization recognizes the existence of natural types that have already been constructed by an audience. Martin Ruef (2000) provides examples from medical care organization.

A full treatment of the emergence of types should take account of the influence of movements and the actions of authorities. Because our framework is already quite complicated, we do not undertake this kind of analysis here. However we do return to issues involving authorization and social movements in Chapter 5.

We must consider the possibility that a member of the audience might try various schemata before deciding that one does a better job than the others in representing the meaning of a cluster. One basis for preferring a particular schema to another is success in reproducing grades of membership in the cluster. Choosing among competing schemata likely involves a tradeoff. Very complicated schemata generally do a better job of representing reality than do simpler ones (schemata of lower dimensionality, for instance). However, complicated schemata require more effort to use and apply only in narrower sets of circumstances. Rosch and collaborators (1976) found that subjects were likely to choose categories at a "basic level" that reflects the actual discontinuities in nature. For instance, "chair" appears to be a basic-level concept to their subjects. The higher-level entry in the taxonomy is "furniture." This category is less useful for subjects (has lower cue validity) because the family resemblance of its constituent elements is lower than is the case for "chair." On the other hand, lower-level types such as "kitchen chair" are less useful (have lower cue validity) because they share most feature values with other subordinate types, such as "living room chair." According to this construction, individuals likely develop schemata at the basic level, which is cast at an intermediate level of specificity. The organizational analog to chair as an intermediate-level schemata is clearly something between, say, "organization" and "small profit-making public firm manufacturing high-end widgets using robotics." But there is much ground between the two descriptions, if indeed that is where individuals choose and where the actual discontinuities occur in the social world.

Empirical social scientists might recognize a parallel between the development of schemata and the development of data coding rules in initially open-ended empirical research.[10] A typical experience is that the researcher first examines some records or makes some observations and attempts to get a sense of the types and range of information available. Then she attempts to dimensionalize the infor-

[10]Another parallel might be drawn to certain types of grading, say, marking student essays, where the grader first reads some essays to get an idea of the range of answers and then develops guidelines about how to systematize the subsequent grading.

mation and test dimensional representations against more records or observations. Finally, she draws distinctions within dimensions, and develops rules about how to classify particular cases.

Chapter Four

Forms and Populations

Building on the conceptual material developed in chapters above, we now turn directly to questions about forms and populations. In our view, it is high time to clarify these concepts. Elaine Romanelli's (1991: 81) review of the literature on the emergence and establishment of organizational forms concluded that "no theoretical consensus exists regarding an approach to the problem . . . the conceptual approaches are diverging." More tellingly, this review also found no generally accepted common definition of the concept. From the proposed theoretical arguments about form emergence, "no overarching themes for integrating these perspectives" could be identified (Romanelli 1991: 100). The diversity of renderings of the concept of organizational form has probably risen since the time of this assessment.

We propose a general characterization of form, one that we hope might gain some wider acceptance. Specifically, we follow much sociological research in defining a form as a category with a high level of legitimation. We use it to develop the theory of form emergence. Given this orientation, it makes sense to begin the chapter with the concept of legitimation. Because the relevant theory and research treat legitimation as a primitive, unanalyzed concept, we try to explicate the core idea and build a model of legitimation.

Our use of the term legitimation refers to only one of its main uses: *constitutive* legitimation, the standing as a taken-for-granted element in a social structure (Berger and Luckmann 1966; Meyer and Rowan 1977; Jepperson 1991). In our view, prior treatments of constitutive legitimation do not make very clear what exactly gets taken for granted and what it means to be taken for granted.

For us, the entity that gets legitimated is a *semantic object:* a concept or category. Furthermore, what it means to us for a concept/category to be taken for granted is that members of the audience generally treat as a default the idea that full-fledged members of the concept/category fit their schemata. Default standing means that agents do not fully inspect or scrutinize each alleged member but instead fill in the feature values that fit their schemata, unless they see evidence to the contrary. We designed a modality to express what it means for a label and an associated schema to be taken for granted.

We define a concept as a type for which an audience member takes for granted that objects to which she assigns the type label satisfy her schemata for the label. A category is defined in parallel at the audience segment level: a category is a class for which the members of the audience segment take for granted conformity to their schemata.

We also explore some of the implications of the conceptual framework for defining organizational populations and for modeling their dynamics. In particular, we examine the implications for the theory of density-dependent legitimation and competition (Hannan and Carroll 1992). This well established theory of long-term organizational population evolution holds that growth in density initially enhances a population's (constitutive) legitimation, thereby raising its founding rate and lowering its mortality rate. These effects initially induce further growth in density. However, persistent growth in density eventually generate intense competition, which depresses founding rates and elevates mortality rates. We show that the reformulated version of the theory preserves the main intuitions but also generates subtle new results.

4.1 TEST CODES AND DEFAULTS

In our view, enthusiasts in an audience segment likely treat their initial schematizations as tentative. Their codifications might be usefully viewed in the way that scientists regard hypotheses—as claims that might or might not be borne out. As evidence accumulates about previously unseen producers and about the behaviors of the producers whose features served as the material for the schematization, the matter might eventually become settled.

Recall that we define a category in terms of agreement about the meaning of a label. The fact that an audience reaches intensional agreement does not imply that a high level of fit to schemata can be taken for granted for all category members. Some schemata will find general—albeit not universal—fit; others will not. Imagine that most organizations that label themselves as "schools" do not now have any enrolled students. We suspect that typical observers would begin to call into question their preconceived understandings of "school." More generally, we conjecture that categories do not prove useful to an audience when the producers claiming membership in the category commonly fail to conform to the codes (schemata) that the agents apply.

On the other hand, widespread fit with the schemata creates the impression that the reality expressed by a category is natural and perhaps even obligatory. Therefore, generic fit and a low frequency of observed misfits lead observers to take for granted the behaviors that fit the schemata. In such cases, schemata become default assumptions of everyday life.

A change to default status leaves the applicability of a schema intact. What changes is that the defaults get used to fill in the many gaps in perceptions that come about from incomplete information, unobservability, and ambiguity. That is, absent evidence to the contrary, agents in default mode assume that they will find behavior and structure consistent with the relevant schemata whenever they encounter an organization to which they have reason to apply the label.

We formalize ideas about taken-for-grantedness with a modal semantics that we constructed for this purpose. Appendix E defines modal operators for perception and default. The modal operator for perception, denoted by $\boxed{\mathrm{P}}$, works as follows. The formula $\boxed{\mathrm{P}}_y \psi$ means that y perceives that the state of affairs represented by the formula ψ is the case. For instance, $\boxed{\mathrm{P}}_y(\mathbf{f}_i(x,t) = \mathbf{v}_i(x,t))$ means that y

perceives that the indexed set of features $\mathbf{f}_i(x,t)$ has the values $\mathbf{v}_i(x,t)$ at time t.

The modality for default is denoted by $\boxed{\text{D}}$. The formula $\boxed{\text{D}}_y\psi$ expresses that y treats as a default that the formula ψ is true. That is, whenever someone lacks evidence to the contrary, he "fills in the fact" that ψ is the case. The modality has a temporal structure. Once an agent has shifted to default mode, she retains the default unless and until there is an update due to a new perception that overrules the default. In an effort to keep the notation from becoming even more byzantine, we leave the temporal parameter in this modality implicit.

In our application, the defaults concern the fit of an entity's actual feature values, $\mathbf{v}_i(x,t)$, to a schema. Suppose that an agent uses the schema $\sigma(l,y,t) = \mathbf{s}_i^l$. Then $\boxed{\text{D}}_y(\mathbf{v}_i(x,t) \rightarrow (\mathbf{v}_i \in \mathbf{s}_i^l))$ means that she accepts, in the absence of information to the contrary, that x's feature values fit the schema $\mathbf{s}_i^l$ at the time point t.[1] It is worth pausing to consider why we use the material implication operator, denoted by $\rightarrow$ in this case. As we noted above, we want to create an expression that tells that the agent treats as a default that the observed feature values fit a pattern allowed by the schema. The conditional $\rightarrow$ has this interpretation (see Appendix C): if the values are as given, then these values fit the schema. This statement is false only when the perceived feature values do not fit the schema.

If multiple labels can be applied to an object, then it is possible that an agent associates several schemata with the set of labels. Suppose that the complex label formed from all the labels that y applies to x is $\oplus l$. As we established in Chapter 3, $\sigma(\oplus l, y, t) = \mathbf{s}_i^{\oplus l} = \mathbf{s}_i^{l_1} \cap \mathbf{s}_i^{l_2} \cdots \cap \mathbf{s}_i^{l_k}$, where k is the number of different labels applied to x. Now suppose that y takes for granted that x's feature values fit each of these schemata:

$$\boxed{\text{D}}_y(\mathbf{v}_i(x,t) \rightarrow (\mathbf{v}_i \in \mathbf{s}_i^{l_1})) \wedge \cdots \wedge \boxed{\text{D}}_y(\mathbf{v}_i(x,t) \rightarrow (\mathbf{v}_i \in \mathbf{s}_i^{l_k})).$$

This means that $\boxed{\text{D}}_y(\mathbf{v}_i(x,t) \rightarrow (\mathbf{v}_i \in \mathbf{s}_i^{l_1}) \wedge \cdots \wedge (\mathbf{v}_i \in \mathbf{s}_i^{l_k}))$. According to the definition of the default modality in Appendix E, each of these modal statements is true if and only if it is true in all of the default alternatives of the actual world. But in that case the conjunction of these statements is also true. This means that we have proven the following theorem.

Theorem 4.1. *If an agent takes for granted that a producer's feature values fit the schematization of all of the (atomic) components of a complex label, then she presumably also takes for granted that the producer's feature values fit the schematization of the complex label.*

$$(\boxed{\text{D}}_y(\mathbf{v}_i(x,t) \rightarrow (\mathbf{v}_i \in \mathbf{s}_i^{l_1})) \wedge \cdots \wedge \boxed{\text{D}}_y(\mathbf{v}_i(x,t)) \rightarrow (\mathbf{v}_i \in \mathbf{s}_i^{l_k}))$$
$$\rightarrow \boxed{\text{D}}_y(\mathbf{v}_i(x,t) \rightarrow (\mathbf{v}_i \in \mathbf{s}_i^{\oplus l})).$$

Induction from a Test

Defaults only matter in the absence of complete information. This is because (perceived) facts override defaults, as we have defined the modality. So we consider

[1]As we explain in Appendix E, a modal operator works in terms of accessibility relations among possible worlds. R^{D} is the default-applicability relation. A world w' is *default-accessible* from the world w if what the agent takes for granted in w is true in w'.

situations in which audience members possess partial information on the feature values of a producer. With only partial information, global fit to a schema cannot be assessed. Incomplete information on the fit of feature values to a schema is common, because only some relevant features can be observed easily. Sometimes all that someone sees is that a producer makes a claim to a label or that some other audience member (perhaps a critic or another kind of gatekeeper) applies the label to the producer. This kind of situation seems to offer the kind of leverage we need to define legitimation.

We begin by formalizing the idea of a test code for fit with a schema, which we will use to define legitimation. We need to introduce some notation for this task.

Notation. As in Chapter 3, we used $\mathbf{f}_i(x,t)$ to denote the indexed set of the i features of producer x at time point t that are relevant for some schema defined over i features and $\mathbf{v}_i(x,t)$ to denote the indexed set of the values of those features for x at t. Let $\mathbf{w}_j$ denote an indexed set of values of some subset of the relevant features: $0 \leq j < i$. We use the expression $[\mathbf{v}_i : \mathbf{w}_j](x,t)$ to represent an alternative indexed set of feature values of x at t with the elements of $\mathbf{v}_j(x,t)$ replaced by the elements of $\mathbf{w}_j(x,t)$. Note that $j = 0$ means that no values are replaced.

With this notation in hand, we can state formally what it means to induce conformity to a schema based on partial information.

Definition 4.1 (Induction from a test). *An induction from a test is a situation in which an agent's perception that producer bears a category label and that its feature values satisfy a test code triggers the agent to apply the default that the untested feature values also satisfy the schema.*

Let $\sigma(l,y,t) = \mathbf{s}_i^l$.

$$\textsc{induc}(\sigma(l,y,t), \mathbf{v}_i : \mathbf{w}_j) \leftrightarrow (l \in \mathbf{lab}(x,y,t)) \wedge \boxed{\text{P}}_y(\mathbf{w}_j, x, t) \\ \rightarrow \boxed{\text{D}}_y(\mathbf{v}_i : \mathbf{w}_j, x, t) \in \mathbf{s}_i^l).$$

In this case we refer to $\mathbf{w}_j$ *as* y*'s* test *for judging conformity to the schema* $\sigma(l,y,t)$*, in notation,* $\textsc{tst}(\sigma(l,y,t), \mathbf{w}_j)$*, and we say that the test has* j *items. An empty test is one with* $j = 0$.

We specialize the argument to the case of "flat" schemata, those in which each feature has equal weight in determining fit. This allows us to conceptualize legitimation in terms of the number of features with certain properties. If a code system is not flat, then we would need to take account of the weights assigned to features.

When a schema pertains to more than two features, an interesting issue arises. How many features would need to be checked before someone treats as a default that the rest of the features fall in a schema-consistent pattern? If every feature must be checked, then nothing is taken for granted. If only a small fraction of the relevant features must be checked, then defaults get used in a powerful way. We think that the latter case suggests that schema conformity is taken for granted, given a small amount of positive information (perhaps only a claim to the label).

These considerations demand that we consider the minimal test for an agent-schema pair, the test that involves the smallest number of features.

Definition 4.2 (Minimal test for induction). *The set of feature values* $\mathbf{w}_j$ *is* y*'s minimal test for induction for the schema for* l *at time* t*, in notation* $\text{MTST}(\sigma(l, y, t), \mathbf{w}_j)$*, if and only if*

1. *it is one of* y*'s tests for conformity with the schema:* $\text{TST}(\sigma(l, y, t), \mathbf{w}_j)$*;*

2. *it uses fewer test features and labels than any other test for the schema:*
$$\forall \mathbf{w}', j' \, [\text{TST}(\sigma(l, y, t), \mathbf{w}'_{j'}) \rightarrow (j \leq j')];$$

3. y *induces satisfaction of the schema* $\sigma(l, y, t)$ *on the untested features from this test:* $\text{INDUC}(\sigma(l, y, t), \mathbf{v}_i : \mathbf{w}_j)$*.*

A good example of a minimal test code comes from the contention between proponents of "traditional" and "modern" wine production for Barolo and Barbaresco, which we mentioned in the previous chapter. The two approaches to wine making diverge on many issues, including practices in the vineyard, degree of control over fermentation, length of maceration (contact of the grape juice with the skins), use of chemical additives, and type of container used for aging. The modernist code appears to have prevailed in the vineyards, as all producers have been switching to practices such as "green harvest" that lower yields sharply (before the modernist insurgency, viticulturists apparently sought to maximize yields). All of the other issues remain contentious.

This debate apparently sharpened the "traditional" code; and it seems to have yielded agreement about its conforming feature values, including sole use of indigenous grape varieties, reliance on wild yeast, minimal intervention in primary and secondary fermentation, long maceration periods, and use of large casks (*botti*) of Slovenian oak for aging, and on an easily observable test code: any use of the French *barrique.* This refers to a barrel with capacity of 225 liters (much smaller than the traditional casks, which means that the wine has more contact with the wood and, therefore, can extract more flavor elements from it and interact more with the gases outside the barrel) made of types of French oak noted for imparting specific tastes to the wine. The traditionalists complain that use of such small barrels creates flavors similar to those of French, Californian, and Australian wines and not characteristic of the local *terroir.* The traditionalists and their supporters now impose the simple test for "traditional" vs. "modern": has a wine been aged in *barrique*? If yes, then it is "modern," and all of the modern practices can be filled in as defaults (Negro et al. 2006). Indeed, some restaurant wine lists in Italy now clearly indicate which wines came from *barrique*, which suggests that this simple test code might be gaining acceptance within the Italian consumer audience.

4.2 TAKEN-FOR-GRANTEDNESS

With these preliminaries in hand, we can now define taken-for-grantedness. Let the function $g(l, x, y, t)$, which maps four-tuples of labels, producers, audience members, and time points to the [0,1] interval, tell the degree to which the audience member takes for granted that the producer conforms to the schema for the label at the time point.

Definition 4.3 (Taken-for-grantedness). *The degree to which an agent takes for granted that the untested feature values of a labeled producer conform to a schema for the label at a time point is the ratio of the untested code to the whole code.*

$$g(l,x,y,t) \equiv \begin{cases} \frac{i-j}{i} & \textit{if } (\sigma(l,y,t)=\mathbf{s}_i^l) \wedge \text{MTST}(\sigma(l,y,t),\mathbf{w}_j) \wedge \\ & \quad (l \in \mathbf{lab}(x,y,t)); \\ 0 & \textit{otherwise}. \end{cases}$$

Note that i indicates the (crisp) cardinality of all of the feature values relevant for the schema, and j indicates the cardinality of the feature values relevant for the minimal test. Therefore, this definition sets $g = 0$ if the agent does not apply the label to the object or needs to see every (nonlabel) feature before making an induction (which is no induction at all); nothing is taken as satisfied by default. It sets $g = 1$ if application of the label by itself is enough to shift the agent to defaults about schema-conformity on all of the other relevant features. In this case, the test on feature values is empty, $j = 0$; and the test is passed automatically whenever the label is applied.

Whether or not someone takes for granted the satisfaction on the untested features of a schema for a label for a single producer does not tell us much. More interesting is the case in which satisfaction is taken for granted generally. If this is the case, then we would conclude that the schema-label pair displays a high degree of taken-for-grantedness for that agent. Making this kind of assessment requires that we consider the levels of taken-for-grantedness across the relevant producers/products in the domain at a time point. The relevant ones consist of those to whom the audience-segment member applies the label at that time point.

Definition 4.4 (Taken-for-grantedness of a label for an agent). *The degree of taken-for-grantedness associated with a label at a time point for y, $G(l,y,t)$, is the average of degree to which the agent takes for granted that the feature values of the producers to which she assigns the label conform to her schemata when the producers pass the minimal tests for their (flat) schemata.*

$$G(l,y,t) \equiv \textstyle\sum_{x \mid l \in \mathbf{lab}(x,y,t)} \frac{g(l,x,y,t)}{|\{x \mid l \in \mathbf{lab}(x,y,t)\}|}.$$

Notice that this definition states that an agent takes a class/category fully for granted when she takes for granted the satisfaction of her schema for the label for *all* of the producers/products to which she assigns the label. The interesting cases are those with very low, but positive GoM in the extension of the label. Recall that we introduced a meaning postulate, M2.1 that equates an object's GoM in an agent's extension of a label with the probability (over occasions) that this same member will apply the label to the object. If a producer has a low but positive GoM in an agent's label, then she will not usually apply the label to it. In those rare cases in which she does apply the label to such marginal cases, she will be unlikely to use defaults about schema satisfaction. Taken-for-grantedness will be low so long as the label is used in such an indiscriminate way. It will rise if the language sharpens.

Consider, as an example, the case of the medical profession in the heyday of its taken-for-grantedness (perhaps the middle of the twentieth century). In that period, "physician" was highly taken for granted legitimated in the sense that knowledge that someone had a license to practice medicine warranted use of defaults on many other feature values. Crucially, the label was applied very crisply. Workers in allied occupations such as faith healer, osteopath, chiropractor, midwife, nurse, paramedic, psychoanalyst had essentially no probability of being assigned the label. Our proposed definition is sensitive to such variations.

We want to capture in our language the changed status of a type when it becomes taken for granted. We use the predicate $\textsc{concept}(l, \sigma(l, y, t))$, which reads as "the pair consisting of a label and schema $\langle l, \sigma(l, y, t)\rangle$ forms a concept for y at t."

Definition 4.5 (Concept). *An audience-segment member's type is a concept if the member treats conformity to her schemata for the type label as taken-for-granted for all those producers/products to which she assigns the label.*

$$\textsc{concept}(l, \sigma(l, y, t)) \leftrightarrow (\langle l, \sigma(l, y, t)\rangle \in \mathbf{ty}(y, t)) \wedge (G(l, y, t) > \mathfrak{g} \approx 1).$$

Note that, as above, we use a threshold construction for such an analytic term.

4.3 LEGITIMATION AND FORMS

Just as a type can become a category if the audience-segment members come to agree about the meaning of the label for a class, so too can a concept become a form if legitimation takes hold in an audience segment. We define the legitimation of a label in an audience segment as the average level of taken-for-grantedness of the label in the segment.

Definition 4.6 (Legitimation of a label for an audience segment). *The degree of legitimation of a label at a time point for an audience segment, $L(l, t)$, is the average (over the members of the audience segment) of the legitimation of the label.*

$$L(l, t) \equiv \frac{\sum_{y \in \mathbf{a}} G(l, y, t)}{|\mathbf{a}|}.$$

Now, we consider form. Earlier, after reviewing the theoretical status of the concept of form in diverse kinds of sociological arguments, we concluded that the form concept can best play its assigned role if a form possesses two properties: it builds on identity and it applies broadly to a class of organizations (Pólos, Hannan, and Carroll 2002). As Becker (1982: 163) explains for art,

> . . . in principle any organization or action can be legitimated as art, but . . . in practice every art world has procedures and rules governing legitimation which, while not clear-cut or foolproof, nevertheless make the success of some candidates for the status of art very unlikely. Those procedures and rules are contained in the conventions and patterns of cooperation by which art worlds carry on their routine activities.

Our prior work stipulated that the set of organizations classified into a form must achieve a certain (form-specific) density. We added this restriction in an attempt to reflect the original density-dependence theory. We argued that tying the emergence of a form in an audience to the growth in the density of the organizational population is an indirect way to represent constitutive legitimation.

Our conceptualization of legitimation provides a simpler, more natural, and more general way to define forms as legitimated cultural objects. The key insight, as we noted above, comes from recognizing that taken-for-grantedness can be equated with broad and strong reliance on defaults. That is, the use of defaults for the members of a category gives a sure sign that the onlooker takes for granted the existence of the category. Therefore, we propose to use the breadth and strength of reliance on defaults about code satisfaction to mark the difference between a category and a form.

We suggest that a form is a highly legitimated category. That is, legitimation, as we now define it, means that the members of the audience treat the satisfaction of their schemata for the label of the category as a default for those producers that pass a test code.[2] Furthermore, we think that the test code is "thin," in the sense that it involves some small subset of the full code.

Definition 4.7 (Form). *A form is a category with a high level of legitimation (a level that exceeds some threshold, denoted by* $\mathfrak{l}$*).*

$$\text{FORM}(l,t) \leftrightarrow \text{CAT}(l,t) \wedge (L(l,t) \geq \mathfrak{l} \approx 1).$$

Our reading of the sociological evidence suggests that the standing of a schema changes when it becomes a set of taken for granteds (conditional on passing a test code). For one thing, people generally express irritation when their default expectations are not met. At the extreme, they treat violation of a default as a moral transgression. Therefore, we mark this difference in our theoretical language. We refer to the schemata associated with forms as *codes.* In this sense, a schema takes on the character of a penal code—not merely an interpretation. Form memberships generally have a rulelike status. So, satisfying or violating the defaults expressing a form entails consequences for an audience's social valuation of any purported member of the form (Meyer and Rowan 1977; Becker 1982; Jepperson 1991).

Notice that a form, as we define it, is a concept. As such, it is a creation of an audience, not an analyst's distinction.

4.4 POPULATIONS

In Chapter 1, we noted that organizational ecology focuses on processes that unfold for organizational populations, e.g., selection among competing forms and organizations. Empirical research attends to the determinants of the flow of entries into and exits from such populations. The import of this work depends crucially on defining populations in a sociologically coherent way. As long as the population concept remains underdeveloped, the link between abstract theory and systematic

---

[2] A definition of form that spells out these considerations would fit the intuitions of the early stages of organizational ecology.

empirical research remains tenuous. Getting the specification of population right surely makes a difference.

As we discussed in Chapter 3, early organizational ecology defined populations as bounded sets of entities with a *common form,* often interacting with each other and struggling over common resources (Hawley 1968; Hannan and Freeman 1977). By this view, population is limited by some social-system boundary, which reflects barriers to the operations of relevant social processes such as the flow of information, organizational competition, natural resource distributions, and governmental regulation. Getting the boundary specification right makes a crucial difference for studying competition and other processes based on mutual dependence; it determines which entities might be seen as possibly interdependent with which others. The most important feature of this now-standard approach is that it defines a population as a time-and-place instantiation of an organizational form.

We argued previously that the standard approach cannot provide a coherent view of a population at the time of its inception (Pólos, Hannan, and Carroll 2002). We find it helpful in thinking about this issue to work backward through the history of a population. As we move backward, we eventually reach the point at which the population-defining form takes hold in the audience. Then imagine pushing the history back further, continuing to the point at which we see the emergence of a consensus about the extension of the label attached to the form.

This is not a purely imaginary exercise. Most contemporary research on the evolution of populations of organizations tries to push observations back to this kind of origin (Carroll and Hannan 2000), partly because we have learned that observations on the very early history are crucial for examining legitimation (Hannan and Carroll 1992). But what is the theoretical status of such a collection of entities before a form has been established? If we define populations in terms of forms, then we lack a warrant for extending a population's history back to the emergence of what will in retrospect be viewed as the pioneers. Obviously, we would prefer to define population in a way that allows meaningful specification of a unitary entity (a semantic object in the new theory) that spans the entire history.

We think that the framework developed here can shed light on these foundational issues. Indeed, a positive sign of the utility of the web of conceptual distinctions made in Chapters 2 and 3 is that a characterization of organizational population arises naturally from it. This definition is based on the assessments of the members of the audience.[3] We suggest that the existence of a *consensual label* (a class label) marks a population of producers/products as an identifiable social object. Therefore, we tie the existence of a population to the emergence of strong extensional consensus about a label.

How should we think about an entity's grade of membership in a population? To this point we have considered grades of membership from the perspectives of individual members of an audience. However, class and category are audience-level constructs. Therefore, we now need to consider an audience segment as a whole in defining GoMs in a class or category as a first step in defining a population.

These considerations lead us to define a producer's GoM in a class by averaging

[3]We compare this definition with others in Chapter 5.

the GoMs assigned to it by the members of the audience segment. If the class happens to be a category, then we average over the producer's GoM in the meaning of the label, with the average taken over the members of the audience segment. We denote this GoM in a class as $\bar{\mu}_{e(l)}(x, t)$ and in a category as $\bar{\mu}_{i(l)}(x, t)$.

Definition 4.8 (Grade of membership in a class/category). *A producer's grade of membership in a class is its average (over the members of the audience segment) grade of membership in the extension of the class label.*

$$\bar{\mu}_{e(l)}(x, t) \equiv \textstyle\sum_{y \in \mathbf{a}} \mu_{e(l)}(x, y, t)/|\mathbf{a}|, \qquad \textit{if}\, \text{CLASS}(l, t).$$

A producer's grade of membership in a category is its average (over the members of the audience segment) grade of membership in the intension of the class label.

$$\bar{\mu}_{i(l)}(x, t) \equiv \textstyle\sum_{y \in \mathbf{a}} \mu_{i(l)}(x, y, t)/|\mathbf{a}|, \qquad \textit{if}\, \text{CAT}(l, t).$$

Researchers studying the evolution of organizational populations will want to define a population in a way that allows for continuity over the possible transition from class to category. Defining a grade of membership in a population such that it equals the GoM in a consensual label if the label pertains to a class that is not a category and equals the GoM in the category otherwise fits this requirement.

Definition 4.9 (Grade of membership in a producer population). *A producer's grade of membership in the population indexed by the label l, in notation $\bar{\mu}_{p(l)}$, equals its average GoM in the class l if there is a consensus about the extension of this label but a weak consensus about its meaning, or its average GoM in the category l otherwise.*

$$\bar{\mu}_{p(l)}(x, t) \equiv \begin{cases} \bar{\mu}_{e(l)}(x, t) & \textit{if}\, \text{CLASS}(l, t) \wedge \neg\text{CAT}(l, t); \\ \bar{\mu}_{i(l)}(x, t) & \textit{if}\, \text{CAT}(l, t). \end{cases}$$

Again we define the dual function for a member of an audience segment. (Recall that we use μ to denote GoMs for producers/products and ν to denote GoMs for audience members.) An audience member's GoM in the consensus supporting a population can be defined in a parallel manner as follows.

Definition 4.10 (Grade of membership in an audience for a population). *An agent's grade of membership in the consensus underlying the population indexed by the label l is its GoM in the extensional consensus for l, $\nu_{e(l)}(y, t)$, if l labels a class but not a category; it equals its GoM in the intensional consensus for l, $\nu_{i(l)}(y, t)$, if the label defines a category.*

$$\nu_{p(l)}(y, t) \equiv \begin{cases} \nu_{e(l)}(y, t) & \textit{if}\, \text{CLASS}(l, t) \wedge \neg\text{CAT}(l, t); \\ \nu_{i(l)}(y, t) & \textit{if}\, \text{CAT}(l, t). \end{cases}$$

Definition 4.11 (Organizational population). *The organizational population associated with a label is the fuzzy set of producers/products in the domain defined by their average grades of membership in the class/category.*

$$\mathbf{pop}(l, t) \equiv \{\bar{\mu}_{p(l)}(x, t)\}, \qquad x \in \mathcal{O}.$$

Again it is useful to introduce constructs for the density and contrast of a population. The density of a fuzzy population can be defined as follows.

Definition 4.12 (Population density). *The density of an organizational population (designated by a label in an audience segment) equals its cardinality.*

$$\bar{n}_{p(l)}(t) \equiv \text{card}\{\bar{\mu}_{p(l)}(t)\} = \textstyle\sum_{x \in \mathbf{o}} \bar{\mu}_{p(l)}(x, t).$$

Note that the variance in GoMs is muted in the two foregoing definitions. A population with an even distribution of organizations with only "near binary" (zeros and ones) GoMs would look similar in these definitions to one where the organizations all had GoMs of 0.5. Because we want to distinguish such cases, we also define the contrast of a population, in parallel to the contrast of a cluster as defined in Chapter 2.

Definition 4.13 (Population contrast). *The contrast of an organizational population (designated by a label) as perceived by an audience segment equals the average contrast of its members as perceived by the audience segment:*

$$\bar{c}_{p(l)}(t) \equiv \frac{\text{card}\{\bar{\mu}_{p(l)}(t)\}}{|\text{supp}\{\bar{\mu}_{p(l)}(t)\}|},$$

if $\text{supp}\{\bar{\mu}_{p(l)}(t)\} \neq \emptyset$; *and it is undefined otherwise.*

The fuzzy construction appears to have great value for ecological analysis. Previous research sought to create classical sets by forcing cases into categories based on the preponderance of evidence. Consider the case of American national labor unions and the classic distinction between craft and industrial unionism. Hannan and Freeman (1987, 1988) viewed the historical literature as revealing that this distinction partitioned the population of unions: each union was treated as one or the other, but not both. Unfortunately, some cases were genuinely ambiguous. Consider the United Brotherhood of Carpenters and Joiners (UBC). This historically important union began as a classic craft union, as the name suggests. After twenty years of operation and some considerable political turmoil, it broadened its claimed jurisdiction to "all that's made of wood," and later added "or that was ever made of wood." In the course of expanding its jurisdiction, it began to organize entire industries such as furniture making. The union became a hybrid. It operated partly as a craft union (in the building trades) and partly as an industrial union (in manufacturing). Forcing this case into either category at the midpoint in its history strains credulity. But there was no alternative, other than to create a "not-otherwise-classified" category for such cases. We find this alternative to be unattractive, because we have no reason to think that any real audience recognized such a category.

Now we would argue differently. It seems that the UBC began as a prototypical craft union (grade of membership of one in this category and grade of membership of zero in industrial unionism). However, in its twentieth year, the UBC began to become less clearly a craft union and more clearly an industrial union. It persisted with what seems like a moderately high grade of membership in craft unionism and a moderate grade of membership in industrial unionism. In other words, it was a member of *both* populations in a nontrivial sense.[4] Forcing it one way or the other runs counter to the facts. This organization contributed to the social reality of each category, but less than more prototypical members. Notice that this approach generalizes; and, therefore, it also allows a coherent treatment of conglomerates.

4.5 DENSITY DEPENDENCE REVISITED

What does the new theoretical framework imply for the dynamics of legitimation and competition? The received theory of density-dependent legitimation contains two core parts. The first holds that higher density initially enhances a population's (constitutive) legitimation, thereby raising its founding rate and lowering its mortality rate. The second part claims that persistent increases in density eventually generate intense diffuse competition, which depresses founding rates and elevates mortality rates of a population.

We now reconsider the latter argument about diffuse competition. What gets preserved of the core insight that diffuse competition grows monotonically with population density?[5]

Density and Diffuse Competition

The original theory assumes classical set memberships. Each organization is either a (full) member of a population or not; and density records the number of full members. Because members are assumed implicitly not to vary in their membership, the theory defines diffuse competition globally for the population and assumes that each member of the population experiences the same level of diffuse competition. In the reformulated theory the picture differs, because members can vary in grades of membership in the population. Therefore, we define diffuse competition as potentially differing for individual organizations due to differences in their grades of membership.

Diffuse competition characterizes the situation in which an organization's rival for an event is chosen at random from the membership of the population (specifically, from the support of the population). Each other member is equally likely to appear as a competitive rival in a particular competitive event. A standard ecological axiom holds that the strength of competition between entities increases with the similarity of their resource utilization (MacArthur 1972). We apply this axiom here. The members of the audience control the relevant resources. Therefore, we consider all triplets consisting of a focal organization, another producer in **o**, and a member of the audience segment **a**.

We explicate the concept of diffuse competition in several steps. We first model an event occurring to a producer at a point in time as a random draw from the set of pairs of audience members and competitors at a time point. The underlying

[4]We take up the issue of multiple category membership more fully in the next chapter.

[5]The theory says more than this. It claims that the functional relation between density and diffuse competition has positive first and second derivatives. The simplified treatment here can be extended in obvious ways to deal with this functional dependence.

conception is that a producer might find itself attempting to appeal to an audience member while another producer is attempting this as well. In this case, there is an event of "rivalry."

The first step defines the competitive pressure exerted by the presence of x' on x in an interaction with the audience member y in the positively valued class/category l. Let $rival(l, x, x', y, t)$ be a function that maps a label, pairs of producers, audience members, and time points to $\{0, 1\}$.

Definition 4.14 (Competitive encounters in a market for a positively valued category).

$$rival(l, x, x', y, t) \equiv \begin{cases} 1 & \textit{if } x \textit{ encounters } x' \textit{ as a rival for the attention} \\ & \textit{of } y \textit{ at time } t \textit{ in the market defined by } l; \\ 0 & \textit{otherwise.} \end{cases}$$

Next we consider the impact of GoMs on competitive intensity. The definition of a positively valued category (D3.10) states that a producer's intrinsic appeal to an agent, $\widehat{ap}(l, x, y, t)$, increases with its GoM in the meaning of the relevant label (at any level of typicality on the agent side). In other words, when a producer with low GoM in the meaning of the label encounters another with high GoM, its intrinsic appeal is much lower than its competitor's. Furthermore, let $comp(l, x, x', y, t)$ be a function defined by comparison of a producer's intrinsic appeal to an agent relative to that of all other relevant producers.

Definition 4.15 (Competitive pressure). *The competitive pressure of x' on x in an interaction with y in positively-valued class/category l is the ratio of the intrinsic appeal of the competitor to that agent as compared to the intrinsic appeal of the focal producer.*

Let l label a positively valued class or category.

$$comp(l, x, x', y, t) = \begin{cases} \frac{\widehat{ap}(l, x', y, t)}{\widehat{ap}(l, x, y, t)} & \textit{if } (\widehat{ap}(l, x, y, t) > 0) \\ & \wedge (rival(l, x, x', y, t) = 1); \\ 0 & \textit{otherwise}; \end{cases}$$

and

$$Comp(l, x, t) \equiv \textstyle\sum_x \sum_y comp(l, x, x', y, t).$$

Next we specify what it means for competition to be diffuse. We use a random-mixing construction. That is, we say that competition in an arena specified by the label l is diffuse if any pair of competitor and audience member is equally likely to be present at an event for a particular organization.

Definition 4.16 (Diffuse competition). *Competition among producers or products is diffuse if and only if each triplet of focal producer, rival producer, and audience member is equally likely to occur in a competitive encounter.*

$$\begin{aligned} \text{DCOMP}(l) \leftrightarrow \forall l, t, x_1, x_2, x_3, y_1, y_2\, [(\bar{\mu}_{p(l)}(x_1, t) > 0) \wedge (\bar{\mu}_{p(l)}(x_2, t) > 0) \\ \wedge (\bar{\mu}_{p(l)}(x_3, t) > 0) \wedge (\nu_{p(l)}(y_1, t) > 0) \wedge (\nu_{p(l)}(y_2, t) > 0) \\ \rightarrow (\Pr(rival(l, x_1, x_2, y_1, t)) = \Pr(rival(l, x_1, x_3, y_2, t)))]. \end{aligned}$$

Notation. It will simplify the formulas that follow to have an expression for the set of ordered pairs of competitors and audience-segment members. Let

$$\mathbf{m}_x = \{\langle x', y\rangle \mid (x' \in \mathbf{o}) \wedge (x' \neq x) \wedge (y \in \mathbf{a})\}.$$

We now also encounter for the first time a logical implication of a nonmonotonic argument. As we will explain in Chapter 6, such an implication has a different standing than the postulates from which it follows. We mark this difference by using a second nonmonotonic quantifier, $\mathfrak{P}$, to tell that a formula states what *presumably* follows from an existing set of premises.

Theorem 4.2. *The expected level of diffuse competition faced by an organization presumably is proportional to the ratio of the total intrinsic appeal of its potential competitors to its own intrinsic appeal.*

Let l be a label for a positively valued class/category, and let diffuse competition be the case.

$$\mathfrak{P}\, l, t, x \left[\mathrm{E}(Comp(l, x, t)) = \frac{1}{|\mathbf{m}_x|} \left(\frac{\widehat{Ap}(l, t)}{\widehat{Ap}(l, x, t)} - 1 \right) \right],$$

where

$$\widehat{Ap}(l, x, t) = \textstyle\sum_{y \in \mathbf{a}} \widehat{ap}(l, x, y, t);\ \textit{and}\ \widehat{Ap}(l, t) = \sum_{x \in \mathbf{o}} \widehat{Ap}(l, x, t).$$

Proof. According to the definition of $comp(l, x, t)$,

$$\begin{aligned} \mathrm{E}(Comp(l, x, t)) &= \mathrm{E}(\textstyle\sum_{x' \neq x} \sum_y comp(l, x, x', y, t)) \\ &= \textstyle\sum_{x' \neq x} \sum_y \mathrm{E}(comp(l, x, x', y, t)). \end{aligned}$$

By the law of total probability, each term in this double summation can be expressed as

$$\begin{aligned} &\mathrm{E}(comp(l, x, x', y, l, t)) = \\ &\mathrm{E}(comp(l, x, x', y, l, t \mid rival(l, x, x', y, t) = 1))\, \Pr(rival(l, x, x', y, t) = 1) \\ &+ \mathrm{E}(comp(l, x, x', y, t \mid rival(l, x, x', y, t) = 0))\, \Pr(rival(l, x, x', y, t) = 0). \end{aligned}$$

According to D4.15, the second summand on the right equals zero in the foregoing. The definition of diffuse competition, D4.16, implies that

$$\Pr(rival(l, x, x', y, t) = 1) = \frac{1}{|\mathbf{m}_x|}.$$

Therefore,

$$\begin{aligned} \mathrm{E}(comp(l, x, x', y, t)) &= \mathrm{E}(comp(l, x, x', y, t \mid rival(l, x, x', y, t) = 1)) \\ &= \frac{1}{|\mathbf{m}_x|} \frac{\widehat{ap}(l, x', y, t)}{\widehat{ap}(l, x, y, t)}. \end{aligned}$$

The second equality above uses the definition of competitive pressure, D4.15. The consequent follows by simple summation:

$$\begin{aligned} \mathrm{E}(Comp(l, x, y, t)) &= \frac{1}{|\mathbf{m}_x|} \frac{\sum_{x' \neq x} \widehat{ap}(l, x', y, t)}{\widehat{ap}(l, x, y, t)} \\ &= \frac{1}{|\mathbf{m}_x|} \frac{(\sum_{x' \in \mathbf{o}} \widehat{ap}(l, x', y, t)) - \widehat{ap}(l, x, y, t)}{\widehat{ap}(l, x, y, t)}. \end{aligned}$$

and rearrangement of terms. □

A key postulate of the standard theory of density dependence now follows as a theorem, but it is restricted to populations based on positively-valued classes and categories.

Theorem 4.3. *The intensity of diffuse competition experienced by a member of an organizational population,* $\mathrm{E}(comp)$, *presumably rises monotonically with population density,* $\bar{n}_p$.

Let l *be the label of a positively valued class or category at times* t *and* t', *and let* $\bar{\mu}_{p(l)}(x,t) = \bar{\mu}_{p(l)}(x',t') > 0$.

$$\mathfrak{P}\,\mathbf{q}, \mathbf{q}' \, [\mathrm{DCOMP} \rightarrow (\bar{n}_p \uparrow \mathrm{E}(comp))(\mathbf{q}, \mathbf{q}')],$$

where $\mathbf{q} = \langle l, t, x\rangle$ *and* $\mathbf{q}' = \langle l, t', x'\rangle$.

Proof. From the definition of the density of a population, D.4.12, we have

$$\bar{n}_{p(l)}(t) = \textstyle\sum_{x \in \mathbf{o}} \bar{\mu}_{p(l)}(x,t).$$

The preamble specifies that $\bar{\mu}_{p(l)}(x,t) = \bar{\mu}_{p(l)}(x',t')$. Therefore, $\bar{n}_{p(l)}(t) \geq \bar{n}_{p(l)}(t')$ guarantees that

$$\textstyle\sum_{b' \in \mathbf{o} | b \neq x'} \bar{\mu}_{p(l)}(b,t') > \sum_{b \in \mathbf{o} | b \neq x} \bar{\mu}_{p(l)}(b,t).$$

The definition of a positively valued class/category, D.3.10, in conjunction with the definition of grade of membership in a population, tells that

$$(\bar{\mu}_{p(l)}(x,y,t) > \bar{\mu}_{p(l)}(x',y',t')) \rightarrow \mathrm{E}(\widehat{ap}(l,x,y,t)) > \mathrm{E}(\widehat{ap}(l,x',y',t')).$$

The consequent follows from linear aggregation over the set of competitors. □

Suppose the situation turned out to be classical, that there is no fuzziness in the sense that every producer has GoM in the population of either one or zero. Then the competitive pressure will be the same for all members of the population, and it equals the "classical" density, the number of members of the population. So the new theory includes the relevant portion of the original theory as a special case.

It is worth noting that fuzziness in memberships implies two ideas about diffuse competition. First, producers with low grade of membership in the population do not exert much competitive pressure. Nonetheless, a large number of population members with low GoM—individually weak competitors—do collectively exert a strong competitive effect. This observation brings to mind Gulliver's account of his waking to find himself bound by an army of Lilliputians.

> . . . I felt something alive moving on my left Leg . . . I perceived it to be a human Creature not six Inches high . . . In the meantime, I felt at least Forty more of the same Kind (as I conjectured) following the first. . . . I was in the utmost Astonishment, and roared so loud, that they all ran back in a Fright . . . However, they soon returned . . . Whereupon there was a great Shout in a very shrill Accent, and after it ceased, . . . I felt above a Hundred Arrows discharged on my left Hand, which pricked me like so many Needles; and besides they shot another Flight into the Air . . . When this Shower of Arrows was over, I fell

> a groaning with Grief and Pain, and then striving again to get loose, they discharged another Volly larger than the first . . . And as for the Inhabitants, I had Reason to believe I might be a Match for the greatest Armies they could bring against me, if they were all of the same size with him that I saw. But Fortune disposed otherwise of me. (Swift 1906 [1726], Chapter 1)

Our rendering of fuzzy population density takes the possibility of Lilliputian competition into account.

The second implication is that producers with low grade of membership experience stronger competitive pressure than those with higher GoM. In any random encounter, low-GoM producers face a big disadvantage from their low intrinsic appeal. This observation has obvious evolutionary implications. If the preferences of audience members remain stable over time, then the producers/products with low average GoMs in a positively valued category will tend to get eliminated from competitive domains with the result that fuzziness will decline. In other words, intense competition tends to make categories into more nearly classical sets.

Contrast and Legitimation

What causes an observer to assume constitutive legitimation? Why would someone assume that producers (products) in a class typically fit their schemata (conditional on passing a test code)? We think that the structures of both the producers and the audience matter for answering this question. If most of the producers (products) encountered fit the applicable schema, then the cases of poor fit will likely come to be viewed as exceptions. The degree to which the members of a class fit an agent's schema is given by the (membership) contrast of the class for the agent. So we postulate that the probability of using defaults increases with the class/category's contrast.

The tendency to shift to defaults will also be stronger when there is greater consensus in the audience about the meaning of a label. Why? When intensional consensus is high, an audience member will less likely be surprised at what she finds upon encountering a producer that another audience member claims is a typical member of the class. If, on the other hand, intensional consensus is low, then the picture will look confused; and the agents are unlikely to treat satisfaction of any given schema as a default for members of the class other than those for which they have direct evidence of fit. But relying on direct evidence means *not* relying on defaults.

Because we assume that the audience members communicate with each other, the segment is the relevant unit for considering the effect of intensional consensus on legitimation. Therefore, we postulate that legitimation increases with the strength of the intensional consensus in the segment, $ic(l, t)$.

Postulate 4.1. *The expected level of legitimation of a class,* $\mathrm{E}(L(l, t))$, *normally grows monotonically with the level of intensional consensus within the audience* *for the class,* $ic(l,t)$.

$$\mathfrak{N}\, l, l', t, t' \,[\textsc{class}(l,t) \wedge \textsc{class}(l',t') \wedge (ic(l,t) > ic(l',t')) \\ \rightarrow (\mathrm{E}(L(l,t)) > \mathrm{E}(L(l',t'))) \vee (\mathrm{E}(L(l,t)) = 1 = \mathrm{E}(L(l',t')))].$$

[The second term in the consequent is needed because L cannot exceed one, which would be implied by this postulate, absent the second term, if it happened that $\mathrm{E}(L(l',t')) = 1$.]

With this postulate, a revised version of the density-dependence claim becomes a theorem. The revised theorem holds that *contrast,* the average grade of membership of the organizations with nonzero GoM—not density per se—matters for legitimation.

Theorem 4.4. *The expected level of legitimation of a class,* $\mathrm{E}(L(l,t))$, *presumably grows monotonically with the average contrast of the population,* $\bar{c}_{p(l)}(t)$.

$$\mathfrak{P}\, l, l', t, t' \,[\textsc{class}(l,t) \wedge \textsc{class}(l',t') \wedge (\bar{c}_{p(l)}(t) > \bar{c}_{p(l')}(t')) \\ \rightarrow (\mathrm{E}(L(l,t)) > \mathrm{E}(L(l',t'))) \vee (\mathrm{E}(L(l,t)) = 1 = \mathrm{E}(L(l',t')))].$$

Proof. The minimal rule chain results from an application of the cut rule[6] to P3.3 (expected intensional consensus increases monotonically with average contrast) and P4.1. (The cut rule does not work directly here because we have the expected level of intensional consensus in the consequent of P3.3 and the level of intensional consensus in the antecedent in P4.1. Chapter 6 introduces a metarule that allows arguments of this form to be chained.) □

No legitimation-based parallel to the Lilliputian-competition story follows directly from this argument. Indeed, a proliferation of marginal members of a population will impede legitimation, not enhance it. More specifically, suppose that we take two identical populations with fairly high contrast and add a bunch of marginal members to one of them. Such an influx causes density to rise of the population with the influx to rise, but it lowers its contrast. According to the theorem, the result says that legitimation falls below that of the unchanged population (or the changed population ex ante.)

This distinction is possible only because we have allowed partial memberships. The original density-dependence theory, by not saying otherwise, followed the nearly universal convention in the social sciences of treating sets, such as populations, as crisp. In such a classical setup, there is no problem of marginal members, and contrast is not in the picture. The intuition that the legitimation of a population depends on its salience naturally focused on the growth of numbers (density in the crisp-set view). The current approach emphasizes the state of the audience, especially its degree of consensus about meanings. We have argued that the likelihood that an audience comes to agreement about meaning depends on contrast, not density.

---

[6] As Appendix C explains, the so-called cut rule of first-order logic is an inference schema for arguments of the following form. Suppose that we have the premises $A \rightarrow B$ and $B \rightarrow C$. By the definition of the language of this logic, it follows that $A \rightarrow C$, which "cuts out" B from the chain. Chapter 6 explains that this inference schema is also valid in the nonmonotonic logic that we use.

Empirical research will eventually determine whether this reformulation of the density-dependence story leads to new insights. The only study we know thataddresses this issue reports encouraging results. Specifically, in studying legitimation among Dutch auditors over the history of the population, Bogaert, Boone, and Carroll (2006) compare the effect on organizational mortality of classic (crisp) density with that of weighted density (fuzzy density) and contrast.[7] They write

> Our findings underscore that population-level legitimation does not automatically derive from density per se. Instead, it became clear that the road to legitimation is strongly hampered when density goes hand in hand with internal population fragmentation. Specifically, we found that both weighted density and contrast lower the hazard of exit from the industry for audit firms. Interestingly, comparative analyses reveal that weighted density seems to "work" better than contrast or the number of associations. As the former measure carries information on density discounted by fuzziness, this suggests that the simultaneous presence of both density *and* contrast (or homogeneity) were necessary to spur taken-for-grantedness. Taken together, legitimacy in the Dutch audit industry did emerge from positive spillovers from increasing density as postulated by classic density dependence theory, but only when fragmentation was low. (Bogaert, Boone, and Carroll 2006: 27)

The distinction between density and contrast also provides a useful way to reframe the issue of "sticky legitimation." The standard density-dependence theory treats the level of legitimation as proportional to density. Yet many observed population histories show a decline in density late in the population's history. It does not seem credible that legitimation falls with a late-stage decline in density, e.g., when the number of automobile producers in the United States dropped from hundreds to dozens. Hannan (1997b) developed a complicated model of population aging (with several interactions of population age and density) to allow legitimation to rise with density in the early history of a population but to become increasingly sticky as a population ages.

We now can address the implications of declining density in a new light. Suppose that the number of (nonzero GoM) members of a mature population declines. What implications does the new theory have for legitimation? The answer depends on what kind of members drop out of the population.

The normal case is one in which the marginal members are more likely to exit (perhaps by mortality), because the theory holds that the strength of competitive pressure is higher for more marginal members. Such a tendency will magnify contrast, while crisp density declines. Theorem 4.3 tells that the loss of marginal members will boost the expected level of legitimation. So perhaps we do not need the

[7] Their research measures the fuzziness of the population of auditors as the evenness of the distribution of memberships among auditors in professional associations holding different schemata for auditing. Then they weight crisp density by fuzziness to create weighted or fuzzy density. They measure contrast as the ratio of fuzzy density to crisp density.

complicated story of population-age interactions to deal with the legitimation of mature populations.

In an exceptional case, the exits might occur to the members with above-average GoM in the population. This, of course, will lower contrast and lower legitimation as a consequence. However, we have not been able to find a real empirical example.

4.6 DELEGITIMATION

We argued that audience-segment members tend to shift to reliance on defaults when they perceive a high level of contrast for a population. This occurs because high contrast implies that most producers conform closely to their schemata for the population label. What then ought to happen when the defaults do not get satisfied in some cases? Abundant sociological research reveals that people get confused, feel awkward, and sometimes get very irritated when this happens.

The situation described above reflects a special kind of lack of fit to a schema, which we call a code violation. We define code violations as situations in which an observer perceives that the minimal test code for a category is satisfied (so that satisfaction of the rest of the code is a default) but then perceives at some later time point that some of the untested code is actually violated. Without introducing a formalization of the idea, we suggest that the violation must be severe or persistent.

Definition 4.17 (Default code violation). *An agent detects a (severe or persistent) violation of a default for satisfaction of a code,* $\text{DCV}(l, \mathbf{s}^l, x, y, t)$*, if and only if*

1. *y has a type given by the label l and schema $\mathbf{s}_i^l$: $\langle l, \mathbf{s}_i^l \rangle \in \mathbf{ty}(y, t)$.*

2. *y employs defaults for satisfaction of the codes in this schema if the producer x passes the minimal test $\mathbf{w}_j$ over the interval of interest. Let t be a point in this interval. Then*

$$\text{MTST}(\sigma(l, y, t), \mathbf{w}_j).$$

3. *y perceives that the producer satisfies the test code over some time before t and does not detect any violation of the remainder of the code in the schema during this time and then perceives that one or more feature values in $\mathbf{v}_i$ fail to conform to the schema:*

$$\exists t_1 \, \forall t_2 \, [(t > t_2 \geq t_1) \rightarrow (\mu_{e(l)}(x, y, t_2) > 0) \wedge \boxed{\text{P}}_y \mathbf{w}_j(x, t_2) \\ \wedge \neg \boxed{\text{P}}_y \mathbf{v}_i(x, t_2) \wedge (\mathbf{v}_i \notin \mathbf{s}_i^l)] \wedge \boxed{\text{P}}_y \mathbf{v}_i(x, t) \wedge (\mathbf{v}_i \notin \mathbf{s}_i^l).$$

A simple way of expressing the consequences of violating a default is by postulating that agents become less trusting, more skeptical, in such situations. We represent this idea in terms of the minimal test code for a category, as defined in D4.2.

Postulate 4.2. *An agent who perceives a default code violation by a producer normally responds by expanding the minimal test code.*

$$\mathfrak{N}\, l, t, x, y\, [\textsc{dcv}(l, \mathbf{s}^l, x, y, t) \wedge \textsc{mtst}(\sigma(l, y, t), \mathbf{w}_j) \wedge \textsc{mtst}(\sigma(l, y, t+dt), \mathbf{w}_{j'}) \rightarrow (j' > j)],$$

where dt is an infinitesimal number.

Finally, we develop the straightforward consequence of this argument. It simplifies exposition to define a function that gives the total number of coded violations that an audience member perceives over an interval. (Because we restrict attention to "flat" codes: sets of codes for which each code (feature-value restriction) is equally important, such a count has a straightforward interpretation.)

Definition 4.18 (Number of default code violations). *The number of violations of defaults associated with a label perceived by an audience member over an interval.*

$$dcv(l, y, t, t') \equiv card(\langle x, y, t'' \mid \textsc{dcv}(l, \mathbf{s}^l, x, y, t'') \wedge (t' > t'' \geq t)\rangle).$$

This definition collects and then counts all of the pairs that correspond to a default code violation perceived by an agent of a producer at a time point within the relevant interval.

Now we want to evaluate the impact of the number of detected code violations. Again we use a closest-possible worlds formulation. We consider an audience member at two time points using the same schema for a label and the same minimal test code.[8]

Theorem 4.5. *The expected taken-for-grantedness of a category to an audience member,* $\mathrm{E}(G)$, *presumably declines monotonically with the number of perceived violations of the defaults,* dcv.

$$\mathfrak{P}\, l, s, t, t', y\, [(\sigma(l, y, t) = \sigma(l, y, t')) \wedge \textsc{mtst}(\sigma(l, y, t), \mathbf{w}_j) \wedge \textsc{mtst}(\sigma(l, y, t'), \mathbf{w}_{j'}) \wedge (j = j') \wedge (dcv(l, y, t, t+s) > dcv(l, y, t', t'+s)) \wedge (s > 0) \rightarrow (\mathrm{E}(G(l, y, t+s)) < \mathrm{E}(G(l, y, t'+s)))].$$

Proof. The antecedent states that the agent's schema for the label is the same at both initial time points. This ensures that the number of relevant feature values (i) is the same at both time points. It also stipulates that the size of the minimal test code is the same at both time points ($j = j'$). These restrictions imply that the level of taken-for-grantedness is the same at both time points: $G(l, y, t) = G(l, y, t')$. According to P4.2, an agent increases the size of the test code upon detecting any code violation, which reduces j by D4.3 and D4.4. The conclusion in the theorem follows directly from aggregation over incidents of perceived violation by the agent within the intervals. □

[8] It might seem that this is an implausible condition, because detected code violations between the two time points would cause the minimal test code to change. This is why we refer to the comparison as involving two close possible worlds: in both worlds the schemata and the minimal test codes are the same but the number of perceived violations differ between the worlds.

Violations of defaults about code satisfaction undermine legitimation in an audience broadly (this follows from aggregation of the result in the foregoing theorem). On the other hand, widespread conformity to defaults tends to strengthen the durability of a category as a cultural object.

DISCUSSION

After (perhaps unexpectedly) bringing individuals into the form-emergence picture, this chapter returns to more familiar issues for ecologists: population, competition, and legitimation. The fuzzy representation provides for partially applicable labels and category schemata; so an organization might be only a partial member of a population and be a member of more than one population.

This chapter presents a reformulation of the well-known ecological theory of density-dependent competition and legitimation in this framework (Carroll and Hannan 2000). In the fuzzy setup, the density of a population is now calculated as a sum of grades of membership of the organizations in the schemata that audience members attach to a label rather than a straight one-for-one count of organizations. However, the reformulation does little to change predictions about diffuse competition; the earlier proposition that the intensity of competition increases with density persists even though the measure has changed. Of course, the empirical status of the new measure still remains largely unexplored; it is natural to wonder whether it will perform as well in systematic tests.[9]

For legitimation, the picture changes considerably. We define legitimation as defaults about conformity of feature values to schemata and a form as a category with a high level of legitimation. We propose that legitimation grows with the level of consensus within the audience about the meaning of a label. With this addition, the theory implies that the legitimation of a population increases with its contrast (the average grade of membership in the class for those with positive grade of membership). So here there is not only a new measure of density but also a new prediction based on an entirely new concept. Again, substantial empirical research on the issues has yet to be undertaken.

An important consideration with respect to this reformulation is that just because density dependence in legitimation does not follow from the new premises, it does not mean that the argument should be dropped, especially because this earlier theory does not contradict the new one. Indeed, this seems to be a case in which further development of the theory should await further relevant empirical knowledge. Both contrast and density might well turn out to matter for the development of legitimation. In the meanwhile, we concentrate on the new insight about contrast dependence.

Finally, we mention some interesting speculations suggested to us by colleagues. These concern various possible combinations of contrast and density. Obviously, many social conditions might produce variations in the density and contrast of a

---

[9]Relatedly, we did not develop ideas about the expected competitive effects of density at founding because it seems that first the effects of diffuse competition should be more settled.

population. Indeed, we have pondered whether it is sensible to interpret the finding of Martin Ruef (2000) that new organizational forms in the health care industry arose in already populated but relatively uncrowded regions of the "identity space" of the environment in this light. It would be interesting to know more about density and contrast in the conditions he highlights. In addition, it has been suggested to us that the combination of low density and high contrast density might produce a prototype structure (e.g., the Oxbridge college form) while the combination of high density and high contrast might produce what psychologists call an exemplar structure (e.g., New York diamond merchants and garment manufacturers).[10] In any event, it is clear to us that contrast provides a new and potentially interesting insight into legitimation and associated processes.

[10]Huggy Rao (personal communication) suggested this interesting line of argument.

Chapter Five

Identity and Audience

with Greta Hsu

The preceding chapters laid the foundation for a perspective on the emergence of forms. We now complete the construction by sharpening the formal connections between form and identity.

We also consider the implications of the new conceptualization of populations for theory and research at the population level. We reconsider the view that forms must be based on identities. And, we argue that this theory of form emergence allows for a sounder treatment of "hybrid" organizations, those belonging to multiple classes, categories, or forms.

In cognitive science research on categorization, the objects to be assigned to categories do not have what we usually regard as identities. An apple is a typical fruit, and an olive is an untypical fruit; and there is no point in inquiring about the distinctive properties of an individual apple or olive. When we think about social entities, the picture changes dramatically. We used many examples to motivate our approach, beginning with a set of organizations that appear to us to differ greatly in terms of grade of membership in the category "university." Our examples of those with very high grade of membership—Bologna, Oxford, and Harvard—are far from interchangeable. This is also the case for our examples of those with positive but low grades of membership in the category—Bob Jones, National Defense, and Maharishi Management.

Each of these organizations comes with a particular social identity to some audience(s). These identities depend partly on the strength of category membership; but they also reflect idiosyncrasy. What we expect to encounter at Oxford is quite different from what we expect to encounter at Bologna or Harvard, for instance. When we speak of social identity, we need to consider the audience-based expectations of both kinds: those based on category membership and those based on an organization's specific history and traditions.

We propose a general formal definition of social identity that follows the usual lines of sociological thought on the subject. Then we show that this definition, along with the conceptual framework of the preceding chapters, bears implications for the relation of certain category memberships and identity. That is, we decided not to make it a matter of definition that form memberships constitute part of social identity; instead we derive this relationship (albeit in a more limited form than we had claimed earlier while working with sets with crisp memberships).

Since this chapter deals with advanced audience-based issues, we also consider certain social structural aspects of the audience: authorization and social-movement support. These important processes often get highlighted in sociological analyses of form emergence. Some of our examples in preceding chapters invoked these processes, e.g., health care forms (authorization) and microbrewers and credit unions (social movements). So, in the last part of the chapter, we present a formal analysis of the ways these two processes might affect form emergence. This theory represents an initial effort at tying these processes to form emergence.

5.1 IDENTITY AS DEFAULT

Characterizing identity in terms of a default modality can make clear the connection between form and identity. In particular, a default modality provides a useful specification of identity as depending on defaults about fit to schemata—but not necessarily schemata that define categories.

Some properties of organizations and other social entities ordinarily change over time; and many changes do not disrupt identity. So looking for social identity in constancy of feature values is fruitless.[1] Therefore, we think that it is essential to incorporate the view that social entities are *intensional objects* and to use a formal language suitable for analyzing intensionality.

As Appendix E points out, the standard approach in logic to dealing with intensional objects uses a possible-worlds formulation. Our modality for defaults follows this approach.

Simply put, an object is intensional if it cannot be fully characterized in terms of the properties it possesses (because it might have different properties in different possible worlds or, even worse, it might not even be present in all possible worlds). Unfortunately, neither the actual values of the properties nor the properties themselves can be the carriers of identity for intensional objects. So what exactly do organizations (and other social actors) preserve when they maintain their identities?

Erving Goffman's (1963: 2) classic work on stigma suggested an answer:

> Society establishes the means of categorizing persons and the complement of attributes felt to be ordinary and natural for members of each of these categories . . . The routines of social intercourse in established settings allow us to deal with anticipated others without special attention or thought. When a stranger comes into our presence, then, first appearances are likely to enable us to anticipate his category and attributes, his "social identity" . . . We lean on these anticipations that we have, transforming them into normative expectations, into righteously presented demands.

Goffman coined the term virtual social identity to refer to these kinds of expecta-

[1]It might be tempting to try to finesse this issue by conceptualizing identity in terms of some temporal functions defined on the properties. Unfortunately, such identification would require complete knowledge of the property values at every time point. Even full knowledge of an organization's past would not be enough. One also has to know its future to define identity in terms of the time path of properties.

tions; and he distinguished virtual from actual social identity, by which he meant the attributes that get revealed by deeper inspection. Our use of the term identity is coreferent with virtual social identity.

The conceptual framework developed above allows us to build on Goffman's imagery and to move beyond the deficiencies of many common conceptions of identity and action. As Claudia Strauss and Naomi Quinn (1997: 9) point out, "most academic discourses on identities tend to assume only two alternatives: Either identities are predetermined and fixed or identities are completely constructed and fluid." The theory developed here embarks on a different route, by tying identities to (taken-for-granted) defaults about schema satisfaction that are subject to change under certain conditions.[2]

Continuing an earlier line of argument, we suggest that an organization's identity (to an agent) can usefully be regarded as a set of defaults about fit to some schema (Pólos, Hannan, and Carroll 2002). In other words, an identity consists of defaults about the satisfaction of a schema that constrains what an organization would or could be and what is expected and not expected of it. The schema used can be collective, in the sense of applying to a class of producers/products, or it can be idiosyncratic.

Identity, as we define it, is a function that maps producers, audience members, and time points to a set of ordered pairs of (composite) labels/names and defaults about the feature values. This general characterization allows many of the identity-based processes that social scientists recognize to operate. For instance, in any fixed context, audience members' defaults about code satisfaction might focus on the distinctive characteristics of an entity or on those that an entity shares with others.

We define identity formally with the function $\mathbf{id}(x, y, t)$. We present the formal definition and follow it with some commentary on our motivations for some of the technical details.

Definition 5.1 (Organizational identity). *An organization's identity (in the eyes of a member of an audience segment at a time point) consists of the composite label (composed of all the labels that the agent applies to the organization) and a minimal superset of the schemata that the agent associates with the composite label such that the agent treats as a default that the organization's feature values satisfy the superset of the set of associated schemata.*

Let $\oplus l$ *be the composition of all the labels that* y *applies to* x *at time* t*, and let* $\mathbf{l}$ *be closed under* $\oplus$*. Assume furthermore that*

$$\mathbf{id} : \mathbf{o} \times \mathbf{a} \times \mathbf{t} \longrightarrow \mathbf{l} \times \mathbf{s},$$

such that

$$\begin{aligned}\langle \oplus l, \mathbf{s}_i \rangle &= \mathbf{id}(x, y, t) \\ &\leftrightarrow (\sigma(\oplus l, y, t) = \mathbf{s}^{\oplus l}) \wedge (\mathbf{s}^{\oplus l}(x, t) \subseteq \mathbf{s}_i) \wedge \boxed{\mathrm{D}}_y(\mathbf{v}_i(x, t) \rightarrow (\mathbf{v}_i \in \mathbf{s}_i)),\end{aligned}$$

[2]Strauss and Quinn (1997) develop a psychological theory of cultural cognition with similar properties.

provided that

$$\forall \mathbf{s}'_i[(\mathbf{s}^{\oplus l}(x,t) \subseteq \mathbf{s}'_i) \wedge \boxed{\text{D}}_y(\mathbf{v}_i(x,t) \rightarrow (\mathbf{v}_i \in \mathbf{s}'_i)) \rightarrow (\mathbf{s}_i \subseteq \mathbf{s}'_i)].$$

This delineation of organizational identity takes account of all of the different aspects from which an audience member looks at an organization. These aspects are reflected in the different labels that this agent attaches to the organization at a given point in time. Each schema that the agent associates with these labels provides a model of what it takes to see the focal organization "as an l." Although each label brings a certain schema into the picture, and the conjunction of these atomic schemata defines the schematization of the complex label, it is possible that compliance with some of the schemata is not taken for granted, that it is not a default assumption of the agent that the organization's feature values fit all of these schemata.

What matters for the sake of the identity is what an audience member actually takes for granted. This is why we did not use $\sigma(\oplus l, y, t) = \mathbf{s}^{\oplus l}$ as the schema for which compliance is taken for granted in the above definition. Fit with only some portion a more permissive schema might be taken for granted, and fit with the rest might not be taken for granted. Because the codes are modeled by the sets within which the feature values are required to fall, a more permissive schema is a superset of a more restrictive one.

Finally, we want the definition of identity to be as specific as possible. This means taking the sharpest, most-restrictive schema that applies, such that compliance is taken for granted. We achieve this with the help of the last clause in the definition.

At this point, we note formally some of the implications of this formalization of identity in terms of the concepts presented in the previous chapter.

Lemma 5.1. *If an audience-segment member treats as a default that an organization's feature values satisfy her schematization of the composite label, then presumably the organization's identity to that agent is a type with the maximal level of taken-for-grantedness.*

$$\mathfrak{P}\, l, \mathbf{s}^{\oplus l}, t, x, y\, [(\langle \oplus l, \mathbf{s}^{\oplus l} \rangle = \mathbf{id}(x,y,t)) \leftrightarrow (\langle \oplus l, \mathbf{s}^{\oplus l} \rangle \in \mathbf{ty}(y,t)) \wedge (g(l,x,y,t) = 1)].$$

Proof. According to D5.1, $l \in \mathbf{lab}(x,y,t)$ and $\sigma(\oplus l, y, t) = \mathbf{s}^{\oplus l}$ when $\langle l, \mathbf{s}^l \rangle \in \mathbf{id}(x,y,t)$. Therefore, $\langle l, \mathbf{s}^l \rangle$ is a type for y according to D3.2. Moreover, the definition of identity, D5.1, holds that the agent treats satisfaction of the schema as a default for the labeled producer. Given the definitions of taken-for-grantedness, D4.3, and minimal test, D4.2, the fact that the default applies to all elements in the schema means that the minimal test is empty ($j = 0$) and taken-for-grantedness, g, equals the maximum possible value of one. (Note that this proof also shows that if $\langle \oplus l, \mathbf{s}'_i \rangle \neq \mathbf{id}(x,y,t)$, then presumably $\exists\, l\, [(l \in \oplus l) \wedge (g(l,x,y,t) < 1)]$. This explains why we restricted attention here (and do the same in the theorem that follows) to situations in which $\mathbf{s}^{\oplus l}$ is part of the identity.) □

What is the relationship between identity and form membership? Both forms and identities, as we define them, involve defaults about code satisfaction. Indeed, we earlier claimed that a core sociological intuition holds that form membership becomes a constituent of identity and derived this relationship as a theorem in their (crisp-set) formulation (Pólos, Hannan, and Carroll 2002). We tuned the new definitions of form and identity so that they might also support such a theorem, revised to fit the fuzzy-set definition. It turns out that they do.

Theorem 5.1. *Fully legitimated forms are collective identities in the sense that form membership is presumably part of an organization's identity to all members of an audience segment.*

Let $\langle l, \mathbf{s}^{\oplus l}\rangle = \mathbf{id}(x, y, t)$.

$$\mathfrak{P}\, l, t, x, y\, [\text{FORM}(l, t) \wedge (l \in \mathbf{lab}(x, y, t)) \wedge (\sigma(l, y, t) = \mathbf{s}^l) \\ \rightarrow (l \in \oplus l) \wedge (\mathbf{s}^{\oplus l} \subseteq \mathbf{s}^l)].$$

Proof. If a label marks a form for an audience segment, the level of taken-for-grantedness for "normal" producers from the perspective of "normal" audience members is one, according to the definition of form (D4.7)—specifically the requirement that L be very close to unity. Because forms are categories and categories are characterized by a very high level of intensional semantic consensus (D3.7), these same "normal" pairs will be such that the agent possesses a schema for the relevant label (otherwise their existence in the segment will diminish the intensional consensus according to D.3.7). In other words, "normal" members of the audience segment hold a type for the label, and the rule chain behind L5.1 applies. □

An organizational identity consists of a pair given by (1) a composite label and (2) all that is taken for granted on the basis of this (composite) label alone. However, what is taken for granted does not always remain constant over time. Some of these codes might occasionally be violated. As we argued earlier (Pólos, Hannan, and Carroll 2002), a violation of identity codes brings about "sanctions." Now we are able to spell out what these sanctions might be. Because identity codes are defaults, a perceived violation of an identity code is a (perceived) violation of a default. In P4.2 we claimed that violations of defaults lead to the expansion of the minimal test code. The (composite) label is no longer sufficient, at least some of the feature values are tested before compliance with schematization of the composite label becomes taken for granted. So the violation of some identity codes leads to heightened scrutiny. Moreover, the identity of the organization in question becomes less sharp.

Theorem 5.2 (Sanctions for violating identity codes). *Agents who detect violations of identity codes presumably expand their minimal test code.*

Let $\oplus l$ *be the composition of all the labels that* y *applies to* x *at time* t, $\langle \oplus l, \mathbf{s}_i\rangle = \mathbf{id}(x, y, t)$, *and let* dt *be an infinitesimally short period of time.*

$$\mathfrak{P}\, l, t, x, y\, [\boxed{\text{P}}_y(\mathbf{v}_i(x, t) \wedge (\mathbf{v}_i \not\subseteq \mathbf{s}_i)) \\ \rightarrow \text{MTST}(\sigma(\oplus l_i, y, t + dt), \mathbf{w}_j) \rightarrow (j > 0)].$$

Proof. Given that $\oplus l$ is the composition of all the labels that y applies to x at time t, and $\langle \oplus l, \mathbf{s}_i \rangle = \mathbf{id}(x, y, t)$, it follows that $\boxed{\text{D}}_y(\mathbf{v}_i(x,t) \rightarrow (\mathbf{v}_i \in \mathbf{s}_i))$. Now suppose that $\boxed{\text{P}}_y(\mathbf{v}_i(x,t) \wedge (\mathbf{v}_i \notin \mathbf{s}_i))$. It is easy to see that $\text{DCV}(\oplus l, \mathbf{s}^{\oplus l}, x, y, t)$. According to P4.2

$$\mathfrak{N}\, l, t, x, y\, [\text{DCV}(l, \mathbf{s}^l_i, x, y, t) \wedge \text{MTST}(\sigma(l, y, t), \mathbf{w}_j, t) \wedge \text{MTST}(\sigma(l, y, t + dt), \mathbf{w}_{j'}) \rightarrow (j' > j)].$$

Given that $\mathbf{s}^l_i$ is part of the identity before the perceived violation,

$$\text{MTST}(\sigma(l, y, t), \mathbf{w}_j) \rightarrow (j = 0).$$

Therefore, $j' > 0$. □

It is interesting to realize that the formal argument does not give any clues about what elements of a schema lose taken-for-granted status, which feature values need to be scrutinized before compliance with the composite code can be assumed. Although one might be tempted to stipulate that the values that led to the violation of the identity codes are the ones that will become scrutinized, we find the underspecificity of the argument more interesting. The uncertainty makes the tighter scrutiny a much more serious sanction. If it is difficult—or impossible—to tell what feature values the agents will now inspect, then organizations with prior code violations face pressure to comply with all of the default codes to secure their identities. Meanwhile, their competitors would still enjoy the benefit of doubt, provided they were not caught in violating identity codes yet.

To spell out what happens to an organizational identity as a result of perceived violation of an identity code, we note the following corollary.

Corollary 5.1. *Violations of code for which satisfaction was treated as a default presumably weaken identities.*

Let $\langle \oplus l, \mathbf{s}_i \rangle = \mathbf{id}(x, y, t)$ *and* $(\sigma(\oplus l, y, t) = \mathbf{s}^{\oplus l})$, *and suppose that* y *perceives that* x*'s feature values do not fit the schema:*

$$\boxed{\text{P}}_y(\mathbf{v}_i(x,t) \wedge (\mathbf{v}_i \notin \mathbf{s}_i)).$$

If $\langle \oplus l, \mathbf{s};_i \rangle = \mathbf{id}(x, y, t + dt)$, *then presumably* $\mathbf{s}_i \subset \mathbf{s}'_i$.

Proof. According to the rule chain behind T5.2,

$$\mathfrak{P}\, l, t, x, y\, [\text{MTST}(\sigma(\oplus l, y, t), \mathbf{w}_j) \rightarrow j = 0],$$

and

$$\mathfrak{P}\, l, t, x, y\, [\text{MTST}(\sigma(\oplus l, y, t + dt), \mathbf{w}_j) \rightarrow j > 0].$$

This means that, if $\langle \oplus l, \mathbf{s'}_i \rangle = \mathbf{id}(x, y, t + dt)$, then $\mathfrak{P}\, l, t, x, y\, [\mathbf{s}_i \subset \mathbf{s}'_i]$. □

In other words, the taken-for-granted codes are less constraining (less is taken for granted) after a perceived violation of identity codes.

Note that the perceived violation of an identity code changes only what is taken for granted of the organization. This allows for the possibility that the codes that the agent is expecting the organization to satisfy remain intact: $(\sigma(\oplus l, y, t) = \mathbf{s}^{\oplus l}) \rightarrow$

$(\sigma(\oplus l, y, t + dt) = \mathbf{s}^{\oplus l})$. In more intuitive terms, this means that perceived violations of an identity code diminish the trust that agents give to producers. We regard the loss of taken-for-grantedness and the shrinking of identity as a form of punishment of violations about default code satisfaction.

The foregoing arguments also point to a second form of punishment of violations. Recall that we defined positively valued categories as those for which a producer's expected intrinsic appeal to audience members increases with the grades of membership that the audience members assign to the producer (D3.10). When an agent detects a violation of a default for code satisfaction, the agent fills in the observed (nonconforming) feature value for the default. Because the default was satisfaction of the schema on the feature(s) for which the violation is now perceived, the producer's grade of membership in the category drops for that audience member. The consequence is a reduction in intrinsic appeal. This is a powerful form of punishment.

As we develop in Part III, a producer's fitness depends upon its intrinsic appeal relative to competitors. Other things equal, a default code violation lowers fitness (and increases mortality). We record the core of this argument in the following lemma and theorem.

Lemma 5.2. *If an agent perceives that an organization violates a default for satisfaction of the schema of a positively valued category, then her or she lowers the organization's grade of membership in the category.*

Let $\text{PCAT}(l, t) \wedge \text{PCAT}(l, t')$.

$$\mathfrak{P}\, l, t, t', x, x', y\, [(\mu_{i(l)}(x, y, t) = \mu_{i(l)}(x', y, t')) \wedge (\mu_{i(l)}(x, y, t) > 0)$$
$$\wedge\, \text{DCV}(l, \mathbf{s}^l, x, y, t) \wedge \neg\text{DCV}(l, \mathbf{s}^l, x', y, t')$$
$$\rightarrow (\mu_{i(l)}(x, y, t + dt) < \mu_{i(l)}(x', y, t' + dt))],$$

where dt is an infinitesimal positive number.
[Read: suppose that the producers x and x' have the same nonzero grade of membership in the positively valued category l. If the agent y perceives that x violates a default for satisfaction of the schema for the category at a time point but does not perceive any such violation by x', then after a short while the grade of membership of x falls below that of x'.]

Proof. In Chapter 3, we defined (informally) $\mu_{\sigma(l)}(x, y, t)$ as the degree to which y's perception of x's feature values fit y's schema σ. Meaning postulate 3.1 equates $\mu_{\sigma(l)}(x, y, t)$ and $\mu_{i(l)}(x, y, t)$. Perception of a default code violation decreases $\mu_{\sigma(l)}(x, y, t)$, because at least one feature value that was "counted" as fitting the schema by default is now perceived as not fitting. □

Theorem 5.3. *A perception by an agent of a violation of a default for satisfaction of a schema for a positively valued category results in a loss of expected intrinsic appeal.*

Let $\text{PCAT}(l, t) \wedge \text{PCAT}(l, t')$.

$$\mathfrak{P}\, l, t, t', x, x', y\, [(\mu_{i(l)}(x, y, t) = \mu_{i(l)}(x', y, t')) \wedge (\mu_{i(l)}(x, y, t) > 0) \\ \wedge\, \text{DCV}(l, \mathbf{s}^l, x, y, t) \wedge \neg\text{DCV}(l, \mathbf{s}^l, x', y, t') \\ \rightarrow (\text{E}(\widehat{ap}(l, x, y, t + dt)) < \text{E}(\widehat{ap}(l, x', y, t' + dt)))],$$

where dt is an infinitesimal positive number.

Proof. A chain rule applied to the definition of a positively valued category and the argument behind L5.2 provides the minimal chain that supports the theorem. □

These two forms of punishment for violating defaults provide a strong inertial force, as we discuss in Chapter 11.

5.2 MULTIPLE CATEGORY MEMBERSHIPS

To this point we have focused on a class, category, or form in isolation. An important issue arises when a producer possesses more than one high-degree category membership. Consider the case of Sony Corp., which presumably holds a grade of membership close to one in the category of consumer-electronics producer and also maintains a very high grade of membership in film production (Sony Entertainment Group, which includes Columbia Tristar Pictures). If Sony has a high GoM in each case but a higher GoM as an electronics producer than as a film production company, what, then, is its identity? A natural reaction claims that Sony's identity includes both category memberships. However, recent psychological research reveals a strong tendency for persons to ignore all but the strongest membership when pressed to make inferences (inductions) about feature values (Murphy 2002: 257–64; Verde, Murphy, and Ross 2005).

Suppose an audience member who knows the facts about Sony's grades of membership is asked to come up with an expectation about its feature values. One can reason about Sony in (at least) two ways. Perhaps it would make sense to use the information about the relative magnitudes of the two grades of membership and come up with a probabilistic assessment of what should be expected.[3] Alternatively, it might make sense to simplify and use only the stronger membership in making the induction. Experimental subjects given such tasks generally take the second route—they go for the stronger membership and ignore the other in making such inferences.

Gregory Murphy and Brian Ross (2005) argue that typicality for individual entities shows two sides. One concerns the *certainty of membership* in a category (a grade of membership in our formalization); and the other concerns *representativeness,* the degree to which the entity shares feature values with other category members (average similarity). Murphy and Ross suggest that certainty (the probability of category membership) depends on the degree to which the object shares

[3]This was—and perhaps still is—regarded as the standard model in cognitive psychology (Anderson 1991).

feature values with members of *other* categories. For instance, the fact that a penguin shares the feature "swims" with fish and with some mammalian species creates uncertainty about its membership in the category "bird." On the other hand, representativeness seems to depend on the degree to which an entity shares features with members of the focal category. A penguin is an unrepresentative bird in that it does not fly.

The experimental evidence suggests that people use both kinds of information in assigning objects to categories. Once the task becomes *induction*—making predictions about unobserved features—people generally consider only representativeness. This is because representativeness affects confidence in inductions. Sony is a very representative electronics manufacturer and a less representative film production company. People would make predictions about unobserved features of Sony based on its membership in the category "electronics manufacturer" of which it is highly representative.

Because we have defined identity in terms of defaults (expectations), such a pattern of induction has implications for how audience-segment members will construct the identities of producers whose feature values fit multiple categories. They will apparently simplify identities in making inductions. There seems to be a disconnection between the tendency to perceive shades of difference in typicality when thinking about a category and the tendency to ignore (much) fuzziness when faced with the problem of making sense of an individual entity. We suspect that this divergence has implications for defining populations, as we discuss below. It would be very valuable to learn whether such a pattern of simplifying memberships in considering identities holds in normal audiences for the producer organizations and their products.

Although people might simplify memberships in making inferences about individual producers/products, multiple memberships do have implications for the legitimation of categories. The possible interference from memberships in multiple categories stems from a principle of allocation (Hsu 2006), as we argue in treating the niche in Chapters 8–10. Producers whose feature values partly fit several categories generally exhibit some values that are not at all characteristic of any focal category. In other words, such multicategory members lack representativeness in any one of their relevant categories (unless the categories are nested). If lack of representativeness lowers confidence about inductions of the values of unobserved features, then less representative objects will tend to lack identity.

Membership in multiple (nonnested) categories likely confuses the audience and makes a producer appear to fit poorly to any of the schemata that an agent applies to the categories. The result is a principle of allocation in fit to schemata that parallels the principle used in niche theory (as we explain in Chapter 8). In support of this view, Hsu (2006) finds that audiences express greater dissensus about the category memberships of films that target multiple categories (genres) as compared to those that target a single genre. Apparently, the perceived fit of a producer with any of the schemata that the agents apply to categories weakens as the producer stretches its focus to incorporate features from a greater diversity of categories. Audience members cannot, as a result, come to agreement about categorization.

This argument meshes with the finding by Zuckerman and collaborators (2003) that Hollywood film actors who are strongly identified with a particular category of work find it difficult to obtain work in other categories. The consequence of this argument is that generalists—those with membership spread over categories—are likely to be judged as having inferior offerings in markets in which specialists can be found in all categories (Hsu, Hannan, and Koçak 2007).

5.3 CODE CLASH

So far, we have defined relationships that are expected to hold across all types of category combinations. Generally speaking, whether a producer will be accepted in a category depends on how clearly it is associated with other categories. Within this general relationship, however, the particular nature of the codes matters. In this section, we consider the impact of clashes between codes.

The sociological literature documents a number of categories that audiences perceive as incompatible with one another. A classic example of clashing categories involves microbrewers and mass brewers in the United States beer industry. Microbrewers produce beer through traditional hand-crafted methods on a small scale, as opposed to the modern industrialized methods adopted by mass producers. Carroll and Swaminathan (2000) found that these two identities are incompatible in the perceptions of beer consumers; consumers of microbrews often reject beverages brewed by mass producers, preferring the tradition and authenticity associated with microbrews. The presence of incompatible categories has also been found in the wine industry (Swaminathan 2001) and the Hollywood film industry (Zuckerman and Kim 2003).

For many category pairings, perceptions of incompatibility are not symmetric. That is, while audiences for one class might perceive membership in the other as incompatible, the converse is not true. This is likely to be the case, for example, for microbrewers and mass brewers. While membership in "mass brewer" is viewed as incompatible with being an "authentic" microbrewer by microbrew fans, consumers of mass beers are unlikely to perceive microbrewers as unsuitable for membership in mass brewing.

Accordingly, we define code incompatibility from the point of view of a focal class. Code incompatibility between classes occurs when agents perceive that the codes for one class clash with the codes for another class in the sense that the perception of a high degree of satisfaction of one code produces a perception of a low degree of satisfaction of the focal code. We define code clash indirectly as follows.

Meaning postulate 5.1. *Normally, the higher a producer's grade of membership in a type whose schema clashes with that of a focal category, the lower the producer's grade of membership in the focal type.*

$$\mathfrak{N}\,\mathbf{q}, \mathbf{q}'\,[\,\text{CLASH}(\sigma(l, y, t), \sigma(l', y, t)) \rightarrow (\mu_{i(l')} \downarrow \mu_{i(l)})(\mathbf{q}, \mathbf{q}')\,],$$

where $\mathbf{q} = \langle l, t, x, y \rangle$ *and* $\mathbf{q}' = \langle l', t, x, y \rangle$.

Now we specialize the argument to the case of positively valued categories: code clash lowers the intrinsic appeal of a producer's offerings in such categories. The extent to which a producer is known and associated with an incompatible category shapes the extent to which its appeal in the focal category is affected. Agents are more likely to identify producers with high standing in an incompatible category as being associated with the other category rather than with the focal category. Their perceived fit to a focal category, and thus intrinsic appeal in that category, will be lower as a result.

Theorem 5.4. *Membership in a clashing type presumably lowers the intrinsic appeal of a producer's offering in a positively valued category.*

Let l mark a positively valued category, $\text{PCAT}(l, t)$*, and let l' mark a class:* $\text{CLASS}(l', t)$.

$$\mathfrak{P}\,\mathbf{q}, \mathbf{q}'\,[\text{CLASH}(\sigma(l), \sigma(l')) \rightarrow (\mu_{i(l')} \downarrow \text{E}(\widehat{ap}(l)))(\mathbf{q}, \mathbf{q}')\,],$$

where $\mathbf{q}$ *and* $\mathbf{q}'$ *are as above.*

Proof. The minimal rule chain uses M5.1 and the definition of a positively valued class, D3.10. □

5.4 IDENTITIES AND POPULATIONS

In Chapter 4, we defined the organizational population associated with a label as the fuzzy set of producers/products in the domain for which a producer's grade of membership in the set is given by its average grade of membership assigned by the members of the audience. Identity does not figure in this definition.

Readers of some of our previous work (Pólos, Hannan, and Carroll 2002; McKendrick and Carroll 2001; Hannan 2005) might recall that we argued earlier that population definitions have the most value for theory and research when they pertain to the most-specific identity applicable to the organizations (or other entities). We contended that a useful specification of a population should mark those organizations that are expected to interact strongly because they both fall within the same system boundary and share a common, highly specific identity. This reasoning led us to propose that populations be defined in terms of minimal identities.[4]

Why the shift? Why do we now want to decouple the definition of an organizational population from identity? Recall the results on the problem of induction for entities with multiple category memberships. These results suggest that Sony's identity continued to include "consumer electronics manufacturer," even after it became a hybrid (because of its higher grade of membership in film production). If we still insisted that forms are specified by minimal identities, then we would place Sony *only* in the "electronics-producer" population. However, had we begun with the categories, we would come to a different conclusion. Given that Sony has at least a moderate grade of membership in its "secondary" category, it would surely

[4]In addition, we also stipulated that only identities to outsiders, to audiences external to the producers, ought to be considered. We made clear in Chapter 2 that we no longer regard the distinction between insiders and outsiders as relevant to the theory.

count as a member of that category. Indeed, no listing of the major producers in the movie industry would fail to include Sony Entertainment Division's Columbia Pictures. Because the concept of population reflects the membership of a category, this seems to be the correct assignment. Populations remain fuzzy even if identities become crisp in induction.

Suppose that a producer displays nearly equal grades of membership in two or more categories. Examples might include LVMH Moët Hennessy Louis Vuitton (a major figure in cosmetics, designer fashion, watches, and wines and spirits) and GE (a major participant in such diverse industries as power plants, medical devices, aircraft engines, television/movies, and financial services). What, then, will an audience conclude about identity in such cases?

The existing psychological research does not (to our knowledge) provide an answer to this question. One possibility is that the organization's identity gets defined at a higher level in a taxonomy, if the relevant audience codifies such a higher level category. In the case of LVMH, the higher level category used by at least some analysts is "luxury goods"; in the case of GE Corp., the higher level is likely "conglomerate." If the audience has indeed constructed the forms "luxury good provider" and "conglomerate," then the identities of these firms include these categorical components. Neither, however, is very constraining and, therefore, neither is very informative. The only way that a producer can fail to fit the putative conglomerate form is by gaining a much higher grade of membership in one of its categories than in all of the others.

More interesting possibilities arise if no more inclusive category has been codified and legitimated. This would be the case, in the examples under discussion, if the audience had not codified "luxury good provider" or "conglomerate." What then? Perhaps such a producer's identity contains only an *organization-specific* schema, and no categorical identity applies. Then visibility to an audience seems to matter. A producer as well-known as GE or LVMH generally has a clear individual identity. On the other hand, an unknown organization that lacks membership in some sharper category is a nonentity (with all of the liabilities entailed in that status—see Zuckerman et al. 2003).

Other interesting possibilities arise when categories come in opposing pairs, as in the case of "microbrewer" and "(industrial) brewer" (Carroll and Swaminathan 2000). When the schemata for categories clash, attempts at spanning them will confuse identities and likely lead to devaluation.

5.5 STRUCTURE OF THE AUDIENCE

At various points in this part of the book, we have referred to the social structure of the audience. For instance, we noted that enthusiasts within the audience likely do the hard work of clustering, labeling, and schematizing. We have also hinted at the roles of authorities and social movements. We now analyze the structure of the audience formally by considering two facets that the sociological literature views as likely to contribute to consensus: authorization and social-movement support.

Authority

Sometimes an agent with authority promulgates a type and an associated code. Authorities might be officials of the state (especially in the modern era), professional bodies, industry associations, or recognized collections of experts. We follow Weber in conceptualizing authority: an agent possesses authority over some realm if others recognize and abide by her claims, including especially her pronouncement of codes. Thus authorization of a category clearly involves a kind of top-down abstraction, especially in comparison to the ground-up process inherent in social-movement support, which we discuss below.

Officials engage in a variety of actions that might generate organizational categories. In the most comprehensive case, officials specify a code for a new type and create incentives that benefit those actors whose features fit the authorized schema. Of course, the specified code can usually only be partial at best. Nonetheless, the official code can serve as a seed around which a cluster forms, especially in cases in which positive and negative sanctions are brought to bear. The presence of a partial code makes the cluster visible and tangible to the audience of a domain.[5]

Attempts at official authorization commonly involve a less comprehensive set of actions. These might include enabling legislation, such as laws that allowed hedge funds to operate. They would also include laws that removed prohibitions on the sale of alcoholic beverages, and judicial rulings that legalized abortion. Other relevant legislation rewards a particular form with tax advantages, thereby shifting the incentives for organizing one way or another. Actions involving officials outside the state apparatus almost always are limited in their coercive power. However, this does not mean that they cannot generate and promulgate codes for categories. Consider professional bodies, for instance, whose self-defined codes usually operate with great force. Or consider the moral sanctioning power of authoritative industry associations such as the International Organization for Standardization (ISO), which accredits businesses according to member-developed codes.

Instances of explicit authorization clustering occurred in the United States in the emergence of "credit union" (Barron 1998), "health maintenance organization" (Strang 1995), and "health systems agency" (Ruef 2000). In the health care sector, Ruef (2000) identified 48 specific organizational forms that emerged in the United States between 1965 and 1994; of these, he attributed 19 directly to regulatory events of authorities, distributed roughly evenly among federal legislative, judicial, and administrative actions and state-level legislation.

A contemporary example of authorization in the domain of education carries the label "charter school." Charter schools receive public financing but are often run outside the conventional public school organizations. Their proponents argue that they would serve as laboratories for reform and would create competition and choice within publicly financed education. Minnesota passed the first state law authorizing such schools in 1991; 40 states had such laws by 2006. Authorization rules and regulations vary by state. More than 3600 charter schools now operate in the United States

[5]This property also makes it easier for researchers to document the origins of a cluster. Ruef (2000) cleverly exploited this property in analyzing the ecology of form emergence.

Another contemporary example, whose outcome in terms of possible form emergence is far less clear, involves those firms and other organizations operating in the tourism domain with ecologically sound practices—commonly referred to as "ecotourism" operators. An emerging authority agency is known as The International Ecotourism Society (TIES). Among other things, this organization attempts to set the principles of ecotourism. The organization's Web page (http://www.-ecotourism.org on December 22, 2005) states that

> TIES defines ecotourism as *responsible travel to natural areas that conserves the environment and improves the well-being of local people.* This means that those who implement and participate in ecotourism activities should follow the following principles: Minimize impact, Build environmental and cultural awareness and respect . . . Provide financial benefits and empowerment for local people . . . Support international human rights and labor agreements.

Of course, it remains to be seen whether TIES can consolidate audiences and organizations in this domain, as well as whether a schematic code for organizations can be articulated and consensually agreed upon.

We define authorization of a class as an endorsement by an agent with Weberian authority. We recognize that many officials of governments and private bodies lack such authority (e.g., TIES). Just because an official with formal authority proposes a code does not mean that the matter is settled, because officials might lack authority as we defined it. Many attempts at official construction of categories produce little in the way of durable categories. Even when official endorsement works, the partiality of the official code leaves great scope for interpretation. In studying organizational responses to an Executive Order authorizing affirmative action and other labor issues, Lauren Edelman (1992; see also Edelman, Uggen, and Erlanger 1999) shows clearly that much of the work of code construction *follows* initial official action and involves considerable action by producers and members of the audience. This means that the initial code merely initiates the process of categorization. Nonetheless, it provides a clear focal point.

Let the predicate $\text{AUTH}(l, t)$ tell that an (unspecified) agent authorizes the class labeled as l for the audience segment at time t and $\text{VET}(l, x, t)$ tell that the agent (an authority) has vetted (validated) x as an instance of l at t.

Definition 5.2 (Authorization). *The label is authorized at time point if and only if*

1. *all (other) members of the audience segment apply the label to a producer (or product) x, $l \in \mathbf{lab}(x, y, t)$, if and only if it has been vetted by the (unspecified) authority:*

$$\forall\, l, t, x, y\, [(l \in \mathbf{lab}(x, y, t)) \leftrightarrow \text{VET}(l, x, t)];$$

2. *if any member of the mass audience attaches a schema to the label, then his minimal test code for applying defaults for schema satisfaction by producer is the empty set, provided that the authority has vetted the producer:*

$$\forall\, l, t, x, y\, [\text{VET}(l, x, t) \wedge \exists\, \mathbf{s}^l\, [\sigma(l, y, t) = \mathbf{s}^l] \rightarrow \text{MTST}(\sigma(l, y, t), \emptyset)].$$

It follows immediately that authorization (support by an authority) implies full legitimation.

Theorem 5.5. *If a label is authorized, then its level of legitimation in the audience segment presumably equals unity.*

$$\mathfrak{P}\, l, t, y\, [\text{AUTH}(l, t) \rightarrow (L(l, y, t) = 1)].$$

Proof. According to D5.4, the members of the mass audience apply the label only when the authority applies it and their test code has a single feature (application of the label by the authority). The definition of legitimation, D4.6, tells that $L = 1$ in this case. Given that all members of the mass audience have the same test code, $L = 1$ for all members of the mass audience: $L(l, t) = 1$, which is at least a great as $\mathfrak{l}$. □

Our characterization of identity allows for the possibility that the legitimation of a label can be high even in the absence of a high level of intensional consensus, because it states that the agents apply their schemata but does not require that the schemata agree. Nonetheless, the definition does imply that an authorized label is a class.

Theorem 5.6. *An authorized label presumably defines a class.*

$$\mathfrak{P}\, l, t\, [\text{AUTH}(l, t) \rightarrow \text{CLASS}(l, t)].$$

Proof. According to D2.10, a class is a label for which the audience segment has achieved a high level of extensional consensus. D5.2 implies that the level of extensional consensus for an authorized label equals unity, because the members of the audience segment apply the label if and only if the authority applies it. This is the maximal possible level, and it therefore meets the threshold. □

Obviously, if the audience segment has also reached a high level of intensional consensus, such that the label defines a category, then an authorized label is also a form.

Theorem 5.7. *A category authorized by an authority presumably is a form.*

$$\mathfrak{P}\, l, t\, [\text{AUTH}(l, t) \wedge \text{CAT}(l, t) \rightarrow \text{FORM}(l, t)].$$

Proof. The minimal rule chain results from the instantiation that l is a category and a cut rule applied to D4.7, which states that a form is a category with a very high level of legitimation, and (the rule chain behind) T5.6. □

Social Movements

Official recognition of a class or category often results from collective action by a social movement that promotes a code. The case of the American "credit union" shows this very clearly (Barron 1998). Something like the current credit-union code (a savings bank owned and operated by its members, usually restricted to a type of common "affiliation," e.g., common employer, coresidence in a community, membership in a church or social club) existed in Germany and Quebec in the nineteenth century. American social reformers, led by Boston merchant Edward Filene, created a movement to promulgate the type in the United States and to gain authorization from state governments. The activists succeeded in this effort by promoting the idea of consumer loans (unavailable at the time) as an antidote to the scourge of loan sharking. Likewise, despite its movement like origins, the brewpub organizational form needed state action, because state laws at the time required ownership separation of production from the sale of alcoholic beverages.

In fact, we find it difficult to identify cases of official recognition of a class that were not preceded at least to some extent by movement like behavior, although the degree to which a potential form's features have cohered into categories prior to official endorsement varies greatly.

In a common occurrence, the movement consists mainly of producers. For example, the collective actions of enthusiasts (especially home brewers) and early entrants into the category shaped the emergence of the modern microbrewer form. Their activities led to the formation of the Institute of Brewing Studies, which claims to speak authoritatively on the boundaries of the claimed organizational form. The movement produced the type labels "microbrewer" and "brewpub" along with agreement about some aspects of the code that specifies the actions consistent with these labels. In an interesting parallel (coded in its name), a club called the Homebrew Computer Club began at Stanford University and held its first meeting in a garage in Menlo Park, California in 1975. This movement organization created the social and technical seed for the personal computer revolution.[6]

Social movements to create organizational categories take on a character broadly similar to those about other social causes. Typically, they get put in motion by a set of activists who possess evangelical beliefs about the value of the activity and its benefits to society. Their motivation appears to be more intrinsic than pecuniary; clearly proprietary efforts do not seem to resonate well with early potential supporters.

Effective social-movement activists prove especially adept at framing issues related to the construction and defense of categories. These frames often point to specific shortcomings of existing forms and hold out the promise of a better set of future arrangements with the yet unrealized new form. For instance, the social union promoting credit unions played to fears of loan sharks (Barron 1998); and health maintenance organizations offered the lure of preventive care in a world driven by reactive medicine. At the extreme, these frames can be openly oppositional in nature (i.e., invoking codes that clash with others), condemning the current practices as hazardous or morally wrong. Clearly, one important component of framing for action around an organizational category—category construction—involves public discourse that proposes and eventually agrees on an essential set of defining features for the form.

Decades of research shows that the success of a social movement depends on the articulation of specific grievances, as well as the ability to mobilize resources and to

---

[6] Steve Wozniak, the cofounder of Apple Computer, provides an account of the importance of this club; see http://www.atariarchives.org/deli/homebrew_and_how_the_apple.php.

gel advocates into a cohesive organizational structure.[7] Resources to be mobilized include attention, financial support, individual members, and support from other organizations, especially powerful and authoritative ones. Organizational structures can be built from the ground up. But if the activities of existing organizations can be redirected, then communities with existing organizational orders are especially attractive as vehicles for mounting protest.

Our reading of the histories of emergence of diverse organizational forms suggests that social-movement activity frequently gives rise to clustering within domains. In addition to credit unions, beer brewing, and personal computing, the documented cases include art museums, automobiles, bicycle manufacturers, cooperatives, health maintenance organizations, labor unions, magazines, newspapers, and telephone companies.

Social movement categorization can also apply to features of products, producers, or both. Movement activists appear to be especially likely to attend to producer characteristics. They frequently seek to impose a categorization of producers within what has been a purely product-based category. Consider the microbrew movement (Carroll and Swaminathan 2000).The category "beer" was conventionally defined purely in terms of features of the product. For instance, the famous Bavarian *Reinheitsgebot* of 1516, still (at least informally if not legally) the prevailing beer code in Germany, specifies that beer must contain only barley, hops, yeast, and water; it says nothing about the features of the brewer. The activists of the contemporary microbrew movement argued for a code concerning the producer (that the brewer not also produce beer by other means or grow beyond a certain size) as well as the product. Similarly, movements such as Fairtrade propose codes to identify appropriate labor practices for small farms (e.g., cacao producers) and plantations (e.g., tea producers) and to identify the products that come from conforming producers. If this movement succeeds, then categories such as coffee, tea, cocoa, and sugar will become differentiated by producer characteristics. Similar processes unfolded in the development of the category "organic food."

Let the predicate $\text{ACT}(l, y, t)$ indicate that y, a member of the audience segment, is a social-movement activist with a schema for the type with label l at time t; and let $\mathbf{act}(l, t) = \{y \mid \text{ACT}(l, y, t)\}$.

Definition 5.3 (Social-movement support). *A social movement supports the label l at time t, $\text{SM}(l, t)$, if and only if*

1. *the set of activists is not a singleton:* $|\mathbf{act}(l, t)| > 1$;
2. *all nonactivists apply the label just in case the set of activists agree in assigning the label*

$$\forall t, x, y\, [\neg \text{ACT}(l, y, t) \rightarrow ((l \in \mathbf{lab}(x, y, t)) \\ \leftrightarrow \forall y'\, [\text{ACT}(l, y', t) \rightarrow (l \in \mathbf{lab}(x, y', t))])];$$

3. *a nonactivist associates a schema with the label and treats as a default that the producer satisfies this schema whenever the set of activists agree in as-*

[7] Snow, Soule, and Kriesi (2004) contains valuable overviews of the relevant research.

signing the label to that producer.

$$\forall t, x, y\,[(\neg \textsc{act}(l, y, t) \wedge \exists\, \mathbf{s}^l\,[\sigma(l, y, t) = \mathbf{s}^l]) \\ \rightarrow \forall y'\,[\textsc{act}(l, y', t) \rightarrow (l \in \mathbf{lab}(x, y', t))] \leftrightarrow \textsc{mtst}(\sigma(l, y, t), \emptyset)].$$

The parallel construction of the definitions of authorization and support by a social movement means that parallels to the three theorems about authorization also follow for movement backing.

Theorem 5.8. *If a label is authorized by a social movement, then its level of legitimation in the audience segment presumably equals unity.*

$$\mathfrak{P}\, l, t\,[\textsc{sm}(l, t) \rightarrow (L(l, t) = 1)].$$

Proof. According to D5.3, the members of the mass audience apply the label only when all of the activists do ($\mathfrak{d} = 1$) and their test code has a single feature (all of the activists apply the label). The definition of legitimation, D4.6, tells that $L = 1$ in this case. Given that all members of the mass audience have the same test code, $L = 1$ for all members of the mass audience: $L(l, t) = 1$, which is at least a great as $\mathfrak{l}$. □

As with authorization, it follows that a label backed by a movement constitutes a class.

Theorem 5.9. *A label supported by a social movement presumably defines a class*

$$\mathfrak{P}\, l, t\,[\textsc{sm}(l, t) \rightarrow \textsc{class}(l, t)].$$

Proof. According to D2.10, a class is a label for which the audience segment has achieved a very high level of extensional consensus. Definition 5.5 implies that the level of extensional consensus for an authorized label equals unity, because the members of the audience segment apply the label if and only if the authority applies it. This is the maximal possible level, and it therefore meets the threshold. □

If the level of intensional consensus is such that the label is a category, then an authorized label is also a form.

Theorem 5.10. *A category supported by a social movement presumably is a form.*

$$\mathfrak{P}\, l, t\,[\textsc{sm}(l, t) \wedge \textsc{cat}(l, t) \rightarrow \textsc{form}(l, t)].$$

Proof. The minimal rule chain uses a cut rule applied to D4.7, which states that a form is a category with a very high level of legitimation, the instantiation in the antecedent that l is a category, and (the rule chain behind) T5.9. □

As we define it, a social movement authorizes a class if and only if the members of the mass audience follow the activists' assessments regarding the types of producers who constitute the class. As noted earlier, consensus over schemata likely affects legitimation. Disagreement over the schemata for a class diminishes the ability of activists to influence the members of the mass audience. Contestation over schemata among the activists works to confuse the mass audiences and lowers the likelihood that they will defer to the activists (because, among other things, it is not clear what it means when the activists do not agree).

Consider, for example, the contestation that currently exists over the fundamental purposes of business schools. Differing conceptions exist over what a business school should aim to be, about "quintessential" goals and practices of a business school. This lack of agreement manifests itself in heated debates in scholarly and practitioner-oriented journals as well as in disagreement over the quality rankings of schools. These differing conceptions contribute to overall confusion in the market. One result is that potential MBAs are unlikely to accept the quality rankings of any one source automatically, but instead consult several sources to reach an overall assessment of each school's quality.

Postulate 5.1. *The probability that a social movement supports a class normally rises with the average level of intensional semantic consensus among the activists,* ic_{act}.

$$\mathfrak{N}\,\mathbf{q},\mathbf{q}'\,[(ic_{act} \uparrow \Pr(\textsc{sm}))(\mathbf{q},\mathbf{q}')\,],$$

where $ic_{act}(l,t)$ *is the level of intensional consensus about* l *among the activists at time* t*, and* $\mathbf{q}$ *and* $\mathbf{q}'$ *are as above.*

Theorem 5.11. *The probability that a social movement supports a class presumably increases with the average contrast of that class to a set of movement activists,* c_{act}.

$$\mathfrak{P}\,\mathbf{q},\mathbf{q}'\,[(c_{act} \uparrow \Pr(\textsc{sm})(\mathbf{q},\mathbf{q}')\,],$$

where $\mathbf{q}$ *and* $\mathbf{q}'$ *are as above.*

Proof. The minimal rule chain supporting this theorem involves a cut rule applied to P3.3, which states that the expected level of intensional consensus in an audience segment increases monotonically with the average contrast experienced by members of the segment, and P5.1. □

DISCUSSION

In concluding our treatment of form emergence and identity, we consider another view about organizational identity and discuss its relationship with ours. Hearkening back to Philip Selznick's (1957: 17) famous observation that certain aspects of formal organization sometimes get "infused with value beyond the technical requirements of the task at hand," a number of recent analysts have observed how organizations and organizational forms sometimes take on great symbolic significance to some audiences.

For instance, in analyzing cultural interpretations of McDonald's Corp. in Asia, James Watson (1997: 38) notes that

> . . . the Golden Arches have always symbolized something other than food. McDonald's symbolizes different things to different people at

> different times in their lives: predictability, safety, convenience, fun, familiarity, sanctuary, cleanliness, modernity, culinary tourism, and "connectedness" to the world beyond. . . . One is tempted to conclude that, in McDonald's case, the primary product is the experience itself.

Likewise, Glenn Carroll and Anand Swaminathan (2000) claim that many Americans are attracted to the sentiments opposing mass production that are inherent in the identities of the microbrewery and brewpub organizational forms rather than to the products themselves. Kolleen Guy (2003: 192) finds that the wine named champagne became part of the identity of France, as distinct from an ordinary product category:

> The champagne industry's ability to successfully mask what were essentially local interests as national concerns convinced the government to protect champagne and other fine wines as national patrimony. AOC laws granted champagne official French citizenship, with special rights and protections within the nation. But in the process of negotiation and compromise, the nation had also become Champagne . . .

Interestingly, Pierre Boisard (2003) makes a similar argument about Camembert (cheese) .

In an analysis of such phenomena, Joel Podolny and Mayra Hill-Popper (2003: 94) contrast a transcendent conception of value, in which "the value that the parties derive from the exchange depends on the extent to which each becomes invested in the vantage that the other has regarding the object" with the hedonic conception in which "a consumer's perception of the value of an exchange offering is contingent on how that offering directly compares to other exchange offerings on a set of abstracted dimensions." They elaborate on the differences as follows:

> The hedonic conception of value is obviously the conception of value that has the strongest affinity with the prevailing view of markets. Indeed, there is a sizeable economic literature on hedonic models of markets, where the value of an object to a particular consumer depends on how that object compares to others on some abstracted, differently weighted dimensions . . . Under the transcendent conception of value, in contrast, other objects may enter into a consumer's assessment of the worth of an object, but they enter in primarily for the purpose of enhancing the understanding of the meaning of the focal work and not for the purpose of developing a common standard against which multiple works may be compared. (Podolny and Hill-Popper 2003: 95)

They go on to say that organizations that attempt to gain advantage through an "authentic identity" typically rely on the transcendent conception of value.

James Baron (2004: 14) makes some related observations in his analysis of organizational identities in the labor market. He too focuses on authenticity as an element of organizational identity.

> . . . authenticity refers to the power of the organization's commitment to clientele and mode of relating to its constituencies, not simply to the

> stability of its product offerings, clientele, and mode of operating. The most authentic identities—or credible commitments—are ones that invoke a non-economic logic for action, inasmuch as they require that actors do certain things that cut against their narrow self-interest (and not do certain things that might further their own interest).

In our view, these are very important insights about organizational identity with great sociological consequence. It is clear to us that authenticity and other symbolic interpretations of categories shape the social interactions that evolve around organizations and affect social sanctioning. It is also clear that these interpretations are audience-based and that the audiences often comprise intensional semantic populations concerning these meanings. In many cases, it is also clear that authorization and social movements have shaped the structure of these semantic populations and the interpretations that they make. One way to think about them in our framework is to regard some parts of the audience as endowed with a "deeper" or more meaningful interpretation than others, perhaps based on its relationship to other categories (e.g., considering oneself to be French).

Of course, a precondition of such "deep" interpretation is social agreement about the existence and meaning of the category. In other words, for a category to become consensually infused with symbolic value, its existence must be recognized and agreed upon. The new theory focuses on the construction of categories and forms rather than on their symbolic interpretations. The conceptual framework advanced here might prove useful in exploring these other issues.

PART 2
Nonmonotonic Reasoning: Age Dependence

Chapter Six

A Nonmonotonic Logic

The chapters in this part introduce and apply the new logic described in Chapter 1: a dynamic, nonmonotonic logic. In logic, nonmonotonicity means that adding a premise to an argument might kill some of its implications (theorems). This chapter provides an informal introduction to the logic. It tells why we designed the logic as we did and how the logic works. (Some potentially useful background on classical first-order logic (FOL) can be found in Appendix C.)

It is customary to identify a logic with a (formal) definition of an inference relation. This might sound like a completely formal exercise, but, in fact, it is not. A sensible inference relation is a formal counterpart of some inference pattern. Of course, such patterns are hard to identify because logics are not intended to account for mistakes. The task of a logic is to describe how people argue when they do it correctly. In other words, there is a certain normative element in definitions of the inference relation.

As we noted in Chapter 1, sociological theorizing often presents a confusing picture as viewed from the perspective of formal logic.[1] The argumentation seems to be erroneous in that the explanatory principles used in different parts of a theoretical program often seem to be inconsistent. A key difficulty originates from incompleteness: typical theories are incomplete and in flux. Carefully constrained explanatory principles are not (yet) available. Formally minded people can easily conclude that the sociological theories are unsystematic and unreliable.

Surely the logic of argumentation in sociology does not always follow the principles of classical logics such as FOL. Nonetheless, we contend that argumentation might fail some classical test and yet still follow systematic logical principles. We want to identify some of these principles, show how they operate in the normal routines of theorizing, and provide a methodology for building theories and testing theoretical claims that fits the actual patterns of argumentation. This effort entails use of dynamic logic, specifically a new nonmonotonic logic developed specifically to fit sociological argumentation. We show that this logic sometimes allows systematic and consistent arguments to be formed even when different fragments of a theory seem to warrant opposing conclusions. In addition, we try to demonstrate that theory building with this logic can strengthen theories in progress and yield novel insights.

We hasten to note that, although our objectives are methodological in a broad sense, we do not deal here with empirical verification of theoretical claims. Instead, we focus on *patterns of argumentation:* how definitions, assumptions, and

[1] Adapted from Pólos and Hannan (2002, 2004).

insightful causal stories get stitched together to reach conclusions when empirical knowledge is partial. Nonetheless, we think that the proposed strategy of theory building can ease the task of making connections between abstract theory and empirical findings. We try to demonstrate this conjecture in sustained substantive applications of our method in the next two parts of the book.

Consider, as an example, the well-studied case of age dependence in organizational mortality. Empirical research provides three different tendencies to be explained. Historically these divergent patterns were explained by separate theory fragments, each selected to explain a subset of empirical findings. Theory fragments were developed under the label of liability-of-newness theories to explain the fact that many populations of organizations exhibited a negative relationship between organizational age and the hazard of mortality. In other populations, organizations were most vulnerable not at founding, but somewhat later. Liability-of-adolescence theory was developed to account for this pattern, especially the initial rise of mortality. Finally, research on some other populations found that older organizations have the highest hazard. Theory fragments, called theories of obsolescence, senescence, and network saturation, were designed to explain these findings.

No one claims that all of these theory fragments hold simultaneously. Nevertheless, even if each fragment is consistent and is supported by some substantial empirical research, the overall picture is disquieting. The relevant empirical work operates at the surface level by establishing parametric relationships between age and the mortality hazard and arguing that certain deeper processes give rise to these relationships. In other words, empirical knowledge on this subject is very incomplete. The present state of knowledge does not supply an answer to the fundamental question: what should be expected of a not-yet-studied population of organizations? Getting to the point where we can answer this question requires some way of unifying the fragments.

Classical FOL does not give enough room to keep all of these theory fragments on board; at most one of them can be true. Hannan (1998) formalized these theory fragments in FOL but was only partly successful in unifying them. The resulting formulation integrated two—but not all three—of the fragments. In other words, the formalization yielded two internally consistent fragments that seemingly cannot be reconciled in FOL. Making sense of this situation and making headway in refining the theories demands a different approach. Perhaps this entails use of a logic that imposes less stringent constraints. We argue that a nonmonotonic approach provides a valuable alternative methodology. (We present this alternative formulation in Chapter 7.)

6.1 BEYOND FIRST-ORDER LOGIC

Use of nonmonotonic logic in theory building constitutes a substantial departure from long-standing practice, as we noted in Chapter 1. When sociologists—or other scientists, for that matter—examine the logic of argumentation in their fields, they invariably employ (often informally) a classical logic, either propositional logic or—if quantification is needed—first-order logic. Such classical logics offer only one way to eliminate inconsistencies: restrict the scope of (some) explanatory principles or discard some principles.

As explained in Chapter 1, the price to be paid for gaining consistency with scope limitations is a limit on explanatory power. Although such a price might be well worth paying, restricting the scope of premises appears to be justified only when the restrictions can be well motivated substantively. Otherwise the cure is ad hoc.

We show that nonmonotonic reasoning offers an appealing alternative methodology. It can allow explanatory principles to remain intact so long as we lack substantive reasons to restrict their scope. Two different lines of explanation pointing in opposite directions might preclude drawing any conclusions, but they might also not yield any contradictions in specified circumstances. And the absence of conclusions might be cured by knowledge showing that (under the specific circumstances) one line of argumentation is more specific than the other. Because the explanatory principles remain intact in this strategy of theory building, so too does the explanatory power of the theory. In fact, we show that the situation is even better in the case of several sociological theories whose explanatory power grows when the theory fragments are integrated using a nonmonotonic logic.

In logic, monotonicity means that the size of the set of conclusions (theorems) that follows from a set of premises grows monotonically as premises are added. In other words, monotonicity means that adding premises cannot overturn conclusions that follow from the original (smaller) set of premises. In contrast, nonmonotonic logics allow that adding new premises (reflecting new knowledge) can overturn existing conclusions. In such logics, introducing premises that would result in contradictions according to FOL do not necessarily create inconsistency. Switches between explanatory principles follow the following generic guidelines:

1. when different principles give conflicting results, inferences should be based on the most specific principles that apply; and

2. when conflicting principles do not differ in specificity, no inference should be drawn.

Since the 1980s, logicians working on applications in computer science designed and studied many nonmonotonic logics. This intense activity led to the vast array of alternatives now available.[2] However, given their typical computer-science motivation, most of these logics are suitable tools for studying reasoning in databases but much less desirable tools for studying patterns of argumentation in theory building. There are two key differences.

First, whether the "rules" are definitions, universally quantified propositions, metaprinciples, insightful causal stories, or auxiliary assumptions obviously matters for representing theoretical arguments. These distinctions ought to be marked in the syntax used to represent a theory. Because these distinctions were not important in modeling the computer-science applications, they do not appear in the syntaxes that were developed for these applications. Second, the database approach

[2]Standard technical references on the subject include McCarty (1980), Makinson (1994), and Veltman (1996); Brewka, Dix, and Konolige (1997) provide an accessible overview of the field of nonmonotonic logic.

treats old information as less valid than new information: one normally updates an entry in a database to override old information that has been found to be incorrect. But we will argue that argumentation patterns are different, that updates add new information but do not vitiate existing information. Hence, we decided that the many available logics are less than ideal for representing patterns of argumentation and theory building.

As far as we know, only Frank Veltman (1991, 1996) rigorously maintained the desired distinctions (among the different kinds of elements that comprise an argument) in designing his nonmonotonic language for update semantics. In formulating our approach, we followed Veltman as closely as possible. Nonetheless, we found that a number of features of his update semantics needed to be altered to fit our problem.[3] So, despite having some qualms about introducing yet another type of nonmonotonic logic, Pólos and Hannan (2002, 2004) concluded that a new logic was needed for representing patterns of theory building.

The new logic should be seen as what we regard as the minimal formalization of the following principles, which we generalized from our studies in building sociological theories.

1. More specific arguments override less specific ones.

2. Specificity differences persist, new information cannot overrule established specificity orders.

3. Whether one argument is more specific than another depends either on factual information or on causal stories.

4. Only the first causal story in an argument chain defines the specificity of the argument. (We will motivate this choice below.)

5. Equally specific arguments pointing in opposite directions eliminate each other's predictions.

6. Arguments that point in opposite directions but whose specificities are not comparable eliminate each other's predictions.

7. Theory building follows the principle of informational monotonicity. Therefore, explanatory principles, causal stories, are not deleted, even when they are partially overruled. Definitions and metaconsiderations are persistent as well.

---

[3]First, Veltman developed the semantics for a propositional language. Theory building requires quantification, that is, at least FOL. Second, he required that the key generic quantifier "normally implies," always be the outmost operator in forming sentences. We found this limitation to be too constraining, especially in forming definitions. Third, he considered inconsistency and incoherence to be similarly damaging. In the context he treated (the study of relatively short natural language discourse), this is indeed justified. For our subject (theory building over several decades) consistency is the most that one can hope for. Fourth, he regarded discourses with the property that generalizations can be completely overridden by more specific considerations as incoherent. On the other hand, this fate does befall explanatory principles in the course of theory building over several decades. So a logic designed to describe reasoning in theory building should not exclude this possibility.

8. Certain operations in FOL that rely on detailed knowledge about the facts (such as modus tollens and contraposition) should not have a counterpart in the new logic.

9. Expansions of the argument should hold. If we establish two causal stories where the first says that "A normally implies B" and the second says that "C normally implies B," then we want to be able to conclude that "A or C normally implies B."

We also want to impose two restrictions on the consequence relation, as we next discuss briefly.

1. The *contraposition* inference schema, sketched in Appendix C, should not hold. In classical logic the sentence "A implies B" is logically equivalent to the sentence "Not-B implies not-A." This equivalence makes the monotonicity statements of functions undesirably strong, and is responsible for some unwanted theorems, as we demonstrated in previous chapters. These theorems are often implied by a pair of premises such as "Inertia grows with size" and "Inertia grows with age." Using contraposition one can prove that size cannot shrink (cannot get smaller with age), otherwise the theory is inconsistent (see Péli, Pólos, and Hannan 2000).

   We do not want even the weaker (generic) form of contraposition either. "A normally implies B" should not logically imply the sentence " Not B presumably implies not A." Such arguments are counterintuitive; and they show that the formalization in a logic where the contraposition holds might not be completely adequate to express how such monotonicity statements are normally meant in theoretical work.

2. The *modus tollens* proof schema (Appendix C) also should not hold. The fact that a causal story establishes the link between A and B in form of "A normally implies B" and we observe "not B" should not license the inference "presumably not-A" in the new logic.

6.2 GENERALIZATIONS

Empirical theories rarely get formalized in the strict sense, even in the mature sciences. Theories are typically presented in a pseudo-formal language, i.e., an extension of a natural language with some field-specific mathematical formalisms. The lack of strict formalization allows for the nature of generality of these theories to remain hidden. Most general considerations in fact appear in the form of bare plural sentences such as those in a famous argument by Stinchcombe (1965): "Routines in young organizations are less well developed than in older organizations," or "Organizations with better developed routines have a lower hazard of mortality," or (the claimed liability-of-newness theorem): "Young organizations display a higher hazard of mortality than older organizations."

These statements are indeed general. But are they universal? Would these sentences be considered false if someone discovered a population of organizations in which young organizations have a lower mortality rate than that the old organizations? No. These claims are general—but *not* universal.

Linguists were puzzled for a long time by the formal grammar of this type of sentence. Gregory Carlson (1980) was the first to argue that these kinds of sentences are *intensional.* As we explain below, an intension is (roughly speaking) a function that tells the extension of a concept in different possible worlds.

Subsequent research by Angelika Kratzer (1995) and Molly Diesing (1995) concluded that these sentences contain a (hidden) generic quantifier in the logical structure. Moreover, Lenhardt Schubert and Jeffrey Pelletier (1988) showed that no context-independent extensional quantifier would assign the appropriate truth conditions to these sentences. This line of research leads to the conclusion that quantifiers for such sentences should be intensional, which means that we must move outside FOL. (Classical logics, such as FOL, are purely extensional.)

The meaning of generically quantified sentences can be approximated by saying that they express *rules-with-exceptions.* Such rules are not sufficient to derive certain truth of objects, but they still might be useful to shape what we expect of unknown individual instances (Veltman 1996). Such expectations might well be the only arguments we have available in the face of the urgency of action. The partiality of available information means that the truth-value assignments occasionally yield truth-value gaps. Moreover, it also creates the possibility that we have only rules-with-exceptions—not strict (universal) rules.

Suppose that the generality of empirical theories often appears in the form of generically quantified sentences. Then, of course, the critical objection to these theories might not be a simple attempt of falsification by finding a counterexample. The possibility of exceptions, counterexamples, is already anticipated. Accidental, unreproducible exceptions might be ignored as mistaken measurements or historical accidents. For example, a study of organizational morality in a population that encounters a political revolution might easily yield a counterexample to the Stinchcombe claim of a liability of newness if the revolution suddenly wipes out all older organizations. Other kinds of exceptions have more serious theoretical implications. For example, one might find that populations to which only large or well-endowed organizations can enter show low mortality even among the young members. Repeated, systematic exceptions of this type create a crisis in a theory, which, in turn, might lead to extensions of the theory.

Theory Building

We treat theories as intensional objects, objects with extended histories. Such histories can usefully be represented as sets of theory stages. A theory stage includes a persistent part and an ephemeral one. The persistent part forms the backbone, the identity of the theory. Following Imre Lakatos (1994), we refer to the persistent part of the theory as its (hard) *core.* We suggest that the core of a theory consists of three elements: (1) metaconsiderations, (2) definitions of key concepts and causal stories (or explanatory principles) linking them, and (3) desiderata concerning implications (desired theorems and nontheorems).

The metaconsiderations are those extratheoretical issues that are treated as nonproblematic for the purposes of developing the theory. They include rules concerned with the structure of legitimate inferences: the logic of the theory. Although these considerations are often left implicit, the theory would be radically different if the logic were changed. Typically the metaconsiderations in our work also include various branches of mathematics, e.g., the calculus, set theory (including fuzzy subset theory), and probability theory.

Definitions and causal stories, or explanatory principles, contain the substantive insights of the theory. These definitions and claims can be either strict rules (universally quantified sentences) or generic sentences, rules-with-exceptions. The latter typically take the form

$$\text{Normally } x\,[\phi(x) \rightarrow \psi(x)].$$

Of course, a core that contains strict empirical rules (universal statements that convey subject-specific insights) also contains the implications of such rules.

The desiderata about implications include two components: what theorems the theory should imply and what theorems should not be implied. Note that this idea reflects Lakatos' (1976) insight that the identity of the theory arises not from the assumptions alone but from the combination of the assumptions, desired theorems, and auxiliary assumptions.

The ephemeral components come in two kinds: auxiliary assumptions and presumptions. Auxiliary assumptions are postulates that theorists introduce into arguments to link the causal stories and metaconsiderations, on the one side, and desired theorems, on the other side. (Of course, such additions are made only in cases in which the argument does not go through without additional specification.) For instance, the classical population genetics of R. A. Fisher and Sewell Wright required a specification of the assignment of mates in the sexual transmission of genes between generations. That is, an auxiliary assumption was needed. The chosen assumption was random mating. Because of their auxiliary nature, such assumptions are treated as subject to replacement by other such assumptions as needed. This suggests to us that auxiliary assumptions ought to be considered as rules-with-exceptions but not as permanent parts of a theory.

The second ephemeral component is the set of theorems (predictions and explanations) that depend on rules-with-exceptions. These implications are either individual sentences or generic sentences. They often take the form

$$\text{Presumably } x\,[\phi(x) \rightarrow \chi(x)].$$

Learning the implications of an argument built on rules-with-exceptions—what is presumably the case—often requires knowing more than the causal stories of the theory's core. As the physicist and philosopher of science Pierre Duhem (1991 [1906]) argued forcefully, certain auxiliary assumptions are generally needed for prediction (and empirical testing). These assumptions might take the form of some simplifying assumptions (descriptions of constraints that make mathematical modeling possible), might carve out mathematical models, or might provide the interface between the causal stories and the models. Sometimes these assumptions describe measurement instructions, operationalizations. *Auxiliary* assumptions stand somewhere between causal stories and presumable consequences. They are not persistent in an evolving theory, because they are assumptions made for special purposes but are not claimed to be causal insights. For example, population biologists who invoke random mating do not claim that this assumption provides an insightful description of the real world. On the contrary, they might be more or less suspicious about the empirical validity of such an assumption. However, this assumption makes it possible to develop precise implications about genetic evolution.

Pólos and Hannan (2002) introduced the quantifiers $\mathfrak{N}$ and $\mathfrak{P}$. An extension of their approach (Pólos and Hannan 2004) introduced the argumentative role of the auxiliary assumptions (they do contribute to the information content, even though the contribution is not persistent) and defined a separate logical form for them. To display their intermediate status in the syntax, they introduced a third intensional quantifier: $\mathfrak{A}$.

There is a further, logical, reason to claim a specific logical form for the auxiliary assumptions. In classical FOL, we can deal with auxiliary assumptions simply by appending them to the set of theoretical premises. In other words, we can condition the argument on the auxiliary assumptions. This follows from the fact that FOL implies that $(\Gamma \cup \{\phi\} \models \psi) \Rightarrow (\Gamma \models (\phi \rightarrow \psi))$, where $\models$ is the standard notation for "provides a model for" (see Appendix C).

We claim that the foregoing derivation does not hold generally for arguments that contain rules-with-exceptions. Therefore, auxiliary assumptions cannot be treated by conditionalization. We need some other way to treat auxiliary information. We designed the quantifier $\mathfrak{A}$ to play this role.

To summarize: causal stories, auxiliary assumptions, and presumptions (or provisional theorems) have a shared responsibility for nonmonotonicity. Nonetheless, causal stories (as we construe them) are informationally monotonic. These considerations set a methodological agenda. The only generalizations that should be added to a theory as causal stories are those that the theorist is prepared to accept as permanent assumptions of the theory. If there are doubts that a generalization will be acceptable in the future stages of a theory, then it does not merit the status of causal story (or empirical generalization).

Theory building, according to this approach, moves from one theory stage to another. (We define a theory stage formally below.) Moves are fueled by critical challenges to the earlier phase/stage of the theory. The already accepted explanatory principles remain intact, but new principles might be adopted. (This appears to be part of normal scientific activity, the conceptual framework remains intact, but considerations are refined.) Figuring out the appropriate response to a critical challenge requires that inferences be made and that these inferences be sound. But sound *according to what logic*?

6.3 NONMONOTONIC REASONING

We distilled some guidelines for both syntax and semantics from our efforts to formalize sociological theories. We argue that theory building ought to conform to the principle of *informational monotonicity:* explanatory principles are not withdrawn, even when their first-order consequences get falsified. Instead, they are maintained; and their effects are controlled by more specific arguments. Thus, explanatory principles clearly differ from classical first-order (universal) generalizations, because they show an informational stability.

What are explanatory principles? As we noted above, at the grammatical surface, explanatory principles typically take the form of bare plural sentences and their normal interpretation is as generic sentences (Krifka et al. 1995). Explanatory principles contain the empirical content of a theory.[4] For these two reasons we referred to these explanatory principles as empirical generalizations in some previous publications. Although such a label is fully justified, it is not quite specific enough. We suggest that explanatory principles should be treated as informationally stable in the sense that already established explanatory principles are maintained in further developments of a theory. Neither their empirical nature nor their genericity accounts for such persistence.

Explanatory principles are generally regarded as persistent in theory building because they provide the key ingredients of theory, the specific causal explanations. In short, they are *causal stories*. Dropping a causal story might be exactly the right thing to do in theorizing. Yet making such a move means that one theory is replaced by another. It will surely be a matter of judgment as to whether a line of theory ought to be preserved. (We discuss issues of falsification below.) The strategy that we outline applies to the line of development of a unitary theory.

The details of our approach differ from previous developments in nonmonotonic logic in how we define specificity orderings of arguments. In particular, we build formal models of arguments involving causal stories (in terms of sequences of intensions of open formulas, as we explain in the next section).

What should be expected of a suitable nonmonotonic logic? To develop some intuition, we begin with a famous example of simple inference pattern with a failure of monotonicity.[5]

Premise 1. Birds fly.

Premise 2. Tweety is a bird.

Proposition. Tweety flies.

Suppose we add three new premises:

Premise 3. All penguins are birds.

Premise 4. Penguins do not fly.

Premise 5. Tweety is a penguin.

---

[4]Metaprinciples are not theory specific, and definitions express only analytical conventions.

[5]This stylized example and the Nixon Diamond (discussed below) are ubiquitous in the technical literature.

What happens to the conclusion that appears to be justified from the first two premises alone? Not only does it now seem unjustified, but we are tempted to derive the *opposite* conclusion "Tweety does not fly."

What is going on here? Compare the two possible arguments about flying. One builds on a premise about birds; the other builds on a premise about penguins. Tweety is both a bird and a penguin; so both premises apply. But the premise about penguins seems to be more relevant for Tweety than the premise about birds. Why? The premise about penguins is more specific than the premise about birds. This difference in the specificity of the premises accounts for the difference in the relevance of the arguments. We want to use the most relevant arguments available, those with greatest specificity. So, we go for the conclusion "Tweety does not fly."

What gives rise to this (implicit) specificity ordering? We argue that it is the third premise "All penguins are birds." One might object that the presence or absence of this premise should not matter much, because our common background knowledge holds that penguins are birds. Yet, another of the logicians' favorite examples—the Nixon Diamond—shows that common background knowledge does not always clarify inferences.

Premise 1. Quakers are doves.

Premise 2. Republicans are hawks.

Premise 3. Dick is a Republican.

Premise 4. Dick is a Quaker.

Proposition. ???

Our background knowledge tells us that no one can be both a hawk (pro-war) and a dove (anti-war). Indeed, the argumentation implicitly assumes that "x is a hawk" is the negation of "x is a dove." Crucially, this background knowledge does not inform us about the specificity of the premises. Lacking a dependable specificity order, we cannot conclude either that "Dick is a dove" or that "Dick is a hawk."

Seeing all of this, one might go back to the Tweety example and decide that the original conclusion might have been unjustified.[6] "Birds fly" is a rule—a rule with exceptions; and we did not know whether Tweety was an exception. Although we should have waited until we learned something about this, we just jumped to the conclusion.

Well, sometimes conclusions must be drawn before all relevant facts are known. The situation imposes what Descartes called the urgency of action. Such urgency always arises in theory building in the empirical sciences, whose knowledge is always partial. A theorist cannot wait until *all* relevant things about a subject are known, but instead must take what is known and draw conclusions on the basis of the available evidence. In fact, this very feature of theorizing accounts for the nonmonotonicity of much argumentation in sociology and other empirical disciplines.

[6]Without doubt, this would be the reaction of some classically minded logicians.

Before we describe the formal language, it is worth pointing out that stories about "Tweety" and "Dick," though time-honored exemplars of nonmonotonic reasoning in logic, raise red flags for social scientists. Any quantitatively oriented scholar surely would object that the statement "birds fly" lacks the specificity needed for a premise to serve as a prop in a scientific argument. This is surely true. The logicians were examining naturally occurring conversations. Scientists operate with semi-formal languages. Given our interest in theory building, we naturally focus on the latter. Indeed, the sociological theory fragments that we model have such a semi-formalized nature (involving statements about probability distributions).

6.4 A PRÈCIS OF THE FORMAL APPROACH

We describe a new language, which we call the language for theory building, which extends the language of FOL (sketched in Appendix C). It contains three nonmonotonic quantifiers on top of the formal machinery of classical FOL.

Some formal machinery is needed for testing claims about what really follows from the premises in a stage of a theory. We represent arguments in the form of regularity chains. These chains are built of links that state strict rules or causal stories. The chains are constructed so that they start with the subject of the argument and terminate with the purported conclusion of the argument (the consequence to be derived). In nonmonotonic inference, different regularity chains—each representing an argument embodied in the state of the theory—might lead to opposing conclusions. The testing procedure determines whether any inference can be drawn at all and, if so, which one. This procedure requires standards for assessing whether a pair of relevant regularity chains can be compared in specificity and thereby determining the specificity differences for comparable chains. It thus provides a method of constructing proofs of the claims of a theory.

We now supply some of the details (but still in a somewhat informal manner); the full details appear in Pólos and Hannan (2004). A logic is a formal definition of a consequence relation. When we consider theorizing, the relevant consequence relations hold among sentences of a language. So, we begin to characterize a logic by defining a language.

We are focusing on nonmonotonicity, the uncertainty that conclusions really follow from the theory as such, although they appear to be conclusions of a given stage of the theory. Uncertainty about what follows in an argument is frightening, and we want to avoid it if at all possible. So long as these dangerous beasts persist, they should be marked clearly. We implement this goal by defining separate languages for the well-behaved part of the theory and the part that misbehaves in the sense of showing signs of nonmonotonicity.

Three relevant kinds of sentences generate failures of monotonicity in theory building: causal stories, auxiliary assumptions, and provisional theorems (propositions derived from causal stories). The differences among them can be seen from their roles in theorizing. Serious causal stories capture some relevant (and valid) insight about the underlying causal mechanisms; they yield the "aha!" feeling that good theories can provide. Neither their validity nor their relevance gets automatically undermined by any accidental counterexample—not even by some systematic exceptions. In fact, the meaning of these causal accounts cannot be properly reproduced by their truth conditions, expressed in term of the number or proportion of positive instantiations. They do not talk about what *is* the case. Rather, their main semantic contribution lies in shaping expectations: what is expected to be the case.

We need extra tools to express default rules. Because they provide insight, we want to treat causal stories as informationally stable. This means that we presume that extensions of a theory keep all causal stories intact.

As a theory develops, new insights might restrict a causal story's domain of applicability. Indeed, this happens as knowledge about exceptions develops, although even new knowledge should not cause us to discard the original insights. Instead, new rules get added to the body of knowledge; and new, more specific rules can—and occasionally do—override older, more general rules.

Auxiliary assumptions are the special claims added to an argument to permit certain kinds of inferences, as in Duhem's account. Clearly these auxiliary assumptions are not intended to persist over the life of a theory.

Provisional theorems also have a haphazard existence. New knowledge might wipe them out without a trace, as we will see. The provisional theorems belong to particular stages of a developing theory—they represent the predictions that can be sensibly formed at that stage.

These considerations set a methodological agenda. The "official" causal stories of a theory should be those that the theorist (or theory group) regards as sufficiently dependable and insightful to serve as permanent assumptions of the theory. A claim does not deserve this status if there are serious doubts about future acceptability.

Part of an evolving theory can sometimes be expressed in the language of FOL (which includes the standard languages of mathematics). This language follows monotonicity. For instance, definitions and strict rules (universally quantified sentences) are generally expressed in this way. Premises stated in this language provide the firm foundation for a theory. Any sentence that can be derived by classical rules from these sentences counts as a dependable proposition of a theory in all stages of the theory. In formal terms, the deductive closure of these classical assumptions is part of a theory.

Study of the linguistic forms of the sentences expressing causal stories reveals that it is unlikely that they can be expressed in the language of FOL. As we noted above, generic sentences are general, but not universal. Their truth conditions cannot be expressed in terms of particular cases. To return to a classic example, even if many kinds of birds do not fly, the claim "birds fly" would still be an acceptable causal story, *provided* that this is a justifiable expectation of a creature with only one known property: it is a bird. These considerations show that causal stories cannot be expressed adequately in the language of FOL, where generality means universal quantification.

The Syntax

Pólos and Hannan (2004) defined a new formal language for theory building, assigned meanings to their (well-formed) sentences, and spelled out the conception of logical consequence that fits these semantics. Here we give an informal sketch of the language.

Designing a language for theory building required that some decisions be made about how to treat the implications of causal stories. Suppose that a theoretical argument contains two causal stories and that these stories can be stated formally as follows

$$\phi \text{ normally implies } \psi: \quad \mathfrak{N}\,\bar{x}\,[\phi(\bar{x}) \to \psi(\bar{x})];$$
$$\psi \text{ normally implies } \chi: \quad \mathfrak{N}\,\bar{x}\,[\psi(\bar{x}) \to \chi(\bar{x})].$$

We obviously want to be able to draw an implication here. That is, we want to have something parallel to FOL's cut rule, which allows ψ to be cut out, giving an implication from ϕ to χ. But what should be the status of the provisional theorem linking ϕ to χ? One answer might be that this too should be regarded as a causal story: ϕ normally implies χ, that is, $\mathfrak{N}\,\bar{x}\,[\phi(\bar{x}) \to \chi(\bar{x})]$.

Recall that we want to reserve the status of causal story for the deep insights of a theory. Whenever the rule linking ϕ to χ is not already contained in the set of causal stories, it is presumably not known and it is to be discovered (as an inference). To mark this distinction, we need a different semantics to express *presumptions,* the implications of causal stories, the theorems generated at a theory stage. This second type of sentence in the new logic is quantified by a "presumably" quantifier, denoted by $\mathfrak{P}$. In the context of the example introduced above, we express the result of applying the so-called cut rule to the pair of causal stories as

$$\phi \text{ presumably implies } \chi: \quad \mathfrak{P}\,\bar{x}\,[\phi(\bar{x}) \to \chi(\bar{x})].$$

Our use of the expressions "normally," "normally implies," "presumably," and "presumably implies" reflects the deep influence of Frank Veltman (1996). Although the research questions suggested a formal semantics that differs from his, the credit for developing some basic, dependable intuitions about a domain, which is normally recognized as very slippery, should go to Veltman.

The Possible-Worlds Semantics

We now turn to the task of assigning meanings to the sentences of the new language. We do so using what logicians call possible-world semantics.[7]

Assigning meaning to sentences in FOL requires specifying what objects the individual constants refer to, what the variables stand for, and what properties or relations the predicates denote. Individual constants refer to and variables stand for elements of the universe of discourse (U). One-place predicates refer to properties that can be represented as subsets of the universe of discourse. Two-place predicates refer to relations represented by subsets of pairs of objects/elements of U, three-place predicates refer to relations represented by subsets of triplets of objects/elements, and so forth.

We can define the semantics for the new language in a systematic manner with *interpretation functions,* which map individual constants to elements of the universe

[7]Valuable background material on the semantics of possible worlds can be found in Dowty, Wall, and Peters (1980) and Gamut (1991b).

of discourse (and n-place predicates to sets of n-long sequences of elements of the universe of discourse). For example, $\text{ORG}(x)$ is a one-place predicate. The interpretation function assigns to it the set of objects that—according to an interpretation—qualify as organizations. This set is called the *extension* of the predicate. Extensions obviously depend upon interpretations.

Not all interpretations are equally useful; some might have very little to do with the real world. Only substantive knowledge can tell which sets the predicates denote. It is not logic that tells us which creatures are organizations or which creatures are subject to norms of rationality. One has to go into the world and find out. When no factual information is available, all denotations of a predicate are equally possible. In other words, we have the whole set of different possible interpretations.

These alternatives are called *possible worlds* in the usual formal language (see Gamut 1991b). If we lack factual knowledge, then we do not know which of the possible worlds is the *actual* world. When more relevant facts and strict rules become known, the set of still-possible worlds shrinks. In other words, the multiplicity of possible worlds characterizes the partiality of our dependable knowledge.

The next step is to identify the sets that each predicate denotes in the various possible worlds. A generalized interpretation of the language assigns (1) references to individual constants and (2) denotation to all predicates in *every* possible world. This makes it convenient to use interpretation functions to characterize the semantics of possible worlds.

The concept of *intension* plays a very important role in possible-world semantics and, therefore, in the logic that we designed. In formal terms, the intension of a predicate is a function that tells the extension of the predicate (the set of those objects for which the predicate is true) in every possible world. This means that an intension maps from worlds to sets. Intensions of expressions give abstract representations of their meanings. As the Gamut collective (1991a, p. 14) put it, "The intension of an expression is something like its conceptual content, while its extension comprises all that exemplifies that conceptual content." In a possible-worlds framework, two predicates are considered to have the same meaning if and only if they have the same intension.

We define causal stories as generic sentences. As we noted above, generic sentences are either true or false; but their truth or falsity generally cannot be expressed in terms of the proportion of positive and negative instances in a world (as the so-called inductivist view argues).

We regard a generic sentence as true when the regularity that it expresses actually holds in the world. Carlson (1995) calls this view the rules-and-regulations approach:

> According to this approach, generic sentences depend for their truth and falsity upon whether or not there is a corresponding structure in the world, structures being not the episodic instances but rather the causal forces behind those instances.

We take advantage of linguistic knowledge in representing such regularities formally. The relevant linguistic research concludes that the underlying structure of a generic sentence contains two open formulas (Carlson 1980; Diesing 1995; Kratzer

1995).

Like generic sentences, causal stories express *conditionality*—they relate antecedents to consequents. Given that we construe the relation between the antecedents and consequents in causal stories as open formulæ, we extended the definition of intension to apply to open formulas (specified with a list of (some of) its free variables).

Definition 6.1 (Intension of an open formula). *The intension of the open formula $\phi(\bar{x})$, denoted by $[\![\phi(\bar{x})]\!]$, gives, for every possible world,*[8] *the (sequences of) objects for which this formula happens to be true in that world.*

We can now specify a core idea underlying our modeling strategy. The ordered pair whose first element is the intension of the antecedent and whose second element is the intension of the consequent provides a useful semantic representation of the regularity expressed by a causal story. The ordering is important, because it tells the *direction* of the relation.

Theory Stages

With these preliminaries in hand, we can define a stage of a theory as a set of ordered pairs: $\langle \mathrm{W}, \mathbf{c} \rangle$. Here W denotes the set of (still) possible worlds, the worlds that can be the real world as far as the first-order part of the theory is concerned; and **c** denotes the set that contains the semantic representations of the causal stories (and nothing else). The idea that a stage of a theory contains both of these components corresponds to the view that both strict rules (premises stated in $\mathcal{L}_F$) and causal stories play an argumentative role in scientific explanations. Strict rules exclude some of the otherwise possible worlds; and causal stories express regularities that are just as real as are the objects, properties, and relations in the world.

Sentences in this new language are to be evaluated in theory stages. The sentences of the first-order part of the theory (the classical premises) can be true, false, or undefined in any stage. Intuitively speaking, a first-order sentence is true in a theory stage if it is true in all of the still-possible worlds, false if it is false in all still-possible worlds, and it is undefined otherwise. (In this context, a world is "still possible" if it has not yet been ruled out by strict rules or causal stories.)

As we noted above, a causal story ought to be modeled semantically by the presence of the corresponding regularity, because the truth or falsity of a rule-with-exceptions cannot be characterized by a universally quantified proposition about the world. Instead of treating causal stories as having to do with truth about the world, we treat sentences expressing causal stories as true if they represent explicit causal claims of the theory and as false otherwise. We characterize the logical impact of causal stories by their role in inference, i.e., in terms of the conclusions they (along with the first-order premises) support. Therefore, we posit that the formula $\mathfrak{N}\,\bar{x}[\phi(\bar{x}) \rightarrow \psi(\bar{x})]$ is true in a stage of a theory if the ordered pair of the intensions of $\langle \phi, \psi \rangle$ is a valid regularity in all of the still-possible worlds at that stage, and it is false otherwise.

[8] If $\phi(\bar{x})$ contains more free variables than are listed in $\bar{x}$, then they too should be valuated.

It is important to realize that we treat universal rules and causal stories as the stable elements of a theory. Once they are posited to be true in a given theory stage, they remain true in any extension. In contrast, the consequences of causal stories can change from stage to stage—a consequence (provisional theorem) provable in one stage might be overruled in a later theory stage.

Semantics of the Language

Lacking a rich semantics for causal stories, we leave the job of characterizing the basic intuitions about inference to the semantics of the (well-formed) sentences of the language. We call an argument based on a causal story a *rule chain.* Loosely speaking, a nonmonotonic test of an argument succeeds if a tentative[9]—but convincing—argument can be constructed from the causal stories (and strict rules) and if the regularity chain that expresses it is more specific than those representing all (tentative) counterarguments.

Because strict comparisons of chains are needed to test arguments, we must define carefully how a chain can be constructed: which rule can follow which other rule in the chain. As a preparatory step, we defined a specificity relation for intensions. Think of the following possible causal claim: Old and small organizations are vulnerable. The formal counterpart is

$$\mathfrak{N}\, x[\text{ORG}(x) \wedge \text{OLD}(x) \wedge \text{SMALL}(x) \rightarrow \text{VUL}(x)].$$

In this case, the antecedent is the formula $\text{ORG}(x) \wedge \text{OLD}(x) \wedge \text{SMALL}(x)$. The intension of this formula is the function that tells, for every possible world, which objects are the old and small organizations in that world. Suppose we have reason to believe that some class of organizations present an exception to this rule, say handcraft producers (in some industry).

All craft producers are old, small organizations:

$$\forall x[\text{CRAFT}(x) \rightarrow \text{ORG}(x) \wedge \text{OLD}(x) \wedge \text{SMALL}(x)];$$

Craft producers are normally not vulnerable:

$$\mathfrak{N}\, x[\text{CRAFT}(x) \rightarrow \neg\text{VUL}(x)].$$

If these premises tell all that we know, then we cannot conclude that the extension of the "craft producer" predicate is smaller than that of the complex predicate "old and small organization" in the actual world. It might be smaller, or it might be equal.

Yet, based on empirical evidence and our general understanding of the world, we might be convinced that the "craft-producer" rule is more specific than the "old-and-small-organization" rule.[10] If so, the relation between the two rules is this: in all still-possible worlds, the extension of the "craft-producer" predicate is a subset of the extension of the "old-and-small-organization" predicate; and the extension of the "craft" predicate is a proper subset in some worlds (where one sees, say,

[9]By tentative, we mean depending upon causal stories instead of simply first-order premises.

[10]This would require a world in which there were no new (young) craft producers.

small, old liberal-arts colleges). This relation can be represented with the following *specificity relation:* the formula ϕ is at least as specific as the formula ψ, formally $[\![\phi]\!] \sqsubseteq_W [\![\psi]\!]$, if and only if the intension of ϕ is a subset of the intension of ψ in every still-possible world.

How to model specificity in our setup? Rules in a rule chain have a conditional form, and their antecedents characterize the subject of the rule. Our main methodological consideration is the following. Because a theory stage, an information state, cannot tell completely how the world looks, a useful characterization of the specificity relationship should be based on what is available in an information state, what we know according to a given stage of a theory. Information states are only partial characterizations of the extensions of predicates—they are open formulas. Suppose that we know of three organizations a, b and c that all are old and that b and c are large. In this information state, all of the known large organizations are old. Now consider two premises:

1. Old organizations are vulnerable.
2. Large organizations are not vulnerable.

Is it justified to conclude that premise 2 is more specific information about organization b than premise 1 under these circumstances (because all known large organizations are old and there is no known old organization that is not large)? No, because new facts can overturn the apparent specificity difference. For instance, we might learn of an organization d that is old and small. On the other hand, suppose that we add two more premises according to which large organizations are always old and there is at least one old but small organization. Then the conclusion that (2) is more specific than (1) is justified. What is the difference? As we noted above, in the first case (with only the first and second premises), new facts might emerge (enlargements of the information state/ theory stage) where the set inclusions of the extensions of "large" and "old" are changed. However, this kind of change is not possible in the second case, because "large organization" is a proper subset of "old organization" in the theory stage that contains all four premises. We use this insight to characterize the specificity relation.[11]

We want to represent arguments as chains of rules (strict rules and causal stories). We define a ϕ–ψ regularity chain as follows. The first component of a chain, γ_1, identifies the subject of the argument. In the case of a ϕ–ψ chain, the first element is the intension of the antecedent ϕ; that is, $\gamma_1 = [\![\phi]\!]$. We build the chain by representing the first-order rules and causal stories to produce a chain of the form $\gamma = \langle \gamma_1, \gamma_2, \ldots, \gamma_k \rangle$, where for each γ_i, γ_{i+1} $(i \geq 1)$, the two components appear in the argument as related by either a first-order rule or a causal story. And the last element in the chain, γ_k, is either $[\![\psi]\!]$ (which means that ψ is true and, therefore, the regularity chain is positive) or $[\![\neg\psi]\!]$ (which means that the regularity chain is negative). In other words, positive chains correspond to (tentative) arguments of a ϕ–ψ relation, negative chains to (tentative) counter arguments.

[11] As we noted in Chapter 1, it might take considerable knowledge of an empirical subject to be able to make clear specificity orderings.

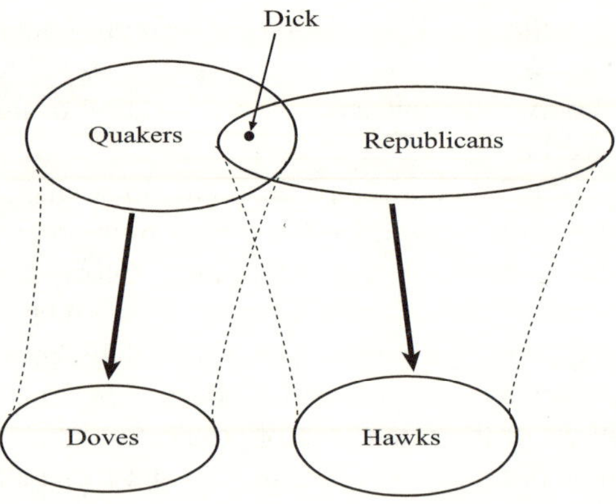

Figure 6.1 Regularity chains for an argument containing a Nixon Diamond

The machinery of FOL allows all sorts of lengthenings of arguments (for instance, by adding tautologies). Adding such irrelevant material to an argument would destroy the possibility of comparing the specificities of arguments sensibly using the length of the chains of argument. In the full-blown statement of the languages, we defined minimal regularity chains, those for which the irrelevant first-order part is cut out. Once the regularity chains are stated in minimal form, specificities can be compared sensibly. Consider the two regularity chains: $\Gamma = \langle \gamma_1, \gamma_2, \ldots, \gamma_k \rangle$ and $\Gamma' = \langle \gamma'_1, \gamma'_2, \ldots, \gamma'_l \rangle$. Comparison of the first elements in different chains tells only whether the arguments concern the same subject. Unless all of the chains have identical first elements ($\gamma_1 = \gamma'_1$ in the case under discussion), comparing them does not make sense. If the first elements are the same, comparison begins with the second elements in the chains. If $\gamma_2 \sqsubseteq_W \gamma'_2$ and $\neg(\gamma'_2 \sqsubseteq_W \gamma_2)$, then Γ is more specific. If these relations are reversed, then Γ' is more specific. If the two sets are incomparable, then specificity cannot be assessed and no conclusions can be drawn. If the sets are comparable and the specificities are the same (e.g., $\gamma_2 = \gamma'_2$), then compare the specificities of the third elements, and so on.

Consider the semantics for the presumably-implies connective. Note that two-element chains can always be constructed for logically true statements, making $\mathfrak{P}$ tests succeed for them.[12] Such a first-order argument (a two-element chain) will always overrule tentative arguments (minimal chains having at least three elements).

The key element in the semantics for this language concerns the truth condition for sentences involving $\mathfrak{P}$. The presumably-implies relation $\mathfrak{P}\,\bar{x}[\phi(\bar{x}) \rightarrow \psi(\bar{x})]$ is true in a stage of a theory if (1) there exist minimal positive two-element ϕ–ψ chains (which means that the relationship is a strict, first-order, rule), or (2) there exist minimal positive ϕ–ψ chains, and, if there also exist minimal negative ϕ–ψ chains, then all minimal positive chains must be more specific than all minimal negative chains. The statement is false otherwise.

---

[12] A sentence is said to be logically true if there is no interpretation that would make it false in any possible world.

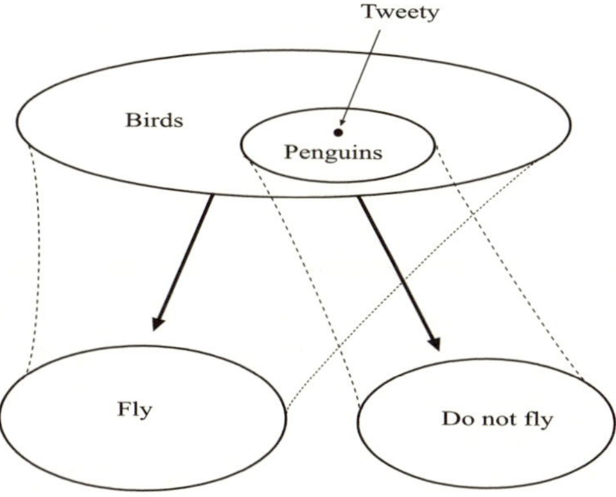

Figure 6.2 Regularity chains for an argument subject to the Penguin Principle

Figure 6.1 illustrates a pair of ϕ–ψ regularity chains that produce a so-called *Nixon Diamond.* The first element in each chain tells the subject of the argument: "Dick." The second elements in the chains are the intensions of "Quaker" and "Republican," and the third elements are the intensions of "dove" and "hawk." The "funnels" connecting the intensions represent the regularities that connect the complex properties—they illustrate that a causal story is modeled as an ordered pair of intensions. The heavy arrows represent the flow of the arguments, linking antecedents to consequents. Here the two regularity chains differ in their implications: the one on the left side of the figure leads to the conclusion "Dick is a dove" and the one on the right of the figure leads to the opposite conclusion (assuming that "hawk" is the negation of "dove"). The two chains have the same length and their specificity cannot be compared (neither "Quakers" nor "Republicans" is a proper subset of the other). Therefore, no conclusion is warranted.

Figure 6.2 illustrates the *Penguin Principle* for ϕ–ψ regularity chains. The situation is just as in figure 6.1 except that the intension of "Penguin" is a proper subset of the intension of "Bird." In other words, the argument represented in the chain on the right side of the figure is more specific than the opposing argument on the left. Therefore, we conclude "Tweety does not fly."

Minimality

Theoretical argumentation takes definitions and premises (stated as strict rules and causal stories) and seeks to establish consequences (theorems). A semantic consequence relation is needed to make sense of such argumentation. In the formal statement of the approach we defined a *regularity-minimal* stage of a theory. Loosely speaking, this refers to a version of the theory for which $\mathbf{c}$ is stripped down to the bare minimum needed to make true all of the sentences of the theory expressing causal stories. In our applications, it suffices to regard the regularity-minimal stage of the theory as the collection of the premises of the theory (and nothing else). With this restriction, we can state the consequence relation as follows: the sentence ϕ is a consequence of a stage of theory if and only if all of the regularity-minimal stages of the theory make ϕ true.

6.5 A METARULE FOR CHAINING PROBABILISTIC ARGUMENTS

In the course of our logical formalization attempts we use premises from a variety of sources. We characterize concepts by definitions and meaning postulates; we state theoretical considerations, theory-dependent insights, as postulates; we borrowed from mathematics, mostly from probability theory and set theory; and we need auxiliary assumptions to complete the derivations of some propositions. The eclectic nature of these premises suggests that we might need some further premises to smooth the transitions among some of these components. There is indeed a challenge in connecting the probabilistic component to the nonmonotonic reasoning.

As we have been discussing, rules with exceptions are represented as formulas quantified by the "normally" quantifier:

$$\mathfrak{N}\, q\, [\phi(q) \rightarrow \psi(q)].$$

In general, ϕ and ψ can be either predicates or functions.

In many of the arguments that we develop, both the antecedents and consequents in these rules-with-exceptions are *random variables.* We think that random variables play different roles in the two positions. The intuitions embedded in the causal stories tell what should normally be the case for the relationship between some factual condition and the *expectation* of the random variable in the consequent position. In other words, the rules with exceptions are rules for determining the average behavior of these random variables. On the other hand, it does not make sense to us to claim that the expectation of a random variable plays a causal role. Instead, the terms in the antecedent in these probabilistic causal stories should be the factual situation—the *realizations* of the relevant random variables. These considerations lead us to form probabilistic causal stories in our theories in the following general form:

$$\mathfrak{N}\, q, q'\, [(\phi(q) < \phi(q')) \rightarrow (\mathrm{E}(\psi(q)) < \mathrm{E}(\psi(q')))];$$

and

$$\mathfrak{N}\, q, q'\, [(\psi(q) < \psi(q')) \rightarrow (\mathrm{E}(\chi(q)) < \mathrm{E}(\chi(q')))].$$

We want to use a "cut rule" here to obtain an implication (theorem) that relates ϕ to $\mathrm{E}(\chi)$. But this is problematic in the nonmonotonic machinery described to this point. This is because we have to form and compare chains of such rules. Chaining the two foregoing formulas is possible only if the intension of $\psi(q) < \psi(q')$ is a (not necessarily proper) subset of the intension of $\mathrm{E}(\psi(q)) < \mathrm{E}(\psi(q'))$. Because these are different types of formulas (one is about the actual values or realizations and the other is about the expected values), they cannot be linked in a chain directly. In what follows we discuss a schema that allows us to establish an indirect linkage.

For the sake of the argument assume that the only information about the values of a random variable at two different positions (for two different objects) is that the expected value for one is smaller than the expected value for the other, i.e., $\mathrm{E}(\psi(q)) < \mathrm{E}(\psi(q'))$. Under these circumstances it is sensible to expect that presumably $\psi(q) < \psi(q')$. In other words,

$$\mathfrak{P}\, q, q' \, [(\mathrm{E}(\psi(q)) < \mathrm{E}(\psi(q'))) \rightarrow (\psi(q) < \psi(q'))].$$

To make sure that this conclusion is available when we need it, we add the following metaschema to our formal assumptions:[13]

$$\mathfrak{A}\, q, q' \, [(\mathrm{E}(\psi(q)) < \mathrm{E}(\psi(q'))) \rightarrow (\psi(q) < \psi(q'))].$$

We call this formula (part of) a schema rather than a postulate because it summarizes (potentially) infinitely many assumptions, depending on what random variables one substitutes for ψ. Instantiations of this schema allow us to form (indirect) linkages between formulas as follows. Suppose that we have available in a theory stage the following pair of causal stories

$$\mathfrak{N}\, q, q' \, [(\phi(q) < \phi(q')) \rightarrow (\mathrm{E}(\psi(q)) < \mathrm{E}(\psi(q')))],$$
$$\mathfrak{N}\, q, q' \, [(\psi(q) < \psi(q')) \rightarrow (\mathrm{E}(\chi(q)) < \mathrm{E}(\chi(q')))].$$

By "plugging in" the formula schema

$$\mathfrak{A}\, q, q' \, [(\mathrm{E}(\psi(q)) < \mathrm{E}(\psi(q'))) \rightarrow (\psi(q) < \psi(q'))],$$

we obtain the implication

$$\mathfrak{P}\, q, q' \, [(\phi(q) < \phi(q')) \rightarrow (\mathrm{E}(\eta(q)) < \mathrm{E}(\eta(q')))].$$

This schema for chaining probabilistic formulas is a metaschema. It makes no empirical or substantive claim. Nor does it require any empirical justification. It is just a bolt needed to make our nonmonotonic machinery tick.

6.6 CLOSEST-POSSIBLE-WORLDS CONSTRUCTION

The notion of possible worlds plays another role in our modeling strategy. Many postulates and theorems have the form that two or more causal factors jointly imply some outcome (consequent). In some analyses, we want to "hold constant" all but one of the causal influences and analyze the effect of the isolated causal factor. In effect, we want to construct a qualitative version of a partial derivative. It turns out that the image of closest-possible worlds provides a way to do so.

The relevant theory in logic concerns what are called *counterfactual conditionals.* A conditional sentence is called a counterfactual if the antecedent of the sentence is presupposed to be false. A typical construction that leads to counterfactuals is the following:

[13]Because this assumption is the only type of rule where the antecedent of the rule compares expected values of a random variable it is easy to see that the impact of this schema is the same as that of

$$\mathfrak{N} q, q' \, [(\mathrm{E}(\psi(q)) < \mathrm{E}(\psi(q'))) \rightarrow (\psi(q) < \psi(q'))].$$

* "Although A is not true,[14] had A been the case, then B would happen."

The material implication ($\rightarrow$) of classical FOL does not adequately express this type of conditionality. This is because a sentence like * is true only if A is false in the actual world, a condition that makes "$A \rightarrow B$" logically true. However, some counterfactual conditionals are false. This indicates that the connective in * is not material implication. Instead it is (say) $\twoheadrightarrow$, whose semantics must differ from the semantics of $\rightarrow$. David Lewis (1973), in his seminal book *Counterfactuals,* argued that the natural analysis of the meaning of sentences like * includes the following insights:

- A is not true in the actual world; and
- if one moved to a world where A was true but was otherwise as similar to the actual world w as possible, then B would turn out to be true in that world.

In other words, the truth conditions for $\twoheadrightarrow$ are as follows: a sentence like * is true in the actual world w if A is false in w, and B is true in (all) the worlds where A is true and are the closest w.

This modeling technique turned out to be useful for providing formal accounts of actions and causal relations as well (see the review by Menzies 2001). Actions can be characterized by the (intended and unintended) changes that they bring about. The unavoidable changes that follow an action can be interpreted as if the action had caused them. Here the key modeling puzzle is how to identify formally the unavoidable changes. The closest-possible-world approach offers a solution. If we want to identify the actual consequences of achieving A, then A must be true in the actual world w. Next we look at the closest alternatives of the actual world w, i.e., the worlds that are the closest to w among those worlds that in which A is true. All of the propositions that were false in the actual world w but happen to be true in all of the closest A-alternatives of w are the unavoidable consequences of A in the actual world.

In this book, we model some of causal stories in a similar style. On the one hand, we try to avoid using new logical constants, such as $\twoheadrightarrow$, while on the other we try to take advantage of Lewis' intuition. To achieve this we use functions with several variables. These variables capture all of the relevant aspects of the situation. Changes are modeled as changes in the values of few, typically one, of these variables. The effect of the change is modeled by the change in the value of one argument of the function. The effect of the change is modeled by the change in the value of the function. In the simplest setup, the only relevant (intended) change concerns the values of the chosen variable. The minimality of the change is expressed by the fact that the values of all the other variables are the same.

More complicated cases arise in our theory of the niche (Chapters 8–10). In these analyses, we define explicitly the closest alternatives that satisfy all the constraints.

---

[14] In the literature of the counterfactual conditionals the falsity of the antecedent is typically presumed rather than explicitly claimed. For the sake of simplicity, we ignore this subtlety here. This allows us to speak of the truth conditions of the counterfactual conditionals rather than of the conditions of their meaningfulness.

It is important to note that this modeling strategy was made feasible by the choice of logic. As we noted above, our nonmonotonic logic excludes modus tollens and contraposition as valid logical principles, i.e., $\{(A \rightarrow B), \neg B\} \not\Rightarrow \neg A$ and $\{(A \rightarrow B)\} \not\Rightarrow (\neg B \rightarrow \neg A)$ do not hold. Had these principles been valid, the closest-possible-worlds modeling technique could lead to unwanted conclusions. For example, one causal story could establish a monotonic relationship between the values of one of the variables and the value of the function, and another causal story could establish a monotonic relationship between the values of another variable and the value of the function. These two premises in a classical FOL would lead to the conclusion that there is a weak monotonic relationship between the values of these two variables, even though this claim could be both empirically and theoretically unjustified. In our nonmonotonic logic, a Nixon Diamond blocks the derivation of the undesirable conclusions.

6.7 FALSIFICATION

Although the impact of developments in the philosophy of science on the actual development of scientific fields is normally quite questionable, there are some exceptions. Karl Popper's (1959) claim that all meaningful empirical theories must be open to empirical test had a lasting, positive impact. Popper argued that theories that cannot potentially be defeated by any critical empirical test cannot be meaningful. A reconstruction of his argument might go as follows:

- Meaningful empirical theories must have general applicability.
- To gain general applicability, empirical theories should contain some general considerations.
- From a formal point of view, such general considerations can be expressed as universally quantified sentences (formulas).
- No universally quantified formula can be empirically proven, provided that the universe of discourse is potentially infinite.
- Although universally quantified formulas cannot be verified empirically, they can well be falsified empirically. If they are not (yet) falsified, then they might have some value; already falsified formulas are useless.
- The status of being "not-yet falsified" is socially meaningful when a theory has survived repeated, serious falsification attempts.
- Repeated and serious falsification attempts are well motivated only for falsifiable theories.
- Finding a false statement in a theory defeats the theory; and it has to be replaced by a new theory that has at least the same explanatory power and is composed of sentences that are not yet falsified.

- If an empirical theory is unfalsifiable, then its not-yet-falsified status is meaningless, and so is the theory.

This argument appears to be convincing and provides a high moral status for the scientific enterprise. It suggests that building an empirical theory is a daring exercise, involving risks of defeat. On the other hand, the critical issue is to decide the source of the social meaningfulness of the not-yet-falsified empirical theories. You know what an empirical theory means if you know what falsification attempts it survived. This high moral status (if one decided to believe in it) did not make it any easier to recognize that the argument leaks at two different points, at least. These leaks can best be characterized by some empirically false premises in the argument above. The two premises we debate are:

- From a formal point of view, such general considerations can be expressed with universally quantified sentences.

- Finding any false statement in a theory means that the entire theory is defeated and has to be replaced by one that has at least the same explanatory power and is made of not-yet-falsified sentences.

We show that the first of these claims is false and that the second is not universally true either. Once we prune these two premises from the argument, the falsifiability criterion for any meaningful empirical theory can no longer be derived in its original form. Nonetheless, we argue that a more general form of the criterion is still justified: Only risk taking and exposure to critical challenges yield meaningful empirical theories. But risks do not come in one form only: theories might (and often do) fail due to their overwhelming intricacy, a feature they might acquire as a response to critical challenges. Sets of sentences whose overwhelming intricacy makes them immune to empirical test would not make meaningful empirical theories.

Critical Challenges to Empirical Theories

Although rules-with-exceptions might be true or false, their truth and falsity cannot be expressed in terms of the truth and falsity of the corresponding sentences about individual instances. The rules are false if the regularities that they express are not present in the world. If one can show that indeed this is the case, then the theory is falsified. It should be discarded, as Popper argued. Think, for example, of the generalization (generally accepted in eighteenth-century science): "In the case of burning, phlogiston leaves the burning material." This statement happens to be false; but the proof of its falsity did (and could) not happen by finding counterexamples, i.e., cases of burning where phlogiston did not leave the burning material (because there is no such thing as phlogiston). Yet proving the *absence* of a regularity is not any easier than proving its *presence*.

Predictions based on generic rules might turn out to be false. Because predictions can pertain to individual instances, proving the falsity of such predictions might be an easier task. But even when such a move succeeds, the theory is not discarded, and it should not be. False predictions indicate that there are exceptions to the regularities, but that is not unexpected. Yet finding the actual exceptions that involve more than accidents—what Popper (1959) called "reproducible" effects—can have a serious impact on the theory. The discovery of exceptions indicates that the set of explanatory principles provided by the theory is incomplete. The theory has to be extended with causal considerations that help to construct *more specific* arguments concerning the individual instance in question.

Successful falsification attempts sometimes point out that the theory is incomplete in a particular respect. Other types of objections might reveal the same information. For instance, a theory might fail to yield a prediction about a question even though the question is expressible in the language of the theory and sits within the intended applicability domain of the theory.

Yet another way to evaluate a theory is to try to figure out if it can generate explanations for observed patterns. The required explanation might not be available from the existing premises for two reasons. First, the desiderata in the core of the theory might not concern the issue; and the set of causal stories likely would not supply the principles required to provide an explanation. In such a case, the failure to explain a pattern would be irrelevant to the theory. The required explanation might have never been in the intended application domain of the theory.

Second, it might happen that an earlier phase of a theory successfully explains the fact in question but that further development of the theory provided equally specific arguments (or arguments with incomparable specificity) that overrule (or block) the rule chain that explained the fact. In such a case, the fact lies within the intended applicability domain and the failure to predict is relevant. The only successful response would be to add new, more specific explanatory principles to provide the explanation.

The tests and objections that we discussed so far might lead to further theory development; but they do not bring down the theory. In normal scientific activity, even successful challenges rarely generate scientific revolutions (Kuhn 1962). How and when would scientific revolutions happen if theory building is viewed as a nonmonotonic process?

Successful challenges demand that an empirical theory be developed further: new explanatory principles must be added as premises of the theory. Although these steps appear to be peaceful enough, they can have an important side effect. The adoption of new explanatory principles typically gets forced in the high(er) specificity area. Such amendments make a theory more *intricate.* If some explanations that were available in a less-developed phase of a theory vanish as a theory develops, it is unavoidable to consider all of the premises in all inferences. The more explanatory principles that must be considered, the more intricate is the theory. Increasing intricacy can paralyze a line of theory. Drawing conclusions gets more and more difficult. The theory becomes less and less useful.

At the same time, responding to critical objections usually requires increasing the complexity of a theory, which makes even the proponents of the theory more and more frustrated. The time becomes ripe for abandoning the theory and trying to find a replacement.

Although most scientific activities intend to make contributions to normal science, they can, and occasionally do, lead to scientific revolutions. It seems that abandoned scientific theories are difficult to find without searches of the archival journals; they are easily forgotten. We believe that the cases that are well documented show that overwhelming intricacy better describes how and why they were abandoned than does Popper's falsification idea. In *Conjectures and Refutations,* Popper (1963) admitted that the replacement of the Ptolemaic system by the Copernican system was not quite on the bases on empirical evidence that favored the later system. Quite the contrary. Copernicus was wrong, because the Earth (and the other planets) did not move on a circular path around the sun but rather on an elliptical trajectory. This (relatively minor) difference made the predictions of the Ptolemaic system superior to those of Copernicus. But the later system was simple, while the former was overwhelmingly intricate.

Toward Falsification of a Theory in Flux

We accept the view that scientific theories ought to be falsifiable. We also recognize that falsifiability is problematic for theories developed in the language we have designed because the key explanatory principles can be—and usually are—stated as rules-with-exceptions. How can an argument be falsified if exceptions are expected? Surely a theory in flux, as we defined it, cannot be falsified directly by finding a pattern of counterexamples. So we propose an indirect strategy that involves "freezing" a theory in flux to provide a set of (restricted) first-order sentences to be subject to empirical testing in the usual sense, meaning that failures of tests are regarded as damaging to the theoretical program.

The idea of freezing a theory in flux is to capture the meaningful theorems of the current stage of the theory in first-order sentences. In general, specificity orderings will have overridden certain causal stories for certain classes of objects. For instance, in formulating a Stinchcombean theory of age dependence in organizational mortality, we might have claimed that populations whose members are large at the time of founding pose exceptions to the causal story. Knowing that a particular population is one in which young members are generally large provides more specific information than knowing that an object is an arbitrary population of organizations. According to the metarule that more specific information overrules less specific information, we would have a rule chain that states that the liability of newness does not (presumably) hold for populations whose young members are large. This stands alongside another rule chain that says that we ought to expect the liability of newness to hold if all that we know is that an entity is a population of organizations. The natural translation of these two nonmonotonic theorems into first-order sentences uses (universally quantified) scope restrictions. This kind of construction ensures that each of the statements to be tested has a counterpart in the underlying theory in flux. This means that tests of these theorems bear directly on the theory.

Once the stage of a theory has been frozen, testing and inference can proceed as usual. (Note that the presence of auxiliary assumptions in the theory stage means that the testing faces the problem identified by Pierre Duhem (1991 [1906]): the tests are joint tests of the combination of the persistent causal claims in the core of the theory and the auxiliary assumptions.) A theory in flux gains empirical credibility if its frozen theorems survive falsification attempts. A theory in flux that does not fare so well needs to be repaired or discarded.

The overall theory-building strategy sets limits on what kinds of operations can be made on the frozen sentences. In particular, some logical operations that would be permissible if the sentences came from a first-order theory should not be allowed in this freezing-and-testing strategy. For instance, the nonmonotonic logic we sketched here precludes use of two argumentation schemata: contraposition and modus tollens. So first-order formulas constructed by applying these operations will not have counterparts in the theory in flux. These considerations suggest that only frozen versions of theorems in the stage of the theory in flux ought to be tested.

Although the material in this chapter is fairly formal by social-science standards, it does not provide the full technical details needed to assess the soundness of the language and its consequence relation. The formal definitions can be found in Pólos and Hannan (2004). The next chapter provides an extended and heavily commented application of this logic to a sociological problem and might give a more tangible sense of the potential value of the logic for the social sciences.

Chapter Seven

Integrating Theories of Age Dependence

The formal logic for theory building presented in the previous chapters might be interesting for its own sake. But does it contribute to our understanding of sociological processes? Here we try to show that it does in the context of theory and research on age dependence in the organizational mortality.[1]

Organization theory possesses too many plausible stories when it comes to the relation of age and mortality. The history of studies of the relationship between organizational age and the probability of mortality goes back three-quarters of a century. Several waves of descriptive studies revealed that young organizations generally face a higher risk of mortality than do older ones (Carroll and Hannan 2000: 36–9). Little, if any, theoretical interpretation was developed for the pattern before the classic paper by Stinchcombe (1965).

Stinchcombe offered four different explanations for the greater vulnerability of young organizations. According to the first of these, new organizations normally lack the technical and social skills needed for smooth functioning. In old organizations members could have learned the required skills and built up loyalty to the organization. They know how to make things happen instead of waiting to be told what to do. Their skills and loyalty can be transferred to new members too. In contrast, new organizations have to depend on general skills in the society at large.

The second argument says that organizations must invent roles, relationships between roles, and structures of rewards and sanctions. In the absence of these roles and structures, organizations cannot function smoothly and reliably. Therefore, new organizations must learn them while in operation. The need for learning-by-doing lowers the performance of young organizations.

Stinchcombe also argued social relations in new organizations often involve relations of strangers. One cannot know for sure if jobs will be completed on time and budget, according to the specifications. In the absence of such knowledge, new organizations face more uncertainty then old ones. Compensating for such uncertainties takes away vital resources from primary processes, and this makes younger organizations more vulnerable than older organizations.

The fourth argument concerns embeddedness. Young organizations normally lack strong social ties with external constituencies. The lack of strong ties makes it harder to mobilize resources and ward off attacks.

All four arguments point in the same direction, therefore, the logical relationship between them is unproblematic. Although each argument would allow for exceptions, very few organizations can escape having at least one of these arguments

[1]Portions of this chapter are adapted from Pólos and Hannan (2002, 2004).

apply to them. In logical terms, Stinchcombe presented four sets of premises and the argument ultimately is as follows: if any of the four sets is applicable to a population of organizations, then the population shows the liability of newness.

Empirical studies exposed the liability-of-newness theorem to empirical testing in many populations of organizations. Much early research found supporting evidence (Carroll and Hannan (2000) provide a review) and made relevant the arguments that, from one postulate-set or another, pointed toward negative age dependence.

Glenn Carroll and Paul Huo's (1988) investigation of the life chances of the local chapters of the Knights of Labor reported that their mortality rates were low at very young ages, rose with subsequent aging, and then began to fall monotonically with further aging. However, they did not propose an explanation for this pattern. Shortly thereafter, two articles appeared that argued that the hazard of mortality peaks not at founding but sometime later (Brüderl and Schüssler 1990; Fichman and Levinthal 1991). The so-called liability of adolescence arises from an overlay of an endowment period (of random length) on the processes described by Stinchcombe. A well-endowed organization can maintain its structures and members even if it cannot continually mobilize resources from the environment.

Endowments matter most in the first months and years of operation. Endowments depreciate unless replenished by continuing positive flows of material and social resources from the environment. Until an endowment has been depleted, the organization's risk of mortality is low. Once the endowment gets exhausted, the risk of mortality jumps. The implications for age dependence in mortality rates are clear. At a given level of endowment, the mortality rate remains low during the period of depletion, and it jumps afterward. That is, mortality rates rise with age initially and then decline. The usual formulation of this idea (as in Brüderl, Preisendörfer, and Ziegler 1996) regards the level of endowment as an unobservable random variable, which makes the length of the period of exhaustion also an unobservable random variable. If the distribution of endowments is (roughly) continuous, one will observe that the hazard of mortality rises smoothly from zero to a peak (the point of exhaustion for the best-endowed organizations).

At this stage of theory development something logically interesting happened: theorists used this idea of overlaying two processes. What does this overlaying mean in logical terms? If the premises put together by Stinchcombe are empirically justified, they imply the liability of newness, i.e., high mortality hazard, for young organizations. Adding more premises that overlay the endowment argument on the Stinchcombe processes would not invalidate the liability of newness. It does, however, produce inconsistency. For such an overlaying to work, the logical principle that adding more premises to the existing set of premises does not invalidate the conclusion—the principle of monotonicity—has to be sacrificed. If sociologists believe that such an overlaying could work, they implicitly departed from classical first-order logic and engaged in a pattern of nonmonotonic reasoning.

Even such a major sacrifice did not discourage research. In fact, a further development leads to a conclusion opposite to Stinchcombe's. This is the theory of obsolescence. According to this theory, a preselection process guarantees that normally only those organizations manage to get founded that are (at founding) aligned with the environment. Among other things this means that at least some typical members of the audience for the organization find the offer appealing. As time passes, the taste of the audience drifts, but the organization remains imprinted by the initial environment.

Although the drift might be slow and the organization might make an effort to keep pace with this environmental drift, the alignment tends to disappear after a certain period due to the inertia of imprinted properties: the organization becomes obsolete or, more precisely starts to be seen as obsolete. Offers from an obsolete organization no longer appeal to typical members of the audience. The organization has to survive on the resources it manages to generate by appealing to atypical members of the audience. Such a life on the fringe is not at all a secure life, in fact the mortality hazard jumps when an organization reaches the age of perceived obsolescence and further declines with age.

Stinchcombe (1965: 153–69) himself laid the foundations for such an imprinting argument, but he failed to recognize its implications for the relationship between age and mortality. As far as we can tell, this connection was made first by Carroll (1983), who argued that imprinting leads to obsolescence if environments drift over time. Given such drifting, organizations locked into the arrangements that prevailed at their times of founding will be less and less well aligned with later environments. In such a scenario, age serves as a surrogate for the magnitude of drift experienced over an organization's lifetime.

The dilemma is that both the theory of obsolescence and the theory of the liability of newness are based on sensible and justified considerations. However, they do not fit together into one theory if the logic is classical first-order logic. In what follows we show that a nonmonotonic logic allows for a happier marriage.

The net consequence of the multiplicity of conflicting stories is that we have no basis for prediction, no way to predict what pattern of age dependence should be expected in a yet-unstudied population of organizations.

The theoretical predicament is sharpened by the fact that systematic empirical studies support each line of reasoning. It seems hard to imagine that the theoretical conflicts will be resolved through further empirical replication. This situation calls for rebuilding the theoretical foundations.

7.1 CAPABILITY AND ENDOWMENT

We want to restrict comparisons to organizations that belong to the same population. Now population enters more directly into the argument, because we need to introduce population-specific parameters. Therefore, we make the notation for organizations and populations explicit here. The predicate $\text{CLASS}(l, t)$ tells that l is the label of a class of organizations at time t. (Chapter 3 defined a class and told what it means to be a member of a class; we do not represent the dependence of the population on the audience in the notation at this point.) The other relevant sorts of variables are organizations. We use an informal sorting of the variables. Specifically, we restrict the variable l to refer to a label, x to point to an organization, and t to point to a moment in time.

Before we launch into the formalization, we must discuss a general methodological issue that arises due to the fuzziness that we introduced into the definitions of classes, categories, and populations. The intuitions on which prior theory and research built came from considering classical sets, as we discussed in the chapters in Part I. Once we generalize the membership functions to allow intermediate grades of membership (those between full membership and nonmembership), we loose our bearings. Do the intuitions apply to comparisons of entities with very different grades of membership in a population? For instance, the classic liability of newness implies that an older member of a population has a lower hazard of mortality than a younger one. Would we still claim that this is the expectation of the theory for a comparison of an older organization with low GoM with a young one with high GoM? We do not think that such an expectation would be well founded. After all, we lack theory and research that addresses such comparisons.

The most conservative modeling strategy would assume that the causal stories from previous theory and research ought to be restricted to apply only to populations with a contrast of unity for all audience-segment members, because then the population is effectively a classical set for each relevant actor. We worry that this stance will reduce the scope of applicability of the theory too much—a single exceptional case (either producer or audience member) would be enough to gainsay applicability. Instead, we suggest that the theory applies so long as the average contrast of the population is high. But how high is "high enough"? Unfortunately, we do not yet know the answer to this question. We think that it will take a lot of work by the research community to provide even a rough answer. Instead of trying to concoct an answer, we use a threshold construction and admit the threshold is now unknown (but potentially knowable).

We implement the threshold idea as follows.

Definition 7.1 (Comembership in a prominent (high-contrast) population). *Let the predicate* $\text{M}(l, x, t)$ *tell that* x *has a nonzero membership in the organizational population labeled* l*:*

$$\text{M}(l, x, t) \leftrightarrow \overline{\mu}_{p(l)}(x, t) > 0,$$

where $\overline{\mu}_{p(l)}(x, t)$ *denotes the average over the members of the audience segment of* $\mu_l(x, a, t)$*; and let the predicate* $\text{PR}(l, t)$ *tell that the population marked with the label* l *is prominent or distinct in the sense that the average contrast of the population to the audience segment exceeds a threshold:*

$$\text{PR}(l, t) \leftrightarrow \text{CLASS}(l, t) \wedge (\bar{c}_{p(l)}(t) > \mathfrak{m}).$$

The comembership of pair of entities in a prominent (or distinct) population at two (possibly different points in time) is defined as

$$\text{CM}(l, x, x', t, t') \leftrightarrow \text{M}(l, x, t) \wedge \text{M}(l, x', t') \wedge \text{PR}(l, t) \wedge \text{PR}(l, t').$$

Capability

As discussed above, a number of distinguishable arguments claim the liability of newness, a monotonic negative relationship between organizational age and the hazard of mortality. Because logical analyses of each argument yield similar results, we treat only one. We chose the argument about capability. In what follows, we usually quantify (nonmonotonically) over organizations and age intervals. Without stating this explicitly, we restrict attention to pairs of organizations in the same population.

We formalize the argument about age-related capabilities using the nonnegative function $cap(l, x, t)$. We represent organization x's age at time t with the nonnegative, real-valued function $a(x, t)$.

Postulate 7.1. *An organization's expected level of capability normally rises with age.*

$$\mathfrak{N}\,\mathbf{q}, \mathbf{q}'\,[\text{CM} \rightarrow (a \uparrow \text{E}(cap))(\mathbf{q}, \mathbf{q}')],$$

where $\mathbf{q}$ *is the indexed set of variables* $\langle l, t, x\rangle$ *and* $\mathbf{q}' = \langle l, t', x'\rangle$.[2] [Read: it is normally the case for all pairs of comembers of a prominent organizational population that the expected level of capability at an older age exceeds that at a younger age.]

According to the standard argument, capability lowers the hazard of mortality.[3]

Postulate 7.2. *Higher capability normally lowers the mortality hazard.*

$$\mathfrak{N}\,\mathbf{q}, \mathbf{q}'\,[\text{CM} \rightarrow (cap \downarrow \omega)(\mathbf{q}, \mathbf{q}')],$$

where $\mathbf{q}$ *and* $\mathbf{q}'$ *are as above.*

Now we want to connect these two postulates, which form a chain—except that the consequent in the first postulate is a comparison of *expected* levels of capability and the antecedent in the second postulate contains a comparison of the *actual* levels of capability. In Chapter 6, Section 5 we argued for a metarule that allows such formula to be chained. Using this metarule, we have the strong-form version of the liability of newness:

Theorem 7.1. *Mortality hazards presumably decline monotonically with age.*

$$\mathfrak{P}\,\mathbf{q}, \mathbf{q}'\,[\text{CM} \rightarrow (a \downarrow \omega)(\mathbf{q}, \mathbf{q}')],$$

where $\mathbf{q}$ *and* $\mathbf{q}'$ *are as above.*

Proof. In the nonmonotonic logic, establishing a proof involves constructing the most-specific rule chains that connect the antecedent and the consequent (Chapter 6). The regularity chains are constructed from the available definitions, postulates, strict rules, and auxiliary assumptions. If the most-specific regularity chain

---

[2]The full (official) version of this formula is

$$\mathfrak{N}\,l, t, t', x, x'\,[\text{CM}(l, x, x', t, t') \wedge (a(x, t) > a(x', t')) \\ \rightarrow (\text{E}(cap(l, x, t)) > \text{E}(cap(l, x', t')))].$$

[3]Perhaps we should note that a hazard is a limit in a probability distribution; an expected hazard would not be well defined.

supports the claim, then the theorem is proven. If among the most-specific regularity chains, some support both the claim and others support the counterclaim, then no conclusion is warranted—the claim is not a theorem. Therefore, we construct the most-specific regularity chains in sketching each proof.

The minimal rule chain comes from a simple cut rule applied to P7.1 (expected capability increases with age) and P7.2 (the hazard of mortality falls with capability). □

We treat this first stage as the default theory. Its postulates will be included in every subsequent theory stage. Notice that, because the (provisional) theorem T.7.1 applies to *all* age intervals, its scope of applicability is extremely unspecific. It will turn out that more specific postulates in the more developed theories usually override this theorem over at least part of the age range.

Endowments

The next development introduced endowments. Organizations often start with considerable seed capital, credit and commitment from others, and political support; these initial resources ensure that organization will exist for at least a minimal period of time. In formal terms, we call these initial resources an endowment, and we claim that an organization begins with a given level of endowment if it possesses immunity after founding, at least for a time. Endowments might be secured by entrepreneurs founding new firms, or obtained from the parent company by managers of a new unit of a firm diversifying laterally (de-alio producers).

In the formal theory, an endowment lasts as long as the initial immunity does. Furthermore, there is a monotonic relation between the level of endowment and the strength of immunity. The higher the level of endowment the stronger the immunity. Let $dow(l, x, t)$ be a real-valued function that tells the level of endowment of organization x in population l at age t; and let $im(l, x, t)$, also a real-valued function, give the level of immunity.

Auxiliary assumption 7.1 (Expected ending of endowment). *The expected age at the ending of endowment is constant within a prominent population of organizations.*

$$\mathfrak{A}\, l, t\, [\mathrm{PR}(l, t) \to \forall x\, [\sup\{a \mid (a(x, t) = a) \wedge (\mathrm{E}(dow(l, x, t)) > 0)\} = \mathfrak{e}_l]].$$

[Read: it is normally the case for every class that there is a ceiling such that the least upper bound (supremum)[4] of the age at which a member of the class retains a nonzero endowment equals the ceiling for the class.]

Note that $\mathfrak{e}_l$ is a population-specific constant. This auxiliary assumption both instantiates the premise that the expected age of ending of endowment is the same for all members of a population and also labels this expectation as $\mathfrak{e}_l$. Henceforth, we let $\mathfrak{e}_l$ denote the expected age of ending of endowment for members of the population labeled as l.

The standard argument holds that organizations normally spend down their initial endowments.

[4]We take the supremum of the set because we assume that age is a real-valued function.

Postulate 7.3. *Expected levels of endowments normally decline monotonically with age within endowment periods.*

$$\mathfrak{N}\,\mathbf{q},\mathbf{q}'\,[\text{CM} \wedge (a(x,t) < \mathfrak{e}_l) \wedge (a(x',t') < \mathfrak{e}_l) \rightarrow (a \downarrow \mathrm{E}(dow))(\mathbf{q},\mathbf{q}')\,],$$

where $\mathbf{q}$ *and* $\mathbf{q}'$ *are as above.*
[Read: normally, if the ages of two organizations (in a class) fall below the expected age of ending of endowment for the class, then the expected level of endowment is larger for the younger organization in the pair. Organizations at the same age have the same expected level of endowment. (Because the formula does not impose the restriction that x is different from x', these variables might refer to the same entity at different ages; therefore, the postulate holds for single organizations as well as for pairs of organizations.)]

Endowments provide immunity and immunity brings a reduction in mortality chances. These postulates hold both for comparisons of an organization at different ages (say before and after the ending of endowment) and for pairs of organizations (say with different levels of immunity).

Postulate 7.4. *During a period of endowment, a larger endowment normally yields a higher expected level of immunity.*

$$\mathfrak{N}\,\mathbf{q},\mathbf{q}'\,[\text{CM} \rightarrow (dow \uparrow \mathrm{E}(im))(\mathbf{q},\mathbf{q}')],$$

where $\mathbf{q}$ *and* $\mathbf{q}'$ *are as above.*

Postulate 7.5. *Mortality hazards presumably fall with increasing immunity.*

$$\mathfrak{N}\,\mathbf{q},\mathbf{q}'\,[\text{CM} \rightarrow (im \downarrow \omega)(\mathbf{q},\mathbf{q}')],$$

where $\mathbf{q}$ *and* $\mathbf{q}'$ *are as above.*

Theorem 7.2. *Mortality hazards presumably rise with age within periods of endowment.*

$$\mathfrak{P}\,l,t,t',x,x'\,[\text{CM}(l,x,x',t,t') \wedge (a(x,t) < a(x',t') < \mathfrak{e}_l) \rightarrow (\omega(x,t) < \omega(x',t'))].$$

Proof. The minimal rule chain arises from a cut rule applied to P7.3 (expected endowment falls with age), P7.4 (expected immunity rises with endowment), and P7.5 (the hazard of mortality falls with immunity) and also uses auxiliary assumption A7.1. □

Theorem 7.3. *Mortality hazards presumably are lower within periods of endowment than afterwards.*

$$\mathfrak{P}\,l,t,t',x,x'\,[\text{CM}(l,x,x',t,t') \wedge (a(x,t) < \mathfrak{e}_l \leq a(x',t')) \rightarrow (\omega(x,t) < \omega(x',t'))].$$

The structure of the proof parallels that for T7.2.

7.2 FIRST UNIFICATION ATTEMPT

At this stage, the two arguments run in opposite directions. According to the default liability-of-newness theory, the hazard declines over all ages; and, according to the endowment fragment, the hazard rises over the initial part of the age axis for endowed organizations and is lower during endowment than afterwards. How can these stories be reconciled?

The usual way of reconciling is to restrict the scope of applicability of *both* theories. Hannan (1998) posited that the default theory applies *only* to periods of nonendowment and (obviously) that the endowment theory applies *only* to periods of endowment. This makes the theory consistent, but it does not really unify. The scope-restriction approach seems less satisfying than alternatives that allow the default theory to apply at all ages.

A second classic alternative would formulate parametric models of the functions relating endowments and immunity to age and capability to age. If knowledge of such functions were available, we would gain precise functional forms of the relationship between age and the hazard under various parameter settings. That is, if available data would allow, one might be able to estimate how organizations of a given population gain capability as they age and similarly how their levels of endowment decline with age. Of course, in the case under discussion, no one has yet succeeded in establishing these relationships. The empirical work has not managed to measure endowments, immunity, or capabilities and, as a result, we have no empirical knowledge about even the functional forms of the underlying processes. What we know comes from studies that establish functional forms in the relationship of age and the hazard and from reasoning about the underlying mechanisms that likely generate these relationships. In other words, our empirical knowledge is partial, at best.

Suppose, contrary to fact, that the task of modeling the subprocesses had been accomplished. Even then, completing the modeling task is far from simple. There are two credible causal stories to tell about how endowment level and capability influence mortality hazards, ceteris paribus of course. One other element would be needed for exposing the combined theory to any reality check: a composition function that tells how to aggregate the contributions of the two component theories. [5] Such a full-blown theory could be used to predict patterns of age dependence in not-yet-studied populations, once it is known how levels of capability and endowment vary in those populations. Getting all the relevant knowledge components at the present state of the art in empirical research is close to impossible.

Therefore, it is worth trying to milk the existing parts of the theory, the available causal stories. Perhaps they play the crucial role in theorizing and therefore can serve as a reliable basis for predicting patterns of age dependence of mortality hazards in not-yet-studied populations. Of course, any such prediction will rely on knowledge of certain population characteristics, but these characteristics are less numerous and definitely less detailed than the functions that the full-blown theory

[5] To find such an aggregation function is not at all a trivial task. For example, the natural choice of addition as a way to combine opposing forces does not work: to get a zero sum of two functions at least one of which is positive one needs a negative component; but negative hazards do not make sense.

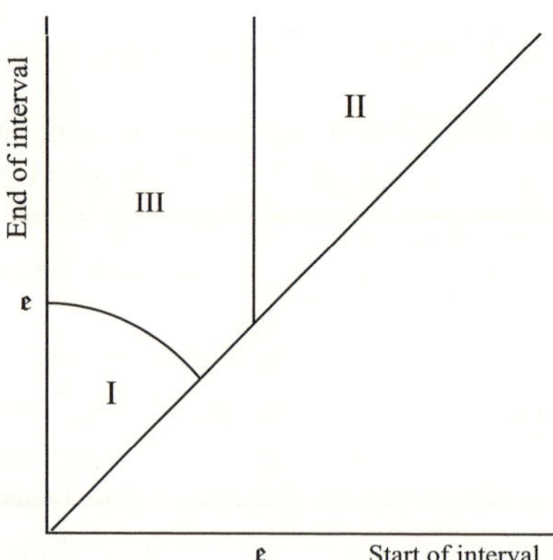

Figure 7.1 Classification of age intervals for translating the endowment theory (𝔢 denotes the expected age of ending of endowment in an unspecified population). Source: adapted from Pólos and Hannan (2002) ©American Sociological Association. Used with permission.

would require.

We have two theory fragments, two lines of argumentation. The subject of each theory fragment is the same: mortality hazards at the beginnings and ends of age intervals. The theory fragments offer opposing propositions. If the arguments are equally specific or have incomparable specificity, then we have a Nixon Diamond; and no theorems can be derived with the logic we use. We do see a straightforward specificity difference here. Endowment considerations apply only before the end of the endowment period while the default theory applies universally. In other words we have a penguin scenario.

So we go for the nonmonotonic approach. A key step in developing such a modeling procedure involves translating the verbal argument into a formal language that enables nonmonotonic testing. It is easy to realize that the claim "Endowment considerations apply only before the end of the endowment period" is not specific enough. Time intervals are extended objects, defined by starting and ending times. Figure 7.1 gives a two-dimensional representation. The horizontal dimension in each gives the start of the interval to be considered, and the vertical dimension gives the end of the interval. So an interval with given start and end points is represented as a point in this space. Because the ending must follow the beginning, only the region above the 45-degree line is meaningful.

We need to consider three cases. An age interval might lie completely within an endowment period, that is, both its start and end times lie before the end of the endowed period (𝔢), the region labeled type I in figure 7.1. Alternatively, the start and end points might lie after 𝔢 completely (type II in figure 7.1). Or the start point might lie before 𝔢 and end after it (type III in the figure). The sentence "Endowment considerations apply only before the end of the endowment period" says that endowment considerations apply to type-I intervals but not to type-II intervals. What about type-III intervals? Both possible translations (that the considerations apply and that they do not apply to type-III intervals) are consistent with the nonmonotonic approach; and in both cases we see a Penguin scenario. Still, one of them might be more in line with the concept of the mortality hazard than the other.

Let us consider first the option: "endowment considerations do not apply to type-III intervals" Under this restriction, only one line of argument applies: the default theory of a liability of newness. According to this theory, the hazard at the beginning of the interval exceeds the hazard at the end of the interval. Due to the immunity considerations, the hazard at the very beginning of an (endowed) organization's life is zero, according to the first translation of the key claim. Now take an interval that begins immediately after the founding of the organization and ends some time after the end of the endowment period. At the end of such a period, the hazard must be *negative.* Although this scenario is a logical possibility, it violates the definition of a hazard.[6] Therefore, this approach does not meet the most basic requirement for a modeling procedure for mortality. The second translation holds that endowment considerations do apply to type-III intervals. This translation does not generate the undesirable result of implying negative hazards. Moreover, we will show that it yields interesting results.

The decision to choose the second translation might engender an objection. Is the endowment rule really as specific as we claim? Note that this rule has implications beyond the ending of endowment in the sense that it predicts that hazards after endowment fall above those during endowment (in the case of type-II intervals). The answer is straightforward: the endowment rule is indeed more specific than the default. The default theory applies to any pair of ages. The endowment theory applies only to those age intervals that start *within* the endowment period (regardless of when they end). In particular, the endowment theory does not offer a prediction for an interval that begins after the endowment period. Hence, our claims about specificity are safe.

The first unification attempt uses all four postulates in the two fragments (according to the strategy we outlined) to yield:

Theorem 7.4. *Mortality hazards presumably rise with age over intervals that begin within expected endowment periods, that is, before age* $\mathfrak{e}_l$.

$$\mathfrak{P}\,\mathbf{q},\mathbf{q}'\,[\text{CM} \wedge (a(x,t) < \mathfrak{e}_l) \wedge (a(x',t') < \mathfrak{e}_l) \rightarrow (a \uparrow \omega)(\mathbf{q},\mathbf{q}')],$$

where $\mathbf{q}$ *and* $\mathbf{q}'$ *are as above.*

Proof. Figure 7.2 depicts the relevant rule chains. One begins with the intension defined for any pair of ages (drawn as the large ellipse at the top of the figure.) This rule chain leads to the conclusion of negative age dependence. The regularity chain drawn on the left emanates from the smaller (more specific) intension that applies only to those age intervals that begin before the expected ending of endowment. This regularity chain leads to a conclusion of positive age dependence. According to the nonmonotonic inference rule, the more specific argument holds.[7] □

---

[6]The hazard is defined as the ratio of two nonnegative functions, the density of the ending durations and the survivor function. Therefore, a negative value of a hazard entails a contradiction.

[7]It might seem from this example that the less-specific regularity chain should dominate because it is shorter. Yet, this is not the case. Length of chains matters for testing only when the chains being compared have the same specificity.

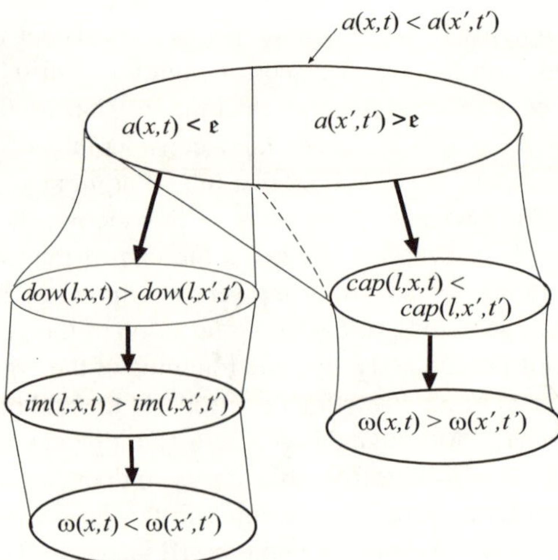

Figure 7.2 Regularity chains in the first unification: combining the first and second theory fragments. Source: adapted from Pólos and Hannan (2002) ©American Sociological Association. Used with permission.

Theorem 7.5. *Mortality hazards presumably decline with age after endowments are exhausted.*

$$\mathfrak{P}\, l, t, t', x, x' \,[\text{CM}(l, x, x', t, t') \wedge (\mathfrak{e}_l \leq a(x,t) < a(x',t')) \\ \rightarrow (\omega(x,t) > \omega(x',t'))].$$

Proof. Examine the most-specific regularity chains that connect the intension of $\mathfrak{e}_l \leq a(x,t) < a(x',t')$ with the intension of $\omega(x,t) > \omega(x',t')$. The antecedent falls only in the right-hand portion of the ellipse at the top of figure 7.2. So the only rule chain that applies is the less specific one (on the right of the figure), which leads to the conclusion of negative age dependence. □

A corollary also follows from T7.4 and T7.5: an overall tendency toward *positive* age dependence, as sketched in figure 7.3. We regard this result as somewhat surprising in the sense that organization theorists, in focusing on the different fragments, did not notice this implication. We shared this limited vision when we set out to construct a model, and we were pleasantly surprised to learn that the postulates as formulated in nonmonotonic logic delivered more than we had expected.

In retrospect, we can realize that the "surprise" arises because the standard endowment story has been told in terms of unobserved heterogeneity: organizations differ in endowments and, therefore, in the lengths of periods of immunity. If one assumes an appropriate mixing distribution on the lengths of immunity periods, then the initial rise in the *average* hazard in a population can be specified as due only to the monotonic decline with age of the fraction of organizations that still possess immunity. In this setup, the organizational-level hazard during immunity

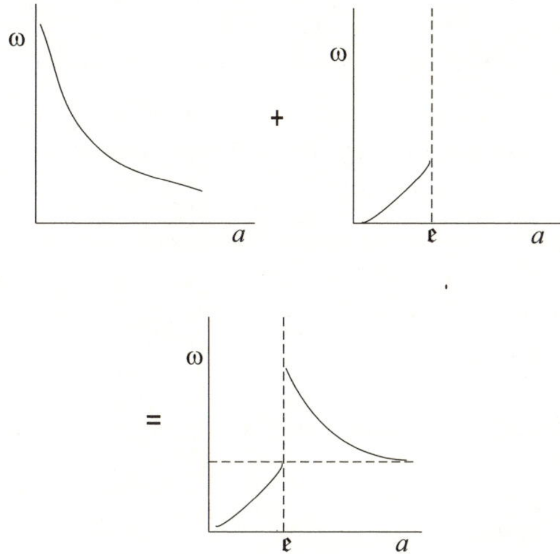

Figure 7.3 The pattern of age dependence of mortality according the first unification ($\mathfrak{e}$ denotes the age of ending of endowment in the unspecified population) Source: adapted from Pólos and Hannan 2002 ©American Sociological Association. Used with permission.

can be lower than at any subsequent age (as we assume), but the average hazard in the population can also decline from the peak.

Our model differs in two important ways. First, we do not mix organization-level and population-level arguments. Second, we introduce age-dependence in the level of endowment. So our endowment effect concerns more than just age-invariant unobserved heterogeneity. The effort to unify fragments in a consistent manner (at the same level of analysis) makes clear the importance of these subtle differences in assumptions.

7.3 OBSOLESCENCE

Now we turn to the other main branch of the theory, which concerns positive age dependence. We concentrate on the version that relies on assumptions about obsolescence. We assume that the total appeal of an organization's offer affects mortality chances. We also assume that organizations are relatively inert, that, in the long run, they cannot follow environmental changes in general and the changes in the tastes of the audience, in particular. So, after a period of given length, they will normally no longer appeal to typical members of their audience. After an organization passes this age, its appeal even to atypical members keeps declining.

The age of onset of obsolescence for an organization is defined as follows:

Definition 7.2. *An organization reaches the onset of perceived obsolescence (as a member of l) at the age when the sum of its expected appeal to typical members* *of the audience (for l) goes to zero and after which its expected total appeal (to typical and atypical members of the audience) keeps declining.*

$ob(l, x)$ is the age of the onset of obsolescence of organization x in population l if and only if $ob(l, x)$ is the smallest age for which the following conditions hold:

$$(1)\, \forall t\, [(a(x,t) \geq ob(l,x)) \rightarrow (\textstyle\sum_{y|\nu_{i(l)}(y,t)=1} \mathrm{E}(\widehat{ap}(l,x,y,t)) = 0)];$$

$$(2)\, \forall t, t'\, [(a(x,t') > a(x,t) \geq ob(l,x))$$

$$\rightarrow (\mathrm{E}(\widehat{Ap}(l,x,t')) < \mathrm{E}(\widehat{Ap}(l,x,t))) \vee (\mathrm{E}(\widehat{Ap}(l,x,t')) = 0 = \mathrm{E}(\widehat{Ap}(l,x,t)))],$$

where $\widehat{Ap}(l,x,t) = \sum_y \widehat{ap}(l,x,y,t)$.

Auxiliary assumption 7.2. *Mortality hazards fall with total intrinsic appeal.*

$$\mathfrak{A}\, \mathbf{q}, \mathbf{q}'\, [\textsc{cm} \rightarrow (\widehat{Ap} \downarrow \omega)(\mathbf{q}, \mathbf{q}')],$$

where $\mathbf{q}$ and $\mathbf{q}'$ are as above.

Note that this premise is stated as an auxiliary assumption. The reason for this is the following. Later, in Chapter 8, we introduce the concept of actual appeal, and we argue that actual appeal requires both intrinsic appeal and engagement. According to our argument in Chapter 9, mortality chances depend on actual appeal, not intrinsic appeal. Differences in intrinsic appeal have mortality implications only if differences in engagement do not run in an opposing direction. It is sensible to assume that obsolete organizations do not increase their level of engagement, so that assuming this auxiliary assumption now makes a couple of theorems easily derivable. Developments in Chapters 8 and 9 will allow us to derive a somewhat more precise theorem with the same general message even in the absence of this assumption.

We can derive general propositions about the impact of aging in populations if we take into account that the change of tastes of the audience is like a glacier, happens slowly, with more or less constant speed. With this imagery, it is straightforward that organizations who are members of the same population lose their intrinsic appeal at approximately the same age. This allows us to define the age of the onset of obsolescence now for the whole population.

Auxiliary assumption 7.3 (Expected onset of obsolescence). *The expected age at the onset of obsolescence is constant within a (prominent) population of organizations.*

$$\mathfrak{A}\, l, t\, [\textsc{pr}(l,t) \rightarrow \forall x, x'\, [\textsc{m}(l,x,t) \wedge \textsc{m}(l,x',t) \rightarrow (ob(l,x) = \mathfrak{o}_l = ob(l,x'))]].$$

where $\mathfrak{o}_l$ is a population specific constant.

These premises imply a pair of theorems.

Theorem 7.6. *Mortality hazards presumably are higher after the expected age of onset of obsolescence than before.*

$$\mathfrak{P}\, l, t, t', x, x'\, [\textsc{cm}(l,x,x',t,t') \wedge (a(x,t) < \mathfrak{o}_l \leq a(x',t'))$$

$$\rightarrow (\omega(x,t) < \omega(x',t'))].$$

Proof. The minimal rule chain uses D7.2, A7.1, A7,2, and A7.3. □

Theorem 7.7. *Mortality hazards presumably rise with age the expected age of onset of obsolescence in a (prominent) population.*

$$\mathfrak{P}\, l, t, t', x, x' \,[\textsc{cm}(l, x, x', t, t') \wedge (\mathfrak{o}_l \leq a(x,t) < a(x', t')) \\ \rightarrow (\omega(x,t) < \omega(x', t'))].$$

The proof parallels that for T7.6.

7.4 SECOND UNIFICATION ATTEMPT

The second unification uses all of the definitions and postulates in the three theory fragments. Again we confront the issue of what to do with intervals for which a specific rule applies to part but not all of an interval. (By definition, the default applies to the whole interval.) Again, we try to avoid having the specific rule made irrelevant. Therefore, we posit that whenever the more specific obsolescence rule applies to the end point of an age interval, the hazard increases over the interval.

In this third stage of the theory, the first theorem from the first unification remains valid. Nonetheless, the substantive reasoning behind the theorem has gotten more complex, because we have introduced an obsolescence process. We can illustrate the proof of this theorem in this unified context with a graphical representation of the argument. Note that all of the theorems concern age intervals. As we noted above, such intervals are two-dimensional objects. Figure 7.4 gives a two-dimensional representation of the domains of the various arguments. Consider this to be a "slice" from the set of possible worlds.[8] The panel on the left represents the case where endowment ends before obsolescence begins; the panel on the right represents the opposite case.

Theorem 7.8. *Mortality hazards presumably rise with age over intervals that begin within expected endowment periods.*

$$\mathfrak{P}\, l, t, t', x, x' \,[\textsc{cm}(l, x, x', t, t') \wedge (a(x,t) < \mathfrak{e}_l) \wedge (a(x,t) < a(x', t')) \\ \rightarrow (\omega(x,t) < \omega(x', t'))].$$

Proof. Intervals that fall in zone I in each panel of figure 7.4 fit the pure endowment story: the entire interval falls within an endowment period. The only rule more specific than the default that applies is "hazards increase within endowment periods." Therefore, the theorem holds in zone I. Zone III in the left panel of figure 7.4 and zone II in the right panel contain the intervals that start during endowment and terminate after the onset of obsolescence. Two specific rules apply: the endowment

[8]The complete proofs examine pairs of intensions. However, this substantive application allows these simpler proofs, because functions of the real line (the inequalities involving ages) are identical in every possible world. And, given a particular (named) organization in a particular population, the other functions in these theorems are also constants over possible worlds. Thus we can conduct nonmonotonic tests in using extensions, rather than with intensions.

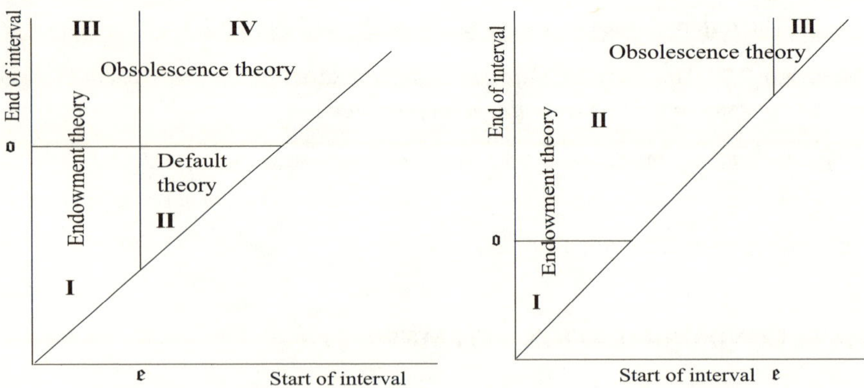

Figure 7.4 Domains of application of the various theory fragments in the second unification when $\mathfrak{e} < \mathfrak{o}$ (left panel) and when $\mathfrak{e} > \mathfrak{o}$ (right panel); $\mathfrak{e}$ denotes the age of ending of endowment in the unspecified population, and $\mathfrak{o}$ denotes the age of onset of obsolescence in that population. Source: adapted from Pólos and Hannan (2002) ©American Sociological Association. Used with permission.

and obsolescence rules. Both rules give the same conclusion: positive age dependence. So the theorem holds in this zone as well. Because only these zones are relevant to the theorem, it is proven. □

Theorem 7.9. *Mortality hazards presumably decrease over intervals that begin on or after the expected end of the endowment and terminate before the expected onset of obsolescence.*

$$\mathfrak{P}\, l, t, t', x, x' \, [\text{CM}(l, x, x', t, t') \wedge (\mathfrak{e}_l \leq a(x,t) < a(x',t') < \mathfrak{o}_l) \\ \rightarrow (\omega(x,t) > \omega(x',t'))].$$

Proof. Only the left panel of figure 7.4 is relevant; the intervals that fit the antecedent in this theorem fall in zone II. Here only the default theory applies. □

Theorem 7.10. *Mortality hazards presumably increase over intervals that end at or after the expected onset of obsolescence.*

$$\mathfrak{P}\, l, t, t', x, x' \, [\text{CM}(l, x, x', t, t') \wedge (a(x,t) < \mathfrak{o}_l \leq a(x',t')) \\ \rightarrow (\omega(x,t) < \omega(x',t'))].$$

Proof. This proof is similar to the proof of T7.9. In zone IV in the left panel and zone III in the right panel in figure 7.4, the only specific rule that applies is the obsolescence rule. This rule gives positive age dependence. In zone III on the left and zone II on the right, both the endowment and obsolescence rules apply. Both lead to the conclusion of positive age dependence. Thus the theorem goes through. □

Again we can derive implications about jumps and maxima in the process—but only when obsolescence follows the end of endowment.

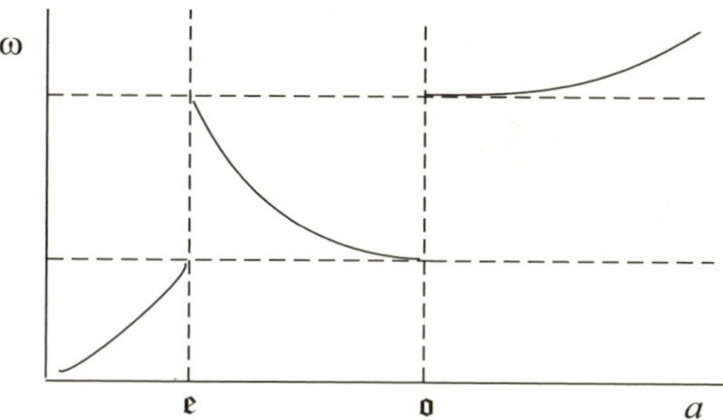

Figure 7.5 Age dependence of mortality according to the second unification for cases in which obsolescence strikes after the expected ending of endowment ($\mathfrak{e}$ denotes the age of ending of endowment in the unspecified population, and $\mathfrak{o}$ denotes the expected age of onset of obsolescence in that population). Source: adapted from Pólos and Hannan (2002) ©American Sociological Association. Used with permission.

Theorem 7.11. *When the expected onset of obsolescence does not occur after the expected end of endowment ($\mathfrak{o} \leq \mathfrak{e}$), an organization's mortality hazard presumably jumps at the end of endowment and at the onset of obsolescence.*

Our model of local behavior yields an unexpected global pattern: positive age dependence. Two cases need to be considered. In the simpler case, when obsolescence strikes before endowments end at the same time ($\mathfrak{e} \leq \mathfrak{o}$), then mortality hazards *increase* with age at all ages. In the left-hand panel of figure 7.4, the default theory (the only one that entails negative age dependence) gets overruled everywhere.

The second, more complex case, involves a delay between the ending of endowment and the onset of obsolescence ($\mathfrak{e} < \mathfrak{o}$). Inspection of the right panel of figure 7.4 reveals an age range in which the default does not get overridden (zone II). So there is a period in which the hazard falls with increasing aging. But due to (the argument supporting) T7.11, the hazard over this range must always exceed the maximum hazard during endowment. The overall pattern for this case has the general form shown in figure 7.5.

Under specific conditions, the general picture reproduces the patterns of age-dependence found in empirical research, as can be seen by consulting figure 7.5.

1. If the organizations in a population lack endowments and occupy environments that change so gradually that obsolescence never strikes, then the default never gets overridden: age dependence is presumably uniformly negative.

2. If the exhaustion of endowments does not occur within an observation period or obsolescence strikes before exhaustion of endowments, then age dependence is presumably uniformly positive.

3. If the organizations in a population are endowed and do not face obsoles-

cence, then the mortality hazard presumably peaks in adolescence.

4. If the organizations in a population are endowed and do face obsolescence at an age later than the ending of endowment, then the mortality hazard presumably has the age profile illustrated in figure 7.5.

DISCUSSION

Now, after seeing how nonmonotonic logic applies in the context of theory construction, it is time to ask whether the new notion of the consequence relation changes our understanding of theory. We claim that it does not. Tarski's view of theory—a deductively closed system of sentences, where deductive closure means closure under the first-order logical consequence—still applies.

The analysis presented in this chapter did not deal with a theory in the Tarskian sense. Instead, it dealt with a theory in flux, which is not a Tarskian theory. At best, it provides the raw material for such a theory. Future research might provide evidence that would gainsay its present conclusions.

How can such a classical theory be built from this raw material? Suppose that enough high-quality empirical work clarified the conditions of occurrence of all the observed patterns of age dependence. Then one would likely be tempted to declare that all the relevant facts are in hand. We would then want to construct a complete classical theory.

Nonmonotonic formalization of a theory in flux can be used to construct what might be called a "frozen" theory, a theory in classical FOL that is not contradicted by any known tendencies. Such a frozen theory can be built as follows. Take all of the causal stories, restrict them to those domains where they were not overridden, and universally quantify them (with antecedents that provide the required restrictions). With this revision, all the derived expectations ("presumably implies" statements) turn into universally quantified—though highly restricted—theorems.

For example, suppose that a theory in flux had been frozen into a restricted classical theory after accommodating (only) considerations about the liability of newness and endowments, that is, at the second stage of the theory. Then the causal stories need to be reformulated as (constrained) universal sentences. The applicability domain of each process must be restricted to the age intervals in which it has not been overridden. The result is a trio of restricted, but universally quantified, theorems that apply to the different relevant segments of the age domain. Because this procedure freezes the theory in flux into a theory proper, these new versions of what had been merely presumptions can freely be used in further derivations. Their inferential behavior follows the rules of FOL (so long as we keep things frozen).

Partly contradictory arguments about age dependence in organizational mortality could be combined by means of a nonmonotonic logic to provide interesting (in part, unexpected) patterns. But extensive further research is needed before freezing a theory becomes a tempting possibility for a research program.

To regain consistency, the argument based on capability has been restricted to ages above the endowment-protected youth of organizations. It is not at all obvious that this restriction is well motivated substantively. Strong intuition suggests the contrary: capability grows more in youth than in old age. So this frozen theory seems both less general and less tuned to substantive considerations than the nonmonotonic version.

To find a consistent way of unifying the arguments and avoiding contradiction of basic intuitions would require dependable knowledge of four functional forms (for all populations of organizations):

1. How (exactly) does aging relate to capability?
2. How (exactly) does capability influence the hazard?
3. How (exactly) does aging relate to the level of endowment?
4. How (exactly) does the level of endowment influence the hazard?

As we emphasized in motivating our approach, the empirical research cannot yet deliver these functional forms, and it does not seem likely that this will change in the near term.

In defining the outcome to be modeled, the hazard of mortality, we emphasized that the new logical machinery is well suited for modeling probabilistic phenomena. Indeed, when probabilistic constructs like the hazard (or other random variables) are embedded in a nonmonotonic argument with its "normally," "assumedly," and "presumably" quantifiers, a theory has a doubled representation of uncertainty, as we discussed in Chapter 1. The underlying stochastic nature of the phenomenon gives rise to uncertainty about the timing of mortality events (given a specified hazard). The nonmonotonic reasoning admits uncertainty about what exactly might be the case for the hazard (given what is "normally" the case). Moreover, our approach treats arguments built on causal stories as tentative, as less informative than those built on universally quantified statements.

Our first illustration of the potential value of these developments involves an application to a well-studied—yet still recalcitrant—problem: age dependence in organizational mortality. We confronted a situation in which several reasonably well developed theory fragments have withstood an attempt to make a coherent single theory expressed in FOL. We took as our challenge to show that representing the arguments with an appropriate nonmonotonic logic would succeed where the classical tools had not.

We claim that our approach has passed this test. We came up with a formalization that incorporates several theory fragments that could not be reconciled in formalizations based upon classical FOL. Moreover, we arrived at a consistent picture that surprised us. We concentrated on getting the local structure right by concentrating on the specific arguments that applied to given phases of an organizational life course, and we did not expect a strongly consistent global structure to emerge. When we shift from a ground-level view to a bird's-eye view, we see that the mortality hazard is higher in each later phase than in each earlier phase, despite the fact that the hazard does not rise monotonically within the phases. This unintended result seems pleasing, because well-designed empirical research has begun to find such a global pattern of positive age dependence (Carroll and Hannan 2000).

PART 3
Ecological Niches

Chapter Eight

Niches and Audiences

The concept of niche has proven to be extremely valuable for specifying competitive processes and environmental dependencies in organizational analysis.[1] However, various strands of organization theory and research define and use the concept in different (occasionally conflicting) ways. Obviously, resolving these differences would help to unify theory and to provide clearer guidelines for empirical research. The chapters in this part of the book report our attempt to integrate several important ecological theories of the niche.[2]

We begin this integration effort in Chapters 8 and 9 by considering three sociological theories of the niche. Niche theory (Hannan and Freeman 1977; Freeman and Hannan 1983; Péli 1997) concentrates on the *fundamental niche,* defined as the region of a resource space in which an organization (or an organizational population) can persist in the absence of competition. Fundamental niches trace the fit between organizations and their environments. The other two theories—resource-partitioning theory (Carroll 1985; Carroll and Swaminathan 2000) and sociodemographic niche theory (McPherson 1983; McPherson and Ranger-Moore 1991; Mark 1998)—work primarily with the *realized niche,* the subset of the fundamental niche in which an entity can sustain itself in the presence of competitors.

The choice of focus—on fundamental or realized niches—carries important ramifications. Specifically, the nonoverlap of two realized niches can have very different interpretations. An empty intersection might occur because (1) the underlying fundamental niches do not intersect (they intrinsically fit nonoverlapping parts of the environment and therefore do not compete with each other) or (2) the fundamental niches do overlap, but intense competition between the organizations has produced a partitioning. Because analysis of realized niches cannot discriminate between these polar cases, we recast the theory in terms of fundamental niches in this part of the book.

Initial research on the niche worked at both the organization level and the population level. For instance, at the organizational level Freeman and Hannan (1983) measured the niches of restaurant organizations by the profile of services that they offered. At the population level, J. Miller McPherson (1983) measured the niches of populations of various types of voluntary associations (such as churches, sports teams, and labor unions) by the distributions of sociodemographic properties of their members.

[1] This chapter retains traces of the formalization in Hannan, Carroll, and Pólos (2003a). However, the formalization is new in most respects.

[2] Dobrev, Kim, and Hannan (2001), Carroll, Dobrev, and Swaminathan (2002), and Dobrev, Kim, and Carroll (2003) make initial efforts in this direction.

Subsequent research tended to work at the level of the organization. For example, J. Miller McPherson, Pamela Popielarz, and Sonja Drobnič (1992) analyzed change in the niches of particular associations by tracing the movements of individuals into and out of organizations. Joel Baum and Jitendra Singh (1994) measured the niches of day-care centers for children by the age ranges that they were authorized to serve and the ranges that they actually served. Joel Podolny, Toby Stuart, and Michael Hannan (1996) treated the niches of semiconductor companies as positions in a technology space as reflected in common dependence on prior technological inventions in research activity (as judged from patent citations). Douglas Park and Joel Podolny (2000) marked the niches of investment banks by the distributions of activity over industries. Jesper Sørensen (2000) traced the niches of local television stations in managerial labor markets by tracing flows of managers between organizations. Stanislav Dobrev, Tai-Young Kim, and Michael Hannan (2001) (and Dobrev, Kim, and Carroll 2003) measured the technological niches of automobile manufacturers by the ranges of engine sizes that they produced.

In many cases, an organization's niche partly reflects the niche of the categories or forms of which it is a member. For instance, Paul Ingram and Tal Simons (2000) note that cooperative organizations in Israel face constraints against using hired labor because of the codes associated with the socialistic cooperative form, even when banks insist that they do rely on hired labor as a condition of obtaining loans. The conflict is driven by a basic difference in schemata and ideologies, not by a policy to undermine cooperatives. In the view of the banks, hiring labor helps lower costs and increase profits; for the cooperatives, the use of hired labor might destabilize the commitment of members and threaten the survival of the organization.[3]

Empirical studies of niches sometimes only implicitly show the dual dependence on both organizational properties and category/form memberships. For example, the niche of a population of newspaper publishers should be delineated partly by the literacy level of the (local) human population as well as by the availability of printing technologies. A study of the emergence of newspaper publishers would surely attend to these dimensions. But studies that compare the success and failure of individual publishers within a population hold these conditions (roughly) constant within a historical period. Naturally, the latter kind of study emphasizes organization-specific properties of the niche.

Hannan and Freeman's (1977) theory of the niche emphasizes the role of competition as a dominant selective force. It offers a framework for thinking about niche width (the generalism–specialism continuum) in terms of environmental dependence and fitness functions. The main insight of this framework comes from recognizing the tradeoff between generalism and specialism in changing environments, called the principle of allocation.[4]

---

[3]Congruence with governmental philosophy also matters. Ingram and Simons (2000) show that the mortality chances of individual workers' cooperatives in Israel vary by organizational form and by the type of government in power. Specifically, cooperatives affiliated with the Merkaz Hakooperatzia (Cooperative Center) of the Histadrut (General Federation of Jewish Workers in Palestine, founded in 1920) experience stronger selection pressure when the Likud party holds power, because Likud has been hostile both to organized labor and the Histadrut.

[4]Péli (1997) formalized this principle in first-order logic with niches defined as classical sets.

In this chapter, we build on this original insight as well as an earlier formalization (Hannan, Carroll, and Pólos 2003a). But we also make two important changes. First, we introduce fuzziness of the kind that we introduced in analyzing clusters, classes, categories, and forms (in Part I). This turns out to be a deep change, and it alters some of the central arguments. It also tightens the connections with the foundational material on categories and forms.

Second, we generalize the treatment to include cases in which the distinctions among positions in the audience are qualitative, e.g., ethnicity, gender, or religion. Previous work considers a special case in which the social distinctions are metric in the sense of mapping to the natural numbers (or even the reals); we learned that this restriction could be relaxed for most of the key results.

We continue to focus on an audience segment, as defined in Part I. Such a segment consists of a bounded collection of agents who value offerings in a domain and control resources to reward the producers conforming to its standards (and punish those that deviate, in some cases). To enhance the conceptual link with prior research on organizational niches, we recast our depiction of an audience, by locating it in a sociodemographic space.[5] Tastes of the audience members are assumed to be a function of position in this structured space.

Perhaps the key modeling question concerns how to define an organization's fundamental niche. This niche specifies what would be observed if the organization did not face competitive pressures. That is, it tells what regions of a resource space an organization would be observed to exploit if potential competitors were absent. In classic biotic applications, a population's fundamental niche summarizes some correspondence between physical attributes of the members of the population and the properties of the resources to be exploited. For instance, beak size limits the sizes of the seeds that birds can harvest. Fundamental niches reflect such limitations, which have nothing to do with (current) competition.

Specifying organizational niches requires finding a parallel between features like beak size and some organizational properties. We develop the parallel using the intrinsic appeal of offerings to social positions and the producers' patterns of engagement. As in Chapter 3, we define the intrinsic appeal of an offering as a match between the characteristics of the offer and the typical local taste or aesthetic. We define engagement by the attention that producers pay to different subaudiences that control parts of the resource distribution. We argue that a durable pattern of engagement converts intrinsic appeal into *actual* appeal.[6]

In this and the chapters that follow, we continue the theoretical strategy, introduced in Chapter 7, of restricting comparisons to pairs of members of a prominent (high-contrast) organizational population.

---

[5]McPherson (2004) calls this "Blau space," after noted sociologist Peter Blau.

[6]It is important to keep in mind that engagement is more malleable than beak size.

8.1 TASTES, SOCIAL POSITIONS, AND OFFERINGS

Organizational niches can be defined for a vast array of environmental properties, including the tastes of potential consumers and members, the availability of various kinds of input (e.g., human and financial capital), and legal and regulatory regimes. Although most contemporary research focuses on consumers in markets for products and services, James Baron (2004) argues that employment relations also powerfully shape niches and identities, especially for organizations whose offering depends critically on the human capital of their members. We see much to be gained from broadening the focus in this way. Potential and existing employees often attend much more strongly to organizational features and to the codes underlying identities and categories than do the potential consumers, who often consider only product features. Therefore, this internal audience might play a very important role in sanctioning code violations; and consumers might regard sanctioning by insiders as a signal of problems with the organization and its offerings. Therefore, we try to tune the theory so that it applies to both consumer markets and labor markets; we do so by adding more specificity to the conception of the audience (beyond what we mentioned in the chapters in Part I).

Audience Reconsidered

Because we want to model the attraction of producers' offerings (in consumer markets and labor markets), we restrict the relevant audience to those in the domain-wide audience with an interest in partaking of the offerings of the set of producers being considered. This means that, in the chapters in this part of the book, we do not consider as part of the audience those agents who develop a high GoM in the intensional consensus that supports a category of producers/products for some purpose other than entering into consumption or employment relations. So, for instance, this interpretation of the concept of audience would exclude occupants of roles that investigate or regulate the actions of producers in a market on the grounds that occupants of such roles might gain a detailed understanding of the distinctions that characterize an intensional consensus without intending to take action in the market for the goods or jobs on offer.[7] This is not to say that the judgments of these specialized critics and regulators do not matter. Indeed, they might prove decisive in shaping the evaluations of consumers/employees. Nonetheless, we elect here to let the influence of these actors operate in the background and to show up in the consumer evaluations that they might affect.

We also now conceptualize the audience as distributed over a social (or sociodemographic) space. We propose a simple model in which the members of the audience differ somewhat in tastes in a way that makes the offerings of category members more or less intrinsically attractive. Extensive research reveals that social-demographic position influences tastes. Nonetheless, the audience members at a social position also generally differ somewhat in tastes. We build a simplified

---

[7] An example here would be a music critic who knows the aesthetics of a particular genre but does not find it attractive, or the police narcotics agent who learns all about the drug underworld but does not intend to participate as a consumer.

model in which each social position possesses a prototypical taste, but the tastes of individual audience members at the position match the prototypical taste to varying degrees.

Audience members can be characterized by values on some features (such as age, educational attainment, income, and wealth) that can be mapped to the natural numbers (or, as in the case of income and wealth, even to the reals). In the usual language of the social and behavioral sciences, these features can be represented as interval (or even ratio) scales, meaning that the mathematical operations of addition and subtraction (and therefore measures of distance) are warranted. Other important dimensions, such as sex, ethnicity, and religion, are purely "nominal" in the sense that distances between the categories or even orderings are not defined. Any general treatment ought to apply to both metric and nonmetric social spaces, to situations in which the social distinctions concern positions on an interval scale as well as to those in which the distinctions apply to unordered social categories.

The intuitions that have developed from prior research on organizational niches come from considering dimensions with interval scales. However, the nonmetric case is more general in the sense that any theory that applies to a set of unordered social distinctions also applies to the same distinctions if they map onto the natural numbers (or, even, the reals). Therefore, we construct the model so that it applies to unordered distinctions, and we push this as far as we can. At a certain point, we need to consider the metric case so that we can address some issues that have figured prominently in prior models that used metric properties, e.g., models that pertain to the distances between social positions.

Sociologists normally regard social space as multidimensional. For instance, McPherson often has considered a space defined by age and years of education. Persons are similar in such a space if they have similar ages and levels of educational attainment. We can represent the argument as pertaining to a multidimensional space. For simplicity in an otherwise complicated model, we restrict attention to only a single set of social distinctions. We introduce a function that ties audience members to locations (positions) in a space induced by the relevant social distinctions.

We use the term position to refer to an audience member's location in the social space. As we noted above, the relevant position in some contexts might refer to a metric space, e.g., age or wealth; in others, position refers to a qualitative feature such as gender or ethnic group membership.

Definition 8.1 (Social position). *Position, $pos(y)$, is a function that maps audience members, $y \in \mathbf{a}$, to social positions:*

Let $\mathbf{p}$ *denote a set of social positions.*

$$pos : \mathbf{a} \longrightarrow \mathbf{p}.$$

When we want to specialize the argument to the metric case, we add the restriction that the set of positions maps to the natural numbers ($\mathbf{p} \subseteq \mathbb{N}$) in a *sociologically meaningful* way.[8] With this restriction, the social distance between any pair

[8]In other words, when we claim that $\mathbf{p} \subseteq \mathbb{N}$, we mean that the assignment of numbers to positions

of positions is Euclidian distance. In this case, if $pos(y) = z$ and $pos(y') = z'$, then $dis(y, y') = |z - z'|$.

Local Intrinsic Appeal

What we call tastes represent abstractly an audience member's aesthetics and preferences; offerings consist of concrete products, services, performances, jobs, political programs, and so forth. Of course, as we noted in defining intrinsic appeal in Chapter 4, tastes can usefully be regarded as pertaining to a comparable class of offerings. For instance, we might compare tastes for offerings within a genre, e.g., comedy (in film or stage production). Likewise, we might consider tastes within a product class, e.g., wine or automobiles. We specify the dependence of tastes on a class of offerings by tying the taste to the label of a class or category. In other words, we consider class-specific (or category-specific) tastes.

We begin by defining prototypical tastes at social positions (for the products of a category). Such prototypical tastes at a position represent the modal tastes of audience members at the positions. For instance, the current modal taste in beer for young American men with at least a high school education and aged 21–25 appears to be a light, watery lager such as that made by Anheuser-Busch (Bud Light) or Miller Brewing (Miller Lite). Of course, some men fitting this description do not subscribe to the typical taste. To model this aspect of taste, we assume that each audience member has a taste that can be compared with the modal taste, and we represent the typicality of a member's taste at the position as a grade of membership in the local audience's taste.

Definition 8.2 (Grade of membership of an audience member in a local taste). *The GoM of an audience member in the typical taste for the category l at its social position $pos(y)$, in formal terms $\rho(l, y, x, pos(y), t)$, maps a label and triplets of audience members, social positions, and time points to* $[0, 1]$.

$$\rho(l) : \mathbf{a} \times \mathbf{p} \hookrightarrow [0, 1].$$

(The symbol $\hookrightarrow$ denotes a partial function, one that is not necessarily defined for all of the objects in the domain of the function. We define $\rho(l, y, z, t)$ as a partial function because it is defined only if $z = pos(y)$.)

An audience member, y, for whom $\rho(l, y, pos(y), t) = 1$, has the prototypical taste for her position; another audience member, y', for whom $\rho(l, y', pos(y'), t) = 0$, does not share the typical aesthetic of the position, and so forth.

Whether an offering attracts a certain taste arguably depends on three factors. The first might be called the sociocultural affinity or fit between the typical offering by a (full-fledged) category member and the prototypical taste of a social position, the degree to which the offering fits the taste, as defined in Chapter 3. We refer to this mapping as the category's fit to the typical local taste at a position. The second fact is the degree to which the producer fits the category, because as we

reflects the underlying social reality (as contrasted with cases in which the assignment is merely a labeling, as would be the case if one assigned numeric values, say 1 and 2, to the social positions occupied by the two sexes).

defined valued categories in Chapter 4, the expected intrinsic appeal of a producer's offering increases with the degree to which the producer fits an audience member's schema for a category. The third factor is the (local) availability of the offer, its mode of presentation, and the organizational identity of the offerer. Offerings that would fit a local taste do not gain actual appeal at a social position if they are unknown or unavailable to persons at that position, are presented in a manner that clashes with their aesthetics, or are presented by organizations that lack conformity with the audience members' schemata.

8.2 CATEGORY NICHE

We analyze the distribution of intrinsic local appeal at two levels: the category and the producer organization (that is, the category member). We start with the category.

The relevant sociological literatures regard offerings as tailored to particular tastes, e.g., political-party platforms directed at particular ideological segments, products designed to fit the presumed needs or desires of some social class, or employment relations designed to suit some group of much sought-after workers. In some cases, the target-taste groups might be broad (as for the Democrat Party in politics or the Toyota Camry in automobiles) and, in others, they might be narrow (as for the Christian Falangist Party of America[9] or the Ferrari Testarossa sports car). Likewise, entertainment offerings, such as films, books, and computer games, are often intended to appeal mainly to positions marked by gender and age.

What would it mean for a category to have a niche in a social space? We find it useful to answer this question by pointing to variations in the intrinsic appeal of category members over social positions. Therefore, we use the concept of intrinsic appeal, denoted by $\widehat{ap}(l, x, y, t)$, as defined in D3.9. But which category members and which audience members ought to be considered in defining a category's grade of membership in a position? The picture is clearest if we consider the typical members on both sides of the role relationship: the full-fledged members of the category and the audience members with the typical tastes of their social positions. This leads us to propose the following definition of a category niche.

Definition 8.3 (Category niche). *The niche of the category l at time point t, in notation $\gamma(l, t)$, consists of a fuzzy set of social positions with a grade-of-membership function that tells the (relative) appeal of the offering of a typical member of the category to a typical member of the local audience at each position.*

Let $z = pos(y)$, $\rho(l, y, z, t) = 1$, and $\mu_{i(l)}(x, y, t) = 1$. Under these conditions the category appeal at position z, $l\_ap(l, z, t) = s$, is defined as follows.

---

[9]Falangists are followers of the authoritarian political views expressed by the Spanish dictator Francisco Franco (The Directory of Politics on www.politics1.com says that the views are, "largely a blend of 1930s fascist ideology, strong nationalism and conservative Catholic theology"). The CFPA is associated with the Lebanese branch of the Falangist movement and is "dedicated to fighting the 'Forces of Darkness' which seeks to destroy Western Christian Civilization."

Let

$$l\_ap(l,z,t) = \mathrm{E}(\widehat{ap}(l,x,y,t));$$

and

$$L\_ap(l,t) = \textstyle\sum_{z \in \mathbf{p}} l\_ap(l,z,t).$$

Then the category niche is

$$\gamma(l,t) = \{z, \gamma(l,z,t)\}, \quad z \in \mathbf{p},$$

where the grade-of-membership function is

$$\gamma(l,z,t) = \frac{l\_ap(l,z,t)}{L\_ap(l,t)}.$$

In other words, a category's niche is a fuzzy set whose grade-of-membership function tells how much of its total expected intrinsic appeal to typical local audience members comes from a focal position. A category with a narrow niche shows a high GoM in one or a few positions and zero GoM in other positions. For instance, a genre in film or fiction might appeal much more to men than to women (e.g., a violent action thriller) or the reverse (e.g., a romantic comedy). Likewise, in devising their coverage of Olympic sports programs, television producers appear to place close attention to gender differences in appeals of sports such as hockey and ice dancing.

Some portions of the theory depend upon the assumption that category niches (and organizational niches) have positions of peak appeal. It is very unlikely that any category has equal intrinsic appeal for all social positions (and the prototypical tastes that they embody). So we assume that for each category—no matter how broad its intended appeal—an associated set of positions (and corresponding prototypical tastes) display greatest intrinsic appeal. Let $\mathbf{pk}_l(t)$ denote the function that records the set of social positions at which the offering of x in the category l has maximum intrinsic appeal at time t. We introduce an auxiliary assumption that posits that every category has a set of positions of peak appeal. (This is an auxiliary assumption instead of a postulate because we do not claim that it models a sociological intuition that deserves to be an enduring part of the theory.)

Auxiliary assumption 8.1. *Each category has a unique nonempty set of positions of peak (very high) local intrinsic appeal with respect to a category, in notation* $\mathbf{pk}_l(t)$.

$$\mathfrak{A}\, l,t\, [\text{P\_CAT}(l,t) \wedge \forall\, z_1, z_2, z_3\, [(z_1 \in \mathbf{pk}_l(t)) \wedge (z_2 \in \mathbf{pk}_l(t)) \\ \rightarrow (\gamma(l,z_2,t) = \gamma(l,z_1,t)) \wedge ((\gamma(l,z_3,t) \geq \gamma(l,z_1,t)) \rightarrow (z_3 \in \mathbf{pk}_l(t)))].$$

This auxiliary assumption does two things: it asserts the existence of a set of peak-appeal positions, and it provides a notation for it.

8.3 ORGANIZATIONAL NICHE

As noted above, most sociological work on the niche has focused at the organizational level. This section lays out an approach to analyzing organizational niches:

we begin by discussing, in turn, intrinsic-appeal niches and engagement; we then shift to actual appeal, which results from a combination of the two and allows us to define the fundamental niche. For analytical clarity, we define these niches in terms of a specific category l of which the organization maintains membership. [10]

Intrinsic-Appeal Niche

We define an organizational niche partly by position-specific intrinsic appeal in a way that parallels our characterization of the category niche.

Definition 8.4 (Intrinsic-appeal niche for an organization). *The intrinsic appeal niche of the producer x with respect to the category label l, in notation $\boldsymbol{\tau}(l, x, t)$, is a fuzzy subset of the set of social positions whose grade of membership equals the share of x's total position-specific intrinsic appeal that arises at each position.*

$$\boldsymbol{\tau}(l, x, t) = \{z, \tau(l, x, z, t)\}, \quad z \in \mathbf{p},$$

$$\tau(l) : \mathbf{o} \times \mathbf{p} \times \mathbf{t} \longrightarrow [0, 1];$$

and

$$\tau(l, x, z, t) = \mathrm{E}(\widehat{ap}(l, x, y, t)),$$

provided that $z = pos(y)$ and $\rho(l, y, z, t) = 1$.

Engagement

The conversion of intrinsic appeal into actual appeal depends, we suggest, on the actions taken by the organization that makes the offering. We refer to such activities as engagement. This term refers to a diverse set of actions, including (1) learning about the idiosyncrasies of the local subaudience and its aesthetics; (2) designing or redesigning features of the offering to make it attractive to that audience; and (3) trying to establish a favorable identity in the relevant subaudience. In many cases of interest, key engagement activities include developing and displaying credible signals of *authenticity* (Carroll and Swaminathan 2000; Baron 2004; Hsu and Hannan 2005).

In formal terms, we define a function $en(l, x, z, t)$, which maps four-tuples of classes or categories, organizations, positions, and time points to the nonnegative real line. This function gives the level of the engagement of producer x at the position z at time t.

We find it useful to represent variations in the strategies of engagement and of catering to local tastes among organizations simply by noting the distributions of shares of engagement over positions. Note that this distribution defines a GoM for engagement.

[10] We recognize that some organizations belong to more than one category and that the niches of such organizations reflect the distributions of engagement and intrinsic local appeal with respect to all of its category memberships. Although we do not analyze this situation here, we think that the framework we have developed can be generalized to deal with these complexities. See Hsu and Hannan (2006).

Definition 8.5 (Engagement niche). *The engagement niche of the producer x with respect to the category label l, in notation $\boldsymbol{\epsilon}(l,x,t)$, is a fuzzy subset of the set of social positions; the grade of membership in a position is the share of x's engagement devoted to the audience at that position.*

$$\boldsymbol{\epsilon}(l,x,t) = \{z, \epsilon(l,x,z,t)\}, \quad z \in \mathbf{p},$$
$$\epsilon(l) : \mathbf{o} \times \mathbf{p} \times \mathbf{t} \longrightarrow [0,1];$$

and

$$\epsilon(l,x,z,t) = \frac{en(l,x,z,t)}{En(l,x,t)},$$

where $En(l,x,t) = \sum_{z \in \mathbf{p}} en(l,x,z,t)$.

Principle of Allocation

As in Hannan and Freeman's (1977) adaptation of Richard Levins' (1968) biological theory of niche width, we assume a tradeoff between niche width and strength of appeal. In particular, we impose the "constant-sum" constraint that increased breadth of a niche comes at the expense of lowered appeal at some positions (Péli 1997; Hsu 2006). Because our model tells that actual appeal depends upon engagement and intrinsic appeal, we pay attention to both in reformulating the principle of allocation.

In particular, we assume that both an organization's total engagement and its total intrinsic appeal over positions normally are the same for all organizations of the same age in a population (at a particular point in time). Here the nonmonotonic logic introduced in Chapter 6 plays an important role. We assume that, lacking any information more specific than that two organizations are typical members of a high-contrast population and have the same age, the default expectation is that they exhibit the same overall capacity for engagement and gaining intrinsic appeal. We render the default version of the principle of allocation as a postulate of the theory.[11] Specifically, we propose that the principle of allocation applies to comembers of a high-contrast population.

Again, when we compare outcomes for (possibly) different organizations in a population, we face the problem that the key intuitions come from analysis of the normal cases. We are unsure what to expect of the unusual ones. Therefore, as in previous chapters, we restrict comparisons to normal members of prominent (high-contrast) populations, using the comembership predicate $\text{CM}(l,x,x',t,t')$—see D7.1.

Postulate 8.1 (Principle of allocation). *The expected levels of total engagement and total intrinsic local appeal over positions normally are the same for all equal-age comembers of a prominent organizational population.*

$$\mathfrak{N}\, l,t,t',x,x' \,[\text{CM}(l,x,x',t,t') \wedge (a(x,t) = a(x',t'))$$
$$\rightarrow (\text{E}(En(l,x,t)) = \text{E}(En(l,x',t'))) \wedge (\text{card}(\boldsymbol{\tau}(l,x,t)) = \text{card}(\boldsymbol{\tau}(l,x',t')))].$$

[11] In modeling resource partitioning in the next chapter, we introduce more specific information about scale that overrides this postulate in some cases.

(Recall that the relation of comembership in a prominent population, in notation $\text{CM}(l, x, x', t, t')$, is given by D7.1.)

Actual Appeal

We propose that an offering's *actual* appeal to the audience members at a social position depends on the offering's intrinsic appeal to the position's prototypical taste and on the intensity of the organization's engagement at that social position. For example, although sports drinks such as Gatorade might have had intrinsic or latent attraction to athletic-minded individuals for much of the late twentieth century in the United States, it was not until Stokeley-Van Camp Inc. introduced and marketed (i.e., engaged the market with) Gatorade in 1969 that actual appeal became positive. Recruitment strategies by firms, universities, political parties, and other kinds of organizations also represent efforts to engage potential audiences in the market for members.

Given that we have defined intrinsic appeal and engagement as grades of memberships in position, we find it natural to define actual appeal as a GoM as well. Now, instead of considering only typical audience members at a position, we consider an arbitrary member of the audience.

Definition 8.6 (Actual appeal). *The actual appeal to the audience member y of the offering x in the category l at time t is a function that maps four-tuples of classes/categories, producers, audience members, and time points to* $[0, 1]$.

$$ap(l) : \mathbf{o} \times \mathbf{a} \times \mathbf{t} \longrightarrow [0, 1].$$

We represent the argument that actual appeal depends upon intrinsic appeal and engagement in two steps. This somewhat circuitous construction reflects our lack of knowledge of any exact function that converts the two inputs into actual appeal. (If we knew this function, then we would provide an exact analytical definition.)

The first consideration is that a producer's offering lacks appeal for audience members at unengaged positions and at positions where its offering lacks intrinsic appeal to typical tastes. In other words, the production function for actual appeal requires nonzero "inputs" of both factors to generate positive actual appeal.

Postulate 8.2. *The expected actual appeal in a category of an offering to an audience member at a social position normally equals zero if*

A. *the organization's expected appeal to the characteristic local taste is zero at the audience member's position:* $\tau(l, x, z, t) = 0$*; or*

B. *the organization's engagement at that position is zero:* $\epsilon(l, x, z, t) = 0$.

Because the offerings of nonmembers of a category lack intrinsic appeal in the category, nonmembers also lack actual appeal.

Lemma 8.1. *Producers that lack standing in a positively valued category presumably do not have intrinsic appeal in that category.*

$$\mathfrak{P}\, l, x, y, t\, [\text{PCAT}(l, t) \wedge (\mu_{i(l)}(x, y, t) = 0) \rightarrow (\mathrm{E}(ap(l, x, y, t)) = 0)].$$

Proof. This is a straightforward implication of M3.1 (producers with zero grade of membership in a positively valued category have zero expected intrinsic appeal in that category), P8.2A (just above), and the metarule introduced in Section 5 in Chapter 6 for linking expected values and realizations of a random variable. □

What can we conclude if nonzero values of the two inputs to actual appeal (engagement and fit to prototypical taste at the audience member's position) are assured? Consider a hypothetical case. Suppose that we know that one organization's offering fits better to the prototypical taste at a specified position than another's; and *all* that we know about engagement is that each organization engages at the relevant position. A sensible inference in such a case, we suggest, yields the default expectation that the offering with the greater intrinsic appeal will also display the greater actual appeal. We think that it is reasonable to treat theses two inputs symmetrically in terms of defaults. Therefore, we will consider pairs of comembers of a high-contrast population, which ensures that the grades of membership in the class/category of the producers being compared are high. This restriction takes care of the requirement in P8.2B.

As mentioned above, we also make another important change. In defining intrinsic appeal, we focused on typical members of the local audience at a position. Now we consider an arbitrary member of the local audience. The intuition behind the postulates introduced here is (1) that if we know that an offering intrinsically appeals to the modal members of a local audience and (2) that the producer engages the local audience enough to support the expectation, then the offering will normally be appealing to an arbitrarily chosen member of that audience. Of course, we treat this claim as a rule-with-exceptions, meaning that there might be subsets of a local audience whose tastes depart strongly from the rest. Knowledge of such patterned exceptions would override the application of the rule.

Postulate 8.3. *The expected actual appeal of an offering normally increases with the fit of the offering to the typical taste at a position and the engagement at the position.*

A. *The expected actual appeal of an offer to an audience member at a position normally increases with the fit of the category to the typical taste at the position (as long as engagement is nonzero):*

$$\mathfrak{N}\, l, t, t', x, x', y, y', z, z' \,[\text{CM}(l, x, x', t, t') \wedge (z = pos(y)) \wedge (z' = pos(y')) \wedge (\epsilon(l, x, z, t) > 0) \wedge (\epsilon(l, x', z', t') > 0) \wedge (\tau(l, x, z, t) > \tau(l, x', z', t')) \rightarrow (\text{E}(ap(l, x, y, t)) > \text{E}(ap(l, x', y', t')))].$$

B. *The expected actual appeal of an offer normally increases with the producer's engagement at the position (as long as the intrinsic appeal of the category to the typical taste at the position is nonzero):*

$$\mathfrak{N}\, l, t, t', x, x', y, y', z, z' \,[\text{CM}(l, x, x', t, t') \wedge (z = pos(y)) \wedge (z' = pos(y')) \wedge (\tau(l, x, z, t) > 0) \wedge (\tau(l, x', z', t') > 0) \wedge (\epsilon(l, x, z, t) > \epsilon(l, x', z', t')) \rightarrow (\text{E}(ap(l, x, y, t)) > \text{E}(ap(l, x', y', t')))].$$

Postulate 8.3 focuses on particular social positions. Part A claims that an improvement in the match of an offer to the prototypical taste at a position (where the producer engages the audience) increases the expected level of actual appeal. Part B claims that more engagement at a position (where there is some degree of match with the local taste) increases the expected actual appeal of an offering.

Analyzing the implications of different niche "strategies" requires considering the implications of restricting or broadening engagement. The principle of allocation tells us that one cannot increase the level of engagement at one position without reducing engagement at other positions. Predicting what benefits would follow from reallocating engagement demands knowledge of the impact of the reallocation on total expected actual appeal. However, the considerations introduced in P8.3 are not strong enough to allow us to deal with the consequences of a reallocation of engagement. The actual appeal drops at one position and rises at another; but what would be the net effect?

We can approach this question if we consider the ratio of the actual appeal at a position to the share of engagement at that position. Normally it is easier to earn actual appeal at positions where the offer matches with the local taste. Therefore, we postulate that this ratio is an upward monotonic function of the fit to the local taste.

Postulate 8.4. *The ratio of the expected actual appeal of an offer at a position to the share of engagement at that position normally increases with the fit of the category to the typical taste at the position:*

$$\mathfrak{N}\, l, t, t', x, x', y, y', z, z' \,[\textsc{cm}(l, x, x', t, t') \\ \wedge (pos(y) = z) \wedge (pos(y') = z') \wedge (\tau(l, x, z, t) > \tau(l, x', z', t')) \\ \rightarrow ((\mathrm{E}(ap(l, x, y, t))/\epsilon(l, x, z, t)) > (\mathrm{E}(ap(l, x', y', t'))/\epsilon(l, x', z', t')))].$$

8.4 FUNDAMENTAL NICHE

The fundamental niche of an organization represents the region of audience space where an entity can potentially operate in the absence of competing entities. Its sociological importance stems from its clear mapping of the relationship between social structures and organizations, unfettered by the complexities of competition for resources. The fundamental niche shows where organizations might feasibly develop rather than where they necessarily will, which depends on outcompeting the other entities that are vying for resources in the same space.

In our view, the fundamental niche should satisfy two properties. First, it should mark the boundary around the positions for which the organization's expected actual appeal remains positive. Second, it should distinguish those positions for which the organization's actual appeal is higher versus those where it is lower. The following definition satisfies the desired conditions.

Definition 8.7 (Fundamental niche). *An organization's fundamental niche with respect the category labeled l in a social space, in notation $\mathbf{f}(l, x, t)$, consists of*

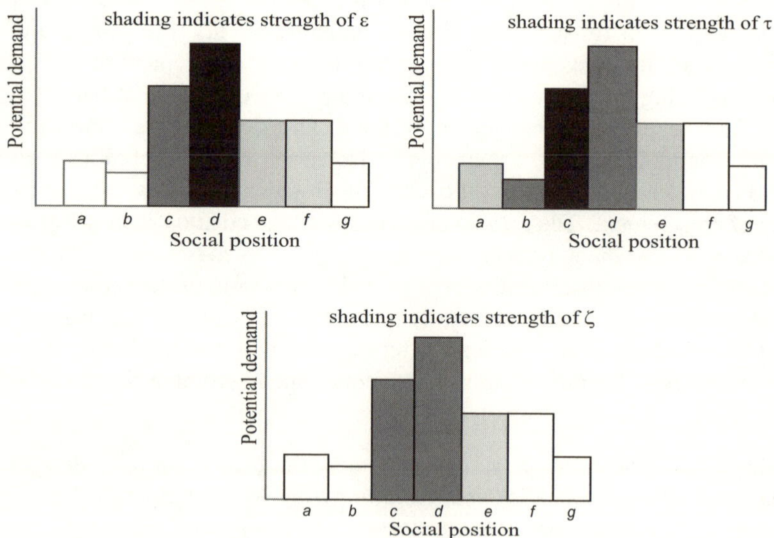

Figure 8.1 Dependence of a fundamental niche on patterns of engagement, ϵ, and of local intrinsic appeal, τ

a (fuzzy) set of social positions; and its grade of membership in a position is its expected actual appeal to agents with the typical taste for a category at the position.

$$\mathbf{f}(l,x,t) = \{z, \zeta(l,x,z,t)\}, \quad z \in \mathbf{p},$$

where

$$\zeta(l,x,z,t) = \mathrm{E}(ap(l,x,y,t) \mid \rho(l,y,z,t) = 1).$$

Figure 8.1 illustrates the construction of a fundamental niche. Each "histogram" shows the distribution of the audience over a set of seven social positions. The height of a bar in the histograms gives the level of potential demand among the audience members at the position. (This aspect of the situation becomes highly relevant in our treatment of resource partitioning in Chapter 10.) The top two graphs of the figure show the grades of membership in engagement (ϵ) and the organization's fit to local taste (τ). (The value of a GoM is indicated by the intensity of the shading.) The bottom graph of the figure shows the resulting fundamental niche. In this illustration, the producer engages a position (f) in which it does not fit the local taste and does not engage two positions (a and b) for which it has a slight fit to the local taste.[12] As a result, the fundamental niche is somewhat narrow (confined

[12]The former case (high engagement but virtually no fit to the typical local taste) resembles

to the three positions shown in the middle in each panel).

It is easy to see that the definition fits the first desired condition. Recall that P8.2 holds that an offering's expected intrinsic appeal to an audience member at a position is zero if $\tau(l, x, z, t) = 0$ or $\epsilon(l, x, z, t) = 0$. Therefore, this definition of the fundamental niche implies that (expected) actual appeal is restricted to positions that lie in the fundamental niche.

Lemma 8.2. *A typical organization in a prominent (high-contrast) population presumably lacks expected actual appeal to typical audience members at positions that lie outside the support of its fundamental niche.*

$$\mathfrak{P}\, l, t, x, y, z\, [\text{M}(l, x, t) \wedge \text{PR}(l) \wedge (pos(y) = z) \wedge (\rho(l, y, z, t) = 1) \wedge (z \notin \text{supp}\, \mathbf{f}(l, x, t)) \rightarrow (\text{E}(ap(l, x, y, t)) = 0)].$$

Proof. This lemma is a straightforward consequence of D8.7 and the definition of the support of a fuzzy niche. □

This new definition also satisfies the second condition, because $\zeta(l, x, z, t)$ lies in the [0,1] interval and might not equal 0 or 1. Therefore, the niche reflects a series of gradations of positions of increasing expected intrinsic appeal. In this respect, the new definition seems better suited to representing sociological ideas about niches than our previous "classical" definition (which satisfies only the first condition). Previously (Hannan, Carroll, and Pólos 2003a) we defined a fundamental niche as a set of positions for which actual appeal is positive. In such a crisp set, a position either lies fully in the niche or falls outside of the niche. Notice, however, that previous treatments of organizational niches (e.g., Hannan and Freeman 1977) use fitness functions in depicting niches. These treatments suggest that niches display a position of maximum fitness and that fitness declines with the distance from that position. The characterization of the niche as fuzzy has the advantage that it allows great flexibility in the shape of a niche. A niche might be "flat" according to this definition, meaning that the GoM does not vary over positions in the support. Alternatively, it might be peaked, with much higher GoM for some positions in the support than others.

We invoke, as an auxiliary assumption, that organizational niches—like category niches—contain sets of positions of peak appeal.

Auxiliary assumption 8.2. *Each typical organization in a population normally has a unique set of positions of peak (very high) local intrinsic appeal with respect*

Gallo Wine's seemingly fruitless attempts to market high-end wines to elite consumers while the latter case (high appeal to taste but no engagement) could reflect the unplanned enormous success of Roederer's high-end Cristal champagne in the hip-hop community. When Frederic Rouzaud, the managing director of Louis Roederer, was asked by a reporter from *The Economist* magazine whether the association of Cristal with hip-hop could be detrimental to the brand, Rouzaud replied "That's a good question, but what can we do? We can't forbid people from buying it" (http://www.economist.com/intelligentlife/luxury/displayStory.cfm?story_id=6905921).

to a category, in notation $\mathbf{pk}(l, x, t)$.

$$\mathfrak{A}\, l, t, x, z_1, z_2, z_3\, [\mathrm{M}(l, x, t) \wedge \mathrm{PR}(l) \wedge (z_1 \in \mathbf{pk}(l, x, t)) \wedge (z_2 \in \mathbf{pk}(l, x, t)) \\ \rightarrow (\tau(l, x, z_2, t) = \tau(l, x, z_1, t)) \wedge ((\tau(l, x, z_3, t) \geq \tau(l, x, z_1, t)) \\ \rightarrow (z_3 \in \mathbf{pk}(l, x, t)))].$$

Although the niches of biotic populations are stable but subject to natural selection, an organization's fundamental niche might be more ephemeral. This would be the case if either tastes or engagement patterns were mercurial. The speed of change in tastes surely varies widely, depending upon the subject matter and the social context. Nonetheless, we think that patterns of engagement experience moderately strong inertial pressures and thus remain reasonably stable over time. (We treat change in the niche below and in Chapter 13.) In any case, our conception of the niche fits both stable and mercurial mappings of organizations to environments.

8.5 IMPLICATIONS OF CATEGORY MEMBERSHIP

As noted at the beginning of the chapter, an organization's fundamental niche is generally constrained by codes. The codes can come from category memberships or from organizational identity (which includes form memberships). Consider, for instance, the American microbrewery population, which has been examined closely by Carroll and Swaminathan (2000) and Pólos, Hannan, and Carroll (2002). The organizational population of microbreweries is defined in part by social codes stressing authenticity in craft production. These codes include such requirements as small-scale production, the use of high-quality, all-natural ingredients, traditional brewing techniques, brown bottles for products, and crowns that do not twist off. Certain styles of beer generally get devalued, mainly light lagers made partly from corn or rice (instead of barley).

We argue below that these codes specify the fundamental niche of an organizational form. Any particular microbrewer claiming membership in the form, e.g., the Anchor Brewing Company of San Francisco, is constrained by these codes. But the organizational-level fundamental niche of any company such as Anchor would be further restricted to those social positions for which Anchor satisfies the typical local taste and that Anchor has engaged. This appears to be a relatively small space on the first dimension. Carroll and Swaminathan (2000: 731) report that Anchor's founder, Fritz Maytag, boasted in an interview that "most people won't like our beer."

The concept of category niche provides a way to formalize these considerations. Recall that the category niche tells how the relative appeal of a typical producer to typical audience members varies over positions. Suppose that a population has high prominence, that its contrast exceeds the relevant threshold. Then an arbitrary member will have a high average grade of membership in the underlying category. So long as the threshold is high, it is safe to reason that the intrinsic-appeal niche of a member of the category will closely resemble the category niche. We introduce this reasoning in the following pair of postulates.

Postulate 8.5. *In the case of a highly prominent organizational population, typical members normally lack local intrinsic appeal at positions that lie outside the support of the category niche.*

$$\mathfrak{N}\, l, t, t', x, x', z, z' \,[\textsc{cm}(l, x, x', t, t') \wedge (\gamma(l, z, t) = 0 = \gamma(l, z', t')) \\ \rightarrow (\tau(l, x, z, t) = 0 = \tau(l, x', z', t'))].$$

Postulate 8.6. *In the case of a highly prominent organizational population, typical members normally have greater local intrinsic appeal at positions with higher grade of membership in the category niche.*

$$\mathfrak{N}\, l, t, t', x, x', z, z' \,[\textsc{cm}(l, x, x', t, t') \wedge (\gamma(l, z, t) > \gamma(l, z', t')) \\ \rightarrow (\tau(l, x, z, t) > \tau(l, x', z', t'))].$$

Then the intuition that a high-GoM member of a category generates more actual appeal at positions that lie more firmly in the category's niche follows as an implication.

Theorem 8.1. *A typical category member's expected actual appeal to typical audience members at a position presumably is zero if the category's grade of membership in the position is zero.*

$$\mathfrak{P}\, l, t, t', x, x', y, y', z, z' \,[\textsc{cm}(l, x, x', t, t') \wedge (z = pos(y)) \wedge (z' = pos(y')) \\ \wedge (\epsilon(l, x, z, t) \geq 0) \wedge (\epsilon(l, x', z', t') \geq 0) \wedge (\rho(l, y, z, t) = 1 = \rho(l, y', z', t')) \\ \wedge (\gamma(l, z, t) = 0 = \gamma(l, z', t')) \rightarrow (\mathrm{E}(ap(l, x, y, t)) = 0 = \mathrm{E}(ap(l, x', y', t')))].$$

Proof. The minimal rule chain results from a cut rule on P8.5 ($\gamma = 0$ implies that $\tau = 0$) and P8.2 (the expected level of actual appeal is zero when $\tau = 0$). □

Theorem 8.2. *A typical category member's expected actual appeal to typical audience members at a position presumably is higher for positions in which a category's grade of membership is higher (as long as engagement is nonzero).*

$$\mathfrak{P}\, l, t, t', x, x', y, y', z, z' \,[\textsc{cm}(l, x, x', t, t') \wedge (z = pos(y)) \wedge (z' = pos(y')) \\ \wedge (\epsilon(l, x, z, t) > 0) \wedge (\epsilon(l, x', z', t) > 0) \wedge (\rho(l, y, z, t) = 1 = \rho(l, y', z', t')) \\ \wedge (\gamma(l, z, t) > \gamma(l, z', t')) \rightarrow (\mathrm{E}(ap(l, x, y, t)) > \mathrm{E}(ap(l, x', y', t')))].$$

Proof. The rule chain supporting this inference results from a cut rule on P8.6 (a producer's intrinsic appeal at a position normally increases with the category's intrinsic appeal at the position) and P8.3A (expected appeal increases with τ). □

8.6 METRIC AUDIENCE SPACE

Now we specialize the argument to the metric case. We do so by adding the restriction that the set of social positions can be meaningfully represented by a subset of the natural numbers: $\mathbf{p} \subset \mathbb{N}$. With this restriction, we bring the model closer to what has been assumed in empirical studies.

Some adjustments are needed. First, we impose the restriction that the set of peak-appeal positions is convex for both categories and organizations. By invoking convexity, we impose the restriction that there is only one contiguous *region* of peak appeal for any organization or any category, which simplifies analysis.

Auxiliary assumption 8.3. *In the case that the distinctions among positions map onto the natural numbers,* $\mathbf{pk}_l(t)$ *and* $\mathbf{pk}(l, x, t)$ *normally are convex.*

Let $\mathbf{p} \subset \mathbb{N}$.

$$\text{A.}\quad \mathfrak{A}\, l, t\, [\text{P\_CAT}(l, t) \rightarrow \text{CVX}(\mathbf{pk}_l(t))];$$

$$\text{B.}\quad \mathfrak{A}\, l, t, x\, [\text{M}(l, x, t) \rightarrow \text{CVX}(\mathbf{pk}(l, x, t))].$$

Our treatment of the sociodemographic space and positions in this space reflects the idea that there is a mapping between the sociodemographic positions and the intrinsic appeal of an offering to a position. Furthermore, this mapping should be relatively simple, something like a monotonic relationship. However, a monotonic mapping is inconsistent with the assumption that every offering has a set of positions of peak appeal. The problem is easy to see in the case in which the appeal function is symmetric around the peak region. Then for any point on the left of the peak region, there is a relatively distant point on the other side of the peak for which the offering has the same intrinsic appeal. We propose instead (as a useful simplification) that an offering's intrinsic appeal to individuals at a position declines monotonically with the distance of the closest position in the region of peak intrinsic appeal.

In examining the popularity of various music genres, Noah Mark (1998) provided empirical evidence consistent with the main lines of this argument. He analyzed individual-level data from the General Social Survey. He defined a genre's niche center as the "region of social space where the type of music is most popular" (Mark 1998: 460), which seems to be an instance of what we call a category niche. This notion of "center" corresponds to what we call the region of peak appeal. Mark's empirical analysis revealed that the probability that a music genre attracts a respondent falls with his or her social distance from the genre's niche center. He explains this pattern by invoking the well-established principle of homophily in social interaction, whereby sociodemographically similar persons are more likely to interact with each other than with dissimilar others. Homophily suggests that sociodemographically similar persons come to acquire similar tastes; and that taste similarity increases monotonically with sociodemographic similarity. So we add an auxiliary assumption that embodies this simplification, which has strategic value in our treatment of niche expansion in Chapter 13. As we understand this argument, it applies to typical producers and typical members of local audiences. Therefore, we represent the idea formally for category niches.

Postulate 8.7. *The grades of membership of a category's niche in positions normally differ more for more distant positions than for more proximate ones, provided that the positions being compared lie on one side of the category's region of peak appeal.*

Let $\mathbf{p} \subset \mathbb{N}$.

$$\mathfrak{N}\, l, t, z_1, z_2, z_3\, [\text{P\_CAT}(l, t) \\ \wedge ((\min \mathbf{pk}_l(t) \geq z_1 > z_2 > z_3) \vee (\max \mathbf{pk}_l(t) \leq z_1 < z_2 < z_3)) \\ \rightarrow (|\gamma(l, z_1, t) - \gamma(l, z_2, t)| < |\gamma(l, z_1, t) - \gamma(l, z_3, t)|)].$$

The antecedent of this postulate restricts comparisons to one side of the region of peak appeal. Because these regions can contain multiple positions, we use either the minimum or maximum of the region as the nearest position for comparison. We treat the two sides of the space separately to avoid imposing the (unwarranted) constraint of symmetry in the distribution of intrinsic appeal around the region of peak appeal.

What about the effect of the distance in audience space, in particular distance of a position from an organization's peak-intrinsic-appeal region and the category's intrinsic local appeal at the position? To derive an implication requires a relationship be established between the region of peak appeal for a category and the region of peak appeal for a member of the category. In P8.6 we asserted a monotonic relationship between the grades of membership in intrinsic local appeal over positions for categories and their members. Based on the same intuition, we make a similar claim about the corresponding peaks.

Postulate 8.8. *Regions of peak appeal of categories and of their typical members normally coincide.*

$$\mathfrak{N}\, l, x, t\, [\text{PR}(l, t) \wedge \text{M}(l, x, t) \rightarrow \forall z\, [(z \in \mathbf{pk}_l(t)) \leftrightarrow (z \in \mathbf{pk}(l, x, t))]].$$

Lemma 8.3. *The values of an organization's grade of membership in local intrinsic appeal presumably differ more for more distant positions than for more proximate ones, provided that the positions being compared lie on one side of the category's region of peak appeal (in the case of typical members of prominent organizational populations).*

Let $\mathbf{p} \subset \mathbb{N}$.

$$\mathfrak{P}\, l, t, x, z_1, z_2, z_3\, [\text{M}(l, x, t) \wedge \text{PR}(l, t) \\ \wedge ((\min \mathbf{pk}(l, x, t) \geq z_1 > z_2 > z_3) \vee (\max \mathbf{pk}(l, x, t) \leq z_1 < z_2 < z_3)) \\ \rightarrow (|\tau(l, x, z_1, t) - \tau(l, x, z_2, t)| < |\tau(l, x, z_1, t) - \tau(l, x, z_3, t)|)].$$

Proof. The minimal rule chain employs P8.6, which holds that a producer's intrinsic local appeal at a position, τ, increases with its category's grade of membership in the position γ, P8.7, which imposes the restriction that regions of peak appeal are the same for categories and their typical members, and P8.8, which holds that the differences in a category's GoM in a pair of positions increase with the distance between the positions. □

Theorem 8.3. *An organization's expected local intrinsic appeal at a position presumably declines monotonically with the distance of the position from the location* *of the closest point in the organization's region of peak intrinsic appeal (in the case of typical members of a prominent population).*

Let $\mathbf{p} \subset \mathbb{N}$.

$$\mathfrak{P}\, l, t, x, z_1, z_2, z_3\, [\text{M}(l, x, t) \wedge \text{PR}(l, t) \wedge ((\min \mathbf{pk}(l, x, t) \geq z_1 > z_2 > z_3) \vee (\max \mathbf{pk}(l, x, t) \leq z_1 < z_2 < z_3)) \rightarrow (\tau(l, x, z_1, t) > \tau(l, x, z_2, t) > \tau(l, x, z_3, t))].$$

Proof. The auxiliary assumption asserting the existence of a set of positions of peak appeal, A8.2, gives immediately that τ is higher at z_1 than at either of the other positions being compared (which do not sit in the set of peak-appeal positions). Then application of P8.7 implies that $\tau(l, x, z_2, t) > \tau(l, x, z_3, t)$ because z_2 is closer to z_1 than is z_3. □

This result carries also applies to distance from the category's region of peak intrinsic appeal.

Corollary 8.1. *An organization's expected local intrinsic appeal at a position presumably declines monotonically with the distance of the position from the location of the closest point in the category's region of peak intrinsic appeal (in the case of typical members of a prominent population).*

Let $\mathbf{p} \subset \mathbb{N}$.

$$\mathfrak{P}\, l, t, x, z_1, z_2, z_3\, [\text{M}(l, x, t) \wedge \text{PR}(l, t) \wedge ((\min \mathbf{pk}_l(t) \geq z_1 > z_2 > z_3) \vee (\max \mathbf{pk}_l(t) \leq z_1 < z_2 < z_3)) \rightarrow (\tau(l, x, z_1, t) > \tau(l, x, z_2, t) > \tau(l, x, z_3, t))].$$

Proof. The most specific rule chain results from a cut rule on (the rule chain supporting) T8.3 and P8.8, just above. □

DISCUSSION

This chapter develops the core ideas for analyzing the niches of organizations. It differs from prior research on niches in representing niches as fuzzy sets. It also introduces the concept of engagement into niche analysis. Both tasks are accomplished within an audience space defined by sociodemographic characteristics.

The main achievements of the chapter involve defining and specifying various types of niches: category niche, local intrinsic appeal niche, engagement niche, and organizational fundamental niche. These formal definitions provide us the tools to model explicit tradeoffs in the allocation of resources, especially in engagement and actual appeal. In general, we argue that tending to a broader and more diverse audience carries with it the cost of less attention paid to each narrower subaudience. In the next chapter, we continue with this analysis, by taking account of competitors in defining the realized niche.

Chapter Nine

Niches and Competitors

As discussed in the previous chapter, the fundamental niche abstracts from the possible implications of competitors: it concerns mainly the relationship between the producer and the environment, as represented by the audience. How does the picture change when competitors are present?

To analyze the impact of competitors, we begin with the concept of fitness, which tells the relation between the appeal of an organization's offering and its viability in the midst of resource competition. Fitness allows us to define formally the realized niche, the traditional way of conceiving how competitors impinge upon the fundamental niche. Here again, our task is complicated (and we think enriched) by our recognition of possible fuzziness of the niche.

In considering competitors, we also analyze overlaps in the niches of two (or more) organizations and their effects on mortality. Niche width, or breadth in product offerings, figures into the analysis of competitors as well, because organizations attempt many ways to approach the audience in trying to outcompete other producers. A special issue about niche width involves niche convexity, or the continuity of the niche in audience space: "gaps" in the niche of an organization might develop (for strategic or unintentional reasons) and this condition appears to be costly, as we demonstrate below. Finally, we consider environmental change in this context.

9.1 FITNESS

Fitness concerns an organization's ability to thrive in the face of competition from other organizations for the resources controlled by the relevant audience. It is tempting to assume that competitive viability gets reflected in summary measures of organizational performance; however, approaches that conflate niche and performance obscure the causal dynamics and also overlook some of the most interesting sociological cases.

For example, consider the declining viability of Catholic schools in the United States. Both scientific and professional observers agree that the average performance of these schools is good: "their students consistently score well on standardized tests, regardless of income or race" (Dwyer 2005: 43; see also Bryk, Lee, and Holland 1993). Yet, more than 3000 Catholic schools have been shuttered over the last 40 years (Sander 2001). In the Brooklyn, New York, diocese alone Catholic enrollments dropped by 11,000 from 1999 to 2005. This decline can be attributed to the lowered number of immigrants from Catholic countries living in dense urban neighborhoods and the rising costs of the teaching staff (and, subsequently, tuition) as lay teachers needed to be hired to replace the religious staff, which suffered from declining enlistments as well.

In our previous formalization of the niche (Hannan, Carroll, and Pólos 2003a), we used a "winner-take-all" notion of fitness at a position. The idea was that the members of the (homogeneous) audience at a position would rank the available offerings by appeal and allocate all of their support (resources) to the offering with the highest ranking (or proportionately to those with highest ranking in the case of ties). This idea seems overly strong when we consider possible heterogeneity in tastes at positions. Although we focus on prototypical tastes, we have explicitly allowed the possibility of variation in local tastes. Audience members at a position can differ in their rankings of offerings by appeal; and there might not be agreement about the "winner(s)." So we change this part of the model. We now propose that each producer gains its proportionate share of the demand at a position, where the proportion equals the ratio of its appeal to the prototypical local taste to the sum of the appeals of all of the members of the producer population at that position.

Definition 9.1 (Fitness at a position and overall).

A. *An organization's relative fitness at a position is its share of the total appeal at the position.*

$$\phi(l, x, z, t) = \frac{Ap^z(l, x, t)}{\sum_{x' \in \mathbf{o}} Ap^z(l, x', t)},$$

where $Ap^z(l, x, t)$ *denotes* x*'s total appeal over social positions at time* t*, i.e.,*

$$Ap^z(l, x, t) = \sum_{y | pos(y) = z} ap(l, x, y, t).$$

B. *An organization's overall relative fitness is the sum over positions of its positional fitness:*

$$\Phi(l, x, t) = \sum_{z \in \mathbf{p}} \phi(l, x, z, t).$$

Note that D9.1A imposes the constraint that relative fitness at a position is zero if actual appeal is zero at that position. In each case, fitness is a grade of membership, because actual appeal is a grade of membership.

An organization's exact relative fitness depends upon the structure of the audience being considered, the distribution of its offering's appeal over the social-position dimension, and the appeal distributions of the competitors. An organization's total appeal might not correspond perfectly with its relative fitness. This was apparently the case with Coors Brewing in California in the 1970s: its very high market share at that time reflected its much higher level of engagement in the state, a situation that eroded considerably after Anheuser-Busch and Miller Brewing created local distribution channels, opened new production facilities, and started advertising aggressively in the state.

Nonetheless, a reasonable default assumption holds that greater total appeal normally translates to higher fitness. That is, if we lack knowledge of the specifics (the distributions of appeal over positions for the relevant competitors), then we would expect that an organization with greater total appeal than another also has higher fitness. Of course, the nonmonotonic logic allows this rule to be overridden by knowledge of the specifics. We state this default explicitly, because we use it below in examining niche width.

Postulate 9.1. *An organization's expected total fitness in a category,* $\mathrm{E}(\Phi)$*, normally increases monotonically with its total appeal,* Ap*.*

$$\mathfrak{N}\,\mathbf{q},\mathbf{q}'\,[\textsc{cm} \rightarrow (Ap \uparrow \mathrm{E}(\Phi))(\mathbf{q},\mathbf{q}')\,],$$

where $\mathbf{q} = \langle l,t,x,y,z\rangle$ *and* $\mathbf{q}' = \langle l,t',x',y',z'\rangle$.

9.2 REALIZED NICHE

At the beginning of Chapter 8 we contrasted lines of sociological theories of the niche by whether they focus on fundamental or realized niches. We defined the fundamental niche in the previous chapter. Now we turn to the realized niche.

An entity's realized niche in Hutchinson's (1957) theory of the niche consists of the subset of its fundamental niche in which it has positive fitness in the presence of its competitors. We adapt this definition slightly to fit the sociological motivations for the model.

Definition 9.2 (Realized niche of an organization). *An organization's realized niche in a category,* $\mathbf{r}(l,x,t)$*, is a fuzzy subset of the set of social positions and the GoM in this set is the organization's fitness at a position.*

$$\mathbf{r}(l,x,t) = \{z, \phi(l,x,z,t)\}, \quad z \in \mathbf{p}.$$

Note that this rendering ensures that the realized niche takes account of the presence of competitors, because fitness depends on appeal relative to competitors. The crisp-set construction we proposed earlier (Hannan, Carroll, and Pólos 2003a) ensured the (desired) property that the realized niche is a subset of the fundamental niche as a strict rule. However, this implication does not hold for fuzzy niches. Instead, this kind of relationship characterizes the *supports* of the two niches, the positions for which the grades of membership are positive.

Lemma 9.1. *The support of an organization's realized niche in a category is a subset of the support of its fundamental niche.*

$$\forall\, l,t,x\,[\mathrm{M}(l,x,t) \rightarrow (\mathrm{supp}\,\mathbf{r}(l,x,t) \subseteq \mathrm{supp}\,\mathbf{f}(l,x,t))].$$

Proof. The definition of realized niche, D9.2, tells that a producer has positive actual appeal at any position that belongs to its realized niche. But expected appeal is zero if either engagement or local intrinsic appeal is zero at the position (P8.2). Given the metarule from Section 6.5, it follows that for any z, $(z \in \mathrm{supp}\,\mathbf{r}(l,x,t)) \rightarrow \zeta(l,x,z,t) > 0$, which is the definition of the support of the fundamental niche as defined in D8.7. □

Note that the preceding lemma is presented in terms of (classical) set-theoretical inclusion for the set of support. When we define width below, a reformulation of this lemma in terms of niche width, i.e., the claim that the fundamental niche is always at least as wide as the realized niche, turns out to be false.

The realized niche can also be tied to membership in a category and the category's niche.

Lemma 9.2. *For typical members of a category, the support of an organization's realized niche in a category is a subset of the support of the category niche.*

$$\forall\, l, t, x\, [\mathrm{M}(l, x, t) \rightarrow (\operatorname{supp} \mathbf{r}(l, x, t) \subseteq \operatorname{supp} \gamma(l, t))].$$

Proof. P8.5 posits that an organization's expected intrinsic local appeal is zero at positions that do not lie in the support of the category niche. □

9.3 NICHE OVERLAP

Competitors have entered the picture only indirectly to this point in this theory of the niche: fitness depends on the appeals of all of the organizations in the domain (see D9.1A). The next steps in the argument attend directly to the competitive dynamics.

What is needed is a characterization of the competitive intensity faced by each organization. For example, today's automobile-producer population in the United States appears to be reasonably competitive, because the major producers offer products intended to appeal across the same broad spectrum of the consumer market. Yet, companies such as Honda and Toyota entered the market initially by targeting less competitive market regions, the consumers who wanted small, less expensive cars. The other (high-priced) end of the market contained such focused producers as Mercedes Benz, Porsche, and Ferrari, which competed among themselves for affluent consumers, although the closer similarity in the identities of Porsche and Ferrari (sports-car makers) likely made their competition more intense. These observations point to the importance of niche overlap in shaping ecological competition.

Overlap of Fundamental Niches

In a classical setup, the overlap of the fundamental niches of a pair of organizations is defined as the fraction of the focal organization's niche covered by the niche of the other (MacArthur 1972; McPherson 1983; Baum and Singh 1994). Each position either falls in the overlap or it does not. We suggest that a reasonable fuzzy-set analog would tell about the *thickness* of overlaps: positions lie in the range of overlap to varying degrees, depending on the patterns of engagement and local intrinsic appeal.[1]

[1] In the world of fuzzy sets, the intersection of a pair of sets, $\{\mu_A\}$ and $\{\mu_B\}$, is defined as $\{\min \mu_A, \mu_B\}$.

Definition 9.3 (Thickness of fundamental niche overlap).

A. *The thickness of the overlap of the fundamental niche of x' on the fundamental niche of x in the category l at time t equals the sum over the positions in the support of x's fundamental niche of the ratio of the intersection of the two niches at the position to the grade of membership of x in the position:*

$$ov(l, x, x', t) = \sum_{z|\zeta(l,x,z,t)>0} \frac{\min(\zeta(l, x, z, t), \zeta(l, x', z, t))}{\zeta(l, x, z, t)}$$
$$= \frac{\text{card}(\mathbf{f}(l, x, t) \cap \mathbf{f}(l, x', t))}{\text{card}\,\mathbf{f}(l, x, t)}.$$

B. *The total overlap thickness experienced by a focal organization equals the sum, taken over all producers in the domain, of the thickness of its overlap with that organization:*

$$Ov(l, x, t) = \sum_{(x' \in \mathbf{o}) \wedge (x' \neq x)} ov(l, x, x', t).$$

According to this definition, allowing fuzziness in overlaps usually gives the sense of considerably less overlap than do calculations based on the assumption that niches are classical sets. Positions on the edges of a pairs of niches will contribute little to total overlap in the fuzzy case but not in the crisp one.

It is interesting to note that the thickness of niche overlaps is asymmetric. Suppose $\zeta(l, x, z, t) < \zeta(l, x', z, t)$. If either the level of the proportional engagement or the intrinsic local appeal of x at z rises such that this inequality gets preserved, then the thickness of the niche overlap for x' does not change. On the other hand, an increase in $\zeta(l, x', z, t)$ alone will increase the thickness of the niche overlap experienced by x in a category.

The intensity of competition facing an individual organization depends on all of its pairwise interactions. We begin to build such a characterization by using the concept from Chapter 4 of the strength of the competition exerted by one organization on another. Recall that we defined a nonnegative, real-valued function, $comp(l, x, x', t)$, that gives the strength of the intensity of the competitive pressure exerted by x' on x in the context of the label l at time t, and we defined $Comp(l, x, t) = \sum_{x' \in \mathbf{o}} comp(l, x, x', t)$, where the summation ranges over all of the producers in the domain, denoted by $\mathbf{o}$.

A standard postulate of ecological analysis holds that the intensity of the competitive pressure exerted by one entity on another is proportional to niche overlap (MacArthur 1972; Hannan and Freeman 1989).[2] We retain this principle; but we adjust it to fit the fuzzy representation of the niche, which allows regions of overlap to vary in thickness.

Postulate 9.2. *The expected intensity of the competitive pressure exerted by one organization on another normally equals zero if their fundamental niches do not*

[2]One might argue that the constants of proportionality vary depending on the identity of the competitor, the population, and the time point (Barnett 1997). The simple formulation we present can easily be generalized to accommodate such arguments.

overlap

$$\mathfrak{N}\, l, t, x, x' \, [\text{CM}(l, x, x', t) \wedge ((ov(l, x, x', t) = 0) \\ \rightarrow (\text{E}(comp(l, x, x', t)) = 0))].$$

Otherwise expected intensity of the competitive pressure rises monotonically with the thickness of the overlap of their fundamental niches.

$$\mathfrak{N}\, \mathbf{q}, \mathbf{q}' \, [\text{CM} \rightarrow (ov \uparrow \text{E}(comp))(\mathbf{q}, \mathbf{q}')\,],$$

where $\mathbf{q} = \langle l, t, x \rangle$ *and* $\mathbf{q}' = \langle l, t', x' \rangle$.

An obvious corollary of P9.2 tells that there is a monotonic relationship between total overlap and competitive intensity.

Corollary 9.1. *Total competitive pressure in a category,* $Comp$*, presumably increases monotonically with the total niche overlap experienced by an organization in that category,* Ov*.*

$$\mathfrak{P}\, \mathbf{q}, \mathbf{q}' \, [\text{CM} \rightarrow (Ov \uparrow \text{E}(Comp))(\mathbf{q}, \mathbf{q}')\,],$$

where $\mathbf{q}$ *and* $\mathbf{q}'$ *are as above.*

Overlaps, Fitness, and Mortality

Now we connect fitness to the main outcome studied in the relevant empirical research: the hazard of organizational mortality. The following meaning postulate provides the motivation for our choice of the term "fitness."

Meaning postulate 9.1. *An organization's hazard of mortality,* ω*, normally falls monotonically with its total fitness in the market associated with its category,* $\Phi(l)$.

$$\mathfrak{N}\, \mathbf{q}, \mathbf{q}' \, [\text{CM} \rightarrow (\Phi \downarrow \omega)(\mathbf{q}, \mathbf{q}')\,],$$

where $\mathbf{q}$ *and* $\mathbf{q}'$ *are as above.*

Next we introduce a second basic premise of ecological theory: intense competition reduces fitness (and thereby elevates the hazard of mortality).

Postulate 9.3. *A producer's expected relative fitness in a category,* $\text{E}(\Phi)$*, normally declines monotonically with the total competitive pressure,* Cp*, that it experiences.*

$$\mathfrak{N}\, \mathbf{q}, \mathbf{q}' \, [\text{CM} \rightarrow (Comp \downarrow \text{E}(\Phi))(\mathbf{q}, \mathbf{q}')\,],$$

where $\mathbf{q}$ *and* $\mathbf{q}'$ *are as above.*

It follows from the foregoing argument (and the absence of any regularity chains running in the opposite direction) that thicker total niche overlap lowers expected fitness.

Lemma 9.3. *A producer's expected relative fitness,* $\text{E}(\Phi)$*, presumably declines monotonically with the total thickness of its niche overlaps,* Ov*.*

$$\mathfrak{P}\, \mathbf{q}, \mathbf{q}' \, [\text{CM} \rightarrow (Ov \downarrow \text{E}(\Phi))(\mathbf{q}, \mathbf{q}')\,],$$

where $\mathbf{q}$ *and* $\mathbf{q}'$ *are as above.*

Proof. The most specific rule chain for the lemma starts with the definition of total overlap, D9.3B. The next element is C9.1, which establishes a link between the niche overlap and competitive pressure. To link them together, we rely on the metaprinciple (introduced in Chapter 6) that allows us to link two arguments, one with the actual value of a random variable in its antecedent and the other with the expected value of the same random variable in its consequent. The final consideration we need is the monotonicity of the addition operation. □

An important caveat needs to be noted here. There is a class of situations in which increasing overlap can improve fitness in contradiction of L9.3. This follows from the standard theory of density-dependent legitimation and competition (Hannan and Carroll 1992). According to this theory, increasing density contributes to the growth of constitutive legitimation (taken-for-grantedness) but the relationship between density and legitimation has a ceiling. When the level of legitimation is well below the ceiling, increasing density contributes more to legitimation than to the opposing force of competition and thereby increases fitness. As legitimation approaches the ceiling, the competition-intensifying effect of increasing density overtakes the legitimation-enhancing effect and further growth in density lowers fitness.

Recall from Chapter 4 that the definition of population preserves the implication that competitive intensity grows with density. But it does not imply that legitimation increases with density. Instead it implies that contrast drives legitimation. Still, as we noted in Chapter 4, the fact that this theory does not imply density-dependent legitimation does not mean that it overturns the earlier result. This is because the new theory is silent on the issue of density dependence in legitimation. Therefore, the standard argument is still relevant and should be considered in the present context.

Because the number of overlaps correlates with density, the original density argument applies to the count of overlaps. When density is very low and legitimation is far below the ceiling, an increase in overlaps (due to an associated rise in density) ought to improve fitness by increasing the legitimation of the form. This result, as noted above, contradicts the lemma. Such a contradiction would be fatal to an integration of the two theories if they were formulated in predicate (first-order) logic. However, this is not necessarily the case for arguments represented in our nonmonotonic logic.

As Chapter 6 explains, a key principle of inference in nonmonotonic logic holds that the most specific argument wins in the case of opposing implications due to different sets of premises of comparable specificity. Here we see a clear specificity difference. The relationship between density (and number of overlaps) and fitness is unspecific. It ought to hold under all conditions. The other side of the argument pertains only to cases in which legitimation lies below the ceiling. When these limited conditions hold, the legitimation argument overrides the argument based on competition (represented in L9.3).

The argument behind L9.3 has obvious implications for the (estimable) average hazard of mortality. In particular, it generates a theorem that has been documented empirically in a number of studies (Podolny, Stuart, and Hannan 1996; Dobrev,

Kim, and Hannan 2001; Dobrev, Kim, and Carroll 2003).

Theorem 9.1. *A producer's hazard of mortality, ω, presumably increases with its total niche overlap in a category, Ov.*

$$\mathfrak{P}\, \mathbf{q}, \mathbf{q}' \,[\text{CM} \rightarrow (Ov \uparrow \omega)(\mathbf{q}, \mathbf{q}')\,],$$

where $\mathbf{q}$ and $\mathbf{q}'$ are as above.

Proof. The minimal rule chain supporting this theorem results from a cut rule applied to (the rule chain behind) L9.3, which links total overlap and fitness, and meaning postulate M9.1, which relates overall fitness to the hazard of mortality. □

As we explained above, this theorem might be overridden (at least below the ceiling on legitimation) by considerations of density-dependent legitimation.

9.4 NICHE WIDTH REVISITED

Distinctions between specialist and generalist forms pertain to niche width. What does niche width mean in the reformulated theory?

Hannan and Freeman (1989: 104), following bioecologist Robert MacArthur (1972), defined niche width as the variance in resource utilization over positions (for the case in which the positions are points on the real line). Other work builds on related ideas. McPherson (1983) defined the (realized) niche of a population of voluntary associations (or of a particular association) by the variance of the sociodemographic characteristics of the members of the associations. McPherson (1983) defined the niche as a hypercube with each side given by a segment of length 1.5 times the standard deviation of the membership's values on the dimension; subsequent research in this tradition has used a variety of multipliers of the standard deviation. Gábor Péli and Bart Nooteboom (1999) developed a model in which width is defined as the radius of a hypersphere in a resource dimension.

In the general nonmetric case that we are considering, the positions are unordered. In the special metric case, the positions map to the natural numbers. We suggest that a useful conception of niche width for both cases is the *diversity* of the GoMs over the social positions.

We choose Simpson's (1949) index of diversity, to represent this idea. This index is a standard measure of the diversity of a distribution over a set of discrete categories. We first convert the grade of memberships into probabilities (relative frequencies) by dividing each GoM by the sum over categories of the GoMs. Then the Simpson diversity index, often represented as $1-D$, is defined as one minus the sum over the social positions of the square of the probability mass at a position. [3]

Definition 9.4 (Width of a fundamental niche). *The width of a fundamental niche of a category, $wd(\gamma)$, or of an organization, $wd(\mathbf{f})$, equals the (Simpson) diversity*

[3] In the case in which the positions are arrayed on the real line, there is no probability mass at any position. Therefore, the proposed definition does not apply to this case. Niche width is more usefully equated with the variance of a grade of membership function over the real line for such cases.

of the GoMs of the fundamental niches of the category/organization over the social positions.

Let

$$\hat{\gamma}(l,z,t) = \gamma(l,z,t)/\textstyle\sum_z \gamma(l,z,t);$$
$$\hat{\zeta}(l,x,z,t) = \zeta(l,x,z,t)/\textstyle\sum_z \zeta(l,x,z,t).$$

Then

$$wd(\boldsymbol{\gamma}(l,t)) \equiv 1 - \textstyle\sum_z \hat{\gamma}^2(l,z,t);$$
$$wd(\mathbf{f}(l,x,t)) \equiv 1 - \textstyle\sum_z \hat{\zeta}^2(l,x,z,t).$$

A parallel definition of the width of the realized niche is based on the fitness function.

Definition 9.5 (Width of the realized niche). *The width of an organization's realized niche equals the (Simpson) diversity of the GoMs of an organization's realized niche over the social positions.*

$$wd(\mathbf{r}(l,x,t)) \equiv 1 - \hat{\phi}^2(l,x,z,t),$$

where $\hat{\phi}(l,x,z,t) = \phi(l,x,z,t)/\sum_z \phi(l,x,z,t)$.

Curiously, although the support of the realized niche is a subset of the support of the fundamental niche (L9.1), an organization's (fuzzy) realized niche can be wider than its (fuzzy) fundamental niche. Suppose, for example, that an organization's intrinsic local appeal and engagement are concentrated in a narrow segment of the fundamental niche, say, where the competition is fierce. The presence of strong competitors might reduce the organization's fitness to a very low level in the region of intense competition, especially if some competitors have very concentrated local appeal and engagement. In this case, the organization might have higher fitness in some of the peripheral parts of its niche where it faces less competition. Although its actual appeal might be low in the periphery of its niche, its fitness still might be close to one, or even exactly one (if the region does not contain competitors). The difference between the distributions of the fitness and the ζ function explains how the fundamental niche can be narrower than the realized niche.

The conception of niches developed to this point retains the implication of earlier treatments about the drawbacks of broad niches. We analyze this implication in terms of the total appeal of an organization's offering.

Consider two typical producers in a prominent population that have exactly the same distribution of intrinsic appeal where one concentrates all of its engagement to its positions of peak appeal and the other engages at certain positions outside of this set. Due to the principle of allocation, these two producers have the same expected total engagement. The engagement of the more concentrated producer earns more expected actual appeal because it engages at positions of high intrinsic local appeal. So the more concentrated producer has higher expected total appeal. Note that the fundamental niche of the more widespread producer is broader than that of the more concentrated producer. We summarize this line of argument in the following lemma.

Lemma 9.4. *A producer that engages only its positions of peak appeal presumably has higher expected total actual appeal than an otherwise similar producer that spreads its engagement beyond its peak-appeal positions (in the case of typical members of a category).*

Consider a pair of comembers of a prominent population, x *and* x'*, that have the same profile of intrinsic appeal over positions:* $\textsc{cm}(l, x, x', t, t') \wedge (\boldsymbol{\tau}(l, x, t) = \boldsymbol{\tau}(l, x', t'))$.

$$\mathfrak{P}\, l, t, t', x, x', z\, [(\epsilon(l, x, z, t) > 0) \rightarrow (z \in \mathbf{pk}(l, x, t)) \\ \wedge \exists z'\, [(z' \notin \mathbf{pk}(l, x', t')) \wedge (\epsilon(l, x', z', t') > 0)] \\ \rightarrow (\mathrm{E}(Ap(l, x, t)) > \mathrm{E}(Ap(l, x', t')))].$$

[Read: if x restricts nonzero engagement to peak-appeal positions, and x' engages at least one nonpeak position, then the expected total (actual) appeal of x presumably exceeds that of x'.]

Proof. The principle of allocation in engagement (P8.1) states that the expected levels of total engagement are equal for comembers of a prominent (high-contrast) population, and the antecedent of the formula above invokes $\textsc{cm}(l, x, x', t, t')$. The preamble to the lemma imposes the constraint that the two organizations have the same profiles of local intrinsic appeal. Provided that x restricts its engagement to its peak-appeal positions and x' does not, A8.1 (existence of unique regions of peak appeal) and P8.4 (returns to engagement are higher at positions of higher intrinsic appeal) jointly imply that the additional engagement that x invests in its peak-appeal positions garners more actual appeal than does the same engagement by x' outside its peak appeal. □

We can also derive a parallel implication for straying outside of the category niche.

Lemma 9.5. *A producer that engages only its positions in the support of its category niche presumably has higher expected total actual appeal than an otherwise similar producer that spreads its engagement beyond the positions in the category niche.*

Consider a pair of comembers of a prominent population, x *and* x'*, that have the same profile of intrinsic appeal over positions:* $\textsc{cm}(l, x, x', t, t') \wedge (\boldsymbol{\tau}(l, x, t) = \boldsymbol{\tau}(l, x', t'))$.

$$\mathfrak{P}\, l, t, t', x, x', z\, [(\epsilon(l, x, z, t) > 0) \rightarrow (\gamma(l, z, t) > 0) \\ \wedge \exists z'\, [(\gamma(l, z', t') = 0) \wedge (\epsilon(l, x', z', t') > 0)] \\ \rightarrow (\mathrm{E}(Ap(l, x, t)) > \mathrm{E}(Ap(l, x', t')))].$$

Proof. The structure of this proof parallels that of L9.4, except that it uses P8.6 (higher γ implies higher τ). □

The life history of *Berkeley Barb*, a weekly newspaper founded in Berkeley in 1965 to promote radical politics, illustrates this process. Although the *Barb* enjoyed high popularity in the late 1960s, with circulation cresting at 90,000 in 1968, it fell on harder times as the political climate changed. Of course, much of the decline must be attributed to changing tastes, in Berkeley and elsewhere, as the attraction of radical politics subsided. But the *Barb* persisted until 1980, fueled in large part by revenues from its expanding business of advertising sex services. By changing its offering in this way, we would suggest, the newspaper moved outside its original fundamental niche and lowered its attractiveness to its original audience (it might have increased its appeal elsewhere).

The declining contemporary fate of the venerable clothing maker Levi Strauss might also be accounted for by such expansion of engagement. This company, of course, made its name and built an empire in the twentieth century by making and selling blue jeans, an item that nearly every teenager came to believe he or she needed to possess in the 1960s and 1970s. Worried about the aging human population and the saturation of its market, Levi Strauss in the 1980s embarked upon an expansion plan intended to widen its consumer base by catering to middle-aged and older adults. The leading product for this effort was a heavily promoted pants product, the khakis branded as Dockers. The effort was wildly successful. By 1998, the company had sold over 150 million pairs of Dockers, and the product comprised over 25 percent of Levi's United States revenues (by one account, 75 percent of American men between ages 18 and 45 owned a pair!).

Alas, the recent hard times of the company derive from its loss of appeal among teenagers for its blue jeans, which are now regarded as passé. It seems that by shifting its base to a staid middle-aged, middle-class consumer group, Levi Strauss undermined its appeal to the original consumer group of teenagers, who wants their jeans to be hip, different from their parents' clothing.

These inferences depend on causal stories stated as rules with possible exceptions, which tell what should be expected if we do not know anything more specific about the cases under analysis. These default rules can be overridden by more specific information. The relevant specific information for an analysis of niche width likely pertains to the exact distribution of tastes within an audience and of engagement by producers. Knowledge that the distribution of actual appeal spikes in the set of positions that an organization engages might override the defaults that would apply to this organization in the absence of such information.

Empirical research, using niches defined as crisp sets, reveals that overlap increases with niche width. For instance, a study of the French automobile manufacturing industry over its early history (Dobrev, Kim, and Hannan 2001, figures 1 and 2) shows that a firm with the narrowest possible niche experienced substantially fewer overlaps than those with only modestly wider niches. This tendency would be more pronounced if this research had defined niches as fuzzy sets. This is because of the variations in thickness of overlap. As a producer broadens its niche, its grade of membership in each position, $\zeta(l, x, z, t)$, will generally decline due to the principle of allocation on engagement. Because $\zeta(l, x, z, t)$ appears in the denominator of the measure of overlap thickness, thicknesses of overlaps will tend to increase with width.

Consider the case in which three organizations in a prominent population have identical distributions of intrinsic appeal, that is, identical τ's. Suppose that each has a region of peak appeal that contains only two positions, say z and z', and that organization x_1 restricts its engagement to z, organization x_2 restricts its engagement to z', but organization x_3 engages both positions. What can we conclude? The niches of x_1 and x_2 do not overlap, but x_3's niche overlaps the other two. Because $\epsilon(l, x_1, z, t) > \epsilon(l, x_3, t)$ and $\epsilon(l, x_2, z', t) > \epsilon(l, x_3, z', t)$ in this example and the three organizations are assumed to have identical τ's, it follows that $\zeta(l, x_1, z, t) > \zeta(l, x_3, t)$ and $\zeta(l, x_1, z, t) > \zeta(l, x_3, t)$. Because ζ appears in the denominator of the formula that defines niche overlap, x_3 has higher overlap with x_1 than does x_1 with x_3 and the same is true for x_3's overlap with x_2. Therefore, x_3 has higher total overlap thickness than the other two organizations.

We postulate that this conclusion holds generally for pairs of organizations that differ in niche width. However, the intuition is most secure in comparisons of organizations that locate in the same regions of the resource space (social positions). Therefore, we restrict the causal story to apply to situations in which the support of the fundamental niche of one of a pair of organizations being compared is a subset of the support of the fundamental niche of the other. This restriction means that the two organizations share a niche but that (only) one also includes positions that the other does not.

Postulate 9.4. *The total thickness of an organization's niche overlaps normally increases with its niche width.*

$$\mathfrak{N}\, \mathbf{q}, \mathbf{q}' \,[\text{CM} \wedge (\text{supp}(\mathbf{f}(l, x', t)) \subseteq \text{supp}(\mathbf{f}(l, x, t))) \rightarrow (wd(\mathbf{f}) \uparrow Ov)(\mathbf{q}, \mathbf{q}')\,],$$

where $\mathbf{q}$ *and* $\mathbf{q}'$ *are as above.*

Suppose that the environment is stable, in the sense that the category niche does not change over time (see below). Then it follows that the broad niches yield poor mortality chances.

Theorem 9.2. *The hazard of mortality presumably rises with niche width in stable environments (unchanging category niches).*

$$\begin{aligned}&\mathfrak{P}\, l, t, t', x, x' \,[\text{CM}(l, x, x', t, t') \wedge (\gamma(l, t) = \gamma(l, t'))\\ &\quad \wedge (\text{supp}(\mathbf{f}(l, x', t')) \subseteq \text{supp}(\mathbf{f}(l, x, t))) \wedge (wd(\mathbf{f}(l, x, t)) > wd(\mathbf{f}(l, x', t')))\\ &\qquad\qquad\qquad\qquad\qquad\qquad \rightarrow (\omega(x, t) > \omega(x', t'))\,].\end{aligned}$$

Proof. The minimal rule chain results from a cut rule applied to (the rule chain supporting) T9.1, which relates total overlap to the hazard of mortality, and P9.4 (just above). □

The literature treats two important exceptions to the pattern in the foregoing theorem. The first involves environmental variation, which we discuss below; and the second involves scale advantages as featured in resource partitioning theory (Chapter 10). We do not expect to see the pattern expressed in T9.2 in environments that change in an uncertain pattern involving large shifts (coarse-grained variation) or in those in which a producer's large scale frees it from the constraints posited in the principle of allocation.

9.5 CONVEXITY OF THE NICHE

One reason why a niche (in a metric space) might be wide is that it contains gaps. In formal terms, a metric niche might lack convexity. Does convexity matter net of width? Several analysts have addressed the question, albeit indirectly. For instance, Mark (1998) argues that network-based social interaction tends to close gaps in distributions of appeal in social space because the homophily principle implies that people near each other in the social-demographic distribution will interact more frequently, thus serving to homogenize their tastes. Although Mark does not consider producers, his reasoning seems to support our argument on the producer side.

By contrast, Dobrev, Kim, and Hannan (2001) and Dobrev, Kim, and Carroll (2003) assume that the gaps reflect latent organizational capabilities (in their case engine sizes that automobile manufacturers could make and offer even though they might not). This approach raises the vexing issue of how to tell latent capabilities before they operate.

The dearth of discussion of the complexities of assessing niche width in general suggests to us that analysts have assumed implicitly that niches do not contain gaps. For some organizational forms, this assumption might not be warranted. For instance, some music recording companies appear capable of segmenting their product offerings to very different social positions and tastes through the use of different labels and semi-autonomous subunits. In the abstract, the audiences engaged by these labels and units could be far from each other in resource space, although the general tendency for corporations to collect a panoply of disparate labels under their roofs suggests a counterforce toward closing gaps. Anecdotal evidence suggests that book publishers, advertising agencies, and law firms might have gaps in their niches.

Nonetheless, for the class of situations considered in this chapter, the assumption that niches normally do not contain gaps appears to be safe, at least as an evolutionary tendency. The absence of gaps can be expressed as the property of convexity.[4]

Definition 9.6 (Convexity of a fundamental niche). *A fundamental niche in a metric space is convex, in notation* $\text{CVX}(\mathbf{f}(l,x,t))$, *if and only if every position that lies between positions in the niche also belongs to the niche.*[5]

Our intuition suggests that an organization with a convex niche has higher fitness than an otherwise similar organization with a concave niche. The intrinsic appeal of an offer declines monotonically with the distance from the closest position in its

---

[4]Here we focus on the convexity of the fundamental niche. This property should not be confused with the property of convexity of the adaptive functions analyzed in niche theory. The latter concerns the difference in the adaptive demands imposed by the alternate states of a variable environment as featured in niche theory (Levins 1968; Hannan and Freeman 1977; Freeman and Hannan 1983).

[5]One might be tempted to define the convexity of the fundamental niche in a more general manner. The fundamental niche of x is convex if the $z \longrightarrow \zeta(l,x,z,t)$ function is convex from above. Our more specific definition makes the following arguments simpler, but these arguments can easily be generalized to deal with other cases as well. We do not think that the greater intricacy of the alternative argument yields any new substantive insights.

region of peak appeal according to A8.2. This, in turn, implies that the intrinsic appeal cannot be concave—an offer cannot have nonzero appeal at two positions but zero intrinsic appeal at some position that lies between them. To get a concave fundamental niche, the organization needs to engage a concave set of positions. If we consider a "hole" in the engagement, the intrinsic appeal of the offer must be higher in the hole than on at least one side of the cavity. Therefore, an organization with a concave niche engages one or more positions where its intrinsic local appeal is lower than in one or more positions that it does not engage or engages less than otherwise. Had it engaged the position(s) in the hole, its actual appeal would have been higher at the positions where its intrinsic local appeal is higher. Hence, given the principle of allocation, organizations with convex fundamental niches have higher expected fitness than those with concave niches.

To turn this line of argument into a formally valid proof requires some preparation (whose details are presented in an appendix to this chapter). It will be useful to be able to talk about cavities in the organization's fundamental niche. If a niche is concave, then it contains (at most countably many) cavities. Let the predicate $\text{CAV}(\mathbf{c}, \mathbf{f}(l, x, t))$ tell that $\mathbf{c}$ is a cavity in the fundamental niche $\mathbf{f}(l, x, t)$ (see the chapter appendix for a formal definition).

For simplicity, we now assume that there is only one cavity. (We make this simplification, because generalizing our findings to more complex cases requires an induction on the number of cavities.) We use a closest-possible-world construction. The appendix to this chapter defines a predicate $\text{CCA}(\mathbf{f}(l, x, t), \mathbf{f}(l, x', t))$, which reads as "the convex niche $\mathbf{f}(l, x', t)$ is a close convex alternative to the concave niche $\mathbf{f}(l, x, t)$." (A formal definition can be found in the chapter appendix.) Figure 9.1 illustrates a concave niche and a close convex alternative. As in figure 8.1, the heights of the bars tell the level of potential demand at the positions and the shading tells the grade of membership. The set of panels at the top of the figure show a concave fundamental niche: there is a position in the center that does not belong to the niche even though the positions to the left and right do. The panels at the bottom illustrate a close convex alternative, in which some engagement has been shifted to fill the cavity.

With the restriction to close convex alternatives, we can now conclude that an organization with a concave niche has lower fitness than an otherwise similar organization with a close convex niche.

Theorem 9.3. *An organization with a concave niche presumably has higher hazard of mortality, ω, than an organization with a close convex alternative (in the case of typical members of a prominent population).*

Let $\mathbf{p} \subseteq \mathbb{N}$.

$$\mathfrak{P}\, l, t, t', x, x' \, [\text{CM}(l, x, x', t, t') \wedge \text{CCA}(\mathbf{f}(l, x, t), \mathbf{f}(l, x', t')) \\ \rightarrow (\omega(x, t) < \omega(x', t'))].$$

Proof. The intrinsic appeal of any offer declines monotonically with a position's distance from the closest position in the peak region. This, in turn, implies that the intrinsic appeal cannot be concave, it is not possible that an offer has nonzero appeal

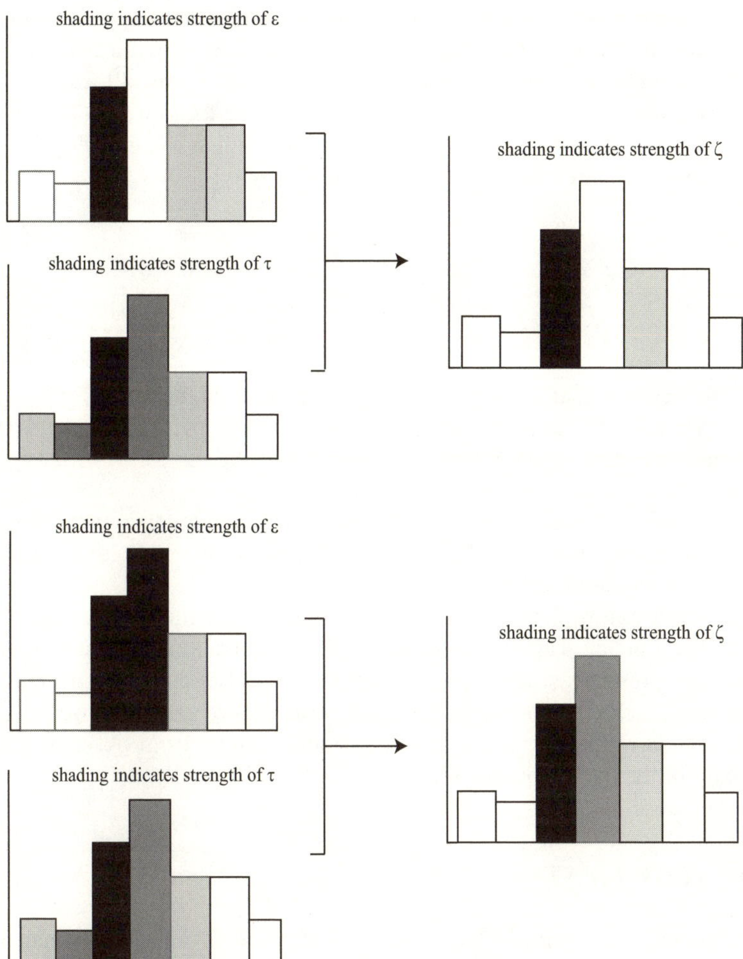

Figure 9.1 An illustration of a concave niche (top set of figures) and a close convex alternative (bottom set of figures)

at two positions but zero intrinsic appeal (to the typical taste) at some position between them. For an organization's fundamental niche to be concave, it must engage a concave set of positions. Concavity means that an organizational niche contains one or more cavities. A strict proof of the theorem requires an induction on the number of cavities in a concave niche. In what follows we show only the initial step of the induction. That is, we assume that there is only one cavity.

Consider the positions in the cavity of the fundamental niche of organization x and consider a "close convex alternative," which is defined in the chapter appendix. In such a comparison, the level of intrinsic appeal to the typical local taste at these positions is higher than at any position where an organization with a close convex alternative fundamental niche has lowest nonzero engagement (D9.A1 in the appendix to this chapter). Suppose that $\mathbf{c}$ is such a cavity: $\textsc{cav}(\mathbf{c}, \mathbf{f}(l, x, t))$. Then we have:

$$\mathfrak{P}\, l, t, t', x, x' \,[\textsc{cm}(l, x, x', t, t') \wedge \textsc{cca}(\mathbf{f}(l, x, t), \mathbf{f}(l, x', t')) \\ \rightarrow \forall z\,[(z \in \mathbf{c}) \wedge (\epsilon(l, x', z, t') < \epsilon(l, x, z, t)) \\ \rightarrow (\tau(l, x, z, t) > \tau(l, x', z, t'))]].$$

P8.4 (which states that the returns to engagement are higher at positions of higher peak appeal), P8.1, the principle of allocation, and M9,1, which relates fitness to the hazard of mortality, complete the minimal rule chain. □

Because selection tends to eliminate less fit entities, organizational populations will display a tendency toward convex niches unless, of course, there is a countervailing force in founding/entry.

It is worth noting that a convex fundamental niche might give rise to a concave realized niche. This might happen if the organization encounters much more competitive pressure at some positions in the central regions of the support of its fundamental niche than it does on the boundaries. More generally, we cannot make inferences about the convexity of a fundamental niche from observations on the convexity of the corresponding realized niche.

9.6 ENVIRONMENTAL CHANGE

Above we restricted certain claims about the survival advantages of a narrow niche to stable environments, and we characterized stability as temporal invariance in the category niche. This is because a narrow niche can be regarded as a very specialized form of adaptation to an environment (an audience and the resources that it controls). An organization acquires a narrow niche by designing its product/service and its identity to appeal strongly to a narrow segment of the audience (one or a few positions in our representation) and by limiting its engagement to the narrow segment. In the imagery proposed by Hannan and Freeman (1977), such a narrow niche corresponds to a narrow strategy, to placing all of the organization's "chips" on a narrow bet. The bet is that the tastes of the focal audience segment will not shift such that the organization loses its appeal to that segment.

In contrast, an organization with a broad niche has generated a product/service and an identity that appeals to diverse subsets of the audience (located at many positions) and has spread its engagement broadly. In a sense, it has hedged its bet with respect to possible change in tastes. Even when tastes do change, the producer is likely to retain some appeal at some of the positions that it engages.

The significance of the principle of allocation, introduced in Chapter 8, is that an organization with a narrow niche generally has higher appeal that an overlapping broad-niche organization. The one with the broad niche pays a price of lowered appeal at any time point relative to the narrow-niche competitor. This price is not compensated if the environment remains stable. But if the distribution of tastes changes over time, then the outcomes for an organization with a broad niche over several periods might be superior to those of narrow-niche competitors. In other words, broad niches might have an evolutionary advantage in changing environments. The tentativeness of the prior sentence ("might") is purposeful, because niche theory (Hannan and Freeman 1977; Freeman and Hannan 1983; Péli 1997) implies that the advantage of a broad niche depends on the pattern of environmental change (reflecting both the likelihood of change and the typical "size" (or grain) of the change).

We think that the new theory can be used to reexamine the niches in dynamic contexts. Change in a fundamental niche has two dimensions, as noted above: change in an organization's fit to local tastes and change in engagement. Because engagement patterns reflect choices directly, it seems more useful to regard changes in tastes as the key environmental dynamic. But an organization's fit to local tastes might also reflect organizational actions, as when a misdeed or an identity-inconsistent action spoils an organization's reputation and lowers its intrinsic appeal. Therefore, we suggest that changes in category niches might be especially useful as a way to represent environmental change. The category niche reflects the distribution of tastes over positions and it is not tied to the actions of any particular organization, as in the examples of the *Berkeley Barb* and Levi Strauss, discussed above. This suggests that work on niche dynamics might profitably link niche width to the stability of category niches (and the audience dynamics that generate stability and change in category niches).

DISCUSSION

At the beginning of Chapter 8 we suggested that it would be valuable to reconstruct the main streams of sociological niche theory on the same conception of the niche. Our motivation was based on our views about the value of theoretical integration, as argued in Chapter 1. Our goal was to build a representation that allows integration of various disparate theoretical usages of niche, including simple propositions about niche position and competition (Baum and Singh 1994), as well as more developed theories such as Freeman and Hannan's (1983) niche theory, Carroll's (1985) resource partitioning theory, and McPherson's (1983) model of niches in sociodemographic space. We next illustrate the suitability of the new theory for this purpose by using it to address resource partitioning.

APPENDIX TO CHAPTER 9

This appendix provides the formal definitions of the concepts used in analyzing convexity/concavity of niches.

Definition 9.A1 *An organization's fundamental niche in a metric space contains the cavity* $\mathbf{c}$*, in formal terms* $\text{CAV}(\mathbf{c}, \mathbf{f}(l, x, t))$*, if and only if*

1. *the set of positions* $\mathbf{c}$ *is convex:*

$$\forall z_1, z_2, z_3 \left[(z_1 \in \mathbf{c}) \wedge (z_2 \in \mathbf{c}) \wedge (z_1 \leq z_3 \leq z_2) \rightarrow (z_3 \in \mathbf{c})\right];$$

2. *for each position in* $\mathbf{c}$ *the organization's offering has a positive intrinsic appeal to the typical local tastes but the organization does not engage the position:*

$$\forall z \left[(z \in \mathbf{c}) \rightarrow (\tau(l, x, z, t) > 0) \wedge (\epsilon(l, x, z, t) = 0)\right];$$

3. *there are positions on both sides of each position in* $\mathbf{c}$ *that belong to the fundamental niche:*

$$\exists z_1, z_2 \, \forall z \left[(z \in \mathbf{c}) \wedge (z_1 \leq z \leq z_2) \wedge (\varsigma(l, x, z_1, t) > 0) \wedge (\varsigma(l, x, z_2, t) > 0)\right];$$

4. *the set of points is the maximal set that satisfies the first three conditions: for any* $\mathbf{c}'$ *such that* $\mathbf{c} \cap \mathbf{c}' \neq \emptyset$ *and* $\mathbf{c}'$ *satisfies 1, 2, and 3, then* $\mathbf{c}' \subseteq \mathbf{c}$.

Definition 9.A2 *The convex niche* $\mathbf{f}(l, x', t)$ *is a close convex alternative to the concave niche* $\mathbf{f}(l, x, t)$*, in notation* $\text{CCA}(\mathbf{f}(l, x, t), \mathbf{f}(l, x', t))$*, if and only if*

1. $\mathbf{f}(l, x, t)$ *is concave and* $\mathbf{f}(l, x', t)$ *is convex;*

2. *the two niches have the same profile of local intrinsic appeal:* $\tau(l, x, t) = \tau(l, x, t)$*;*

3. *the cavity of engagement is "filled" with engagement taken from positions where the intrinsic local appeal is lower than the intrinsic appeal within the cavity:*

$$\forall z \left[\text{CAV}(\mathbf{c}, \mathbf{f}(l, x, t)) \wedge (z \in \mathbf{c}) \rightarrow (\epsilon(l, x', z, t) < \epsilon(l, x, z, t)) \rightarrow (\tau(l, x', z, t) > \tau(l, x, z, t))\right].$$

Chapter Ten

Resource Partitioning

The connections between niche theory (Hannan and Freeman 1977) and resource-partitioning theory (Carroll 1985) are somewhat unsettled.[1] Although both lines of theory build explicitly on the niche concept, they define specialism/generalism differently and make different assumptions about the possible tradeoff between peak fitness and the breadth of adaptive capacity.[2] Given these differences, whether the two theories differ fundamentally or can be integrated into a unified theory remains an open question. We seek to provide an answer by building a formal model of partitioning that incorporates the key assumptions about the structure of the niche presented in the previous chapter. We present a formulation that indeed unifies the theories.

The original niche theory builds on the premise that a specialist (narrow-niche organization) designed well for a particular environmental state will always outperform a generalist (broad-niche organization) in that same state, as we discussed in the previous chapter. This is so because the generalist organization must carry extra capacity—appearing as slack at any point—that allows it to perform adequately in other environmental states. By this argument, the specialist "maximizes its exploitation of the environment and accepts the risk of having that environment change" while the generalist "accepts a lower level of exploitation in return for greater security" (Hannan and Freeman 1977: 948). This theory predicts that specialists do better in stable or certain environments and in environments where change has fine grain (short durations in environmental states). It also predicts that if environmental variation is high and coarse-grained (long durations in states), specialists have trouble outlasting the long unfavorable periods and the generalist strategy conveys advantage.

Resource partitioning theory holds that generalists might actually benefit from participating in multiple activities if they can achieve larger scale. These scale economies might be strong enough to outweigh any overhead costs of having a broad niche, thus giving the overall advantage to generalist organizations.[3]

---

[1]Portions of this chapter were adapted from Hannan, Carroll, and Pólos (2003b); but they have been changed considerably to reflect the new theory of the fuzzy niche and other changes in niche theory.

[2]Carroll, Dobrev, and Swaminathan (2002) note that they also make different assumptions about the environment. The original niche theory treats situations in which clumps of environmental resources and conditions are disjointed or highly dissimilar (Freeman and Hannan 1983; Péli 1997). Resource partitioning theory treats situations in which the different pockets or conditions do not differ greatly in adaptive demands. This difference means that the two theories might apply in different circumstances. But this does not mean that the theories clash in the sense that they make different predictions for the same circumstances.

[3]This might be the case even when the environmental states do not vary over time.

Work on the two theories has focused on different kinds of niches. Research based on the original niche theory focused on the *fundamental* niche; and research based on resource partitioning theory generally treats the *realized* niche. If scale provides strong advantages, then (as we demonstrate below) a large organization will generally have a larger realized niche than a smaller organization with the same fundamental niche. Therefore, larger organizations tend to have broader realized niches—but not necessarily broader fundamental niches. Research on partitioning pays attention mainly to realized niches. Therefore, it often conflates generalism and large size. In contrast, research based on the original niche theory focuses on fundamental niches in characterizing generalism. This difference sometimes leads to confusion.

This chapter seeks to resolve the seeming tension between the usual interpretations of the two theories by creating a unified theory. In particular, we take advantage of the fact that most of the action in resource partitioning theory comes from considering changes in the realized niche. Using the niche theory presented in the previous chapters, we reformulate core aspects of partitioning theory in terms of fundamental niches. In our view, the integrated theory clarifies previously murky issues and paves the way for integration with other theory fragments in organizational ecology. The gains to resource partitioning theory include the explicit incorporation of the principle of allocation (a tradeoff between niche width and strength of appeal), a central tenet of Hannan and Freeman's (1977, 1989) theory.

As the capsule summary of the argument makes clear, a market must possess several properties for partitioning to operate. We formalize four such properties: (1) scale advantage, (2) a market center, (3) a partition of the market into a (set of) center(s), near centers, and a periphery, and (4) crowding. The next three sections offer formal renderings of these conditions. We tuned these conceptual developments to preserve the target theorem that holds that concentration in the center of a market with scale advantage improves the life chances of organizations on the periphery. All of the results of this chapter can be developed for the general case in which the distinctions that define the audience positions do not necessarily follow an ordering, that the audience space is nonmetric.

10.1 SCALE ADVANTAGE

A scale advantage exists when the returns to some activity grow with the scale at which it is done. The canonical example concerns situations in which conducting an activity involves both a fixed cost, independent of the number of items produced, and a variable (per-item) cost. Then the marginal cost of producing an item declines with scale, as the ratio of fixed to variable costs declines. Carroll (1985) argues that organizations generally use scale advantages to improve the price/quality of offerings relative to those of competitors. A straightforward way to translate this idea to the framework of Chapter 8 claims that growth in scale normally gets converted into greater engagement—a rise in scale inflates an organization's appeal distribution by increasing its expected level of total engagement.

We do not want to assume that a scale advantage holds in all markets; indeed some markets might be characterized by scale *dis*advantage (at least above some minimum scale). Therefore, we define a predicate $\text{SA}(l)$, which reads as "scale advantages can be realized by members of the focal population l (in the relevant market)," which we use to mark the part of the argument that depends upon the presumption of scale advantages. (For simplicity, we do not treat temporal variations in the availability of scale advantage.) We also introduce a nonnegative, real-valued function, $s(l, x, t)$, that records the scale of x in the activities relevant to category l at time t.

Definition 10.1 (Scale advantage). *The market experienced by typical members of an organizational population is characterized by scale advantage if and only if an organization's expected total engagement in the activity connected to a class label, $En(l, x, t)$, normally increases with its scale in that activity, $s(l, x, t)$.*

$$\text{SA}(l) \leftrightarrow \mathfrak{N}\,\mathbf{q}, \mathbf{q}'\,[\text{M}(l, x, t) \wedge \text{M}(l, x', t') \rightarrow (s \uparrow \text{E}(En))(\mathbf{q}, \mathbf{q}')\,],$$

where $\mathbf{q} = \langle l, t, x\rangle$ *and* $\mathbf{q}' = \langle l, t', x'\rangle$.

Note that invoking scale advantage can override one aspect of the principle of allocation (P8.1), the part that holds that the expected level of total engagement does not vary among the producers in a market. The principle would be overridden when scale advantages operate and specific information about scale differences is available. We do not alter the assumption that the principle of allocation holds for intrinsic appeal to local tastes, because we think that this insight gets preserved even in partitioned markets. The continuing relevance of allocation constraints on intrinsic appeal generally prevents a single giant organization from monopolizing a domain.

The second premise of Carroll's model holds (in the language used here) that a producer's expected total appeal increases with its scale. With a fairly mild auxiliary assumption, we can derive this premise as an implication. It might be helpful to recap. The definition of scale advantage, D10.1, tells that expected total engagement increases with scale in markets with scale advantage. The principle of allocation, P8.1, tells that all (high grade of membership) producers in a prominent population have the same level of expected total appeal over social positions. We defined total appeal in previous chapters as

$$Ap(l, x, t) = \textstyle\sum_z \sum_{y|(pos(y)=z)} ap(l, x, y, t),$$

where we use the following shorthand: $\sum_z \equiv \sum_{z\in\mathbf{p}}$.

Lemma 10.1. *In markets with scale advantage, the expected total appeal of a producer's offering in a category, $Ap(l, x, t)$, presumably increases with the producer's scale in the category, $s(l, x, t)$, when considering organizations with the same distributions of expected local intrinsic appeal and of proportional engagement.*

Let $\text{SA}(l) \wedge (\boldsymbol{\tau}(l, x, t) = \boldsymbol{\tau}(l, x', t)) \wedge (\boldsymbol{\epsilon}(l, x, t) = \boldsymbol{\epsilon}(l, x', t))$.

$$\mathfrak{P}\,\mathbf{q}, \mathbf{q}'\,[\text{CM} \rightarrow (s \uparrow \text{E}(Ap))(\mathbf{q}, \mathbf{q}')\,],$$

where $\mathbf{q}$ *and* $\mathbf{q}'$ *are as above.*

Proof. The antecedent states that the two organizations being compared have identical distributions of intrinsic appeal to typical audience members at a position and of distribution of engagement over positions. The minimal rule chain that links the antecedent and consequent uses the definition of share of engagement: $\epsilon(l, x, z, t) = en(l, x, z, t)/En(l, x, t)$. If the two organizations have identical shares of engagement at each position, then the one with greater total engagement has higher engagement at each position. The definition of scale advantage (D10.1) tells that the organization with larger scale has a higher level of expected total engagement. Finally, P8.4 completes the chain. □

Unfortunately, the result in L10.1 is too narrow to support the partitioning theory, because it assumes that the organizations being compared have identical niches. We have to add a specification of the social structure of the market to complete the job.

Below we develop a simple model of the market that distinguishes a center, near-center, and periphery. We will argue that organizations with the same location are affected similarly by changes in the structure of the market. This means that we cannot rely wholly on the model in Chapter 8; we must supplement it with additional premises. We do so by elaborating the concept of niche overlap so as to take account of the effect of scale differences.

Scale-advantage was not yet in the picture in Chapter 8. Therefore, we treated all overlaps of given thickness as alike in affecting competitive intensity in modeling competition. Now we must refine this view for markets that allow scale advantage so that we can take account of the effects of scale. In such markets, larger competitors pose more danger than do smaller ones, because they can use their scale to generate high levels of engagement and thereby heighten actual appeal (in positions in which their offerings have nonzero intrinsic appeal).

We address the implications of scale for competitive intensity by considering *scale-weighted* overlaps. Recall that D9.3 specified the thickness of the overlap of the niche of x' with the niche of x for the label l as

$$ov(l, x, x', t) = \frac{\text{card}(\mathbf{f}(l, x, t) \cap \mathbf{f}(l, x', t))}{\text{card}\, \mathbf{f}(l, x, t)}.$$

The motivation for this definition builds on the presumption that the organizations being compared have the same total engagement so that their proportional engagement at a position, $\epsilon(l, x, z, t)$, captures the relevant facts about engagement. In other words, under the principle of allocation introduced in Chapter 8, there is no need to consider actual *levels* of engagement at positions. However, if scale-advantage overrides the principle, then the implications of overlaps depend upon the scale differences of the organizations being considered, because a producer's expected total engagement grows with its scale in markets with scale advantage according to D10.1. This implies that the ratio of expected total engagement of a pair of organizations is proportional to the ratio of their scales in a market with scale advantage.

We use this implication in defining scale-weighted overlap as ordinary overlap (as in D9.3) multiplied by the ratio of the scales of the two organizations.

Definition 10.2 (An organization's scale-weighted niche overlap).

A. *The pairwise scale-weighted overlap thickness for a pair of producers is*

$$s\_ov(l, x, x', t) = ov(l, x, x', t) \cdot \frac{s(l, x', t)}{s(l, x, t)};$$

B. *the total scale-weighted overlap thickness for a producer is*

$$s\_Ov(l, x, t) = \textstyle\sum_{x' \neq x} s\_ov(l, x, x', t).$$

Organizations whose niches overlap with those of other organizations can see their fates affected by what happens to those other organizations. When, for any number of reasons, an overlapping organization grows in scale, the scale of a focal organization becomes harder to sustain; it experiences competitive pressure. We propose a parallel to L8.3, which holds that expected fitness declines with total niche overlap.

Postulate 10.1. *In markets with scale advantage, a producer's expected total fitness in a category,* $\Phi(l, x, t)$*, normally decreases with its total scale-weighted overlap thickness,* $s\_Ov(l, x, t)$*.*

$$\mathfrak{N}\, \mathbf{q}, \mathbf{q}' \left[\text{SA} \wedge \text{CM} \rightarrow (s\_Ov \downarrow \mathrm{E}(\Phi))(\mathbf{q}, \mathbf{q}') \right],$$

where $\mathbf{q}$ *and* $\mathbf{q}'$ *are as above.*

Next we identify a set of segments of a market and link the dynamics of the producers in the different segments. Because the partitioning argument features scale, we decided to link the fates of organizations in different segments in terms of scale. For this purpose, we need to postulate a feedback from fitness to scale. We argue that a drop in an organization's fitness causes its scale to decline but that the decline might involve some delay.

Notation. At this point in the argument, we need to consider monotonic relationships with some delay. We use the following notation. The delayed monotonic positive relationship $f \Uparrow g$ holds if and only if any difference between the f values of two organizations that is sustained for a long enough period results in a similar difference between their g values (provided that their g values were equal at the beginning of the period in consideration). Appendix D provides the formal details.

Postulate 10.2. *In markets with scale advantage, a producer's expected scale,* $\mathrm{E}(s)$*, normally increases with its fitness,* Φ*, with some delay.*

$$\mathfrak{N}\, \mathbf{q}, \mathbf{q}' \left[\text{SA} \wedge \text{CM} \rightarrow (\Phi \Uparrow \mathrm{E}(s))\, (\mathbf{q}, \mathbf{q}') \right],$$

where $\mathbf{q}$ *and* $\mathbf{q}'$ *are as above.*

Lemma 10.2. *In markets with scale advantage, a producer's expected scale,* $\mathrm{E}(s)$*, presumably declines (with some delay) as its scale-weighted total overlap,* s_Ov*, increases.*

$$\mathfrak{P}\, \mathbf{q}, \mathbf{q}' \left[\text{SA} \wedge \text{CM} \rightarrow (s\_Ov \Downarrow \mathrm{E}(s))\, (\mathbf{q}, \mathbf{q}') \right],$$

where $\mathbf{q}$ *and* $\mathbf{q}'$ *are as above.*

Proof. The minimal rule chain results from a cut rule applied to P10.1 and P10.2. □

Before we use these constructions to build a model of partitioning, it is worth noting that the conceptualization presented to this point can sort out some of the confusion that has surrounded the discussion of specialism–generalism. Work based on the original niche approach has defined generalism by the width of the fundamental niche. Work in the partitioning line equated generalism with wide niche breadth in the market center, which is strongly associated with scale. This divergence has led to debate about the association between size and width. Some analysts wondered what to think of a firm like Ford Motor Company during the Model-T era. Ford was one of the world's largest companies at that time; but it had an extremely narrow product range, which would suggest that it be coded as a specialist in product space (see Dobrev, Kim, and Hannan 2001). On the other hand, Ford's Model T appealed to a very large (and broad) market segment, which would suggest that it was a generalist, as we define niches here. Therefore, whether this organization should be considered as a specialist or a generalist depends upon the dimension used in specifying the niche.

Suppose that we maintain the focus on appeal over social positions (which makes Ford in the 1920s a generalist). Does Ford's capture of half the world's sales of automobiles at that time mean that its fundamental niche was broader than that of other automobile manufacturers (or of Ford Motor Company at the time that it originally introduced the Model T)? We can gain some insight about this question by thinking about markets that contain many competitors and have high levels of niche overlap. Due to niche overlap, realized niches in such a market will generally be narrower—often much narrower—than fundamental niches. However, in markets that allow scale advantages, some organizations might manage to grow large. If this happens, the large organizations will gain appeal over positions in their fundamental niches such that their realized niches will tend to widen, even if their fundamental niches remain constant. In such a scenario, size and the width of realized niches will be positively correlated, even if size is uncorrelated with the width of the fundamental niche.

Such reasoning convinced us that clarity might be gained by weakening reliance on the terms specialist and generalist. Instead, we concentrate on the widths of fundamental and realized niches (in the chosen dimension).

10.2 MARKET CENTER

The next condition to be considered is the presence of a market center. A center of a market is a set of social positions in which a producer can attain large scale because the intrinsic appeal of the category is high at each position and there is a large audience at each position. For instance, Christophe Boone, Glenn Carroll, and Arjen van Witteloostuijn (2002) show that consumer demand for newspaper markets in the Netherlands concentrate around strong peaks or modes along the dimensions of age, education, religion, and politics. Because the intrinsic appeal of newspapers does not vary strongly over the social space, these peaks in the socio-demographic space likely constitute a market center. Likewise Carroll, Dobrev, and Swaminathan (2002) show that the probability that an American drinks beer display a unimodal joint distribution when classified by age and political outlook. The positions in which the probability is high and the audience is large are the center of the American beer market.

We formalize this notion using the grade-of-membership function for the category niche from D8.3, $\gamma(l, z, t)$, and the size of the audience at the position z: $|\{y \mid pos(y, t) = z\}|$. Let the potential size of the demand for the offerings of prototypical producers in category l at position z at time t be denoted as:

$$\theta(l, z, t) = f(\gamma(l, z, t), |\{y \mid pos(y, t) = z\}|), \quad p \in \mathbf{p},$$

and f is monotonically increasing in both arguments.

For a position to lie in a market center, $\theta(l, z, t)$ should be far above the average over all positions. How far above the average this should be is not relevant to the argument; but this is an important question in empirical applications. Let $\mathbf{ctr}(l, t)$ be a partial function that maps populations to sets of social positions and that identifies the positions of unusually high levels of $\theta(l, z, t)$. (The function is partial because some markets might lack a center.)

Definition 10.3 (Market center). *The market center for the population l, in formal terms* $\mathbf{ctr}(l, t) = \mathbf{z}$*, consists of those social positions at which the potential size of the demand for the offerings of prototypical members of the category* l *exceeds the average across social positions in the market by some (unspecified) criterion* $\mathfrak{p}$ *at time* t.

$$\mathbf{ctr} : \langle \mathbf{l}, \mathbf{t} \rangle \hookrightarrow \mathcal{P}(\mathbf{p}),$$

and

$$z \in \mathbf{ctr}(l, t) \leftrightarrow (\theta(l, z, t) - \bar{\theta}(l, t) > \mathfrak{p}),$$

where $\bar{\theta}(l, t)$ *is the average level of* $\xi(l, z, t)$ *over the set of social positions and* $\mathfrak{p}$ *is a threshold.*

(As elsewhere, the symbol $\hookrightarrow$ denotes a partial function and $\mathcal{P}$ denotes the power-set, the set of all subsets of a set.)

10.3 MARKET SEGMENTS AND CROWDING

Perhaps the most important decision in building a formal model of partitioning concerns how to represent the linkage between concentration in the center and the fates of organizations in the periphery.

We adapt an approach used by Hannan (1979) to explain the resurgence of regional ethnic identities in later stages of national development (e.g., the upsurge of Welsh, Scottish, Breton, Catalan, and Québécois separatist movements in the middle of the twentieth century). This earlier argument, like the one developed here, focuses on the tension between scale advantage and appeal. It assumes that movements based on localized identities have greater appeal, ceteris paribus, than those based on larger-scale identities because the local movements can tune their engagement to the idiosyncrasies of the local social structure. But it also assumes that larger-scale movements have better chances of succeeding in contention with the political center. It asserts that the continuing salience of highly localized identities impedes mobilization on the basis of a regional identity. "As long as the smallest scale identities remain strong and salient to collective action, the likelihood of effective and sustained action on the basis of widely shared ethnic identities is low" (Hannan 1979: 255). Various processes of economic and political development, loosely called modernization, tend to eliminate the idiosyncratic conditions that preserve local differences with the result that the salience of local identities declines. This decline tilts the competitive balance toward organizations built on regional identities (which have the advantage of potential large scale) and allows an upsurge of organizational mobilization based on regional identities.

For our purposes, the key insight in this story concerns the process of *competitive release.* Population biologists use this term to refer to situations in which an event improves the viability of a focal population by diminishing the viability of its predators or competitors. For instance, application of broad-spectrum pesticides in an effort to eliminate a certain "pest" sometimes prove more effective at eliminating its predators and competitors with the result that the population of pests actually proliferates. In the case at hand, we use the term competitive release to refer to conditions that debilitate a population of organizations that had effectively precluded the emergence and growth of a focal population.

We rely on a competitive release mechanism to explain the resurgence of organizations in the periphery. One reading of Carroll's (1985) original argument suggests that the demise of relatively large organizations that competed partly in the periphery sparks this resurgence. We formalize a version of this argument by distinguishing three locations in a market:

1. *center positions,* occupied by organizations whose positions of peak (intrinsic) appeal lie in the market center and whose fundamental niches intersect the market center,

2. *near-center positions,* occupied by those whose peak-appeal positions lie at least partly outside the market center but whose fundamental niches intersect a market center, and

3. *peripheral positions,* occupied by those whose fundamental niches do not intersect the market center.

According to the view of partitioning that we offer, the growth of very large, dominant organizations in the center (concentration) comes at the expense of organizations in the near-center and the demise of near-center organizations removes a powerful competitive constraint on organizations in the periphery.

With these preliminaries, we define formally the (disjoint) positions in the market.

Definition 10.4 (Center-market position). *An organization occupies a market-center position if and only if all of its peak-appeal positions lie in the market center* *and its fundamental niche intersects the market center.*

$$\text{CENT}(l, x, t) \leftrightarrow \text{M}(l, x, t) \wedge (\mathbf{pk}(l, t) \subseteq \mathbf{ctr}(l, t)) \\ \wedge (\mathbf{f}(l, x, t) \cap \mathbf{ctr}(l, t) \neq \emptyset)].$$

(The conjunct in the second line in the foregoing formula excludes as a center-position organization one that has peak appeal in the center but, for some weird reason, does not engage in the center (which would make its fundamental niche lie outside of the market center.)

Definition 10.5 (Near-center position). *An organization has a position in a near-center if and only if it has a position of peak appeal that lies outside the market center but its fundamental niche intersects a market center.*

$$\text{NC}(l, x, t) \leftrightarrow \text{M}(l, x, t) \wedge (\mathbf{pk}(l, t) \setminus \mathbf{ctr}(l, t) \neq \emptyset) \\ \wedge (\mathbf{f}(l, x, t) \cap \mathbf{ctr}(l, t) \neq \emptyset),$$

where $\setminus$ denotes set subtraction.

Definition 10.6 (Peripheral position). *An organization lies in the periphery if and only if its fundamental niche does not intersect the market center.*

$$\text{PER}(l, x, t) \leftrightarrow \text{M}(l, x, t) \wedge (\mathbf{f}(l, x, t) \cap \mathbf{pk}(l, t) = \emptyset)].$$

Figure 10.1 illustrates the distinctions among market niches. This illustration assumes that the audience is distributed over four positions, labeled a, b, c, and d. The panel in the upper left of the figure shows a possible distribution of the potential population demand (θ) over positions (the vertical axis). As this figure is drawn, this potential demand is much higher at the position a than the others, so much more that a qualifies as the market center. The other three panels in the figure illustrate possible center, near-center, and peripheral niches in this market. In each case, the vertical axis, ζ, is the grade of membership of a position in an organization's (fundamental) niche. For simplicity, we restricted the set of peak-appeal positions to a singleton in each case.

The top-right panel in this figure illustrates a center niche, because the position of peak appeal falls in the market center, position a. The bottom-left panel illustrates a near-center niche, because the position of peak appeal (b) falls outside of the market center a but the grade of membership of a in the niche is positive. Finally, the bottom-right panel illustrates a peripheral niche: the niche has a zero grade of membership in the market center a.

Market centers provide opportunities to grow large because, by definition, positions in a market center combine high intrinsic appeal for the relevant product and a large local audience. The organizations with the best position to capture these opportunities are those whose peak appeal lies in a market center. Therefore, the expected scale of an organization in a center exceeds that of an organization outside any center. (More specific information about the intensity of competition in the center can, of course, override this assumption, as we see below.) Peripheral organizations operate in the least-rich portions of the resource distribution (because

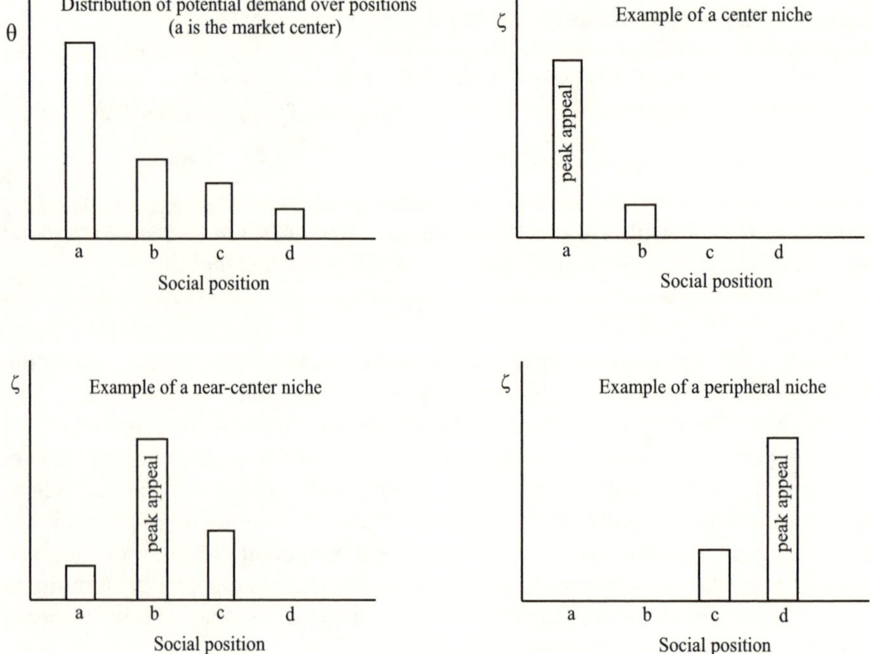

Figure 10.1 Illustration of center, near-center, and peripheral niches in a market whose center is position a

their fundamental niches do not cover any of the most resource-rich segments). Therefore, the expected scale of a near-center organization normally exceeds that of a peripheral organization. We record these expectations in a meaning postulate.

Meaning postulate 10.1. *Typical organizations located in a market center normally have larger expected scale than those located in a near center; and those in a near center have larger expected scale than those in the periphery.*

$$\mathfrak{N}\, l, t, x_1, x_2, x_3\, [\text{CENT}(l, x_1, t) \wedge \text{NC}(l, x_2, t) \wedge \text{PER}(l, x_3, t) \\ \rightarrow (\text{E}(s(l, x_1, t)) > \text{E}(s(l, x_2, t)) > \text{E}(s(l, x_3, t)))].$$

Throughout much of its history in the second half of the twentieth century, the population of American beer brewers reflected this expected pattern. In the center, the mass production brewers such as Anheuser-Busch and Miller made beers appealing to taste found most frequently in the market, light lagers mainly. These organizations possessed mammoth scale (literally tens of millions of barrels per year) compared to others in the market, fostering a common joke that each spills more beer in a day than other brewers make in an entire year. In the periphery, the microbreweries flourished by offering "full-flavor" malt beverages such as porter and stout, appealing to a much rarer taste. Microbreweries sometimes made only several thousand barrels of beer per year. In the near center, many older regional breweries such as Pittsburgh Brewing, New York's Rheingold Brewing, and Cincinnati's Hudepohl Brewing struggled to survive by emphasizing their historic ties to the region, and most did not survive. The average scale of the regional brewers fell in the middle ground between the mass producers and the microbreweries.

Partitioning depends upon chains of interactions among the outcomes to organizations in different segments of the market. Such chaining of dynamics requires a certain level of intensity of competition, which depends upon a certain level of average total thickness of niche overlaps.

We restrict the argument about partitioning dynamics to apply to markets with intense competition using the predicate $\text{CROWD}(l, t)$, which reads as "the market for population l is crowded." We define this predicate in terms of an unspecified level of average niche overlap, given by the parameter $\mathfrak{k}$.

Definition 10.7 (Market crowding). *A market is crowded at a time point if and only if the expected level of the thickness of niche overlaps of center organizations on near-center organizations and of near-center organizations on peripheral organizations each normally exceed certain thresholds.*

$$\text{CROWD}(l, t) \leftrightarrow \mathfrak{N}\, l, t, x_1, x_2, x_3\, [\text{CENT}(l, x_1, t) \wedge \text{NC}(l, x_2, t) \wedge \text{PER}(l, x_3, t) \\ \rightarrow (\text{E}(ov(l, x_2, x_1, t)) > \mathfrak{w}_1) \wedge (\text{E}(ov(l, x_3, x_2, t)) > \mathfrak{w}_2)].$$

The illustration in figure 10.1 depicts a potentially crowded market. (Whether it is actually crowded depends on the actual thresholds.) This is because the center and near-center niches overlap, as do the near-center and periphery niches.

Unlike the case of diffuse competition analyzed in Chapter 4, the partitioning story holds that competition gets localized, by tastes, identities, or categories. For instance, in the American beer population, the mass producers fought each other for market share in the center by attempting to convince consumers that their light lager was the best tasting, least filling, or sexiest and by developing nationwide distribution systems to make the beer widely available. Microbreweries competed within category by offering similar traditional styles of beer that differed radically from those of the mass producers. Near-center regional breweries typically offered beers closer in taste to those of the mass producers along with claims of traditional regional ties. The identities of these types of breweries also came strongly into play, as the microbrewers fostered a social-movement-like following that defined the (center market) mass producers as evil and their products as inauthentic and even harmful.

We interpret this argument as meaning that (1) niches generally overlap across segment boundaries but (2) niches generally do not overlap across more than one segment boundary. We implement this notion in a meaning postulate that indirectly defines the relation between the center and the periphery.

Meaning postulate 10.2. *Fundamental niches of center organizations normally do not overlap those of peripheral ones (in a prominent population).*

$$\mathfrak{N}\, l, t, x, x' \left[\text{PR}(l,t) \wedge \text{PER}(l,x,t) \wedge \text{CENT}(l,x',t) \rightarrow (\text{E}(ov(l,x,x',t)) = 0)\right].$$

The illustrations in figure 10.1 conform to this meaning of center–periphery, because the periphery and center niches do not overlap.

10.4 DYNAMICS OF PARTITIONING

We have now developed a conceptual structure that allows us to derive theorems that state the main conclusions of resource partitioning theory. The key dynamic of partitioning involves growth in the scale of the largest organizations in the market. As noted above, Carroll (1985) argued that the rise to dominance of a large-scale organization in the center frees resources in the periphery. This comes about as the dominant organization destroys other organizations in the center but does not completely cover their realized niches.

The theory presented here elaborates this argument to apply to the proposed three-way partitioning. We begin by defining the average scales realized in the center and near-center at a point in time.

Definition 10.8 (Average scale).

A. *The average scale in the market center is*

$$\bar{s}^c(l,t) = \textstyle\sum_{x|\text{CENT}(l,x,t)} s(l,x,t)/|\{x \mid \text{CENT}(l,x,t)\}|;$$

B. *the average scale in the near-center is*

$$\bar{s}^n(l,t) = \textstyle\sum_{x|\text{NC}(l,x,t)} s(l,x,t)/|\{x \mid \text{NC}(l,x,t)\}|.$$

Notation. The portion of the theory that follows involves comparisons of pairs of producers of the same age in the same population in a crowded market with a center and scale advantage. Therefore, we need to instantiate all of these conditions in the antecedents of all relevant formulas. To simplify formulas, we introduce the following notation:

$$\mathcal{Q}_1 \leftrightarrow \text{SA}(l) \wedge \text{CROWD}(l,t) \wedge \text{CROWD}(l,t') \wedge (\mathbf{ctr}(l,t) \neq \emptyset) \wedge (\mathbf{ctr}(l,t') \neq \emptyset) \\ \wedge \text{CM}(l,x,x',t,t') \wedge (a(x,t) = a(x',t')) \wedge (Ov(l,x,t) = Ov(l,x',t')).$$

Because the niches of near-center organizations generally overlap those of some center organizations in crowded markets, the emergence of one or more very large organizations in the center greatly amplifies the competitive pressure on some—perhaps all—near-center organizations. This rise in competitive intensity in the center generally causes near-center organizations to lose their footholds in the center. As a result, near-center organizations lose opportunities in the resource-rich segment of the market and their expected scale declines. A parallel argument applies for the near-center and periphery.

Lemma 10.3. *If the total thicknesses of scale-weighted overlaps of near-center (peripheral) organization is the same at two time points and the average scale of center (near-center) organizations is greater at one time point than the other, then the expected scale-weighted overlap of the near-center (peripheral) organization presumably is higher at that time point.*

A. $\mathfrak{P}\,\mathbf{q},\mathbf{q}'\,[\,\mathcal{Q}_1 \wedge \text{NC}(l,x,t) \wedge \text{NC}(l,x',t') \rightarrow (\bar{s}^c \uparrow \text{E}(s\_Ov))(\mathbf{q},\mathbf{q}')\,];$

B. $\mathfrak{P}\,\mathbf{q},\mathbf{q}'\,[\,\mathcal{Q}_1 \wedge \text{PER}(l,x,t) \wedge \text{PER}(l,x',t') \rightarrow (\bar{s}^n \uparrow \text{E}(s\_Ov))(\mathbf{q},\mathbf{q}')\,],$

where $\mathbf{q}$ *and* $\mathbf{q}'$ *are as above.*

Proof. Part A: The minimal rule chain begins with D10.7, the definition of crowding, which tells that a near-center organization's expected overlap with a center organization is positive. If the total overlap thickness is the same at two time points and the average scale in the center grows, then the expected scale of at least some overlapping organizations increases for a near-center organization and the consequent follows.

The proof of part B follows the same lines. □

Now we can begin to spin out some of the rich implications of this simple story.

Theorem 10.1. *In a crowded market with a center and scale advantage, increased average scale in the center presumably lowers (with some delay) the expected fitness of organizations in the near-center.*

$$\mathfrak{P}\,\mathbf{q},\mathbf{q}'\,[\,\mathcal{Q}_1 \wedge \text{NC}(l,x,t) \wedge \text{NC}(l,x',t') \rightarrow (\bar{s}^c \Downarrow \text{E}(\Phi))(\mathbf{q},\mathbf{q}')\,],$$

where $\mathbf{q}$ *and* $\mathbf{q}'$ *are as above.*

Proof. The minimal rule chain results from a cut rule applied to (the rule chain supporting) L10.3 and P10.1 ($SA \rightarrow (s\_OV \Downarrow \Phi)$); as elsewhere we invoke the metarule for chaining expected values and realizations of random variables (Section 6.5). □

A study of Dutch newspapers (Boone, Carroll, and van Witteloostuijn 2002) provides empirical support for T10.1. It finds that as the center consisting of national papers located in the Dutch Randstad became more concentrated, the growth rates and profitability of distant provincial newspapers increased but the growth and profitability of local newspapers situated in the Randstad declined. The facts of the case make clear that local Randstad newspapers qualify as near-center organizations.

The same kind of dynamics plays out between the near-center and periphery according to the theory.

Theorem 10.2. *In a crowded market with a center and scale advantage, increased average scale among near-center organizations presumably lowers (with some delay) the expected fitness of organizations in the periphery.*

$$\mathfrak{P}\,\mathbf{q},\mathbf{q}'\,[\,\mathcal{Q}_1 \wedge \text{PER}(l,x,t) \wedge \text{PER}(l,x',t') \rightarrow (\bar{s}^n \Downarrow \text{E}(\Phi))(\mathbf{q},\mathbf{q}')\,],$$

where $\mathbf{q}$ *and* $\mathbf{q}'$ *are as above.*

Proof. The minimal rule chain results from a cut rule applied to (the rule chain supporting) L10.3 and P10.1 ($SA \rightarrow (s\_OV \Downarrow \Phi)$) and the metarule for chaining expectations and realizations. □

Now we can derive a set of theorems that capture the chain of effects across the market segments, the main insight of partitioning theory.

Lemma 10.4. *In a crowded market with a center and scale advantage, increased average scale in the center (near-center) presumably lowers (with some delay) the expected scale of organizations in the near-center (periphery) with some delay.*

A. $\mathfrak{P}\,\mathbf{q},\mathbf{q}'\,[\,\mathcal{Q}_1 \wedge \text{NC}(l,x,t) \wedge \text{NC}(l,x',t') \rightarrow (\bar{s}^c \Downarrow \text{E}(s))(\mathbf{q},\mathbf{q}')\,];$

B. $\mathfrak{P}\,\mathbf{q},\mathbf{q}'\,[\,\mathcal{Q}_1 \wedge \text{PER}(l,x,t) \wedge \text{PER}(l,x',t') \rightarrow (\bar{s}^n \Downarrow \text{E}(s))(\mathbf{q},\mathbf{q}')\,],$

where $\mathbf{q}$ *and* $\mathbf{q}'$ *are as above.*

Proof. The minimal rule chain results from a cut rule applied to (the rule chain supporting) L10.3A for part A (and L10.3B for part B) and (the rule chain behind) L10.2 ($\text{SA} \rightarrow (\Phi \Uparrow \text{E}(s))$) along with the metarule from Section 6.5. □

Lemma 10.5. *In a crowded market with a center and scale advantage, increased average scale in the center presumably boosts (with some delay) the expected fitness of organizations in the periphery.*

$$\mathfrak{P}\,\mathbf{q},\mathbf{q}'\,[\,\mathcal{Q}_1 \wedge \text{PER}(l,x,t) \wedge \text{PER}(l,x',t') \rightarrow (\bar{s}^c \Uparrow \text{E}(\Phi))(\mathbf{q},\mathbf{q}')\,],$$

where $\mathbf{q}$ *and* $\mathbf{q}'$ *are as above.*

Proof. The minimal rule chain results from a cut rule applied to (the rule chains supporting) L10.4A (increasing scale in the center lowers the expected scale of organizations in the near center), L10.3B (increased scale in the near center lowers the expected scale-weighted overlap of organizations in the periphery), and P10.1 (expected fitness declines with scale-weighted overlap). □

This theorem states an instance of competitive release, as noted above. Concentration in the center improves the life chances of peripheral organizations by diminishing the vitality of those organizations that impose greatest competitive constraint on them.

Now we develop the implications of the argument for (estimable) hazards of mortality and the hazard of founding.

Theorem 10.3. *In a crowded market with a center and scale advantage, growth in the average scale in the center presumably amplifies (with some delay) the hazard of mortality of organizations in its near center, and growth in the average scale in the near center presumably amplifies (with some delay) the hazard of mortality of organizations in the periphery.*

A. $\mathfrak{P}\,\mathbf{q}, \mathbf{q}'\,[\,\mathcal{Q}_1 \wedge \mathrm{NC}(l, x, t) \wedge \mathrm{NC}(l, x', t') \rightarrow (\bar{s}^c \Uparrow \omega)(\mathbf{q}, \mathbf{q}')\,];$

B. $\mathfrak{P}\,\mathbf{q}, \mathbf{q}'\,[\,\mathcal{Q}_1 \wedge \mathrm{PER}(l, x, t) \wedge \mathrm{PER}(l, x', t') \rightarrow (\bar{s}^n \Uparrow \omega)(\mathbf{q}, \mathbf{q}')\,],$

where $\mathbf{q}$ *and* $\mathbf{q}'$ *are as above.*

Proof. The minimal rule chains for these theorems use the minimal rule chain supporting L10.4 and the meaning postulate that tells that the hazard of mortality is inversely proportional to fitness (M9.1). □

Finally, we can state and prove a parallel to the most celebrated result on partitioning. Carroll (1985) predicted that the mortality hazard of specialist organizations declines as a market (with a center) concentrates; and he found such a result for populations of American newspaper publishers. This result has been replicated in many kinds of markets (Carroll and Hannan 2000; Carroll, Dobrev, and Swaminathan 2002). Given Carroll's characterization of specialists as organizations located in the periphery (and given that concentration is proportional to the size of the largest organization in the market), this result entails a negative relationship between the size of the largest organization and the hazard of mortality for organizations located in the periphery. This relationship follows from the theory.

Theorem 10.4. *In a crowded market with a center and scale advantage, growth in the average scale in the center presumably lowers (with some delay) the mortality hazard of organizations in the periphery.*

$$\mathfrak{P}\,\mathbf{q}, \mathbf{q}'\,[\,\mathcal{Q}_1 \wedge \mathrm{PER}(l, x, t) \wedge \mathrm{PER}(l, x', t') \rightarrow (\bar{s}^c \Downarrow \omega)(\mathbf{q}, \mathbf{q}')\,],$$

where $\mathbf{q}$ *and* $\mathbf{q}'$ *are as above.*

Proof. The minimal rule chain results from a cut rule applied to (the chain supporting) L10.4 and M9.1 (and the metarule on chaining). □

Implications of Partitioning

While the periphery segment in populations of newspaper publishers appears to have developed significantly through differential mortality of the kind modeled here, in other partitioned populations (such as beer brewing) it appears to result primarily from new foundings. Extending the theory to apply to foundings seems both possible and plausible; but this does require additional assumptions about the rate at which organizations enter a population.

Hazards of founding (or entry) can be defined for each region of the market. Let $\lambda^n(l,t)$ and $\lambda^p(l,t)$ denote the hazards of entry or founding in the near-center and periphery, respectively. The standard theory of density dependence holds that the hazard of founding in a population is proportional to the legitimation of the form that underlies the population and inversely proportional to the intensity of competition faced by the members of the population (Chapter 4). We now deal with situations in which the forms underlying populations are (nearly) fully legitimated, that the categories are forms (as explained in Chapter 4). Therefore, systematic variation in hazards of founding over time (given full legitimation) reflects changes in the intensity of competition.

To this point we have treated competitive intensity at the organization level. We have assumed that this competitive intensity is proportional to the average scale of the organizations whose niches overlap that of the focal organization. We now need a parallel construct at the segment level. Let $Comp^n(l,t)$ and $Comp^p(l,t)$ denote functions that record the average level of competitive pressure in the near-center and periphery of the market, respectively. And we rely on the following notational shorthand:

$$\mathcal{Q}_2 \leftrightarrow \text{PR}(l,t) \wedge \text{PR}(l,t') \wedge \text{SA}(l) \wedge \text{CROWD}(l,t) \wedge \text{CROWD}(l,t') \\ \wedge (\mathbf{ctr}(l,t) \neq \emptyset) \wedge (\mathbf{ctr}(l,t') \neq \emptyset).$$

Postulate 10.3. *The expected competitive force on entry in the near-center (periphery) normally rises monotonically with the average scale in the center (near-center).*

$$\text{A.} \quad \mathfrak{N}\,\mathbf{q},\mathbf{q}'\,[\,\mathcal{Q}_2 \rightarrow (\bar{s}^c \uparrow \text{E}(Comp^n))(\mathbf{q},\mathbf{q}')\,];$$
$$\text{B.} \quad \mathfrak{N}\,\mathbf{q},\mathbf{q}'\,[\,\mathcal{Q}_2 \rightarrow (\bar{s}^n \uparrow \text{E}(Comp^p))(\mathbf{q},\mathbf{q}')\,],$$

where $\mathbf{q} = \langle l,t\rangle$ *and* $\mathbf{q}' = \langle l,t'\rangle$.

Postulate 10.4. *The hazard of entry in a segment, λ, normally declines monotonically with the average level of intensity of competition in that segment.*

$$\text{A.} \quad \mathfrak{N}\,\mathbf{q},\mathbf{q}'\,[\,\mathcal{Q}_2 \rightarrow (Comp^n \downarrow \lambda^n)(\mathbf{q},\mathbf{q}')\,];$$
$$\text{B.} \quad \mathfrak{N}\,\mathbf{q},\mathbf{q}'\,[\,\mathcal{Q}_2 \rightarrow (Comp^p \downarrow \lambda^p)(\mathbf{q},\mathbf{q}')\,],$$

where $\mathbf{q}$ *and* $\mathbf{q}'$ *are as above.*

Lemma 10.6. *The hazard of entry in the near-center (periphery) presumably declines monotonically with the average scale in a market center (near-center).*

$$\text{A.} \quad \mathfrak{P}\,\mathbf{q},\mathbf{q}'\,[\,\mathcal{Q}_2 \rightarrow (\bar{s}^c \downarrow \lambda^n)(\mathbf{q},\mathbf{q}')\,];$$
$$\text{B.} \quad \mathfrak{P}\,\mathbf{q},\mathbf{q}'\,[\,\mathcal{Q}_2 \rightarrow (\bar{s}^n \downarrow \lambda^p)(\mathbf{q},\mathbf{q}')\,],$$

where $\mathbf{q}$ *and* $\mathbf{q}'$ *are as above.*

Proof. The minimal rule chains results from a cut rule applied to P10.3 and P10.4 (and the metarule on chaining). □

Finally, we can derive the target theorem linking scale in the center to enhanced entry in the periphery.

Theorem 10.5. *The hazard of entry in the periphery presumably increases monotonically (with some delay) with the average scale in a market center.*

$$\mathfrak{P}\,\mathbf{q},\mathbf{q}'\,[\,\mathcal{Q}_2 \rightarrow (\bar{s}^c \Uparrow \lambda^p)(\mathbf{q},\mathbf{q}')\,],$$

where $\mathbf{q}$ *and* $\mathbf{q}'$ *are as above.*

Proof. The minimal rule chain results from a cut rule applied to P10.3, P10.4, and (the rule chain behind) L10.6 (and the metarule on chaining). □

The next part of the argument requires that we define the "classical" density (numbers) of organizations in the three market segments. We treat these as crisp sets, because the distinctions among market segments are *analytical* distinctions, not categories used by the audience. These definitions characterize the sets of organizations defined by segment type. So, for instance, we define the total scale in the center as the total scale of all organizations with a center location, not the scale in the market center for all organizations in the market.

Definition 10.9 (Segment density). *"Classical" organizational density by segment:*

$$N^c(l,t) = |\{x \mid \text{CENT}(l,x,t)\}|;$$
$$N^n(l,t) = |\{x \mid \text{NC}(l,x,t)\}|;$$
$$N^p(l,t) = |\{x \mid \text{PER}(l,x,t)\}|.$$

We need to use a basic result on stochastic processes that relates density to the hazards of founding and mortality.

Postulate 10.5. *The classical density in a population normally is an increasing function of the hazard of founding,* λ, *and a decreasing function of the average hazard of mortality,* $\bar{\omega}$.

$$\text{A.}\quad \forall\,\mathbf{q},\mathbf{q}'\,[(\lambda \Uparrow \mathrm{E}(N))(\mathbf{q},\mathbf{q}')\,];$$
$$\text{B.}\quad \forall\,\mathbf{q},\mathbf{q}'\,[(\bar{\omega} \Downarrow \mathrm{E}(N))(\mathbf{q},\mathbf{q}')\,],$$

where $\bar{\omega}(l,t)$ *is the average hazard of mortality of those in the population defined by* l *at risk at time* t, *and* $\mathbf{q} = \langle l,t\rangle$, *and* $\mathbf{q}' = \langle l,t'\rangle$.

Theorem 10.6. *The expected classical density in the near-center (periphery) presumably declines monotonically (with some delay) with the average scale in the center (near-center).*

$$\text{A.}\quad \mathfrak{P}\,\mathbf{q},\mathbf{q}'\,[\,\mathcal{Q}_2 \rightarrow (\bar{s}^c \Downarrow \mathrm{E}(N^n))(\mathbf{q},\mathbf{q}')\,];$$
$$\text{B.}\quad \mathfrak{P}\,\mathbf{q},\mathbf{q}'\,[\,\mathcal{Q}_2 \rightarrow (\bar{s}^n \Downarrow \mathrm{E}(N^p))(\mathbf{q},\mathbf{q}')\,],$$

where $\mathbf{q}$ *and* $\mathbf{q}'$ *are as above.*

Proof. The minimal rule chain for part A uses the rule chains behind T10.3A (the hazard of mortality in the near-center increases monotonically with the average scale in the center) and T10.6A (the hazard of entry in the near-center decreases monotonically with the average scale in the near-center) along with P10.5 (the relationship of density to the underlying hazards). The rule chain for part B uses the B parts of the two theorems. □

We can now derive another target theorem that links scale in the center to the density in the periphery.

Theorem 10.7. *The expected classical density in the periphery presumably increases monotonically (with some delay) with the average scale in the center.*

$$\mathfrak{P}\, \mathbf{q}, \mathbf{q}' \, [\, \mathcal{Q}_2 \rightarrow (\bar{s}^c \Uparrow \mathrm{E}(N^p))(\mathbf{q}, \mathbf{q}') \,],$$

where $\mathbf{q}$ *and* $\mathbf{q}'$ *are as above.*

Proof. The minimal rule chain results from a cut rule applied to (the rule chains supporting) T10.3, T10.6, and P10.5 (and the metarule on chaining). □

10.5 IMPLICATIONS OF CATEGORY MEMBERSHIP

The dynamics treated in the preceding section can partition a market by decimating the near-center. Can such a partitioning persist? Persistence depends on the existence of some force that prevents the giant organizations in the center from expanding to claim the entire market.

The analysis to this point has considered a single population of producers (in a crowded market with a center and scale advantage). In particular, we have not assumed that three subsets (center, near-center, and periphery) constitute populations in the sense that they reflect different audience constructions of classes/categories.

In other words, we have treated the distinctions among the three sets as an analytical distinction as contrasted with a distinction made by members of the audience. So we have treated the relevant audience as applying a common schema to all members of the population members in all segments, despite the local taste differences within the audience. As long as there is a reasonably continuous gradation of appeal over subaudiences and market segments, the absence of sharp discontinuities allows the audience to regard the population as unitary. The shadings of difference do not challenge a sense of commonality.

Partitioning creates a discontinuity that sometimes disrupts this picture. Microbrewing is a case in point. Operators of microbreweries and brewpubs have worked hard to create a separate identity from mass-production breweries. They attempt to present themselves as handcraft artisanal producers who make malt beverages with traditional methods using high-quality ingredients while mass producers use automated systems. Boutique wineries, chocolate manufacturers, and bread bakers also have arisen as a result of partitioning and the creation of new schemata; and they are potential organizational forms.

The relevant discontinuity arises as the near-center organizations succumb to the competitive pressures imposed by the winners of the scale-based competitive struggle in the center. Such partitioning eliminates the near-center organizations that are responsible for the perceived unity of the population, and it therefore sets the stage for clustering, labeling, and codifying the set of producers in the periphery. Because this account is mainly a conjecture on our part at this point, we sketch it verbally rather than present a formalization.

Using ideas from prior chapters on category and form emergence, we could conceive of the process as governed by a set of hazards (to the audience): (1) a hazard of similarity clustering by the focal audience of the organizations in the periphery (at an unspecified time point); (2) a hazard of labeling; and (3) a hazard of codification (schematization).

We would then argue that increasing contrast and density in the periphery coupled with decreasing density in the near-center generally increases (1) the hazard of similarity clustering for the set of organizations in the periphery; (2) the hazard of labeling for the peripheral organizations in the market; (3) the hazard of codification for peripheral organizations in the market; and (4) the expected legitimation for the peripheral organizations in the market. Why?

Clustering in a partitioned market makes codification likely at the time of clustering. The audience already has a code (for the full set of organizations in the population, distributed over segments) that it can modify. It also has a natural way to decide on modifications of the code: apply as code the observable fact that the realized niches of the peripheral organizations are restricted to the periphery. This might be enough to turn a peripheral cluster into a category. Whether such a category survives the perceptions of code violations by existing peripheral organizations and the inflow of claimants remains an open question. Therefore, we restrict the claim about codification to the time of initial clustering.

Conditions are also favorable for legitimation in the periphery after partitioning. The existing model tells that the contrast and density of the set of peripheral organizations rises as the center of the market concentrates. The structure of the partitioning is such that the peripheral organizations will conform to the new code; so legitimation can be achieved more easily.

Codification and legitimation of the peripheral form relies on a distinction vis á vis the center; the resulting collective identity possibly will have an oppositional character (as in the case of microbrewing). The rise of such an identity can stabilize the partitioning.

DISCUSSION

This chapter developed a formal model of partitioning. We think that the reinterpretation of the process clarifies some important issues and enlightens several others related to partitioning. For instance, the newly specified theory contains more detailed guidance for empirical testing. Rather than rely simply on concentration and a summary measure of niche width (often using size as a surrogate), empirical analysts now might explore how to use information on location vis-à-vis the center and crowding to specify empirical tests.

Likewise, the model advanced here also shows new potentially fertile veins for previously neglected empirical issues, such as the limits on niche expansion from the center. Among the theoretical gains to resource partitioning theory is the explicit incorporation of the principle of allocation (a tradeoff between niche width and strength of appeal), a central tenet of the original niche theory that had previously been treated by reference to diseconomies of scope.

In our view, core aspects of resource partitioning theory are now more clearly articulated and also more readily amenable to integration with niche theory. As we have seen, a gain of integration to resource partitioning theory is the explicit incorporation of the principle of allocation Among the potential similar gains of integration to niche theory is a consideration of scale advantages.

PART 4
Organizational Change

Chapter Eleven

Cascading Change

A considerable body of empirical research generally supports the main implications of ecology's theory of structural inertia, namely that change in a core feature raises the hazard of organizational mortality (Hannan and Freeman, 1984; Barnett and Carroll 1995; Carroll and Hannan 2000). However, the theory has not advanced in parallel with the empirical work; further progress in understanding inertia and change requires attention to theoretical foundations.

The inertia story began, somewhat indirectly, with Stinchcombe's (1965) observation of a "correlation of age and structure" across industrial segments. Stinchcombe argued that the stability of organizational structures was partly responsible for the fact that organizations at any age tend to reflect the circumstances of their origins. Subsequent work noted that two principles explain why mature organizations display imprints of the conditions that they experienced in their early days. First, the conditions at time of founding must shape organizations. Second, strong inertial forces must keep organizations from changing (some of) their imprinted feature values; otherwise the imprint would not be recognizable years—even decades—later.

In developing the theory, Hannan and Freeman (1977, 1984) argued that organizations can change, but that certain characteristics display great inertia in the sense that attempts at changing them appear to be onerous, slow, and risky (in the sense of raising the hazard of mortality). The most frequently used part of their theory connects change and mortality; it gets used mainly to motivate studies of the effects of various types of change on the hazard of organizational mortality.

Hannan and Freeman's (1984, 1989) inertia theory deals with changes in the core features of organizations, not peripheral ones. In this formulation, four organizational features constitute a generalized core: the organization's mission, its form of authority (along with the nature of the exchange between the organization and its members), the basic technology used to transform inputs into outputs, and the general marketing strategy. This specification of inertial forces rests on assumptions about the contention, cost, and disruption caused by changing specific domains. Hannan and Freeman (1984) also assert that the list is hierarchical. The most difficult organizational elements to alter, in descending order of flexibility, are mission, form of authority, core technology (including employee skills), and marketing strategy (ways of relating to external constituencies). These elements are "core" precisely because efforts to change them "raise fundamental questions about the nature of the organization" (Hannan and Freeman 1984: 156).

Limiting the scope of the theory in this way—to a set of purported canonical features—now seems ill-founded. Moreover, this limitation on scope does not discipline empirical research very much. Reviews of studies testing the main implications of the theory show that researchers claim a wide variety of organizational features as corelike (Barnett and Carroll 1995; Carroll and Hannan 2000).

Accordingly, in the chapters in this part of the book, we reformulate and extend structural inertia theory (Hannan and Freeman 1977, 1984). In doing so, we pursue two broad objectives. First, we develop a formal language that is suitable for expressing the insights of the original theory and for supporting efforts to deepen and broaden it. Second, we use this language to embed the original arguments in a richer model of organizational structure. We show that some key assumptions of the original theory can be derived as theorems in the new one. This effort involves elaborating what might be called microfoundations for organizational ecology.

The theory building that we undertake illustrates vividly the value of logical formalization in uncovering the hidden assumptions buried in an insight taken as a theoretical principle. That is, we regard the idea that core change in an organization elevates the hazard of mortality as a "target theorem" (in the sense discussed in Chapter 1); and we use the task of formalization to help us uncover some assumptions required to derive it.

Development of inertia theory carries dual significance in organizational ecology. On one hand, the theory proposes explanations for observable features of the organizational world—it predicts scenarios than can turn out to be false empirically. On the other hand, the arguments about inertia help justify the larger enterprise of organizational ecology. To see this, consider the biotic case. An evolutionary theory of population bioecology makes sense because the genes that define species persist across time. If any individual organism could change its genes in response to circumstances it encountered, it would be hard to tell what part of the population originated from adaptation and what came from selection.

Structural inertia theory also plays a deeper, subtler, role in organizational ecology. It develops a mechanism that can explain the common observation that organizations of many types seem to be unable or unwilling to initiate changes in core or "deep" features. The evolutionary story claims such changes imperil organizations and that change-prone organizations run the risk of getting into serious trouble and perhaps failing. The more difficult the job of tuning reorganizations to environmental changes, the greater is the danger of engaging in frequent changes in core features. An evolutionary consequence holds that resistance to fundamental change will characterize organizational populations (unless this tendency is counterbalanced by an inflow of change-prone organizations or selection pressures are very weak). In due course, selection eliminates organizations that attempt to change their core features too often. In so doing, selection provides the guarantee for the (relative) persistence of relevant organizational characteristics, and that, in turn, provides the conditions for evolution.

11.1 IDENTITY AND INERTIA

At least four types of processes can delay—and often prevent—change in organizations: (1) institutional processes, involving identities and the "moral" character of structural arrangements, (2) structural processes, including the consequences of intricacy and viscosity (sluggishness of response), (3) political processes, involving interests and interest-group politics, and (4) learning processes, involving feedback over time. Although any specific major organizational change likely activates several, or even all, of these processes, dealing with them separately clarifies the analytical picture. In following developments in organizational ecology, in this book we consider mainly the first two processes; we defer the others to future research.

Notions of identity played an important part in shaping the original inertia argument (but that aspect of the argument has largely been forgotten in contemporary renderings). For instance, Hannan and Freeman (1984: 155–6) motivated their argument with the example of the university: although some features, such as textbooks, constantly change in an adaptive way, changing a curriculum from liberal arts to vocational training would be extraordinarily difficult.

> The curriculum is difficult to change, then, because it represents the core of the university's organizational identity and underlies the distribution of resources across the organization. In these ways, it can be said to lie at the university's "core."

Thus, an identity-based understanding of inertia holds that organizational changes go to the core when they challenge a well-established identity.

Part I of the book already offers insight into why changing features that are part of identity codes is generally difficult and risky. Identities are specified as defaults about codes that include form memberships. The analysis shows that if a particular change violates such a default about code satisfaction, then test codes shrink (P4.2) and taken-for-grantedness falls (D4.3). The consequence is that default code violations shrink identities (C5.1). As we discussed in Chapters 4 and 5, the loss of taken-for-grantedness and the shrinking of identities means that organizations get subjected to more scrutiny. We interpreted such a shift on the part of the audience as a loss of trust.

Organizational changes that violate codes that specify categories and forms diminish the violator's grade of membership in the category or form. If the category or form is positively valued, then the drop in GoM causes the intrinsic appeal of the organization's offer to decline (D3.10). That is, violation of codes results in a loss of expected intrinsic appeal (T5.3).

Recall that fitness depends on an organization's intrinsic appeal relative to competitors (D9.1) Therefore, code violations that diminish expected intrinsic appeal also generally reduce fitness (assuming that not all of the competitors also are perceived as violating codes). The result is a higher hazard of mortality (M9.1). For these reasons, mortality hazards likely rise following change in features tied to identity.

A test of these ideas using information about changes in the premises of the employment relation in young, high-technology firms finds that such changes did indeed destabilize the organizations, raising the outflow of employees (Baron, Hannan, and Burton 2001). These changes also decreased the growth of market capitalization and increased the hazard of mortality (Hannan, Baron, Hsu, and Koçak 2006).

A structural perspective on inertia holds that even changes that do not violate identities might prove problematic. We think that it is useful to develop the implications of this idea because many studies have data on organizational changes but (given the current state of the art) lack data on the specifics about the codes that apply as defaults to the organizations. Perhaps a structural theory will yield predictions for such cases.

Structural changes often trigger further, unanticipated changes (Barnett and Carroll 1995). That is, in complex organizations, altering a feature might imply many additional alterations—initiating a cascade of changes. The feature in question might reasonably be regarded as a core feature because it prompts a lengthy reorganization that absorbs resources. Conversely, a feature that can change without further implications should be considered as peripheral.

The two kinds of processes are more tightly intertwined than it might seem at first glance. Changes that violate identity codes surely set off cascades in most instances. Consider the example of curriculum change: serious reorganization of a curriculum requires changing employment models, staffing plans, budgets, and possibly even physical facilities. Moreover, codes are deeply held—attempting to change feature values in a way that violates such codes often prompts resistance; and this will burden the reorganization further. Structural features of the organization that carry identity-based interpretations for constituents are especially prone to this reaction.

Given that we already elaborated the implications of changes tied to identity in Part I, we now turn our attention to a structural alternative to specifying coreness. We examine changes in an organization's architecture (represented as a code system associated with audiences) and analyze their impacts in terms of the cascades of subsequent changes throughout the organization.

We follow the original theory in positing that such architectural changes initiate reorganization periods. Our analysis examines the impact of structural conditions such as intricacy (a strong and complex pattern of interconnections among an organization's component units), opacity (visibility of unit interconnections to those initiating a change) and asperity (cultural restrictiveness about allowable architectural features).

Notation. Notation in this chapter and the next is complicated because we specify parallel functions and random variables at the level of the organizational unit and the organization. In particular, we specify processes for the units of an organization, and we derive implications at the organization level. To keep this distinction straight, we use the following notational convention. Functions and random variables that are defined for a unit in an organization are expressed in lowercase strings; and those defined for an entire organization are in uppercase strings. Functions and random variables that pertain to cascades with specified origins have arguments for the organization and the unit that initiates the cascade; those of cascades in which the initiating unit is chosen at random do not have an argument slot for the unit. The predicate $\text{U}(u, x)$ tells that u is a unit of the organization x.

11.2 ORGANIZATIONAL ARCHITECTURE

In developing a structural approach to analyzing change, we concentrate on changes in an organization's architecture. We represent architectures as codes, following the line of argument in the previous chapters. This means that we can utilize the conceptual framework that we developed for schemata in Chapter 3 to represent architectures.

Architectural features include the formal structures for assigning work, that is, the specification of the units that undertake the tasks in the organization's division of labor. Architectural codes also specify the means of coordinating members and units, monitoring them, and allocating resources and rewards. In other words, architectures can be regarded as collections of sentences pertaining to ontology (e.g., delineation of the units in an architecture) and codes (e.g., rules that state which units have authority over which other units). We define an organizational architecture as a code that discriminates between the allowed and disallowed feature values for the organization. That is, an architecture imposes constraints on feature values, limiting the values that they can legitimately take.

Codes clearly differ in importance. Some codes matter greatly in the sense that violations get punished very severely while others are handled with a lighter touch. (Consider, for instance, the distinction made in legal systems between felonies and misdemeanors.) We restrict the theory to apply to serious codes. Henceforth, when we refer to architectural codes, we always mean only the serious ones, those for which observable violations bring strong sanctions. In most cases, an organization's architectural code includes many codes taken from the identity of the organization and especially from its memberships in different categories and forms. That is, the architectural codes for any specific organization come at least partially from the codes that stem from its category and form memberships.

We consider two kinds of architectural schemata. The first is the global organizational schema. We refer to this code as $\breve{\sigma}(x, t)$. This global architectural code defines a set of units and specifies for each pair (1) whether one has authority over the other and, if so, which one is dominant or (2) that neither has authority over the other. The coded superordination/subordination relation among units can reflect the formally specified lines of authority. They can also arise from conventions and norms that have arisen in managing the flow of work, or from any similar relation that allows one component of the organization to impose constraints on another. Organizations differ in the extent to which they explicate formal architectural rules and enforce them. In cases in which organizations have a "strong" architecture, the superordination relations can be read from a set of organization charts. However, even the most detailed architectural specifications must leave open some of the details about control. Many, perhaps most, organizations leave much of the detail about implementation of control to informal arrangements and organizational culture. In such cases, detailed knowledge of the overall culture and its local variants is needed to decipher the structure of control.

An important class of coded interunit relations in the global architectural code concerns subordination in choice of architecture. We represent this notion formally with the relation $u_i \Vdash u_j$, which indicates that "u_i and u_j are units in the same organization and that u_i is superordinate to unit u_j in the sense that u_i's choices of architectural feature values impose architectural code restrictions (binding constraints) for u_j."[1]

The second kind of architectural code is local: it tells the ranges of feature values that are permissible for a unit. In general, we regard the features as possessing a set of possible values. We can then represent an architecture as a set of approved/required feature values. We represent the prevailing schema for a unit's local architecture with the function $\sigma(u, x, t)$, which refers to the schema for the unit u in the organization x at time t.

In this kind of two-level construction, the overall architectural code of an organization that has structured itself into n units is an $n + 1$-tuple of the form

$$\boldsymbol{\sigma}(x, t) = \langle \breve{\sigma}(x, t), \sigma(u_1, x, t), \sigma(u_2, x, t), \ldots, \sigma(u_n, x, t) \rangle.$$

11.3 CASCADES

The situations that we analyze begin with a change in the architectural code by an identifiable unit. The initiating unit might sit anywhere in the organization. The reasons for this initial change are not pertinent to our theory. They could encompass a wide variety of possibilities including changes in external opportunities and constraints, executive tinkering, and internal strife. The specific change undertaken might be sensible in that it would likely improve organizational alignment and functioning. But we do not assume that this is so—changes surely can also degrade performance.

It is valuable to focus on architectural changes as initiators, because architectural rules are more malleable to management and to individual decision makers than are cultural rules or identity. Changing an element of an architecture often requires only a directive from someone in authority; members of an affected unit often accept the directive.

We represent an architectural change with a random variable, $ch(u, x, t)$, which equals one if u, a unit in organization x (in notation $\mathrm{U}(u, x)$), changes its architecture just after t and equals zero otherwise. When we wish to refer to a change by any of an organization's units, we use the random variable $Ch(x, t)$, which equals one if any unit in organization x experiences architectural change at (just after) time t and equals zero otherwise.

Inconsistencies between new and existing codes normally become salient and consequential when the arrangements or actions that would have satisfied the old code do not satisfy the new one. We use the random variable $vl(u_i, u_j, x, t)$, which maps triplets of units, organizations, and time points to $\{0, 1\}$.

Definition 11.1 (Induced code violation). *A unit experiences induced violation of new architectural code if and only if an induced change in architectural code*

[1]The symbol $\Vdash$ is used in logic for a very different purpose; but, as we do not use it for any other purpose, this should not cause confusion.

results causes its feature values to be in violation of an architectural code when no violation existed prior to the change.

$vl(u_i, u_j, x, t) = 1$ *if and only if*

1. u_i *is a unit in the organization* x*, that is,* $\mathrm{U}(u, x)$*; and* u_j*, another unit of the same organization,* $\mathrm{U}(u_j, x)$*, is subordinate to* u_i*; that is,* $u_i \Vdash u_j$*;*
2. *the unit* u_i *initiates an architectural change at time* t*; that is,* $ch(u_i, x, t) = 1$*;*
3. *just before the change, the collection of architecturally relevant feature values of another unit,* u_j*, conforms to all of its applicable architectural code:* $\mathbf{f}(u_j, t) = \mathbf{v} \subset \sigma(u_j, t)$*;*
4. *after the change, the (not-yet-changed) feature values of* u_j *do not conform to the newly imposed architectural code.* $\mathbf{f}(u_j, t) = \mathbf{v} \not\subset \sigma(u_j, t + dt)$*, where* dt *is an infinitesimal positive number.*

$vl(u_i, u_j, x, t) = 0$ *otherwise.*

We assume that units experience pressure to resolve imposed architectural-code violations. The reasons vary, depending on he source of the subordination relation. In some cases, there is pressure to respond to organizational authority and the implicit threat that official sanctions will be brought to bear if compliance does not occur; in other cases, the pressure is cultural. Of course, if the existence of architectural-code violations does not prompt an effort to resolve them, then changes will not cascade.

It appears that organizational changes do frequently generate cascades of related changes in the sense that a single initial change often begets a series of subsequent changes. For instance, consider Alfred P. Sloan's (1963: 50) description of the architectural change at General Motors in 1920 that implemented its fabled decentralized organizational structure:

> The principles of organization... thus initiated for the modern General Motors the trend toward a happy medium in industrial organization between the extremes of pure centralization and pure decentralization. The new policy asked that the corporation neither remain as it was, a weak form of organization, nor become a rigid, command form. But the actual forms of organization that were to evolve in the future... what exactly, for example, would remain a divisional responsibility and what would be coordinated, and what would be policy and what would be administration—could not be deduced by a process of logic from the "Organization Study" [the plan].

Sloan goes on to describe in detail how product policy, coordination mechanisms, and financial policy had to be altered to make them consistent with the new basic architectural structure.

Why do such cascades occur? Suppose that the code violations arising from an architectural change can be reduced by changing a subset of other codes or by changing a feature value. Then the initial architectural change can be said to induce change in this second set of codes or in the feature value. Seeking to remove the code violations created by an architectural change might often proceed by boundedly rational search. The members of the affected units search locally to find whether change in any other set of codes or feature values might eliminate the code violations. The search operates locally in the sense that it takes the initial change as given. It follows bounded rationality in the sense that it stops whenever it finds a simple adjustment that eliminates the code violation (even if other, more distant changes might do this as well and also provide some other benefits).

Such search and adjustment can yield a cascade of changes. Each time that a unit decides to implement a set of conforming changes, these new changes play the role of (second-order) changes. They initiate a new local boundedly rational search, perhaps in other units, for ways to eliminate code violations (conditional on the initial change and the second-order changes) by changing yet other elements. At this step, those involved in the search process might consider trying to undo the original change.

It is often extremely difficult to restore the status quo ex ante, to "put the Genie back in the bottle." This is because local search and adjustment "in reverse" would frequently not retrace the initial path of changes.

The presence of hidden codes provides another possible source of cascades. Architectural codes often take a conditional form: the codes consist of formulas stating that if a certain set of conditions holds, then certain other conditions should also hold. Suppose that the antecedent in a conditional code does not obtain. Then the code is satisfied vacuously, whatever the condition on the consequent. If a code has been inactive for a long time, then it likely gets forgotten and the code becomes hidden. An architectural change that activates the antecedent in a hidden code might create a new (unforeseen) code violation.

How might cascades of architectural code changes be represented formally? We would begin with a code change in a particular unit and trace out the chains of induced changes in subordinate units.

We analyze cascades at three levels of detail. The most refined level is an actual cascade that was initiated by a particular architectural change in an identifiable unit. At this level of detail, we trace the sequence of impelled changes. At an intermediate level of detail, we analyze the set of possible cascades that might be initiated by a particular initial change. Here we characterize the average properties of the cascades in the set of possibilities. At the least refined level, we consider the expected properties of the set of cascades that result from an initiating event in a random unit. This more aggregated characterization allows us to compare changes (and to assess their expected impacts) across organizations without having to specify the exact details about what codes or features values get changed.

Detailed Structure of a Specific Cascade

At a microscopic level, we pay attention to the exact sequence of code changes that comprise a cascade.

Definition 11.2 (Cascade). *A particular cascade of resolutions of induced violations of architectural code in organization x that begins at time t with a change initiated by unit u, in notation* $\mathbf{cas}(u, x, t)$*, is a set of "steps" or "stages" constructed as follows.*

Step 0: The unit u, not in violation of any of its applicable architectural code, initiates the cascade at time t by changing architectural code and that change induces architectural-code violations in one or more subordinate units ;

Step 1: A unit with an induced violation in step 0 changes its architecture such that conformity eliminates the induced violation, but this change in architecture induces a violation in one or more subordinate units;

⋮

Step L: The only unit with an unresolved induced violation (generated by the previous steps in the cascade) eliminates the violation at time z_L, and this architectural change does not induce a violation in any unit.

This particular cascade need not be the only cascade that might be initiated by the change in step 0. At each step, the unit resolving an imposed architectural violation might have a choice among several alternative resolutions. These choices determine which other units experience an imposed violation, which in turn shapes the direction of the cascade. At any step a change might induce multiple branches in the cascade.

A cascade can be characterized by (1) its number of stages, (2) the number of units that experience induced violations during the cascade, and (3) its temporal character, including the time elapsed from origin to conclusion and the total time units spend reorganizing even if in parallel. A step (or stage) in a cascade begins each time that a change by one unit induces violations recognized and accepted by the members of one or more other units, a cascade with no indirect effects has only one stage, a cascade in which the adjustments to the first stage induce violations that have no indirect effects has two stages, and so forth. Thus we can measure the number of stages in a cascade by the number of units whose changes induce violations in one or more units.

This kind of detailed account highlights the precise connections that animate a cascade. Such a description might be useful for close study of a small number of cascades. Yet it would likely prove too cumbersome as a device for comparing change processes in different organizations (whose code systems and architectures likely differ). For this reason, we strip much of the detail from the story. We focus on the most comparable elements of cascades, and we introduce probabilistic considerations explicitly.

11.4 ORGANIZATIONAL ARCHITECTURE AND CASCADES

Now we begin to abstract from the details of the actual code substitutions. We use a specific design idea: generally speaking, organizations with more complicated

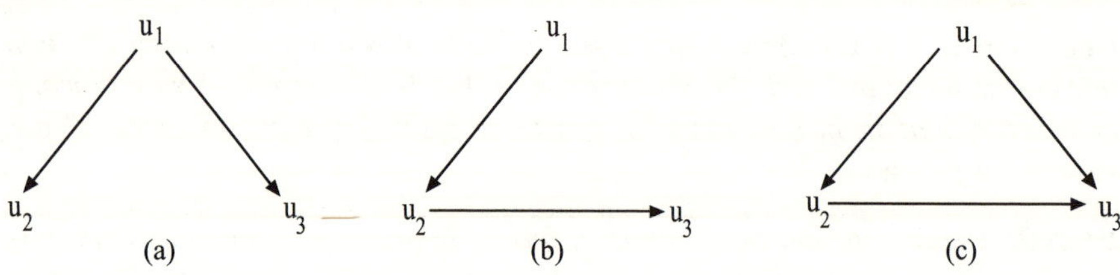

Figure 11.1 Illustration of three different patterns of connections among units. Source: Hannan, Pólos, and Carroll (2003b) ©Institute for Operations Research and the Management Sciences. Used with permission.

patterns of interconnections among their units will generate longer cascades. This is because a change in a unit likely affects many other units when the pattern of interconnectedness is complex (Simon 1962).

We formalize this reasoning in terms of the pattern of relations among units. A pattern of interunit relations shapes the variety of possible cascades for any initial architectural change. We relate the level of coupling among units in the organization to the likely pattern of cascades. This framework allows us to make predictions about certain characteristics of a cascade, including the (expected) total time in reorganization.

Unit Interconnections

Consider the examples of the three architectures depicted in figure 11.1. Here the directed lines indicate the constraints embedded in the architectural codes. An arrow directed from u_i to u_j indicates that $u_i \Vdash u_j$. On the left in the figure, figure 11.1a, we see a flat hierarchy (a star network): unit u_1 directly constrains u_2 and u_3, which are otherwise unconnected. The middle, figure 11.1b, is a vertical hierarchy. In this case, u_1 constrains u_2 directly and u_3 indirectly. In figure 11.1c, u_1 constrains u_2 and u_3 directly and u_2 constrains u_3 directly. Thus u_1 constrains u_3 both directly and indirectly.[2] This architecture shows a violation of the classic attribute of hierarchy—unity of command—which means that each unit should have one and only one direct superior.

Consider the likely effect of an architectural change by the dominant unit (u_1) in each case. In figure 11.1a, units u_2 and u_3 can act independently in solving the problem, changing local architectures, and resolving the violation. Thus the cascade has only one stage. The temporal span of the cascade is simply the maximum of the durations of the unresolved code violations in the two units. The cascade in the three-level hierarchy, figure 11.1b, has two stages: one in which u_2 adjusts to the initial change and another in which u_3 adjusts to the induced change in u_2. In this case, the temporal span is the sum of the durations of the unresolved code violations in the two units.

Finally, the nonhierarchical case, figure 11.1c, also unfolds in two stages. As in

[2]This case, unlike the other two, cannot be described as a lattice.

figure 11.1a, the temporal span is the maximum of the two durations. However, the resolution time for u_3 will generally be longer in the nonhierarchical case than in the others. Consider two scenarios. First, u_3 resolves the inconsistency induced by the change in u_1 before u_2 does. At this point, the duration of the resolution for u_3 is the same as it would have been in the structure in figure 11.1b, the vertical hierarchy. But it still must adapt to the not-yet-completed change in u_2. So its total resolution time will be greater. In the second scenario, u_2 completes its adjustment to the change by u_1 before u_3 does. This means that additional constraints on u_3 get imposed in the midst of an ongoing reorganization. We expect that this will complicate the adjustment and lengthen the period of resolution.

These simple considerations suggest two lessons for building a model of the process. First, we should attend to the number of stages of a cascade. Both the total time spent reorganizing and the temporal span of a cascade generally increase with its number of stages. Second, we should pay attention to the complexity of the pattern of connections among organizational units. The time spent reorganizing in a cascade will generally be longer the more that the pattern departs from simple hierarchy. We now formalize these intuitions.

Unit Centrality and Organizational Coupling

Recall that two units are connected in an architectural sense if decisions by one govern and constrain the architectural codes that apply to the other. In particular, one unit constrains another architecturally if the feature values (and choices allowed by the codes) of the former are accepted as an external constraint (as codes) on the latter. So, although the constraint might be imposed as an authoritative or imperative command, what matters for our purposes is the occurrence (or not) of compliance.

Let U_x denote the number of units in organization x. Consider a $U_x \times U_x$ adjacency matrix $\mathbf{B}(x, t)$ for which $b_{ij}(t) = 1$ if unit i constrains unit j architecturally at time t (that is, if $u_i \Vdash u_j$), and it equals zero otherwise.

The nuances recognized above in discussing figure 11.1 can be captured by representing the pattern of connections in an organization's architecture with an eigenvector measure of centrality. Such measures have the general form that a unit's centrality in the architecture depends upon the centrality of the units that it constrains.[3] A unit is central to the extent that it constrains units that are themselves central. Thus, the most central unit in the flat hierarchy has lower centrality than does the most central unit in the vertical hierarchy in figure 11.1.

An architectural change by a unit might or might not induce a violation in a subordinate unit. This depends upon the details of the codes—both the relational codes governing interactions among units and the changes in the local code. Given this complexity, we opt for a probability model. We concentrate on the probability that a change in one unit induces an architectural code violation in another: $\Pr(vl(u_i, u_j, x, t))$, which we call the *induction probability.* Differences in typical induction probabilities among organizations arguably correspond with variations in

[3] Wasserman and Faust (1994) present a useful overview of such measures.

the tightness of coupling. Loosely coupled organizations presumably tend to have lower induction probabilities than do more tightly coupled ones.

In general, induction probabilities might vary among pairs of units and over time. At a later stage in the development of this theory, it might prove useful to analyze probability models that allow them to vary in specified ways among dyads. At this point, we want to characterize the typical situations for sets of organizations. Accordingly, we assume that induction probabilities vary between organizations but not over dyads within an organization or over time for an organization. In other words, we assume that each organization has a characteristic induction probability. This premise has the status of analytical convenience rather than of a claim about the organizational world. As we explained in Chapter 6, we refer to the simplifying premises that we expect to see relaxed in further developments of the theory as auxiliary assumptions; and we refer to the real causal claims of the theory as postulates. Therefore, we mark the simplifying assumption of constant induction probabilities as an auxiliary assumption.

Auxiliary assumption 11.1. *The probability that an architectural change by a unit induces an architectural-code violation in a subordinate unit normally does not vary over pairs of units or time points; it is an organization-specific constant,* π_x*; and* $0 < \pi_x < 1$.

$$\mathfrak{A}\, t, x, u, u' \left[(ch(u', t) = 1) \rightarrow \Pr(vl(u, u', x, t)) = \begin{cases} \pi_x & \textit{if}\, u \Vdash u'; \\ 0 & \textit{if}\, u \nVdash u'. \end{cases} \right];$$

and $0 < \pi_x < 1$.

[Read: assumedly for each organization in a domain there is an organization-specific parameter π_x such that, for every pair of units in the organization and every time point, if one unit initiates an architectural change at that time, then the probability that the other unit experiences an induced architectural-code violation at that time equals π_x if the unit is constrained architecturally by the initiator and it equals zero otherwise.]

We added the restriction that $\pi < 1$ because we think that $\pi = 1$ means that the two units involved are effectively one unit.

Next we define an index of the centrality of unit, in formal terms $cen(u, x, t)$, using a variation of Philip Bonacich's (1987) measure of centrality and making a probabilistic interpretation.

Definition 11.3 (Unit centrality). *The vector containing the centralities of the units of organization* x *is*

$$\mathbf{cen}(x) \equiv \textstyle\sum_{k=1}^{\infty} \pi_x^k\, \mathbf{B}(x)^k\, \boldsymbol{\ell},$$

where π_x *is the organization's induction probability,* $\mathbf{B}(x)$ *is the adjacency matrix that records the dominance relations between pairs of units, and* $\boldsymbol{\ell}$ *is a* $(U_x \times 1)$ *vector of ones.*

Applying this measure to the three cases illustrated in figure 11.1 provides a sense of how the measure works. The matrices that record the $\Vdash$ relations for these cases are

$$\mathbf{B}_a = \begin{pmatrix} 011 \\ 000 \\ 000 \end{pmatrix} \quad \mathbf{B}_b = \begin{pmatrix} 010 \\ 001 \\ 000 \end{pmatrix} \quad \mathbf{B}_c = \begin{pmatrix} 011 \\ 001 \\ 000 \end{pmatrix}$$

The squares of these matrices are

$$\mathbf{B}_a^2 = \begin{pmatrix} 000 \\ 000 \\ 000 \end{pmatrix} \quad \mathbf{B}_b^2 = \begin{pmatrix} 001 \\ 000 \\ 000 \end{pmatrix} \quad \mathbf{B}_c^2 = \begin{pmatrix} 001 \\ 000 \\ 000 \end{pmatrix}$$

Because $\mathbf{B}^k$ is a matrix of zeros for $k \geq 2$ in all three cases depicted in figure 11.1, we can calculate the vector of centrality scores as follows:

$$\mathbf{cen}_a = \begin{pmatrix} 2\pi_x \\ 0 \\ 0 \end{pmatrix}; \quad \mathbf{cen}_b = \begin{pmatrix} \pi_x + \pi_x^2 \\ \pi_x \\ 0 \end{pmatrix}; \quad \mathbf{cen}_c = \begin{pmatrix} 2\pi_x + \pi_x^2 \\ \pi_x \\ 0 \end{pmatrix}.$$

The centrality scores in these examples vary with the architecture, as will generally be the case. It is easy to see that the centrality scores generally also depend upon the number of units. For instance, adding a third subordinate unit to case (a) in Figure 11.1 but keeping the architecture otherwise unchanged magnifies the centrality of the dominant unit from $2\pi_x$ to $3\pi_x$. Adding another vertical link at the bottom of the hierarchy in case (b) causes the centrality score of the dominant unit to rise from $\pi_x + \pi_x^2$ to $\pi_x + \pi_x^2 + \pi_x^3$, and so forth. In other words, the centrality scores reflect the density and pattern of ties among units as well as the number of units in the organization.

This characterization provides a useful representation of a marked random cascade of induced architectural changes. (By "marked" we mean that the initiator of the cascade is known.) A cascade begins with an architectural change by a unit at a time point. The marked cascade induced by this change can be regarded as a realization from the probability model in A11.1 and the centrality score of the initiating unit.

One of the important characterizations of a cascade is the number of induced violations. Let $V(u, x, t)$ denote a random variable that records the number of induced violations in the cascade initiated by unit u at time t in organization x, that is, in $\mathbf{cas}(u, x, t)$.

Definition 11.4 (Induced violations during a cascade). *The number of induced violations of architectural codes in organization x during the marked cascade initiated by unit u at time t is*

$$V_u(x, t) \equiv |\mathbf{cas}(u, x, t)|.$$

(As in previous chapters, $|\cdot|$ denotes the cardinality of a (crisp) finite set, the number of distinct elements it contains, and $\langle .,. \rangle$ denotes an ordered pair.)

Our reason for choosing this representation of centrality can now be seen clearly. The centrality score of a unit in architecture gives the expected number of induced violations in a cascade initiated by an architectural change in that unit, according to the probability model. This is the key to our model. Because this relationship plays an important role in the analysis that follows, we make it explicit.

Lemma 11.1. *The expected number of induced violations of architectural codes in a marked cascade, $V_u(x,t)$, presumably equals that the centrality of the initiating unit, $cen(u,x)$.*

$$\mathfrak{P}\, t, u, x\, [\mathrm{U}(u,x) \rightarrow (\mathrm{E}(V_u(x,t)) = cen(u,x))].$$

Proof. The expected number of induced violations in a marked cascade initiated by the unit u, $\mathrm{E}(V_u(x,t))$, can be expressed as the sum of the expected number of violations at each path length. That is, $\mathrm{E}(V_u(x,t)) = \sum_{k=1}^{\infty} \mathrm{E}(V^k(u,x,t))$, where $\mathrm{E}(V^k(u,x,t))$ is the expected number of induced violations at step k of the cascade (that is, at path length k). The joint probability of k inductions along a path, under auxiliary assumption A11.1, is given by π_x^k. Because inductions must follow the subordination relation, $\mathrm{E}(V^k(u,x,t)) = \sum_{u \neq u'} \pi_x^k\, z_{u,u'}^k$, where $z_{u,u'}^k$ equals the number of distinct k-step paths connecting u and u'. Inspection of the terms in the powers of $\mathbf{B}(x)$ reveals that $z_{u,u'}^k$ is the (u,u') entry in $\mathbf{B}(x)^k(z)$. □

Temporal Aspects of a Cascade

The temporal dimension of a random cascade in an organization decisively shapes its possible consequences, as we explain below. We considered two different ways to represent the temporal dimension. The first, the *temporal span* of a cascade, measures the time elapsed from the initiating event to the event that terminates the cascade, as in D11.1. The second, the *total time reorganizing,* is the sum of the times spent by the individual units in reorganization mode (changing codes and feature values so as to eliminate induced violations). The total time reorganizing is calculated by summing the durations of all of the reorganizations by the units reached by a cascade, even if they occur simultaneously.

Both ideas have substantive promise. A protracted period of change presumably complicates organizational action and diverts the attention of at least some members over the whole period—the first idea; and the disruption caused by change ought to be proportional to the time spent by units (and their members) in working out the consequences of changes—the second idea. Given that we model processes at the unit level, the argument goes more smoothly when we focus on the second concept for the whole organization, the total time reorganizing. Nevertheless, we have to bring temporal span back into the picture when we derive implications about the affects of cascades on organizations.

Now it might happen that different branches of a cascade hit a unit at different times. This would mean that one effort to eliminate an induced violation gets interrupted by another induced violation. We must make clear what we assume for such situations. Start with the simple case of no interruption. Suppose, next, that a reorganization does get interrupted. What should we expect about the duration of the reorganization for this unit? We think that the normal case is one in which the duration of the overlapping reorganizations lasts (at least) as long as the sum of the two uninterrupted durations. Consider two scenarios. In one, the problem of eliminating the second induction gets postponed until the effort to eliminate the first finishes. In the other, some attention gets shifted from the first reorganization to the second. In both cases, the amount of work to be done arguably does not differ. In the first case, some of the work of the first reorganization might have to be undone in the second, which would tend to lengthen the process. However, the second case involves a more highly constrained adjustment (because it deals with constraints coming from different sources). So there does not seem to be a strong argument that either would generally take longer. We simplify and assume that the expected time elapsed during the two overlapping reorganizations equals the sum of expectations of the durations of the two uninterrupted ones.

Again we opt for simplicity in characterizing the probability model. We analyze $d(u, x, t)$, a nonnegative, real-valued random variable that records the duration of an *uninterrupted* spell of reorganization in unit u in response to an architectural-code violation that was induced at time t. We assume that an organization's units have a common expected duration for eliminating induced violations, that this expected duration varies among organizations but not over episodes within organizations. We label this common reorganization duration in organization x as $\eta(x)$.

Auxiliary assumption 11.2. *The expected unit-level duration of an induced violation of an architectural code normally does not vary over units or over time in an organization; it is an organization-specific constant,* η.

$$\mathfrak{A}\, t, u, u', x\, [(vl(u, u', x, t) = 1) \rightarrow (\mathrm{E}(d(u, x, t)) = \eta(x))].$$

How should we think about $\eta(x)$? A large value of this constant means that it typically takes a long time for a unit to correct induced violations. To use a physical analogy, an organization in which things work slowly has high *viscosity*—think of the difference between stirring honey and water. Viscosity is often defined (loosely) as the resistance in a material to changes in form. Because this analogy seems to fit the organizational context, we refer to η as *viscosity*.

Now we shift from the duration of a unit's reorganization to a cascade's total reorganization time.

Definition 11.5 (Total duration of reorganizations in a marked cascade). *The total of the durations of the unit-level reorganizations triggered in a marked cascade,* $D_u(x, t)$, *is defined as the sum of the durations of all reorganizations triggered by a cascade that initiates in unit* u *at time* t.

$$D_u(x, t) \equiv \sum_{\langle u', t' \rangle \in \mathbf{cas}(u, x, t)} d(u', x, t').$$

Note that total time that units spend reorganizing differs from the temporal span of the cascade; we return to this difference below.

The model of a marked random cascade yields an important substantive insight.

Lemma 11.2. *The expected total time reorganizing by an organization's units during a cascade that originates in a known unit presumably equals the product of the initiating unit's centrality and the organization-specific viscosity.*

$$\mathfrak{P}\, t, x, u\, [(ch(u, x, t) = 1) \rightarrow (\mathrm{E}(D_u(x, t)) = \eta(x) cen(u, x))].$$

Proof. The most specific regularity chain uses A11.1 (the probability model for violation induction) and A11.2 ($\mathrm{E}(d(u, x, t)) = \eta(x)$ for all units in x), and the regularities that support L11.1 ($\mathrm{E}(D_u(x, t)) = \eta(x) cen(u, x, t)$ for all units in organization x). □

11.5 COMPARING RANDOM CASCADES: INTRICACY AND VISCOSITY

To this point we have considered marked cascades, those for which the initiating unit is known. This allowed us to relate properties of the initiating unit (such as centrality) to the kind of cascade that should be expected. We now abstract further so that we can characterize an entire organization by its propensity to generate long cascades. We do so by treating the origin of the cascade within the organization as random.

Based on the reasoning used in discussing the alternatives in figure 11.1, we propose that the mean centrality score in an organization provides a useful way to express intuitions about likely cascade lengths. A unit has high centrality if and only if it dominates units that themselves have high centrality; and cascades are more likely to hit more units in an organization with a high mean centrality. Indeed, mean centrality provides a characterization of the *intricacy* of the organization's design.[4] The nonnegative real-valued function $I(x)$ records the intricacy of the design of organization x.

Definition 11.6 (Intricacy). *The intricacy of an organization's design is the mean of the centralities of its units.*

$$I(x) \equiv \sum_u cen(u, x)/U_x.$$

(Here and elsewhere in this chapter and the next, $\sum_u$ stands for $\sum_{u|\mathrm{U}(u,x)}$.)

Building a model at the organizational level requires a characterization of the distribution over units of the probability of being the initiator, conditional on a change being initiated in the organization. We express this idea with the hazard of initiating change. Let $\delta(u, x, t)$ and $\Delta(x, t)$ denote these hazards at the unit level and organizational level, respectively.

Definition 11.7 (Hazard of architectural change). *The hazard of initiating an architectural change in unit x at time t is defined as*[5]

$$\delta(u, x, t) \equiv \lim_{dt \downarrow 0} \frac{\Pr(ch(u, x, t + dt) = 1)}{dt}.$$

An organization's hazard of experiencing architectural change by one of its units at time t is the sum of the hazards of its units.

$$\Delta(x, t) \equiv \sum_u \delta(u, x, t).$$

As with other aspects of the probability model, we go for simplicity by invoking a set of simplifying auxiliary assumptions. In particular, we assume homogeneity among the units within an organization, but we allow variation over time. Although it might seem more natural to assume that units closer to the top are more likely to

---

[4]The *Oxford English Dictionary* defines intricate as "perplexingly entangled or involved; interwinding in a complicated manner."

[5]We make the standard assumption that two or more events cannot occur at the same instant.

initiate changes, this version of the argument is actually stronger than needed. The general line of argument holds that cascades that start in units with high centrality last longer, and, as a result, they create more serious problems. All of the lemmas and theorems would hold (in modified form due to the greater complexity of implementing this assumption) if we substituted this alternative auxiliary assumption. Nonetheless, we want to make the auxiliary assumptions as innocuous as possible. We can show that the argument is sound even when we make the weaker assumption that each unit is equally likely to initiate a change.

Auxiliary assumption 11.3. *The hazard of initiating an architectural change normally does not vary over units within an organization or over time; it is an organizational hazard, which we label as* δ_x.

$$\mathfrak{A}\, t, t', u, u', x \; [\mathrm{U}(u, x) \wedge \mathrm{U}(u', x) \rightarrow (\delta(u, x, t) = \delta_x = \delta(u', x, t'))].$$

In developing proofs, we will encounter expressions for the probability that a particular unit initiates a change, given that some unit in the organization initiated a change. In this respect, it is useful to record a straightforward consequence of A11.3.

Lemma 11.3. *The probability that any chosen unit is the one that initiated a change (given that one unit in the organization did initiate a change at a time point) presumably equals* $1/U_x$.

Proof. This result follows from standard calculations in probability theory. It is easy to show that $\Pr(ch(u, x, t) = 1 \mid Ch(x, t) = 1) = \delta(u, x, t)/\Delta(x, t)$. (Just sum both sides over all the units in the organization and note the second equality in D11.7.) Given D11.7 (the definition of the hazard of change) and A11.3 (the probability that a given unit initiates an observed change equals $1/U_x$), the right-hand side of the foregoing formula can be written as $\delta_x/(\delta_x U_x) = 1/U_x$. □

Notation. We will repeatedly encounter expectations of functions of (unmarked) random cascades. These functions involve summations over all of the induced violations in a cascade. In the standard case, in which the size of the set of elements in the summation is deterministic, the calculation uses the straightforward rule that the expectation of a sum of functions of random variables is the sum of the expectations. In the case of cascades, however, the number of terms in the summation is itself a random variable, $V_u(x, t)$. Consider the case in which the initiating unit is chosen at random (as specified in the auxiliary assumptions). Given the notational convention introduced above, the random variables characterizing a cascade with random origin are expressed as the unconditional versions of the parallel terms for the cascade with known origins. That is, the number of induced violations in a cascade with random origin at time t is denoted by $V(x, t)$, the total amount of reorganization time in such a cascade as $D(x, t)$, and the temporal span by $T(x, t)$. Note that each of these terms has only two argument slots, for the organization and the time point—the notation does not contain a reference to the initiating unit, u.

The probability model developed to this point implies a relationship between the expected number of violations in a cascade and intricacy for the case of a cascade with random origin.

Lemma 11.4. *The expected number of induced violations of architectural codes in a cascade with a random origin in an organization at a time, V, presumably equals the organization's intricacy, I.*

$$\mathfrak{P}\, t, x\, [(Ch(x,t) = 1) \rightarrow (\mathrm{E}(V(x,t)) = I(x))].$$

Proof. According to the law of total probability [6] (and given that a change did occur at t),

$$\mathrm{E}(V(x,t)) = \textstyle\sum_u \mathrm{E}(V_u(x,t))\, \mathrm{Pr}(ch(u,x,t)).$$

Under the auxiliary assumption that the hazard of change is constant for all units in an organization at a point in time (A11.3) and the regularities behind L11.2, the right-hand side of this equation can be written as $\sum_u \mathrm{E}(V_u(x,t))/U_x$. According to the regularities that warrant L11.1 and L11.2, this expression reduces to $\sum_u cen(u,x,t)/U_x$, which, by D11.6, equals $I(x)$. □

With this result in hand, it is straightforward to derive the expected total time reorganizing during a cascade with a random origin.

Theorem 11.1. *The expected total time reorganizing in a cascade with a random origin presumably equals the product of the organization's intricacy, I, and viscosity, η.*

$$\mathfrak{P}\, t, x\, [(Ch(x,t) = 1) \rightarrow (\mathrm{E}(D(x,t)) = \eta(x) I(x))].$$

Proof. According to the notation we introduced above, $D(x,t)$ equals the sum of all of the durations of reorganization within a cascade with random origin. By the regularities behind L11.4, the number of episodes of reorganization equals the organization's intricacy, $I(x)$; and A11.2 asserts that the expected duration of each episode is $\eta(x)$. □

11.6 MISSED OPPORTUNITIES

Why do long cascades damage organizations? During periods of reorganization, attention, time, and energy get devoted to adjusting features and codes to eliminate incompatibilities, thereby diverting the members from the tasks that generate revenues. Management attention gets focused on the change, production gets disrupted, relations with customers are left unattended as responsibilities are reallocated, and so forth. For instance, before the spin-off at Agilent Technologies, the CEO of the parent company (Hewlett-Packard) warned that the units involved had to ensure to "keep the plane flying" during the reorganization. His comment refers to a tendency in early aviation for pilots and copilots to get obsessed with fixing

[6] For the discrete case, the law of total probability states that

$$\mathrm{Pr}(X \leq x) = \textstyle\sum_y \mathrm{Pr}(X \leq x \mid Y = y) \cdot \mathrm{Pr}(Y = y).$$

the "problem" when cockpit lights and buzzers went off and to forget about actually flying the plane, thereby causing tragic accidents (Chang, Barnett, and Carroll 2001)., These problems become more serious as reorganization lengthens.

During a period of adjustment, agents pay considerable attention to the fate of the new architecture. Unlike normal functioning in which managerial attention to architectural conformity is partial and episodic, violations of newly added code generally get noticed during a reorganization period.

The resulting diversion of attention causes an organization to miss opportunities during reorganizations. Therefore, any protracted change generally entails substantial opportunity costs.

Tying structural change to missed opportunities requires a specification of the flow of opportunities and of the probability of missing an opportunity. We denote the hazard of the arrival of opportunities to unit u at time t as $\psi(u, x, t)$ and the hazard of the arrival of opportunities to organization x at time t as $\Psi(x, t)$. Thus the expected flow of opportunities to a unit over a period for the (half-open) interval $[s, t)$ equals $\int_s^t \psi(u, x, v)dv$; and for an organization it equals $\int_s^t \Psi(x, v)dv$.

We continue to specify the basic process at the unit level; but now we face a slight complication. Two otherwise similar organizations might structure themselves into different numbers of units. Simply creating more units ought not, by itself, amplify the flow of opportunities. Hence, it makes sense to specify that opportunities are experienced by units in a way that reflects the degree of division of the organization into units.

Auxiliary assumption 11.4. *An arriving opportunity to an organization normally is equally likely to hit any of its units.*

$$\mathfrak{A}\, t, u, x\, [\, \Psi(x, t) = \psi(u, x, t)\, U_x].$$

We will compare cascades at (possibly) different times in (possibly) different organizations. Such comparisons are simplest when the arrival of opportunities is stationary. If the hazard of arrival of opportunities stays constant over the period being considered, then we expect similar flows for different organizations over equal-length intervals located at different points within the period. Given this motivation, we add the auxiliary assumption that the arrival process is stationary. We also follow the practice, introduced in Chapter 7, of restricting the claim to apply to all comembers of a (prominent) population (the typical members of a population with high contrast).

Auxiliary assumption 11.5. *Opportunities normally arrive at the same constant hazard, Ψ_l, for all organizations in the (prominent) population labeled l.*

$$\mathfrak{A}\, l, t, t', x, x'\, [\mathrm{CM}(l, x, x', t, t') \rightarrow (\Psi(x, t) = \Psi_l = \Psi(x', t'))].$$

It will simplify formulas to have a notation for the unit-level hazard in an organization. We use the following:

$$\psi_x = \Psi_l / U_x.$$

It is also helpful to have the predicate, $\mathrm{RE}(u, t)$, which reads as "unit u is reorganizing at time t." Moreover, we let $miss(u, t)$ denote the random variable that equals one if unit u misses an opportunity that arises at time t and equals zero otherwise.

Because reorganization deflects attention from work, a unit is hampered in taking advantage of new opportunities while it is reorganizing. We instantiate this intuition as follows.

Postulate 11.1. *A unit's probability of missing an arriving opportunity normally is higher while it is in the midst of reorganization.*

$$\mathfrak{N}\, t, t', u, u', x\, [\mathrm{U}(u, x) \wedge \mathrm{U}(u', x) \\ \rightarrow (\Pr(miss(u, t) \mid \mathrm{RE}(u, t)) > \Pr(miss(u', t') \mid \neg\mathrm{RE}(u', t')))].$$

Notation. To avoid repeating a very complicated expression in a series of lemmas and theorems, we introduce some notational shorthand.

1. $\mathcal{T} = \max(T(x, t), T(x', t'))$, the maximum span of the two cascades being compared.

2. The formula $\mathcal{Q}_3$ stands for the following: the entities being compared, x and x', are comembers in a prominent population, have the same age, experience architectural changes at times t and t', respectively, and neither experiences another (uninduced) architectural change until the end of the longer of the two cascades.

$$\mathcal{Q}_3 \leftrightarrow \mathrm{CM}(l, x, x', t, t') \wedge (a(x, t) = a(x', t')) \wedge (Ch(x, t) = 1) \\ \wedge (Ch(x', t') = 1) \wedge \forall s[(t < s < t + \mathcal{T}) \rightarrow (Ch(x, s) = 0)] \\ \wedge \forall s'[(t' < s' < t' + \mathcal{T}) \rightarrow (Ch(x', s') = 0)].$$

We now focus on missed opportunities. Let the random variable $miss(u, x, s, t)$ give the number of opportunities missed by unit u during the (half-open) interval $[s, t)$, and let the organization-level counterpart be given by

$$M(x, s, t) = \textstyle\sum_u miss(u, x, s, t).$$

The main intuition of this portion of the argument is contained in the following lemma.

Lemma 11.5. *The expected number of opportunities missed by an organization during a cascade,* $\mathrm{E}(M)$*, presumably increases with the total time spent reorganizing by its units during the cascade,* D*.*

$$\mathfrak{P}\, \mathbf{q}, \mathbf{q}'\, [\mathcal{Q}_3 \rightarrow (D \uparrow \mathrm{E}(M))(\mathbf{q}, \mathbf{q}')],$$

where $\mathbf{q} = \langle l, t, x \rangle$ *and* $\mathbf{q}' = \langle l, t', x' \rangle$.

Proof. The most specific rule chain uses the definition of $\mathcal{Q}_3$, A11.5 (opportunities arrive at the same constant rate for all organizations in a population), the notation that we introduced in defining $D(x, t)$, and P11.1, which holds that a unit's probability of missing an opportunity is higher during reorganization. □

Again we simplify the probability model. Because we have assumed that all comembers of a (prominent) population face the same opportunity structure, we assume that the probability of missing opportunities (in reorganization or outside of reorganization) does not vary among them or over time.

Auxiliary assumption 11.6. *The probability that a unit misses an opportunity while not reorganizing normally does not vary over time or among units in any typical organization in a prominent population; it equals* κ_l*. Likewise, the probability that a unit misses an opportunity while reorganizing does not vary over time or among units in any typical organization in such a population; it equals* $\kappa_l + \widetilde{\kappa}_l$*.*

$$\mathfrak{A}\, l, t, t', u, u', x, x' \,[\textsc{cm}(l, x, x', t, t') \wedge \textsc{u}(u, x) \wedge \textsc{u}(u', x') \\ \rightarrow (\Pr(miss(u, t) \mid \neg\textsc{re}(u, t)) = \Pr(miss(u', t') \mid \neg\textsc{re}(u', t')) = \kappa_l) \\ \wedge (\Pr(miss(u, t) \mid \textsc{re}(u, t)) = \Pr(miss(u', t') \mid \textsc{re}(u', t')) = \kappa_l + \widetilde{\kappa}_l)].$$

As an obvious consequence of P11.1 and A11.6, we have $\widetilde{\kappa}_l > 0$.

It follows that reorganization elevates the probability of missing opportunities.

Theorem 11.2. *The expected number of opportunities missed in a typical organization in a prominent population during a random cascade presumably equals the sum of (1) the baseline expected number that would be missed over the time interval had no reorganization taken place and (2) an excess expected number that grows monotonically with the product of the organization's viscosity,* η*, and intricacy,* I*.*

$$\mathfrak{P}\, l, t, x \,[\textsc{m}(l, x, t) \wedge \textsc{pr}(l, t) \wedge (Ch(x, t) = 1) \wedge (T(x, t) = v) \\ \rightarrow (\mathrm{E}(M(x, t, t + v)) = \Psi_l\, \kappa_l\, v + \psi_x\, \widetilde{\kappa}_l\, \eta(x)\, I(x))].$$

Proof. According to A11.5 and A11.6, the expected number of arrivals of opportunities to the organization in an interval of length v equals $\Psi_l v$. (Here, and below, we use the basic result that the occurrence of the random arrival process with (constant) hazard over the period of exposure is simply the product of the hazard and the exposure period.) According to T11.1, the expected time spent in reorganization during a cascade with random origin equals $\eta(x)I(x)$. Because any unit is equally likely to be in reorganization during a cascade, the probability that the arrival during the interval of length v hits a reorganizing unit equals $\eta(x)I(x)/vU_x$, where vU_x is the total time at risk of experiencing reorganization taken over all of the units of the organization for the relevant duration. The probability that it hits a unit not in reorganization equals $1 - \eta(x)I(x)/vU_x$.

The probability that an organization misses an arriving opportunity can be expressed as

$$\kappa_l \left(1 - \frac{\eta(x)I(x)}{v\,U_x}\right) + (\kappa_l + \widetilde{\kappa}_l)\,\frac{\eta(x)I(x)}{v\,U_x},$$

using the conditional probabilities of an opportunity being missed from A11.6. Applying this expression to the expected number of arriving opportunities over the interval, $\Psi_l v$, gives the result in the theorem by simple algebraic substitution (and the relationship $\Psi_l = \psi_x U_x$, which follows from A11.4 and A11.5). □

A subtle issue needs attention in comparing cascades: a pair of cascades might differ in temporal span. This means that we need to compare experiences over the span of the longer cascade to get the full scope of both cascades. Things get very complicated if we allow the possibility that the organization with the shorter cascade starts another cascade within the period of comparison. So we restrict the comparison to the case in which no subsequent initiations of cascades occur within the period of comparison.

We focus on missed opportunities because failing to capitalize on opportunities generally degrades an organization's position in the market (relative to competitors) for attracting members of the audience. In the terms used in analyzing organizational niches in Chapters 8 and 9, missing opportunities means missing chances to build and sustain engagement and to sustain or strengthen intrinsic appeal to the audience. The time of senior managers (and other organizational members) spent on changing feature values and codes limits their availability to manage relations with key constituencies. The consequence of missing such opportunities, if some competitors do not, is that the expected appeal of the organization's offering (relative to competitors) falls. Appeal relative to competitors defines fitness (D9.1). So we can state the main implications of the argument in terms of fitness. We begin by tying missed opportunities to fitness.

Postulate 11.2. *If one organization in a population misses more opportunities over the interval than the other, then its expected fitness is normally lower.*

$$\mathfrak{N}\, \mathbf{q}, \mathbf{q}' \, [\textsc{cm} \rightarrow (M \downarrow \mathrm{E}(\Phi))(\mathbf{q}, \mathbf{q}')\,],$$

where $\mathbf{q}$ *and* $\mathbf{q}'$ *are as above.*

Turning back to the example of the architectural decentralization in General Motors, one might naturally wonder how the company managed to survive, even dominate, if these theoretical claims are accurate. After all, the structural change and associated cascade introduced in 1920 should have caused the firm to miss opportunities. Sloan (1963: 50) suggests an answer:

> Even mistakes played a large part in the actual events...and if our competitors—Mr. Ford among them—had not made some of their own of considerable magnitude, and if we had not reversed certain of ours, the position of General Motors would be different from what it is today.

It is reasonable to think that what Sloan regards as "mistakes" are related to the organization's induced code violations and subsequent adjustments. We interpret his statement as recognizing that adjustment costs were significant and would have damaged the company severely if its competitors had not been experiencing similar difficulties. Given the massive expansion of the automobile market at the time, it seems plausible that the main competitors were all suffering from reorganization pains.

This argument has an obvious implication for fitness in situations in which not all competitors reorganize.

Lemma 11.6. *An organization's expected fitness,* $\mathrm{E}(\Phi)$*, presumably declines with the total time spent reorganizing,* D*, during a cascade with a random origin.*

$$\mathfrak{P}\, \mathbf{q}, \mathbf{q}' \, [\mathcal{Q}_3 \rightarrow (D \downarrow \mathrm{E}(\Phi))(\mathbf{q}, \mathbf{q}')\,],$$

where $\mathbf{q}$ *and* $\mathbf{q}'$ *are as above.*

Proof. The most specific rule chain results from a chain rule applied to (the arguments behind) L11.5 ($D \uparrow \mathrm{E}(M)$), P11.2 ($M \downarrow \mathrm{E}(\Phi)$), and the metarule for chaining probabilistic arguments from Section 6.5. □

11.7 CHANGE AND MORTALITY

At this point, we have a clear point of contact with the original inertia theory. Indeed, a slight restatement of Hannan and Freeman's (1984) key Assumption 9 now follows as a theorem (when restricted to apply to comembers of a prominent population of organizations).

Theorem 11.3. *An organization's excess hazard of mortality due to reorganization presumably rises monotonically over a period of reorganization.*

$$\mathfrak{P}\, l, t, t', v, x, x' \,[\textsc{cm}(l, x, x', t, t') \wedge (a(x,t) = a(x',t')) \wedge (Ch(x,t) = 1) \\ \wedge (T(x, t_1) = v) \wedge \forall w[(0 < w \leq v) \rightarrow (Ch(x', t' + w) = 0)] \\ \rightarrow (\omega(x, t + w) < \omega(x', t' + w))].$$

Proof. The most specific rule chain uses M9.1, which states that increasing fitness lowers the hazard of mortality, and the regularities behind L11.6, which holds that expected fitness declines monotonically with the duration of reorganization. The minimal rule chain follows by application of the cut rule and the chaining metarule. □

Note that another line of argument, from the age-dependence fragment in Chapter 7, leads to the opposite conclusion because an organization is older while in a change than it was before it initiated the change. The times at which mortality hazards are compared for an organization are for (otherwise) unspecific ages in the sense that they do not tell that one or the other time is before or after the normal age of exhaustion of endowment (or the age of onset of obsolescence). Therefore, the fragment on the liability of newness applies. Recall that the rule chain behind the liability-of-newness theorem tells that the mortality hazard at a later age is lower than that at a younger one, which would contradict the theorem. Which argument applies depends upon specificity considerations. In our interpretation, the liability of newness argument is entirely unspecific in that it applies to any age segment. The antecedent in the foregoing theorem is, however, specific: it tells that the times being compared lie within the span of a cascade. Hence, in cases where the period in question falls within an interval of known reorganization, the cascade argument overrides the age-dependence argument. The nonmonotonic logic eliminates an apparent contradiction.

The main line of argument identifies conditions that lengthen cascades. If stocks of resources fall monotonically during cascades, then the factors that lengthen cascades make change more risky. We provide a formal statement of these implications for pairs of organizations that experience architectural changes and differ in the structural factors that affect expected cascade length. The key results depend upon the expected time reorganizing. According to the model, the product of intricacy and viscosity gives the expected time reorganizing. Therefore, the central theorem in the argument relies on comparisons of ηI between organizations.

Theorem 11.4. *The increase in the hazard of mortality due to an architectural change presumably rises monotonically with the product of intricacy and viscosity,* ηI.

$$\mathfrak{P}\,\mathbf{q}, \mathbf{q}'\,[\mathcal{Q}_3 \rightarrow (\eta I \uparrow \Omega)(\mathbf{q}, \mathbf{q}')\,],$$

where $\Omega(x, t+T) = \int_t^{t+T} \omega(x, v)dv$, *and* $\mathbf{q}$, $\mathbf{q}'$ *are defined as above.*

Proof. The most specific regularity chain begins with the intension of $\eta(x)I(x) > \eta(x')I(x')$. Given $\mathcal{Q}_3$, the regularities behind T11.2 give the equality $\mathrm{E}(D) = \eta(x)I(x)$; the regularities behind L11.6 give $D \downarrow \mathrm{E}(\Phi)$; and M9.1 gives $\Phi \downarrow \omega$ Application of the cut rule and the chaining metarule completes the chain. □

Empirical researchers might want to focus on η or I, not their product in some cases. For instance, they might be in a position to characterize the intricacies of a set of organizations but lack information on their viscosities. Indeed, the original inertia theory made a claim that can be rendered as a claim about intricacy: Hannan and Freeman's (1984) Theorem 5 states "Complexity increases the risk of death due to reorganization." The following translation of this theorem also follows as an implication of the current stage of the new theory.

Corollary 11.1. *The increase in the hazard of mortality due to an architectural change presumably grows monotonically with intricacy (so long as levels of viscosity do not complicate the relationship).*

$$\mathfrak{P}\,\mathbf{q}, \mathbf{q}'\,[\mathcal{Q}_3 \wedge (\eta(x) \leq \eta(x')) \rightarrow (I \uparrow \Omega)(\mathbf{q}, \mathbf{q}')\,],$$

where $\mathbf{q}$ *and* $\mathbf{q}'$ *are as above.*

Proof. The most specific rule chain connecting the antecedent and consequent uses the regularities behind T11.4. □

Hannan and Freeman (1984) concluded that the arguments about the effect of organizational size on the risk of mortality due to change present what we would now call a Nixon Diamond (see Chapter 6). Larger organizations are normally more intricate and normally have more resources. Reasoning about intricacy leads us to expect that change would be more hazardous for larger organizations. Reasoning about resources would lead to the opposite conclusion. Neither argument is more specific than the other: this is a Nixon Diamond, and no conclusion is warranted.

DISCUSSION

It makes sense at this point to ask what, if any, implications of the revised theory differ from the original. Several differences between the initial theory and the reformulation deserve note. One difference concerns the role of architecture. The original argument treated architecture as "plastic" and relatively insignificant for understanding inertia and change. Our revised theory allows for the possibility that architectural change might be very important. In providing a list of features constituting the core, the original theory did not allow any exceptions, and it did not provide any guidance for dealing with exceptions if they are encountered. In these respects, we believe that the new theory constitutes an advance.

The reformulation also provides different, specific advice for conducting empirical research on structural inertia. Rather than look at a single type of change in a population of organizations (such that each experiences as single shock), the theory implies that the subsequent cascading changes and their temporal dimensions should be studied as well. In current empirical studies, a commonly observed pattern suggests that mortality hazards jump when changes get undertaken but that they then decline with the time elapsed from the change. On the basis of the new theory, it now seems important to know whether a studied architectural change is the initiating change in a cascade or simply one episode in a longer sequence. But how much does this matter?

The typical contemporary study traces the mortality consequences in a complete organizational population of a single type of structural change, say a change in the basic product design for a manufacturer (see Carroll and Hannan (2000) for a review). Although this design represents a definite advancement over previous studies with outcome-biased samples, it cannot record information on the cascades of changes brought on by the initial adjustment. As a result, none of the following are visible: the total time reorganizing, the temporal span of the cascade or the end of the period of reorganization. This means that commonly estimated duration effects about the shape of the hazard following a change, based simply on time elapsed since the initial change, might not be very meaningful. To see the impact of this, assume for the moment (for ease of interpretation) that the studied change is the initiating event in a cascade and that there is a positive association of the total time reorganizing and the temporal span of a cascade. Under these assumptions, the hazard of mortality rises with the duration of the reorganization. But empirical studies, which have not sought to disentangle reorganization effects from processes that operate after reorganization, generally find that the hazard falls monotonically following the initial jump at the time of the change. We suggest that this common pattern might arise solely from the design of these studies. A design that records subsequent changes and measures better the temporal aspects of reorganizing might very well yield different findings.

From a methodological point of view, this chapter might be instructive as an example of how to use logic to reveal assumptions needed to derive an already accepted substantive insight, taken as a target theorem (see Chapter 1). In this case, we took, as the theorem-to-be-derived, the proposition that core structural change generates higher than usual mortality chances. Our particular formalization effort of this idea led to the elaboration of certain central concepts such as cascade and reorganization period. This effort required that we invoke many auxiliary assumptions explicitly. (In prior work on this issue, such assumptions appear to be implicit.) Of course, the theory will generate different predictions if these auxiliary assumptions are altered or discarded.

Chapter Twelve

Opacity and Asperity

We can gain deeper insight about the risk of organizational change by building a more complex model of internal organization and by introducing organizational culture into the picture. We find it insightful to consider the implications of two specific factors: (1) structural limits on the foresight of those initiating a change (which we call opacity) and (2) restrictiveness of the organization's culture with respect to architecture (which we call asperity). Considerations of culture bring issues of identity back into the picture.[1]

12.1 LIMITED FORESIGHT: OPACITY

The structural theory presented in Chapter 11 provides a framework for explaining why certain architectural changes in certain contexts increase an organization's chances of failure. But recognizing such possibilities raises a question: Why would any organization undertake a change that likely takes a long time to complete and thereby causes it to miss many opportunities and risk failure?

A general answer typically offered by organizational theorists says that the rationality of the agents is bounded in these contexts and that such outcomes are unanticipated (March and Simon 1958; Cyert and March 1963). This assessment seems sound, but it does not go far enough. We need more specification of how bounded rationality manifests itself in the initiation of architectural changes with potentially dire results.

The initial change in a cascade-gone-wrong presumably involves miscalculations rather than perverse intentions. Although many possible forms of miscalculation could produce this result, we focus on one that is only subtly connected to the outcome and that can be addressed in the model. This is what we call the opacity of the organization (from the perspective of the initiators of architectural changes) and the limited foresight that results. In particular, we assume that reduced foresight about the exact structure of connections among units impairs the ability to calculate accurately in advance the costs and benefits of an architectural change to those in the initiating unit. This miscalculation can give a rosier-than-justified expectation and thus prompt agents to undertake some changes with potentially deleterious results.

Limitations on foresight produce a systematic tendency to underestimate the length of reorganizations and thus to underestimate the costs and risks of change.

[1]Portions of this chapter are adapted from Hannan, Pólos, and Carroll (2003b); however, the formalization has been adapted to fit the revised conceptions of audiences and codes.

Given such systematic underestimation, managers can easily choose to enter into changes that cost far more than the expected benefits of successfully completing the change. For example, analysts generally agree that the management of Xerox Corporation underestimated the difficulty of a transformation it undertook in 1999 in an attempt to improve its cost structure and provide better service.[2] At a time when the company was doing very well by most observable measures (increasing profits and stock price; absence of high-end competitors with comparable products), Xerox simultaneously reorganized the architecture of its sales and billing functions. The billing reorganization consolidated 36 administrative centers into 3. The sales reorganization shifted its staff of 15,000 persons from units based on geography to those based on industry, moving from local generalists to national product specialists. The results proved disastrous. Billing errors proliferated, and the sales staff spent much of its time resolving problems rather than learning new roles and making contacts with prospective buyers. Staff turnover rose, sales dropped, and customers moved to competitors. Within 18 months the losses had become so substantial that a recently installed CEO was ousted, and the business press speculated that the company would not survive.[3]

In many cases, an organization's structure imposes limits on what can be known. Information about some parts of an organization is often unavailable in other parts, what Oliver Williamson (1975) calls information impactedness. For instance, Stinchcombe (1990: 75) observes that local information usually does not "have to flow anywhere in a hierarchy, except in very aggregated form as a budget estimate." Sometimes the hindrance to information flow arises from differences in the languages used in different parts of the organization, which make it difficult for those outside a unit to interpret a full-disclosure description of the activities in an organizational unit. Other times, lack of transparency arises due to strategic withholding of information.

Stinchcombe (1990: 81) notes that pools of local knowledge might facilitate cultural developments that heighten opacity:

> When a large share of the information used in a given activity is such local knowledge, a subculture grows that is more or less isolated from the rest of the organization. The subculture is organized in a large measure around the information system that is of little use or interest to anyone else and so is adapted to particular concrete features... uses an arcane language or system of notation and resists invasion by standards from larger and more uniform information systems.

Although opacity might have many potential meanings in an organizational context, we use the term here in a specific sense. We say that one component of organization is structurally opaque to another if the interunit connections that flow from the former cannot be readily seen by the latter. For example, suppose that the interdependencies among the subunits of a research and development division in a

[2]For instance, the *Wall Street Journal* noted that "retraining to sell and service such intricate machines proved more difficult than the company anticipated" (Periera and Klein 2000).

[3]At the same time, Xerox faced stiff new competition on its previously unrivaled high-end copiers from both Heidelberger Druckmaschinen AG and Canon Inc.

firm cannot be perceived by those in divisions such as manufacturing, sales, and marketing. Then the R&D division in the firm is opaque to the others. Or, alternatively, suppose that the firm's architecture has a regional basis and that the North American division cannot perceive the interconnections within the Asian division. Then the former is opaque to the latter.

Notation. We distinguish what can be (or is) foreseen when an initial change is undertaken from the factual situation with the following notation. We mark predicates and functions that refer to foresight with an asterisk, and we do not add such a mark to those that refer to the facts (as they emerge). This means that $V^*(u, x, t)$ denotes the random variable that records the number of induced violations of architectural codes resulting from a cascade initiated by unit u in organization x that can be foreseen by the relevant actors in unit u at time t; $D^*(u, x, t)$ is the random variable that records the foreseen length of the cascade beginning at time t from the vantage of the actors in the unit u in organization x, and so forth.

Now consider again the binary matrix $\mathbf{B}(x)$, which records the code in the high-level architecture that tells the superordination relations among the units that comprise the organization, which we denoted in Chapter 11 by $\breve{\sigma}(x, t)$ for the organization x at time t. To model the effects of opacity, this factual information needs to be combined with the potentially clouded vision from the vantage points of the various units. To this end, we define the matrix $\mathbf{B}^*(u, x)$, the matrix of architectural relations in the organization from unit u's (potentially opaque) vantage point. We use the perception modality used in previous chapters (and defined formally in Appendix E) to distinguish the architectural connections that are perceived (not obscured) from those that are not.

Definition 12.1 (Matrix of perceived architectural connections). *The matrix of architectural connections in an organization from the point of view of the decision makers in a unit, in notation $\mathbf{B}^*(u, x)$, is the $U_x \times U_x$ matrix whose (i, j)th element, $b^*_{i,j}$, is defined as follows.*

$b^*_{i,j} = 1$ *if and only if*

1. *the architecture is such that u_j actually constrains u_i architecturally at time t, that is, $b_{i,j} = 1$; and*

2. *the decision makers in the focal unit correctly perceive this architectural constraint, in formal terms $\boxed{\text{P}}_u(b_{i,j}(t) = 1)$, where we use the informal notation $\boxed{\text{P}}_u$ to denote the perception of the agent making decisions about architecture in the unit u.*

Otherwise $b^*_{i,j}(t) = 0$.

The consequences of opacity can be seen by considering the centralities based on $\mathbf{B}^*(u, x)$.

Definition 12.2 (Obscured centrality of a unit). *The (partially) obscured centrality scores of unit u at time t is*

$$cen^*(u, x) \equiv \mathbf{d} \sum_{k=1}^{\infty} \pi_x^k \, \mathbf{B}^*(u, x)^k \, \boldsymbol{\ell},$$

where $\mathbf{d}$ *is a* $(1 \times U_x)$ *vector with* $d_i = 0$ *for* $i \neq u$ *and* $d_i = 1$ *for* $i = u$.

[Note that premultiplying by $\mathbf{d}$ simply picks out the uth element in the vector of partial centrality scores from the vantage point of unit u.]

By combining the concept of obscured centrality with the argument of the previous chapter, we have a parallel to L11.1, which states that the expected number of (actual) induced violations in a marked cascade increases with the centrality of the initiating unit.

Lemma 12.1. *The expected number of foreseen induced violations of architectural code in a marked cascade presumably equals the initiating unit's partially obscured centrality.*

$$\mathfrak{P}\, t, u, x\, [\mathrm{U}(u, x) \rightarrow \mathrm{E}(V^*(u, x, t)) = cen^*(u, x)].$$

Proof. The proof follows the lines of the proof of L11.1 but uses D12.1 instead of D11.6 as the definition of centrality. □

We define a unit's opacity as the difference between its actual and partially obscured centralities.

Definition 12.3 (Opacity at the unit level).

$$op(u, x) \equiv cen(u, x) - cen^*(u, x).$$

With this definition in hand, we obtain a lemma that parallels L11.1, which states that the expected number of induced violations in a cascade with known origin equals the centrality of the initiating unit.

Lemma 12.2. *The expected number of induced violations of architectural codes in a marked cascade initiated by unit* u *at time* t *that are unforeseen from the vantage of the initiating unit presumably equals the level of opacity of the view of the initiator:* $op(u, x)$.

$$\mathfrak{P}\, t, u, x\, [(ch(u, x, t) = 1) \rightarrow (\mathrm{E}(V_u(x, t) - V_u^*(x, t)) = op(u, x))].$$

Proof. The expected foreseen number of induced violations, expressed as $\mathrm{E}(V_u^*(x, t) \mid ch(u, x, t) = 1)$, is given by the sum of the expected foreseen number of violations at each path length. That is, $\mathrm{E}(V_u^*(x, t)) = \sum_{k=1}^{\infty} \mathrm{E}(V_u^{*\,k}(x, t))$, where $\mathrm{E}(V_u^{*\,k}(x, t))$ is the expected foreseen number of induced violations at step k of the cascade (that is, at path length k). The joint probability of k inductions along a path is π_x^k. Because inductions must follow the subordination relation, $\mathrm{E}(V_u^{*\,k}(x, t)) = \sum_{u \neq u'} \pi_x^k\, z^{*,k}(u, u')$, where $z^{*\,k}(u, u')$ equals the number of distinct k-step foreseen paths connecting units u and u'. Inspecting the terms in the powers of $\mathbf{B}^*(x)$ reveals that $z^{*\,k}(u, u')$ is the (u, u') entry in $(\mathbf{B}^*)^k(x)$. Hence, the expected foreseen number of induced violations equals $cen^*(u, x)$. Use of D12.3 and the chaining metarule completes the regularity chain. □

Developing the organization-level implications of opacity requires aggregating opacities over units within the organization. Lacking any information on the appropriate aggregation, we opt for simple averaging.

Definition 12.4 (Obscured intricacy). *The partially obscured intricacy in an organization is the mean of the partially obscured intricacies of its units.*

$$I^*(x) \equiv \sum_u cen^*(u,x)/U_x.$$

We use the term organizational opacity to refer to the average level of opacity over an organization's units.

Definition 12.5 (Opacity at the organization level). *An organization's level of opacity is the difference between its actual intricacy, $I(x)$, and its perceived intricacy, $I^*(x)$.*

$$O(x) \equiv \sum_u op(u,x)/U_x = I(x) - I^*(x).$$

Note that $O(x) = 0$ if and only if the centralities are not obscured for any unit, which we call full transparency.[4]

Next we consider the implications of opacity for cascades with random origins.

Lemma 12.3. *The expected number of unforeseen induced violations of architectural codes in a random cascade presumably equals the organization's level of opacity.*

$$\mathfrak{P}\, t, x\, [(Ch(x,t) = 1) \rightarrow (\mathrm{E}(V(x,t) - V^*(x,t)) = O(x))].$$

Proof. The expectation of a sum of random variables equals the sum of their expectations: $\mathrm{E}(V(x,t) - V^*(x,t)) = \mathrm{E}(V(x,t)) - \mathrm{E}(V^*(x,t))$. According to the regularities that ensure L12.3, $\mathrm{E}(V(x,t)) = I(x)$. By the law of total probability,

$$\mathrm{E}(V^*(x,t)) = \sum_u \mathrm{E}(V^*(u,x,t)) \Pr(ch(u,x,t)).$$

According to L11.2, $\Pr(ch(u,x,t)) = 1/U_x$, which gives

$$\begin{aligned} \mathrm{E}(V^*(x,t)) &= \sum_u \mathrm{E}(V^*(u,x,t))/U_x \\ &= \sum_u cen^*(u,x)/U_x = I^*(x), \end{aligned}$$

where the equality on the second line of the foregoing formula is warranted by the regularities behind L12.1; and the equality on the third line comes from D12.4. Finally, D12.5, which equates O and $I - I^*$, completes the regularity chain. □

When we refer to differences in opacity in deriving results on the expected durations of cascades, we will need an expression that tells the probability that the initiating unit foresees an induced violation. Let $v^*(u_i, u_j, x, t)$ be a random variable that equals one if the pair $\langle u_j, t_j \rangle$ is one of the induced violations in the cascade $\mathbf{cas}(u,x,t)$ and the occurrence of this induced violation is foreseen from the vantage point of unit u, the initiator of the cascade and that equals zero if it is not foreseen.

The intuition behind this argument is the recognition that induced violations take longer to deal with when they are unforeseen. When violations cannot be foreseen, agents cannot plan comprehensively for reorganization, and they cannot undertake as many adjustments in parallel. The fact that the unforeseen architectural code violations show up in midchange slows adjustment, thereby extending (actual) periods of reorganization.

---

[4]It is also worth pointing out that $I(x) = 0$ logically implies that $O(x) = 0$, because $I(x)^* = 0$ under this condition.

Postulate 12.1. *The expected duration of an unforeseen violation of architectural codes for a unit normally exceeds that of a foreseen one.*

$$\mathfrak{N}\, t, u_1, u_2, u_3, x\, [(ch(u_1, x, t) = 1) \wedge (v^*(u_1, u_2, x, t) = 1) \\ \wedge (v^*(u_1, u_3, x, t) = 0) \rightarrow (\mathrm{E}(d(u_2, x, t)) < \mathrm{E}(d(u_3, x, t)))].$$

Finally, we need to characterize the probability that an actual violation is foreseen so that we can characterize random cascades in opaque organizations. As with the auxiliary assumptions used in building the probability model in Chapter 11, we simplify as much as possible. Accordingly, we introduce the auxiliary assumption that each induced violation is equally likely to be foreseen and that this probability equals the fraction of foreseen induced violations to total induced violations.

Auxiliary assumption 12.1. *The probability that the initiating unit in a cascade foresees that a violation will be induced in another unit normally does not vary over units or over time; it equals the ratio of obscured intricacy to actual intricacy.*

$$\mathfrak{A}\, t, t', u_1, u_2, u_3, u_4, x\, [(ch(u_1, x, t) = 1) \wedge (ch(u_2, x, t') = 1) \\ \rightarrow (\Pr(vl^*_{u_1}(u_3, x, t)) = I^*(x)/I(x) = \Pr(vl^*_{u_2}(u_4, x, t')))].$$

We will use this auxiliary assumption, along with the foregoing argument, to derive implications of opacity for the consequences of organizational changes. But first we develop the parallel arguments concerning organizational culture.

12.2 CULTURAL OPPOSITION: ASPERITY

Our second major extension to the structural model of cascading changes in Chapter 11 revisits the theme in inertia theory that changes that break codes specifying identities are especially problematic. Here we develop an argument that such changes generally encounter cultural opposition. According to the general reasoning about codes introduced in Chapters 2–5, perceived code violations produce normative reactions and sanctions. These reactions could emanate from a variety of possible sources including local tradition, professional norms, organizational form membership, or other identity constraints. From our point of view, the important observations are that (1) cultural opposition generates turmoil and (2) turmoil likely lengthens reorganization periods.

Cultural opposition signifies a shift in the meaning of a proposed architectural change. It implies that what was likely evaluated by those initiating the change in a dispassionate cost-benefit calculation is, in fact, a normative matter. In Philip Selznick's (1957) words, such situations are likely to occur when architectural features have become infused with moral value. For instance, when officials at Ben & Jerry's Ice Cream proposed relaxing their fixed salary distribution ratio specifying the maximum range of compensation allowed by the firm, there was a strong cultural reaction against this architectural change (Lager 1994).

The strength of cultural opposition can be difficult to anticipate if those that initiate a change do not share in the organizational culture (intensional consensus) of the members. So newly hired executives run a high risk of making this mistake. For example, at Apple Computer in 1997 CEO Gilbert Amelio introduced a centralized architecture to a culture that "always championed the individual and stressed freedom to act unilaterally" (Amelio 1998). Amid much strife, Apple's transformation continued down a stormy path until Amelio was ousted and replaced by cofounder Steve Jobs.

We make use of the conceptual apparatus developed in Part I to characterize organizational culture. Here we consider the membership of an organization and the members of its units as the relevant audiences. As in our formalization of categories, we define for each audience member, $y \in \mathbf{a}_u$, a grade of membership in a consensus about the local architectural code, about what feature values are consistent with a member's architectural code for the unit and which are not. It again makes sense to distinguish extensional and intensional consensus. As we see it, an extensional reading of an architectural code corresponds to what is generally called the "letter of the law," its literal meaning. In contrast, an intensional reading corresponds to the "spirit of the law." Because codes are generally highly simplified and cannot provide a complete specification of an architecture, intensional consensus is much more important to smooth functioning than extensional consensus. Therefore, we focus on the former.

We define agreement about architectural schemata with the function is, which we introduced in Chapter 3 to tell the degree of agreement of one schema with another.[5] (Of course, now the schemata give the architectural codes that hold for a unit.)

Definition 12.6. *A unit member's grade of membership in an intensional consensus about the rules that apply to the unit is the degree to which his or her schema for the architectural rules for the unit agrees with those of other members of the unit.*

Let $\sigma(y, u, t) = \mathbf{s}_u$ *and* $\sigma(y', u, t) = \mathbf{s}'_u$ *be a pair of schemata for the architecture of the unit* u *at a time point* t.

$$\nu_{i(u)}(y, t) \equiv \frac{\sum_{y' \neq y} is(\sigma(y, u, t), \sigma(y', u, t))}{|\mathbf{a}_u| - 1},$$

where is *is the intensional agreement function (similarity) from D3.5 and* $\mathbf{a}_u$ *denotes the set of members of the unit* u.

These grades of membership allow a simple representation of the cultural homogeneity (with respect to architectural matters) of the audience for a unit.

Definition 12.7 (Cultural consensus about architectural rules). *The degree of cultural consensus about the meaning of the architectural rules that apply to a unit*

---

[5]This formulation exhibits a formal similarity with the formal treatment of enculturation by J. Richard Harrison and Glenn Carroll (2006). However, the interpretations differ. Whereas the Harrison–Carroll enculturation score reflects the degree to which an organization's management assesses an individual as ideal according to management's cultural preferences, the GoM defined here represents agreement with fellow audience members. Nonetheless, cultural consensus in the two models represents similar situations, those in which agreement among members is high.

is the average among its members of the grades of membership in the consensus about the architectural schemata for the unit.

$$cul(u, x, t) \equiv \overline{\nu}_{i(u)}(t) = \frac{\sum_{y \in \mathbf{a}_u} \nu_{i(u)}(y, t)}{|\mathbf{a}_u|}.$$

How much each unit's membership agrees about architectural issues matters enormously for the unit's functioning. A unit whose membership represents a homogeneous culture for the architectural rules presumably operates effectively and without great conflict. In contrast, a unit whose membership lacks cultural consensus about the architecture would seem to be dysfunctional and ineffective.

From the perspective of imposed architectural changes, cultures should be distinguished by the likelihood that an arbitrary set of architectural feature values will fail to correspond to the architectural schemata of the unit's membership. A restrictive architectural schema excludes many architectural possibilities. We call the level of such restrictiveness *asperity*, relying on the dictionary definition of asperity as "severity or rigor." We denote asperity by the random variable $asp(u, x)$, which varies from 0 to 1 inclusive. (For tractability we ignore possible variation over time in asperity in what follows.)

As we see it, an aspere culture displays two defining characteristics. First, the cultural code must be restrictive in the sense that it allows only a narrow range of possible rules, structures, or behaviors; many possibly functional alternatives are considered not morally acceptable (e.g., a newspaper publisher requiring editorial staff to consult with advertising staff before running stories about key advertisers). Second, the membership must understand and embrace the culture and also be willing to enforce sanctions when violations of the code are detected. In our representation, this means that the membership has a high level of cultural agreement about the architecture. So we define asperity indirectly with the following meaning postulate.

Meaning postulate 12.1 (Asperity). *The cultural asperity of the membership of one unit is higher than that of another (in the same organization) if it has greater (or equal) cultural homogeneity and a higher average degree of restrictiveness in members' schemata.*

Let $strict(u, y)$ give the probability that a set of architectural feature values for unit u chosen at random fails to conform to the architectural schema of the unit member y and $Strict(u, x)$ denote the average of $strict(u, y)$ over the membership of the unit.

$$\mathfrak{M}\, t, u, u', x\, [\mathrm{U}(u, x) \wedge \mathrm{U}(u', x) \wedge (cul(u, x) \geq cul(u', x)) \wedge (Strict(u, x) > Strict(u', x)) \rightarrow (\mathrm{E}(asp(u, x)) > \mathrm{E}(asp(u', x)))].$$

Asperity and Resistance to Induced Change

We have been considering situations in which units experience induced violations of architectural codes and take actions to modify the local architectures to conform to the newly imposed external constraints. Now we incorporate the notion of cultural resistance to the imposed changes. We use the random variable $rst(u, x, t)$, which equals one if unit u mobilizes cultural resistance to resolving an induced violation of architectural code that is created at time t and equals zero otherwise.[6] When an attempt to eliminate an induced architectural code violation comes into conflict with local cultural code, the new architecture becomes morally suspect in the eyes of a unit's members (the most relevant audience for the local cultural code). We believe that this was the case when CEO Amelio attempted to centralize Apple Computer and when top management of Ben & Jerry's Ice Cream attempted to expand the internal salary ratio. Note that in such cases, there might be nothing operationally or mechanically wrong with the new code; indeed, the architectural change might very well prove beneficial except for the cultural reaction.

In analyzing cultural opposition, we build on the concept of asperity. Recall that we suggested that cultural codes vary in asperity, the fraction of possible architectures that they rule out. Above, we defined asperity at the unit level. Because an aspere culture rules out many of the alternative possible architectures, efforts to modify architecture are more likely to violate cultural codes in organizations with more aspere cultures (Sørensen 2002). With this insight, we can provide a deeper characterization of asperity with another meaning postulate. We first define the binary random variable $rst(u, x, t)$, which equals one if cultural resistance occurs and zero otherwise. We then postulate that the probability of cultural resistance is given by the level of asperity.

Meaning postulate 12.2. *The probability that an induced architectural change mobilizes cultural resistance to local architectural change normally equals the asperity of a unit's culture.*

$$\mathfrak{N}\, t, u, u', x\, [(vl(u, u', x, t) = 1) \rightarrow (\Pr(rst(u, x, t)) = asp(u, x))].$$

Cultural opposition resists ready resolution for at least three reasons. First, cultural violations might produce intense moral reactions that cause individuals to fight harder and longer. Second, the cultural nature of the opposition might not be easily recognizable as it is often difficult to articulate as such. So resolution efforts might focus mistakenly on noncultural matters perceived to be the source of opposition. Third, organizational culture provides a potential basis for very broad resistance. If so, the proponents of the changes cannot count on many members of the organization to use their specialized knowledge to facilitate the many local adjustments required to implement the changes. In such situations, change and adjustment requires more direct managerial control. Given limits on managerial time and effort, reliance on managerial control puts sharp limits on the pace of adjustment. Accordingly, we hold that cultural resistance slows adjustment.

Postulate 12.2. *It normally takes longer for a unit to eliminate an induced violation of an architectural code when cultural resistance is stronger.*

$$\begin{aligned}\mathfrak{N}\, t, t', u_1, u_2, x\, [&\mathrm{U}(u_1, x) \wedge \mathrm{U}(u_2, x) \wedge (rst(u_1, x, t) > rst(u_2, x, t')) \\ &\wedge \exists\, u_3, u_4\, [(vl_{u_1}(u_3, x, t) = 1) \wedge (vl_{u_2}(u_4, x, t') = 1)] \\ &\rightarrow (\mathrm{E}(d(u_1, x, t)) > \mathrm{E}(d(u_2, x, t')))].\end{aligned}$$

[6]We do not attempt to specify exactly when the cultural code violation occurs, other than to assume that it occurs after the induced violation of architectural code.

At this point we aggregate to the organizational level under the simplifying auxiliary assumption that asperity in an organization does not vary among units or over time.[7]

Auxiliary assumption 12.2. *Each organization normally has a characteristic level of asperity, A, that applies to all of its units.*

$$\mathfrak{A}\, u, u', x \left[\mathrm{U}(u,x) \wedge \mathrm{U}(u',x) \rightarrow (asp(u,x) = A(x) = asp(u',x))\right].$$

12.3 OPACITY, ASPERITY, AND REORGANIZATION

We next develop arguments about the role of opacity and asperity in shaping the time it takes for a unit to resolve an induced architectural violation. The first stage of the theory (Chapter 11) uses the auxiliary assumption that the expected duration of an induced violation does not vary over units or over time for an organization (A11.2). This common level is labeled $\eta(x)$ and called viscosity (sluggishness). At this point, we take advantage of the nonmonotonic logic to override that premise with premises that apply to situations of greater specificity. The original assumption of constant viscosity remains in the theory and it is not overridden if *all* that we know is that an organization is a typical member of a prominent population. If we know more than this, specifically if we have information on opacity and asperity, then the auxiliary assumption stated below replaces the original default.

Our conceptual framework highlights four conditions: an induced architectural violation for a unit can be either foreseen or not, and it can either trigger cultural resistance to change or not. One way to model this situation is to assume additivity of effects of opacity and asperity. Then only three organization-specific parameters are needed: a baseline duration for the situation in which neither complication occurs, an effect of opacity, and an effect of asperity. The reasoning that would support this kind of model is that the effect of opacity does not depend upon asperity. Because this reasoning might not apply to at least some cases of interest, we impose a four-parameter specification. The fourth parameter, labeled β_4 below, can be either positive or negative (but in this case its value is constrained, as we explain below). A negative value would mean that the combination of complications can be dealt with more quickly than one would expect based upon what is typical when the complications are encountered one at a time. A positive value means that the combination is worse (in terms of lengthening durations) than would be expected from knowledge of the separate effects. We think that positive values of this parameter are likely in real situations.

Auxiliary assumption 12.3. *The expected duration of reorganization for a unit (the elapsed time from induction of an architectural code violation to elimination) depends on whether the induced violation is foreseen and whether the response to*

---

[7]The extensive literature on organizational culture that posits the existence of unitary cultural characteristics would seem to support this simplification. Of course, organizations that lack a unitary culture might not conform to this simplifying assumption.

the induced violation encounters cultural resistance. Within combinations of these two conditions, the expected duration normally is constant over pairs of units and over time points for all organizations in a population.

Violation foreseen	Cultural resistance	Expected duration
yes	no	β_1
yes	yes	$\beta_1 + \beta_2$
no	no	$\beta_1 + \beta_3$
no	yes	$\beta_1 + \beta_2 + \beta_3 + \beta_4$

Because a duration cannot be negative, $\beta_1 \geq 0$. Recall that P12.1 states that unforeseen induced violations take longer to resolve than foreseen ones. This implies that $\beta_2 > 0$ (otherwise P12.1 would be violated). Similarly, P12.2 states that induced violations whose attempted resolution meets cultural resistance last longer than those that do not encounter such resistance. This argument implies that $\beta_3 > 0$ and $-\beta_2 < \beta_4$.

Reorganization Periods

The central intuition underlying our argument recognizes that opacity and asperity lengthen the expected duration of a reorganization in a random cascade. In the case of opacity, this occurs because the initiators of the change cannot know a priori all of the adjustments required to eliminate architectural code violations in an opaque organization. As a result, not all changes can be done in parallel. Only when a cascade of adjustments within one part of the organization has played itself out can a downstream unit begin to undertake adjustments to those changes. Hence, induced violations will arise at random. A unit might be well on its way to resolving an induced violation when another violation gets induced (coming over another path in the pattern of architectural dominance relations). In Chapter 11, we argued that resolving a pair of uncoordinated and interacting violations takes at least twice as long as an otherwise similar uninterrupted spell of resolution.[8]

For example, when Hewlett-Packard spun off what became known as Agilent Technologies, the corporate headquarters of the new organization consolidated and centralized certain shared functions such as information technology that had been fully decentralized in the parent company. For most functions, completing the consolidation apparently took several months. The implications of these changes for the various businesses will take much longer to work out, because the various transaction units are somewhat opaque to the central administration. A real danger for

[8]A potentially promising way of thinking formally about the length of the period of reorganization in these cases views the subject as a queuing problem. Queuing theory, of course, provides a framework for analyzing the behavior of queues including waiting times with uncertain (stochastic) arrivals. In the usual queuing problem setup, the main modeling choices concern: (1) the rate and stochastic form of arrivals to the system; (2) the rate at which arrivals get served and the corresponding waiting times; and (3) the number of service agents available. There are also endless potential complications having to do with queue discipline, waiting behavior, and the like.

the company is that the tightening of local resources might diminish innovation in the long run, because the units historically had almost full autonomy and did not need to ask for resources to attempt experimental projects as they might now.

Above we argued that asperity increases the time required to resolve each induced violation because (1) the reactions are more intense and (2) the broad basis of opposition might require more managerial attention to fine-tuning the structure in adjustment. Of course, holding constant the number of induced violations, this implies that the total time in reorganization will lengthen. Coupling these ideas with the argument about intricacy of organizational design in Chapter 11 yields the following theorem.

Theorem 12.1. *The expected total time spent in reorganization by an organization's units during a cascade with a random origin presumably increases monotonically with intricacy, I, opacity, O, and asperity, A.*

$$\mathfrak{P}\, t, x\, [(Ch(x,t) = 1) \\ \rightarrow (\mathrm{E}(D(x,t)) = \beta_1 I(x) + \beta_3 O(x) + A(x)(\beta_2 I(x) + \beta_4 O(x)))].$$

Proof. The proof again involves application of the law of total probability. The key information appears in the following table. (Recall that, by P12.2 and A12.2, $A(x)$, the level of asperity, equals the probability that an induced violation sparks cultural opposition.)

Foreseen	Resistance	Expected count	Expected duration
yes	no	$I^*(x)(1 - A(x))$	β_1
yes	yes	$I^*(x)A(x)$	$\beta_1 + \beta_2$
no	no	$O(x)(1 - A(x))$	$\beta_1 + \beta_3$
no	yes	$O(x)A(x)$	$\beta_1 + \beta_2 + \beta_3 + \beta_4$

The expected duration equals the sum over the four conditions (rows) of the products of the entries in the third and fourth columns. Taking this sum and using the identity $O = I - I^*$ gives the result.[9] □

Consider the relevant cases in light of this theorem. The expected total time reorganizing during a random cascade equals the sum of three terms. The first, $\beta_1 I(x)$, gives the expected duration for a fully transparent organization, that is one with $O(x) = 0$, whose organizational culture admits all possible architectures, $A(x) = 0$. This result shows that the result for Stage 1 of the theory persists as a special case of transparency and no cultural restraint.

Suppose that transparency is incomplete, $O(x) > 0$, but cultural restraint is lacking, $A(x) = 0$. Then the theorem states that the expected total time reorganizing equals $\beta_1 I(x) + \beta_3 O(x)$. Given the definition of opacity and the regularities behind L12.3, this result tells that the expected total time rises monotonically with opacity in the absence of cultural restraint.

[9]A more complete formal proof can be found in Hannan, Pólos, and Carroll (2003b).

Finally, let us bring asperity into the picture. The final term to be considered, $(\beta_2 I(x)+\beta_4 O(x))A(x)$, shows that asperity interacts with intricacy and opacity in affecting the expected time reorganizing. The coefficient of the intricacy–asperity effect, β_2, is the expected duration of a foreseen induced violation that involves a cultural violation. The coefficient of the opacity–asperity effect, β_4, is the expected duration of an unforeseen induced violation that involves a cultural violation. A12.3 and L12.3 tell that all of the parameters, other than β_4, are positive. Even if $\beta_4 < 0$, the combination of L12.3 and the definition of $O(x)$ imposes that the overall effects of $O(x)$ and $A(x)$ are positive. Hence the expected total time reorganizing strictly increases with asperity, intricacy, and opacity.[10]

12.4 CHANGE AND MORTALITY

We argued in the previous chapter that devoting attention, time, and energy to reshaping an organization diverts its members from the tasks that generate revenues. We specified the consequences of missed opportunities for expected fitness. Organizations experience a relative decline in fitness during periods of reorganization, both because reorganization imposes costs and also because directing resources and attention away from production causes a drop in revenue (a failure to acquire new resources).[11]

According to the probability model we have developed to this point, opportunities arrive at the same constant rate, Ψ_l, for all typical organizations in the (prominent) population l. We focus on the expected difference in the number of opportunities missed over an interval for a reorganizing unit and an otherwise identical not-reorganizing one. The interval considered is the full span of a cascade, which we labeled $T(x, t)$ in Chapter 11.

At this point we can see the advantage of the simplifying assumptions: they allow us to provide an algebraic characterization of the expected number of opportunities missed during a full cascade.

Theorem 12.2. *The expected number of opportunities that an organization misses during a full cascade presumably equals the sum of (1) the baseline expected number that would be missed over the time span had no reorganization taken place and (2) an excess expected number that grows monotonically with the organization's intricacy, I, opacity, O, and asperity, A.*

$$\mathfrak{P}\, l, t, v, x\, [\mathrm{M}(l, x, t) \wedge \mathrm{PR}(l, t) \wedge (Ch(x, t) = 1) \wedge (T(x, t) = v) \\ \rightarrow (\mathrm{E}(M(x, t, t + v)) = \kappa_l\, \Psi_l\, v + \widetilde{\kappa}_l\, \psi_x(\beta_1 I(x) + \beta_3 O(x) \\ + A(x)(\beta_2 I(x) + \beta_4 O(x))))].$$

[10]It is, nonetheless, important to remember that these three factors might not vary independently. In particular, intricacy and opacity are definitionally dependent—a nonintricate organization cannot be opaque.

[11]The decline is relative in the sense that the organization's fitness falls below what would have been the case absent the architectural change.

Proof. According to the regularities that support T11.2, each unit contributes $\kappa_l \psi_x v$ expected missed opportunities, the baseline that holds for all units, whether reorganizing or not (where $\psi_x = \Psi_l / U_x$). This portion of the process therefore contributes $\kappa_l \psi_x v \, U_x = \kappa_l \Psi_l v$ expected missed opportunities. Next consider the additional expected missed opportunities due to reorganization. The expected total time spent reorganizing in a complete cascade equals $\beta_1 I(x) + \beta_3 O(x) + A(x)(\beta_2 I(x) + \beta_4 O(x))$ according to the regularities behind T12.1. The expected excess in the number of opportunities missed during reorganization is this expected time multiplied by $\widetilde{\kappa}_l \psi_x$. □

If fitness falls monotonically during cascades, then the factors that lengthen cascades make change more risky, as we showed in Chapter 11. We provide a formal statement of these implications for pairs of organizations that experience random cascades and differ in the structural and cultural factors that affect expected cascade length. These key implications of the argument focus on the integrated hazard of mortality over the relevant period:

$$\Omega(x, t, t + \mathcal{T}) \equiv \int_t^{t+\mathcal{T}} \omega(x, v) \, dv,$$

where, as in Chapter 11, $\mathcal{T}$ denotes the maximum of the temporal spans of the cascades being compared.

Theorem 12.3. *The increase in the hazard of mortality due to an architectural change over the longer of a pair of cascades, $\Omega(x, t, t + \mathcal{T})$, presumably grows monotonically with intricacy, opacity, and asperity.*

A. $\mathfrak{P}\, \mathbf{q}, \mathbf{q}' \, [\, \mathcal{Q}_3 \wedge (O(x) \geq O(x')) \wedge (A(x) \geq A(x')) \rightarrow (I \uparrow \Omega)(\mathbf{q}, \mathbf{q}') \,]$;

B. $\mathfrak{P}\, \mathbf{q}, \mathbf{q}' \, [\, \mathcal{Q}_3 \wedge (I(x) \geq I(x')) \wedge (A(x) \geq A(x')) \rightarrow (O \uparrow \Omega)(\mathbf{q}, \mathbf{q}') \,]$;

C. $\mathfrak{P}\, \mathbf{q}, \mathbf{q}' \, [\, \mathcal{Q}_3 \wedge (I(x) \geq I(x')) \wedge (O(x) \geq O(x')) \rightarrow (A \uparrow \Omega)(\mathbf{q}, \mathbf{q}') \,]$,

where $\mathbf{q}$ *and* $\mathbf{q}'$ *are as above.*

Proof. The proofs of the three theorems follow the lines of the proof of T11.2, except that the last step in the rule chains utilizes the regularities behind T12.1 □

DISCUSSION

We have attempted here to offer an explanation for why things so often go badly awry when organizations seek to change their architectures. This chapter examined the implications of opacity, defined as limited foresight about unit interconnections, and asperity, defined as normative restrictiveness to certain architectural features for organizational change. We argued that opacity leads actors to underestimate the lengths of periods of reorganization and the associated costs of change, thereby prompting them to undertake changes with adverse consequences. As with organizational intricacy, both opacity and asperity serve to lengthen the total time that the organization spends reorganizing and to the associated opportunity costs. The central theorems state that the likely deleterious effect of a change in architecture on mortality hazards strengthens with the intricacy of the organizational design, the organization's opacity, and the asperity of its culture.

In Hannan, Pólos, and Carroll (2003b), we provide a detailed interpretation of how this theory might plausibly explain (at least in part) the spectacular collapse of Barings Brothers bank in February 1995. Although widely blamed on a single "rogue" trader who worked in Singapore, the conditions under which such activities could occur and persist undetected appear consistent with the theory. To wit, the Barings organization was in a period of reorganization (as we define the term), a fact acknowledged later by the Singapore inspectors, who ultimately blamed the failure of the bank on the chaotic conditions created by this state. Insider accounts of Barings at the time also suggest that the centuries-old Barings had produced an aspere traditional culture that would not readily accept the architectural changes initially put in place to motivate the entrepreneurial group in Asia; cultural opposition from the more traditional parts of the bank generated a cascading change that attempted to rein them in, that is, reintegrate this autonomous group. Furthermore, it appears that opacity in the organization caused leading Barings officials in London and elsewhere to underestimate the costs of the reintegration effort.

Chapter Thirteen

Niche Expansion

At this point, we can advance the project of integrating aspects of various theory fragments we have considered: categories and forms, age dependence, the niche, and structural change. We do so by considering the consequences of expansion of an organization's niche.

Recent empirical research examines the consequences of niche change (see Dobrev, Kim, and Hannan 2001; Dobrev, Kim, and Carroll 2003). Generally speaking, this research shows that niche change typically induces deleterious outcomes. In particular, it raises the hazard of mortality in the period following the change.

In seeking to reconcile this empirical work with theory, we focus exclusively on niche expansion. We ignore other kinds of shifts in the niche (e.g., niche contraction and change in the center of their niche) because we think the theoretical issues involving expansion are more tractable given the current state of knowledge.

We argue that expanding the niche leads to higher mortality in the period following expansion for at least two general reasons. First, it takes time to establish engagement at a new position, and resources get diverted from ongoing activities during the transition. Second, expansion often entails architectural reorganization as well, which retards the gaining of appeal at newly engaged positions. Both stories imply that niche expansion generally raises an organization's hazard of mortality. We develop these basic arguments and then elaborate them by considering characteristics of both the organization's structure and its niche. Again, we present most aspects of the model for the general nonmetric niche theory. Some key results concern the distances of expansions, whose analysis requires defining the audience space as metric so that distance is well defined.

13.1 EXPANDED ENGAGEMENT

An organization expands its fundamental niche when it adds one or more social positions to its niche and does not drop any. Clearly efforts to broaden an organization's fundamental niche entail costs. The direct costs involve the resources that must be devoted to building engagement at new positions and developing intrinsic appeal to the typical audience members at those positions. These activities require learning about the audience at that position, devising methods for bringing the offering to their attention, and fashioning the means to deliver it. Sometimes it also requires developing authenticity to the local audience at the position.

According to our niche theory, an organization does not fully control its fundamental niche. The distribution of actual appeal over social positions depends both upon the distribution of the intrinsic appeal of the offering over positions (which a producer does not control directly) and on the organization's distribution of engagement. In this framework, an organization cannot expand its niche directly. But it can expand its engagement. Accordingly we cast the argument as involving expansions of engagement. We define a set, $\epsilon^{+}(l, x, t)$, that contains the positions at which organization x has newly engaged just after time t. Recall that $en(l, x, z, t)$ tells x's level of engagement at position z at time t, and $ap(l, x, y, t)$ gives the level of x's actual appeal to the audience member y at position z at time t with respect to class/category l.

Definition 13.1 (Expanded engagement). *$\epsilon^{+}(l, x, t)$ equals, by definition, the set of positions that the organization x adds to its portfolio of engagement in the class/category l just after time point t.*

$$\epsilon^{+}(l, x, t) \equiv \{z \mid (\epsilon(l, x, z, t) = 0) \wedge (\epsilon(l, x, z, t + dt) > 0)\},$$

where dt is an infinitesimal positive number.

We consider expansions position by position. That is, we analyze situations in which the set of newly engaged positions is a singleton. The first set of results shows the consequences of any expansion. The second set of results compares pairs of expansions that differ in theoretically interesting ways. Both sets of results can be applied to more general expansions—involving more than a single position—by working out the implications position by position.

A key assumption in our model of expansion concerns the *latency* (or delay) in gaining positive results from a new engagement. An organization normally does not immediately experience returns at newly engaged positions. For example, in an attempt to consolidate and dominate the fragmented U.S. national ice-cream market, Dreyer's Grand Ice Cream Co. embarked upon a strategic expansion plan in 1994. The plan included significant additional engagement of consumers in the market, based on product innovation, expanded product lines, increased spending to build brand equity, and the construction of a national direct-store-delivery distribution network. The costs of this expansion were significant and despite company achievement toward the strategic goals, in 1998 Dreyer's faced a financial crisis and did not recover until 2000 (Chang, Chatman, and Carroll 2001). Although this six-year delay might be unusually long, we believe that it illustrates a common condition.

We argue that this kind of delay is generally the case, that it takes time for engagement to generate local intrinsic appeal at a position. During this period, appeal can be said to be latent in the sense that the organization has begun to engage the position and the offering has local intrinsic appeal.

Postulate 13.1. *Normally there is delay before engagement and intrinsic appeal produce nonzero expected actual appeal at a newly engaged position.*

$$\mathfrak{N}\, l, t, x, z\, [(z \in \epsilon^{+}(l, x, t)) \wedge (\tau(l, z, t) > 0) \rightarrow \exists\, w\, \forall\, s, y\, [(w > s > 0) \rightarrow \mathrm{E}(Ap^{z}(l, x, t + s)) = 0\,]],$$

where $Ap^{z}(l, x, t) = \sum_{y \mid pos(y) = z} ap(l, x, y, t)$.

Of course, many delay periods satisfy this condition, e.g., if the foregoing formula is true for some w, then it is also true for w' that satisfy $0 < w' \leq w$. This means that we must consider a set of segments on the real line. The most relevant segment is the supremum of the set of w for which the foregoing postulate is true: [1] We refer to the supremum of the set of waiting times that fit this condition as the latency.

Definition 13.2 (Latency). *The latency for gaining nonzero expected local appeal at a newly engaged position is the shortest time span after new engagement after which expected actual appeal is positive.*

$$w(l,x,z,t) \equiv \sup\{w \mid (z \in \boldsymbol{\epsilon}^{+}(l,x,t)) \wedge (\tau(l,x,z,t) > 0) \\ \wedge \forall\, s\,[(w > s > 0) \rightarrow \mathrm{E}(Ap^{z}(l,x,t+s)) = 0]\}.$$

We again use the modeling strategy of using a "closest-possible-worlds" construction, which we sketched in Chapter 6 and used in Chapters 5 and 9 in dealing with multiple memberships and niche convexity, respectively. We construct a scenario that defines an identical pair of typical members of a prominent population of organizations. We posit that the pair is identical in the sense that they have the same values of age, scale, pre-enlargement profile of engagement over positions, and profile of local intrinsic appeal over positions. One expands its engagement at the time point and the other does not change its engagement over an ensuing interval equal to the expected duration of latency. We add the restriction that the distributions of local appeal of the two organizations remain constant over the interval being considered.

Notation. It will simplify formulas to use the following notational shorthand to represent this situation. We introduce a shorthand, $\mathcal{Q}_4$, for the formula that states that one of a pair of otherwise-identical organizations in a prominent population expands its niche and the other does not.

$\mathcal{Q}_4$ is the case if and only if

1. the two comembers of a prominent population have the same age and scale:
$$\mathrm{CM}(l,x,x',t,t') \wedge (a(x,t) = a(x',t')) \wedge (s(l,x,t) = s(l,x',t'));$$

2. the two organizations have the same pre-expansion profile of engagement over positions:
$$\boldsymbol{\epsilon}(l,x,t) = \boldsymbol{\epsilon}(l,x',t');$$

3. the two organizations have the same time-invariant profile of local intrinsic appeals: $\boldsymbol{\tau}(l,x,t) = \boldsymbol{\tau}(l,x',t')$;
$$(\boldsymbol{\epsilon}^{+}(l,x,t) = \{z\}) \wedge (|\{z_1\}| = 1) \wedge \forall s\,[(w(l,x,z,t) > s \geq 0) \\ \rightarrow (\boldsymbol{\epsilon}^{+}(l,x',t'+s) = \emptyset)].$$

---

[1] Because we are considering points on the real line, we must focus on the supremum of the set, the least upper bound.

What are the implications of a delay in generating positive returns for an expanding organization's viability in its pre-expansion niche? While resources are being used to build engagement at new positions, some engagement gets diverted from positions in the pre-expansion niche. As long as appeal stays at zero at the newly engaged positions, there are no returns at the new position to compensate for the losses in the pre-expansion niche due to a reduction in engagement. That there is a reduction follows from the principle of allocation, P8.1, which holds that the expected total engagement equals a constant for all typical members of a prominent population. (Because we have assumed that the organizations being compared have the same scale, this principle does not get overridden by D10.1 which states that expected total engagement increases with scale in markets characterized by scale economies).

Lemma 13.1. *Expanded engagement over positions presumably yields a period of reduced engagement in the pre-expansion fundamental niche (in a class or category).*

$$\mathfrak{P}\, l, t, t', x, x', z, z' \,[\, \mathcal{Q}_4 \wedge (w(l, x, z, t) > s > 0) \\ \rightarrow (\mathrm{E}(\textstyle\sum_{\mathrm{supp}\, \mathbf{f}(l,x,t)} en(l, x, z, t+s)) < \mathrm{E}(\textstyle\sum_{\mathrm{supp}\, \mathbf{f}(l,x',t')} en(l, x', z, t'+s)))].$$

Proof. Organization x's added engagement at some new position requires diversion of engagement from some other position(s) in the pre-expansion realized niche, according to the principle of allocation (P8.1). The result follows from the restrictions stated in $\mathcal{Q}_4$. □

Given the assumed relationship between intrinsic local appeal, engagement, and actual appeal (P8.2 and P8.3), a parallel result holds for actual appeal in the original niche as long as the distribution of intrinsic appeal remains constant over the interval being considered, as is imposed by $\mathcal{Q}_4$.

Lemma 13.2. *Expanded engagement presumably initiates a period of reduced total expected actual appeal.*

$$\mathfrak{P}\, l, t, t', x, x', z, z' \,[\, \mathcal{Q}_4 \wedge (w(l, x, z, t) > s > 0) \\ \rightarrow (\mathrm{E}(Ap(l, x, t+s)) < \mathrm{E}(Ap(l, x', t'+s)))].$$

Proof. The rule chain behind L13.1 tells that expansion comes at the expense of engagement in the pre-expansion niche; and P8.2 and P.8.3 tell that an organization's appeal at a position increases monotonically with its engagement at the position. Consequently, the expanding organization's expected total appeal within the pre-expansion niche falls below that of the nonexpanding organization. P13.1 states that the expected appeal garnered at newly engaged positions is zero until the duration of engagement reaches $w(l, x, z, t)$. No gain at the new position can offset the loss at an initially engaged position over the interval being considered. □

Because an organization does not receive any benefit in the expanded part of the niche during the latency period, we have a stronger implication for fitness—stronger in the sense of holding more broadly. It pertains to the entire niche, not just to the newly added portion. These results imply that expansion heightens an organization's vulnerability to competition in its original niche. Moreover, if the length of the latency period exceeds the delay in converting returns into scale, then there is also a negative feedback process: a drop in scale lowers appeal, which lowers return still further.

Theorem 13.1. *Expanded engagement presumably initiates a period of increased hazard of mortality.*

$$\mathfrak{P}\, l, t, t', w, x, x' \,[\, \mathcal{Q}_4 \rightarrow (\Omega(x, t, t + w) > \Omega(x', t', t' + w))].$$

Proof. By (the rule chain behind) L13.2, the total appeal of the niche-expanding organization in its pre-expansion niche falls below that of the nonexpander; P13.1 and D13.2 imply that the expander has zero expected appeal in the newly occupied space until its tenure there equals $w(l, x, z, t)$. According to D9.1, an organization's fitness at a position is zero if its appeal at that position is zero. This means that fitness is zero in the newly occupied space before tenure equals $w(l, x, z, t)$ (by the chaining metarule). Other things equal, a fall in appeal at some positions in the pre-expansion niche lowers fitness at those positions (D9.1). No rule chains imply that fitness increases at any position in the pre-expansion niche. M9.1 states that $\Phi \downarrow \omega$ for any pair of time points. Integration over the relevant time points in the comparison completes the chain. □

We next analyze the effects of organizational architecture, culture, and the distance of the expansion for the implications of niche expansion. In these analyses we compare two organizations (with possibly different architectures and cultures) that expand their niches (possibly by greater or smaller distances). It is helpful to develop the implications of the foregoing argument for the situation in which two otherwise-identical organizations expand their niches at the same time point (a closest-possible-worlds analysis).

Notation. Again it simplifies formulas to introduce a shorthand. Now we introduce a symbol that tells that two otherwise-identical organizations expand their niches to different positions (with possibly different latencies).

Let $\mathcal{W} = \max(w(l, x, z_1, t), w(l, x', z_2, t))$.

$\mathcal{Q}_5$ is the case if and only if

1. two same-aged, same-scale comembers of a prominent population have the same time-invariant profile of local intrinsic appeal:

$$\textsc{cm}(l, x, x', t, t') \wedge (a(x, t) = a(x', t')) \wedge (s(l, x, t) = s(l, x', t')) \wedge (\boldsymbol{\tau}(l, x, t) = \boldsymbol{\tau}(l, x', t')) \wedge (t = t');$$

2. both expand their niches to single positions as the same time point:

$$(\boldsymbol{\epsilon}^+(l, x, t) = \{z_1\}) \wedge (|\{z_1\}| = 1) \wedge (\boldsymbol{\epsilon}^+(l, x', t') = \{z_2\}) \wedge (|\{z_2\}| = 1);$$

3. they do not expand their niches during the periods $(t, t + \mathcal{W})$ and $(t', t' + \mathcal{W})$:

$$\forall s'[(\mathcal{W} > s' > 0) \rightarrow (\boldsymbol{\epsilon}^+(l, x, t + s') = \emptyset) \wedge (\boldsymbol{\epsilon}^+(l, x', t' + s') = \emptyset)];$$

4. they have the same profile of engagement in their pre-expansion niches over all time points in the pre-expansion and post-expansion periods:

$$\forall s\,[(\mathcal{W} > s \geq 0) \rightarrow (\epsilon(l, x, t+s) = \epsilon(l, x', t'+s))].$$

Lemma 13.3. *If two otherwise identical organizations expand their niches, then the excess hazard of mortality due to expansion presumably is greater for the organization with the greater latency.*

$$\mathfrak{P}\, \mathbf{q}, \mathbf{q}'\, [\, \mathcal{Q}_5 \rightarrow (w \uparrow \Omega)(\mathbf{q}, \mathbf{q}')\,],$$

where $\mathbf{q} = \langle l, t, x, z \rangle$ *and* $\mathbf{q}' = \langle l, t', x', z' \rangle$.

Proof. The proof follows the same lines as the proof of T13.1. The only difference is that the premises imply that the hazard of mortality is the same for the two organizations so long as neither has yet gained appeal at the newly added position. From the time point at which one of the pair has gained actual appeal at the new position, the rule chain that stands behind the theorem is the same as for T13.1. □

We use the causal chain supporting this theorem as the basis for the extensions of the argument. We tie the other relevant conditions to the expected length of the latency period.

13.2 ARCHITECTURAL AND CULTURAL CONTEXT

At this point we take advantage of an opportunity to integrate niche theory and the theory of architectural change. Our point of departure is the recognition that efforts at expanding niches generally entail architectural reorganization. For example, when Gannett Newspapers launched its national newspaper *USA Today,* the organization added a new subunit to oversee the planning and operation of the activities directed to the new market. Indeed, organizations typically tinker with their architectures when expanding their activities. These observations suggest another avenue of plausible argumentation that links niche expansion and mortality. Expansion often entails architectural reorganization and, by the theorems of Chapters 11 and 12, this should elevate the mortality hazard. So the first step in this part of the formalization links expanded engagement and architectural change.

Postulate 13.2. *Expanded engagement generally normally entails architectural reorganization.*

$$\mathfrak{N}\, l, t, t', x\, [(\epsilon^{+}(l, x, t) \neq \emptyset) \rightarrow (Ch(x, t) = 1)].$$

($Ch(x, t)$ is the random variable that equals 1 if a unit in organization x initiates an architectural change at time t and equals 0 otherwise, as defined in Chapter 11.)

Chapters 11 and 12 argue that organizations experience cascades of changes from initiating architectural changes and that the durations of cascades shape the mortality consequences of change. We invoke a parallel argument here. As long as an organization's units are working out the sequence of induced architectural changes that stem from the actions taken by one or more units to expand engagement, the organization will be hampered in its ability to learn about the audience at the new position and to tailor the offering to fit that audience. A delay in gaining the benefits of engagement is a kind of missed opportunity. If one organization experiences a protracted cascade of architectural changes and another does not, then the organization with the shorter cascade generally realizes the gains from expanded engagement before the organization with a longer cascade does. We can formalize this intuition using the concept of latency.

Postulate 13.3. *The expected latency (delay in gaining positive appeal) at a position normally increases monotonically with the duration of a random cascade of architectural reorganization in the organization,* $D(x, t)$.

$$\mathfrak{N}\, \mathbf{q}, \mathbf{q}' \, [\, \mathcal{Q}_5 \rightarrow (D \uparrow \mathrm{E}(w))(\mathbf{q}, \mathbf{q}')\,],$$

where $\mathbf{q}$ *and* $\mathbf{q}'$ *are as above.*

Much empirical research on organizational change, including studies of niche change, shows that the consequences of change often depend on an organization's structure. For instance, Dobrev, Kim, and Carroll (2003) find that the effects of niche change vary by organizational size: large firms are more likely to experience mortality when undertaking niche change (see also Carroll and Teo 1996; Dobrev, Kim, and Hannan 2001). These findings suggest that certain organizational contexts make expanded engagement more precarious; here we build on three such contexts developed above: intricacy, opacity, and asperity.

An intricate organization faces greater coordination problems when expanding its niche than does a simpler one. It takes longer to develop a plan for expansion, to get agreement on how to execute the plan, to transfer the necessary information and resources, to get accurate feedback about activities, and to make adjustments as a cascade unfolds.

Similarly, opacity should also delay positive returns from expanded engagement, because opacity creates uncertainty about the effects both of anticipated actions and of the unanticipated actions that get induced by the anticipated ones. In other words, expansion in an opaque organization likely turns out to be more complicated and time-consuming than can be anticipated.

Finally, high asperity implies that expanded engagement more likely causes contention within the organization. Contention about change surely lengthens reorganization and makes it less likely that proposed changes become fully embraced and implemented well.

These considerations imply that returns to expansion take longer in more intricate, more opaque, and more aspere organizations, thereby heightening the mortality hazards that accrue to niche expansion.

Theorem 13.2. *Intricacy, I, opacity, O, and cultural asperity, A, presumably exacerbate the effect of niche expansion on the hazard of mortality.*

A. $\mathfrak{P}\, \mathbf{q}, \mathbf{q}' \, [\, \mathcal{Q}_5 \wedge (O(x) \geq O(x')) \wedge (A(x) \geq A(x')) \rightarrow (I \uparrow \Omega)(\mathbf{q}, \mathbf{q}')\,];$

B. $\mathfrak{P}\, \mathbf{q}, \mathbf{q}' \, [\, \mathcal{Q}_5 \wedge (I(x) \geq I(x')) \wedge (A(x) \geq A(x')) \rightarrow (O \uparrow \Omega)(\mathbf{q}, \mathbf{q}')\,];$

C. $\mathfrak{P}\, \mathbf{q}, \mathbf{q}' \, [\, \mathcal{Q}_5 \wedge (I(x) \geq I(x')) \wedge (O(x) \geq O(x')) \rightarrow (A \uparrow \Omega)(\mathbf{q}, \mathbf{q}')\,],$

where $\mathbf{q}$ *and* $\mathbf{q}'$ *are as above.*

Proof. According to the rule chains securing T12.1,

$$\mathrm{E}(D(x,t)) = \beta_1 I(x) + \beta_3 O(x) + A(x)(\beta_2 I(x) + \beta_4 O(x))$$

in a random cascade. The result follows from application of the chain rule to T13.1 and P13.3 and the chaining metarule. □

13.3 AGE AND ASPERITY

We next explore the possibility of tying the argument to a feature that is generally observable in large-scale empirical studies, organizational age. According to a famous argument by Selznick (1957), as organizations age, their structures get reified and their feature values become endowed with symbolic moral value. In many manifestations of this, the structure gets reproduced regularly without justification or rationalization other than the statements such as "that's the way we do things here" or (for example, at Hewlett-Packard "that is the 'H-P way'." Accordingly, attempts to try new or different ways of doing things are dismissed without analysis of the potential costs and benefits.

Such institutionalization constrains architectural possibilities. From the point of view of the theory developed above, cultural asperity increases with aging. The automatic advocacy of tradition and the dismissal of alternative proposals clearly indicate a heightened cultural asperity. Thus we introduce the Selznick argument formally as pertaining to age and asperity.[2]

Postulate 13.4. *Cultural asperity normally grows with age.*

$$\mathfrak{N}\,\mathbf{q}, \mathbf{q}'\,[(a \uparrow A)(\mathbf{q}, \mathbf{q}')\,],$$

where $\mathbf{q} = \langle l, t, x\rangle$ *and* $\mathbf{q}' = \langle l, t', x'\rangle$.

This leads immediately to an implication that can be tested straightforwardly with available data.

Theorem 13.3. *The effect of niche expansion on the hazard of mortality increases with age (so long as differences in intricacy and opacity do not run in the opposite direction).*

$$\mathfrak{P}\,\mathbf{q}, \mathbf{q}'\,[\,\mathcal{Q}_5 \wedge (I(x) \geq I(x')) \wedge (O(x) \geq O(x')) \rightarrow (a \uparrow \Omega)(\mathbf{q}, \mathbf{q}')\,],$$

where $\mathbf{q}$ *and* $\mathbf{q}'$ *are as above.*

Proof. The minimal rule chain results from a cut rule applied to P13.4 and (the rule chain behind) T13.2C. □

---

[2]The following postulate differs syntactically from what we have presented in parallel cases, because we did not define A as a random variable. In the previous pair of chapters, we wanted to derive the implications of cascades given fixed organizational characteristics such as intricacy, opacity, and asperity. To simplify the analyses, we treated these properties as deterministic so that we did not have to try to characterize the full joint distributions of organizational properties and characteristics of cascades. Given the way in which we defined these properties, it would be meaningless to refer to expected values. Therefore, the postulate refers to the level of asperity in the consequent.

13.4 DISTANT EXPANSION IN A METRIC SPACE

In Chapter 8 we noted that building engagement at a market position demands learning about the audience at the position, developing means of marketing and distributing the offering at that position, and, possibly, gaining authenticity to the audience at that position. The speed with which engagement translates into appeal likely differs for close and distant positions. Obviously, analyzing such scenarios requires the assumption that the audience positions are distributed over a metric space.

We develop two stories about distance. One concerns the distance of the new position from the region of the peak appeal of the organization's offer and from the peak appeal of the category; the other concerns distance from the support of the organization's (fundamental) niche. The two notions can differ, and they presumably do so, especially for organizations with broad niches.

The definition of the set of positions of peak appeal allows for cavities (that is, concave sets of positions of peak appeal). A concave set of peak-appeal positions can be interpreted as meaning that the market has multiple regions of peak appeal. The argument that we develop is much more straightforward for the single-peak-region case. We specialize the argument to this case with the following auxiliary assumption, which uses the predicate for convexity of a niche, D9.6.

Auxiliary assumption 13.1. *A category's/organization's set of positions of peak appeal (in a metric space) normally is convex.*

$$\text{A.}\quad \mathfrak{A}\, l, t, x\, [(\mathbf{p} \subset \mathbb{N}) \rightarrow \text{CVX}(\mathbf{pk}_l(t))];$$

$$\text{B.}\quad \mathfrak{A}\, l, t, x\, [(\mathbf{p} \subset \mathbb{N}) \rightarrow \text{CVX}(\mathbf{pk}(l, x, t))].$$

At positions close to an organization's region of peak local intrinsic appeal, its offer generally has higher intrinsic appeal than at more distant positions. This means that less work is needed to tailor the offering and its mode of presentation to make it attractive. With less work to be done, presumably less time is needed to accomplish it. Tactics with which the organization has experience have a reasonable probability of succeeding for similar audiences; and authenticity ought to transfer more readily. But this reasoning does not carry over to the case in which the newly added position lies far from the point of peak appeal.

Consider the case in which each organization adds a newly engaged position, but the intrinsic appeals of the organizations' offerings differ at the newly added positions. We posit that it takes longer to gain actual appeal at positions at which an offering has lower intrinsic appeal.

Postulate 13.5. *The expected latency for generating actual appeal at a newly engaged position normally decreases with the level of intrinsic appeal to the typical taste at that position.*

$$\mathfrak{N}\, \mathbf{q}, \mathbf{q}'\, [\, \mathcal{Q}_5 \rightarrow (\tau \downarrow \text{E}(w))(\mathbf{q}, \mathbf{q}')\,],$$

where $\mathbf{q}$ *and* $\mathbf{q}'$ *are as above.*

Recall that our simple model of preferences, when specialized to the case of a metric space, holds that the intrinsic local appeal of an organization's offering declines monotonically with distance from its region of peak appeal (A8.3). This means that the waiting time for expected actual appeal at a newly added position grows with the distance of the position from the organization's region of peak appeal. In expressing this postulate, we use the following notation to express the distance of a position from the region of peak appeal:

$$d\_pk(l, x, z, t) = \min_{z' \in \mathbf{pk}(l,x,t)} d(z, z'), \qquad \text{where } d(z, z') = |z - z'|.$$

Lemma 13.4. *Latency at a position presumably increases with the distance of a position from the (closest point in the) organization's region of peak appeal of the producer's offering.*

$$\mathfrak{P}\, \mathbf{q}, \mathbf{q}' \, [\, \mathcal{Q}_5 \wedge (\mathbf{p} \subset \mathbb{N}) \rightarrow (d\_pk \uparrow \mathrm{E}(w))(\mathbf{q}, \mathbf{q}') \,],$$

where $\mathbf{q}$ *and* $\mathbf{q}'$ *are as above.*

Proof. According to the rule chain behind L8.3, the expected intrinsic appeal to a local taste at a position declines monotonically with distance of the position from a point of peak appeal. Therefore, expansion to positions further from a peak means moving to positions of lower expected local appeal. P13.4 says that the expected latencies are longer for positions at which intrinsic appeal is lower. (The chaining metarule is used to connect these premises.) □

Now a parallel chain of reasoning yields an implication about the increase in the mortality hazard due to expansion. We skip the intermediate steps and present the final theorem.

Theorem 13.4. *The rise in the hazard of mortality due to expansion presumably is greater when the expansion lies further from an organization's region of peak appeal.*

Let $d\_pk_l(z, t) = \min_{z' \in \mathbf{pk}_l(t)} d(z, z')$.

$$\mathfrak{P}\, \mathbf{q}, \mathbf{q}' \, [\, \mathcal{Q}_5 \wedge (\mathbf{p} \subset \mathbb{N}) \rightarrow (d\_pk_l \uparrow \Omega)(\mathbf{q}, \mathbf{q}') \,],$$

where $\mathbf{q}$ *and* $\mathbf{q}'$ *are as above.*

Proof. The minimal rule chain uses T8.3 (an organization's expected intrinsic appeal at a position decreases with the distance of the position from its offer's region of peak appeal), P8.3a (the expected actual appeal increases with local intrinsic appeal, when the conditions stipulated in $\mathcal{Q}_5$ are met), and D9.1 (fitness at a position increases with actual appeal at that position). The remainder of the rule chain is as given in the proof of T13.1. □

Under the assumptions made in Chapter 8 about the relationship of regions of peak appeal for categories and their members, a parallel line of argument holds for the distance of an expansion from a category's positions of peak appeal.

Theorem 13.5. *The rise in the hazard of mortality due to expansion for a typical category member presumably is greater when the expansion lies further from a category's region of peak appeal.*

$$\mathfrak{P}\, \mathbf{q}, \mathbf{q}' \, [\, \mathcal{Q}_5 \wedge (\mathbf{p} \subset \mathbb{N}) \rightarrow (d\_pk \uparrow \Omega)(\mathbf{q}, \mathbf{q}') \,],$$

where $\mathbf{q}$ *and* $\mathbf{q}'$ *are as above.*

Proof. The proof is similar to that of T13.4 except that it also invokes P8.1 (regions of peak appeal of prominent categories and of their members normally coincide). □

A similar line of argument applies to the distance of a newly engaged position from the (support of an) organization's niche. The greater this distance, the less applicable is previous learning to the local audience. Because more has to be learned, it likely takes longer for an organization to develop actual appeal at a position far from the support of its niche. Let $d\_\mathbf{f}(l, x, z, t) = \min_{z' \in \text{supp}\, \mathbf{f}(l,x)} d(z, z')$.

Postulate 13.6. *Latency at a position normally increases with the distance of a position from the support of the organization's niche.*

$$\mathfrak{N}\, \mathbf{q}, \mathbf{q}' \, [\, \mathcal{Q}_5 \wedge (\mathbf{p} \subset \mathbb{N}) \rightarrow (d\_\mathbf{f} \uparrow \mathrm{E}(w))(\mathbf{q}, \mathbf{q}')\,],$$

where $\mathbf{q}$ *and* $\mathbf{q}'$ *are as above.*

Theorem 13.6. *The rise in the hazard of mortality due to expansion is greater when the expansion lies further from the support of an organization's fundamental niche.*

$$\mathfrak{P}\, \mathbf{q}, \mathbf{q}' \, [\, \mathcal{Q}_5 \wedge (\mathbf{p} \subset \mathbb{N}) \rightarrow (d\_\mathbf{f} \uparrow \Omega)(\mathbf{q}, \mathbf{q}')\,],$$

where $\mathbf{q}$ *and* $\mathbf{q}'$ *are as above.*

Proof. The minimal rule chain links P13.5 (the expected latency at a position increases with the distance of the position from the fundamental niche) and the rule chain that warrants L13.3 (the hazard of mortality due to niche expansion increases with the latency at the newly engaged position), the chaining metarule, and the aggregation stated in the proof of T13.1 □

13.5 EXPANSION AND CONVEXITY

As we noted above, niche expansion commonly requires architectural adjustments as well as learning about new portions of the audience. Many organizations seek to produce and market offerings in new markets or market segments by building new subunits devoted to those markets. We think that architectural modifications for distant expansions are likely to be extensive. The activities required in a distant new market typically differ qualitatively from those of existing markets. This makes it harder to coordinate them efficiently with the same routines and in the same subunit. This observation suggests that distant expansions are especially likely to exacerbate opacity and intricacy, with the implication that hazards rise further.

We have treated organizational properties such as intricacy, opacity, and asperity as time independent. We have not introduced any theoretical considerations concerning the nature and direction of their changes over time. Now we can add some considerations that, in our view, might be parts of a future theory concerning these changes.

It is obvious that organizational actions generally influence all three of the abovementioned features and that niche expansions, in particular, have implications for intricacy, opacity, and asperity. To spell out some of these implications, we consider four types of niche expansions, depicted in figure 13.1. The figure again uses the conventions set forth in figures 8.1 and 9.1. Each "histogram" shows the distribution of the audience over a set of seven social positions. The height of a bar in the histograms gives the level of relevant resources controlled by the audience members at the position. For each type I–IV, the leftmost graph of the row shows the grades of membership in engagement (ϵ, the engagement niche) and the center graph shows the organization's fit to local taste (τ, the intrinsic appeal niche). The value of a GoM is indicated by the intensity of the shading. The rightmost graph of each row shows a fundamental niche that is consistent with the distributions of engagement and intrinsic appeal (ζ).

Starting with the top row and proceeding downward, the figure shows:

Type I: Continuous expansion. A niche expansion is continuous if the number of cavities in the niche is the same before and after the expansion. An expansion is continuous only if it adds social positions to the niche on the edge of the ex-ante niche. This boils down, in practice, to new engagement at positions next to already engaged positions.

Type II: Distant expansion. A niche expansion is distant if the positions added to the earlier niche are separated from the earlier niche by a cavity. Another way to characterize the result of a distant expansion is to say that the number of cavities in the new niche is the number of cavities in the old niche plus one and that the new cavity lies outside of the ex-ante niche.

Type III: Gap-creating continuous expansion. Another type of expansion is continuous in that positions are added on the edge of the previously existent niche. However, the principle of allocation predicts that the total appeal and engagement are fixed, so adding positions to the ex-ante niche lowers the engagement or the appeal at some positions that belonged to the earlier niche. The lowered engagement (or appeal) might turn out to be zero, in which case a gap emerges in the previously existent niche. In more formal terms, a type III expansion is such that the number of cavities in the new niche exceeds the number of cavities in the previously existent niche, and all of the extra cavities lie within the previous niche.

Type IV: Gap-creating distant expansion. This type of expansion is distant because positions are added further away from the previously ex-ante niche. The lowered engagement (or appeal) creates a gap in the previously existent niche. In more formal terms, a type-IV expansion is such that the number of cavities in the new niche exceeds by at least two the number of cavities in the previous niche and some, but not all, of the extra cavities lie outside the previous niche.

We assume that a type-I niche expansion that is not too radical might even be an exception to P13.2, in the sense that this type of niche expansion does not usually imply architectural changes. Such cases would violate the general claim of P13.2.

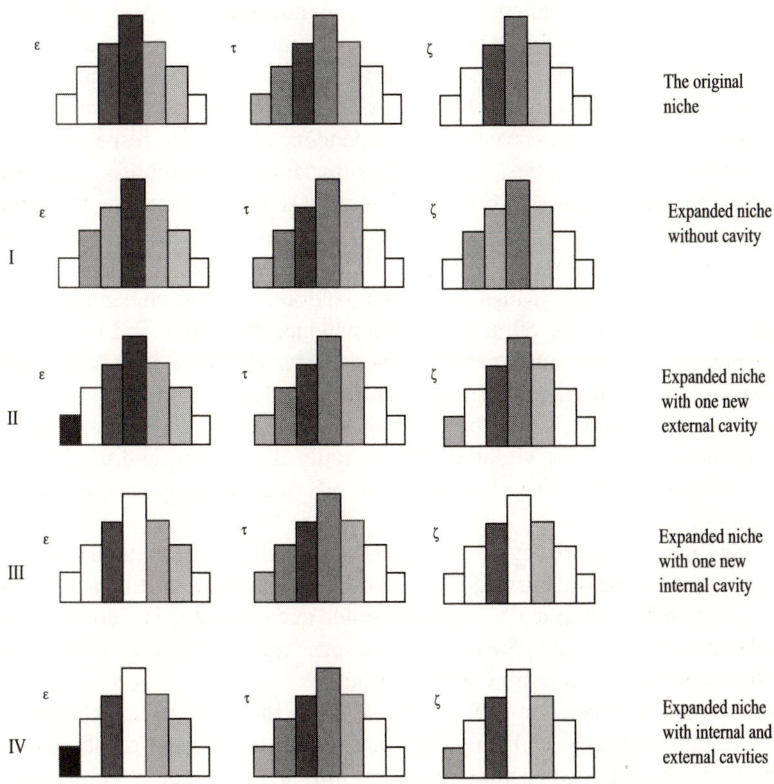

Figure 13.1 Four different types of niche expansion

On the other hand, type-II through type-IV expansions do not provide exceptions to P13.2. These types of expansions trigger architectural change; and the resulting reorganizations are not even completed when the latency at the newly engaged positions ends. Instead, they linger for a while. In what follows we spell out what changes of intricacy, opacity, and asperity might be brought about by the different types of niche expansions.

If the expansion is of type II, then it is likely that new organizational units have to be created to bring together the expertise required to secure engagement and appeal at the newly added positions. Adding new units might increase the opacity of the organization. One might believe that they also contribute to an elevated level of intricacy, though in general this is not at all clear. Under some circumstances, adding units does not increase the intricacy. For instance, consider the acquisitions that led to the growth of Johnson & Johnson, the diversified medical products company. The newly added units preserved their independence in several respects, including profit-and-loss responsibilities. The result is that Johnson & Johnson has a simple organizational structure for an organization of its size. It is tempting to argue that the way the niche expansion is implemented determines whether the adding of new units increases or does not increase the intricacy of the structure.

If, as a result of niche expansion, an organization abandons engagement at some positions, then the change often makes knowledge, personnel, and organizational units redundant. Such changes generate uncertainty. The more culturally imprinted the organization is with the engagement at the abandoned positions, the more cultural opposition is triggered by these changes. The cultural opposition highlights the cultural codes that are violated or potentially threatened, and the heightened salience of these norms bring about higher levels of asperity against any organizational change.

Breaking up existing structures, eliminating organizational units that connected the engagement of the organization, makes the subordination relation among the remaining units more complicated, even unsettled occasionally. The consequence of a type-III expansion of the niche is increased intricacy even if the new engagement, in itself, did not require a more complex structure.

Finally, type-IV expansion of the niche leads to the most radical change of the organizational features. With this type of change, we get the combined effects of type-II and type-III expansions: asperity, intricacy, and opacity all increase as a consequence of a type-IV expansion. Asperity rises because the redundancies that follow the elimination of engagement at certain social positions, intricacy gets elevated because the breaking up of connecting units, and opacity grows due to the relative isolation of the new units that provide the engagement at new and distant positions.

Now we can compare the impact of the different types of niche expansions on the mortality hazards of otherwise similar organizations. The mortality hazard increases least if the expansion is of type I. In such a situation, architectural change is normally not required, so the moderate rise in the mortality hazard in this case is due only to the latency period. A type-II expansion yields increased opacity, which makes the ongoing architectural changes hard to predict. We argued in Chapter 11 that the unforeseen delays contribute to the rise in mortality during structural reorganization. Type-III expansions are still worse. Now architectural changes take place in the context of increased asperity and intricacy. Type-IV expansion leads to a rather dramatic boost in the mortality hazard; it has the combined effect of types-I, -II, and -III niche expansions.

A type-IV expansion might seem the most risky strategic move that an organization might consider, and this is almost true. As it happens, one cannot be so deep as to be unable to dig a hole. If a type-IV niche expansion also goes beyond a category niche, then the mortality hazard shoots even higher.

One option not considered so far when an initially concave niche undergoes an expansion that fills the cavity. In this case, the expansion does the least damage. There is no reason why asperity, intricacy, or opacity should grow, and the more desirable convex niche can soon compensate for the effects of the latency. It is not surprising that several niche expansions are motivated by arguments that are intended to demonstrate that the niche expansion actually eliminates a cavity in the niche. It is important to note, though, that this does not make the argument sound. The complementarity argument only shows that this type of niche expansion can be almost as good as neutral, at least in the longer run.

DISCUSSION

This chapter considered an organization's expansion of its niche as a kind of organizational change. We modeled the effect of enlargement of the niche on the hazard of mortality in the period following expansion. According to our theory, expansion magnifies this hazard for two reasons. First, it takes time to establish engagement at a new position and to reap gains from the expansion. In the meantime, resources get diverted from ongoing activities during the transition. Second, expansion often requires architectural reorganization; and reorganization slows the development of actual appeal at newly engaged positions. Both arguments imply that an organization's hazard of mortality rises with niche expansion. Moreover, the latency of returns at a newly engaged position depends on the speed with which an organization can revise its architecture to exploit new opportunities. Because this speed depends upon properties of the organization's architecture (intricacy and opacity) and culture (asperity) and asperity grows with age, the risk of niche expansion depends on these properties as well. The resulting theory shows how the theoretical foundations developed here can be used to integrate various theoretical fragments that might previously have borne no obvious relationships.

Chapter Fourteen

Conclusions

In Dr. Seuss's classic children's book *Green Eggs and Ham*, a pesky character named Sam persistently implores his companion, a circumspect character with a rumpled top hat, to eat an offering of green eggs and ham. In a battery of insistent propositions, Sam tries many arguments, asking his companion variously would he be willing to eat them "here or there, with a mouse or in a house, with a fox or in a box, in the dark, in a tree, in a car, in the rain or in a train, on a boat or with a goat." To each impassioned plea, the companion responds "No" in unequivocal terms and with a mocking tone, even regularly referring to the offerer as "Sam-I-Am." Finally, realizing that Sam's boundless energy means that he might never stop, the companion offers to sample the food should Sam be willing to cease his overtures. Sam agrees. His companion tastes the green eggs and ham and quickly decides that he actually likes them. In a burst of ebullience, he declares that he will eat them under any of the conditions that Sam previously offered by reciting each of them individually.

We realize that some readers might very well liken us to Sam, as annoying characters who persistently and insistently offer formal (especially dynamic) logic and nonstandard set theory in a variety of ways to those who do not think they will like them or benefit from using them in their theoretical work. While we cannot claim to match Sam's evangelical spirit, we can only hope that we should be so lucky in the result. Would you, could you, should you try to make the logic in your arguments explicit? If even some of those to whom we address our entreaties partake of the offerings and find the experience to their liking, then we will be gratified; obviously, we also think that sociological theory will likely be enhanced.

Of course, the decisions we speak of should not (and likely will not) be chosen by scientists simply on the basis of taste. Instead, the choice should be based on the power of the methodological tools on offer as compared to the standard tools used in sociological analysis. Accordingly, after making general arguments about the appeal of formalization using modern logics in the Preface and Chapter 1, we set out in the body of the book to demonstrate these claims by formalizing several vibrant strands of theory in organization theory by, among other things, incorporating considerations of partiality and vagueness and using nonmonotonic logic and fuzzy-set theory. The obvious question to ask in this last chapter is whether the effort has been worthwhile. Have the advances we achieved lived up to the general claims? Does the progress achieved merit the significant investment required in new technical concepts and skills? And, perhaps most important, would other theoretical domains in sociology (and other social sciences) also profit from employing the same tools?

To begin to answer these questions, we again take a bird's-eye view. We first review briefly the general claims that we made about theoretical unification. We then review some of the specific theoretical developments reported in the foregoing chapters that we believe benefited from the use of the new tools. We subsequently discuss the implications of these developments by highlighting some of the resulting changes in theoretical propositions and arguments. Finally, we consider the next steps, both in term of unresolved theoretical issues and newfound empirical issues.

14.1 THEORETICAL UNIFICATION

Most contemporary sociological theory constructs what Merton called theories of the middle range, what we call theory fragments. These sets of theoretical statements about certain specific sociological contexts display a moderate level of abstraction that might carry their application into other contexts, but they are not derived deductively from a highly abstract general theory. Middle-range theory has proven very useful and has made sociology highly productive. Among other things, it has helped spur the rapid growth of sociological knowledge because a middle-range focus allows new arguments and insights to diffuse through the scientific community without undue delay.

But we contend that the middle-range strategy of theory building allows knowledge to cumulate only so far. To progress beyond the initial ideas brought on by a burst of new middle-range theory, a substantive area eventually needs some disciplined integration. Otherwise, the coexisting (potentially inconsistent) theory fragments might be treated as equals, yielding different (or even contradictory) predictions for yet-unstudied cases. Before unification, the relation of any particular empirical finding to a set of fragments often cannot be determined.

Integration might lead to the wholesale tossing of some theory fragments and to the reformulation of others. All things considered, unification requires initially determining if and how the various relevant fragments fit together, and then figuring out how some fragments must be altered to make them consistent while still preserving their basic insights. Obviously, not all social science theory would currently benefit from attempts at unification; success in this endeavor presupposes a degree of confidence in the constituent fragments. Otherwise, unification might merge valid and invalid ideas in a difficult-to-separate way.

In this book, we dealt with efforts to build and integrate theories in the face of three kinds of complications: (1) the existence of partial knowledge about the relevant causal processes; (2) inherently stochastic processes; and (3) fuzzy boundaries characterizing the social units. The first and second complications concern mainly the theorist; presumably more information would clear these up. The third complication concerns the agents whose actions the theory characterizes. Accordingly, we represent the first complication as partiality of the kind that linguists and logicians call genericity (and we develop quantifiers that can deal with genericity). The second complication is well described by probability theory. We represent the third complication as a kind of partiality based on graded membership in the categories used by the agents to whom the theory applies.

Because standard formal languages do not aid theory construction that deals with the first and third complications, we developed what we believe to be a more appropriate language. To address the first complication, this language builds on an alternative dynamic (specifically nonmonotonic) logic that is designed to deal with systematic reasoning about arguments that contain generic rules with exceptions. In this language, "exception" does not mean stochastic variation; rather, exceptions involve deviations from general patterns in the underlying probability distributions. In this language, the degree of specificity controls which (if any) of several possibly applicable arguments applies. The principle of inference used is that the most specific applicable argument prevails and that no conclusion follows if equally specific or incomparably specific arguments lead to opposing conclusions. This logic eases the task of integrating partly conflicting fragments while still allowing the theorist to "calculate" (e.g., prove theorems).

A common way to deal with some of the issues we raise involves restricting the scope of explanatory principles and causal claims. Indeed, this is the only solution offered by classical logics, such as predicate (or first-order) logic. So, when research identifies exceptions to an argument, theorists generally delineate tighter scope conditions. But usually these conditions are tentative, as sociologists often make clear in their expositions of the arguments. The nonmonotonic logic that we propose in this book specifies this tentative state of theoretical knowledge in a clearer, more systematic, and more parsimonious way.

To address the third complication, we used a different foundational set theory. Standard set theory defines sets as the collections of objects in a universe of discourse that satisfy a given predicate. The main alternative, fuzzy-set theory, describes situations in which set membership can be partial, a matter of degree. It defines a grade of membership, a function that maps from elements of the universe of discourse to the [0,1] interval. This function tells the degree to which an entity belongs to the set. For grades of membership between zero and one, the values tell the degree to which an agent categorizes the object in the set (e.g., cluster, class, category, form, or population).

Organizational Ecology

The bulk of the book describes a unification project using a body of sociological theory and research commonly called organizational ecology. As we sketched in Chapter 1, this theory examines interactions within and between populations of organizations. Progress within the ecological research program has been driven by systematic empirical research conducted on a variety of distinct theory fragments. Theory fragments typically arose from some core insight or intuition about a phenomenon and persisted so long as the intuitions remained viable or fruitful. Many remain active today.

Nonetheless, the relationships among ecology's fragments had remained largely unexamined. As a result, major points of apparent conceptual intersection appear ambiguous and possibly inconsistent at points—they require clarification.

Our approach to unification within this tradition did not attempt to fit all available fragments into a single whole or to insist on the priority of the initial theoretical statements. Instead, we tried to retain what seemed valuable in the early efforts and those that followed. This strategy led us to highlight social codes in ecological analysis. In our usage, a social code denotes and connotes both cognitive recognition and imperative standing. A social code can be understood as (1) a set of interpretative signals, as in the "genetic code," and (2) a set of rules of conduct, as in the "penal code." Some of the most interesting and important processes are those that convert interpretative schemata into imperative codes.

In taking stock of what the unification effort has wrought, we distinguish four types of theoretical activity: (1) construction of a common conceptual core across fragments; (2) resolution of inconsistencies within and across fragments; (3) development of theory about previously unattended processes; and (4) development of arguments that integrate ideas from several fragments. We briefly review some of our accomplishments within each, recognizing that classification of this kind is certainly incomplete. We also remind that any such description betrays the depth and subtlety of the full treatments contained in the above chapters.

14.2 COMMON CONCEPTUAL CORE

Previous ecological (and other organizational) theory relies heavily on the concept of organizational form. But even a cursory look at the literature reveals little agreement about the meaning or usage of the concept. That the form concept can be found in use in virtually all the theory fragments of ecology shows how central it is. In reconstructing it, we needed to take into account (1) the possible emergence of forms out of more primitive structures such as clusters and categories; (2) the varying degrees of fuzziness of organizational memberships in categories and forms; (3) the social fact that organizational forms can be treated in interaction as identities; and (4) the composition of the audience(s) making the observations and assignments.

The language we developed deals directly with vagueness in agents' concepts, that is, fuzziness. We suggest that individuals and other actors often experience social entities as only partly satisfying applicable codes. Many of our main applications concentrate on the codes that define organizational categories, which we see as arising when audience members come to partial agreement about the meanings of memberships in these categories.

In the social world, local audiences construct and rely on categories that involve both typicality judgments and vagueness or fuzziness in category boundaries (Hampton 2005). Based on available evidence, we propose that agents often detect shades of difference and decide that some producers (or products) fit neatly within a category, some do not fit at all, and others fit to a greater or lesser degree.

The unification effort builds on the insight that forms are (socially agreed-upon) categories for which most members of an audience treat as a default that objects bearing the category label will fit the schemata that they apply to the category. That is, forms are ways of classifying organizations that are taken for granted by contemporaneous agents who observe them and interact with them. Social codes, that is schemata, play a central role in this framework.

Our reconstructed notion of form involves taking account of the specific audiences that populate particular social domains. Audiences are composed of actors and agents of all kinds who possess an interest, material or otherwise, in a domain. A domain is a culturally bounded segment of the social world containing producers/products, audiences, and a language that tells to whom these distinctions apply and what they mean. The reformulation attends to certain basic perceptual and cognitive processes of the members of the audience. In particular, vagueness often characterizes how audience members classify organizations and develop defaults about satisfaction of the codes (schemata) that they apply to category members.

Because of the centrality of the form concept in ecology, the reconceptualization potentially has far-reaching consequences. Here we used it to build a theoretical account of the form emergence process (Chapters 2–5), to reconcile and extend theories of niche width and resource partitioning (Chapters 8–10), and to reformulate and extend theories of structural change and inertia in organizations (Chapters 11–13).

Reconceptualization

Received organizational ecology contains widely used theories of legitimation, age dependence, competition, and inertia. We attempted to use the insights behind these theories to develop deeper conceptualizations, ones that will reveal additional implications for both the theory and empirical testing. Of course, the real test of whether we have succeeded in this vein will be determined by the future actions of researchers—do they find the additional ideas intriguing and do they reveal new empirical patterns? Nonetheless, we think that the unification process has in many spots generated a conceptual apparatus that can support new lines of empirical inquiry.

Consider, for instance, that legitimation has until now been treated as a primitive, a basic concept that stands alone based on its stated definition. In the revised theory, there is now much more underlying conceptualization: legitimation exists when a consensus of agents in the audience apply a very simple test code to check fit to their category-relevant schemata. The test code works as follows. The agent checks an organization's values on a few features. If the checked features fit the schema, then the agent fills in as a default that the organization's other features fit as well. (The default modality that we use to express this idea allows for positive perceptions to overrule defaults.) We defined taken-for-grantedness as the size of the (minimal) test code used by an agent relative to the size of the schema (number of features that a schema considers). The maximum possible value of unity obtains when mere possession of the label causes audience members to apply defaults. Then we define the legitimation of a category to an audience as the average level of taken-for-grantedness over all pairs of audience members and organizations.

Likewise, the reformulated theory offers an account of a series of processes by which forms emerge from a simple cluster. The list of similar elaborated conceptualizations in the theory includes age dependence, density dependence (including competition), niche competition, structural inertia, and niche change.

14.3 INCONSISTENCIES RESOLVED

Age Dependence

Perhaps our most thorough illustration of the potential value of nonmonotonic logic involves its application to age dependence in organizational mortality, a well-studied—yet still recalcitrant—problem. The current scientific situation includes inconsistent empirical findings and several associated theory fragments that cannot be brought together to make a coherent single theory expressible in first-order logic.

To demonstrate that nonmonotonic logic might succeed where the classical tools had not, we developed a formalization that incorporates several of the otherwise incompatible theory fragments (see Chapter 6). The following general theoretical picture emerged; it reproduces the patterns of age dependence found in empirical research:

1. If the organizations in a population do not possess endowments and inhabit environments that do not induce obsolescence, then age dependence is presumably uniformly negative.

2. If the endowments do not get burned up within an observation period or obsolescence strikes before endowments burn up, then age dependence is presumably uniformly positive.

3. If the organizations in a population possess endowments but run no risk of obsolescence, then the mortality hazard presumably peaks in adolescence.

4. If the organizations in a population possess endowments and face obsolescence after the endowment is burned up, then the mortality hazard presumably changes with age as follows: the hazard rises over an initial age interval, jumps at the start of the next age interval and then declines, and then rises over the final age interval.

The effort also yielded an overall pattern picture that surprised us. In particular, the mortality hazard is higher in each of the defined later phases of an organization's life as contrasted with each earlier phase, despite the fact that the hazard does not increase within all of the phases. This result is attractive, because much well-designed empirical research finds such a global pattern.

Niche

The concept of niche commands center stage in many ecological analyses; it allows analysts to specify environmental dependencies of organizations and competitive processes among organizations. However, two productive theory fragments—niche width theory and resource partitioning—defined and used the niche concept in different ways. We sought to unify the fragments.

Both theory fragments in question used the terms generalism/specialism in describing and analyzing organizational niches. Due to a difference in focus, however, the theorists who worked with the different fragments applied the terms differently, which generated confusion. In the formulation presented in Chapters 8 and 9, we tried to clarify the situation. But, in doing so, we abandoned the terms generalism/specialism. Instead, we theorized about niche locations, niche width, and niche overlap. We also cast the theory in terms of fundamental niches rather than realized niches, which had been the approach of resource partitioning.

The new niche theory treats fundamental and realized niches as fuzzy subsets of a social space. The grades of membership for these sets tell the degree to which a position in the social space belongs to the niche. We incorporated a version of the principle of allocation in this framework. This principle states that full-fledged members of a prominent (high-contrast) organization population face common "budgets" of total engagement and total intrinsic appeal. This principle represents the inherent tradeoff between a broad allocation of engagement and intrinsic appeal and the level of engagement and intrinsic appeal at any given social position.

These reformulations allowed us to build a theory of fuzzy niches that has a conceptually consistent core yet still retains many insights and predictions of the two fragments. In the end, resource partitioning theory gained an explicit incorporation of the principle of allocation, a central tenet of niche width theory that had previously been treated by reference to diseconomies of scope. Among the gains to niche width theory is a consideration of scale advantages. Moreover, the new theory also shows new potentially fertile veins for previously neglected empirical issues, such as the limits on niche expansion from the center due to category boundaries.

Niche Overlap and Competition

A subtle problem in integrating the fragments on the niche involved how the fitness function might vary over the niche. The initial formulations of niche theory assumed that niches contained regions of high fitness and that fitness declined to zero near the boundaries of the niche. This means that members of a population are more vulnerable to competition near the boundaries of a niche than near its center.

Other work, including most empirical work, treats fitness functions as flat over a niche. Under this kind of a scenario, vulnerability to competition does not vary over the niche.

The difference between these two views comes into sharp relief when we examine the implications of niche overlap for viability. Consider a case in which the niche of one organization is a proper subset of the niche of the other. Suppose that the social space is metric (so that distance between positions is well defined). The usual approach to measuring overlaps is as the proportion of the focal organization's niche that is covered by the other. Then the overlap for the narrow-niche organization in the example is one, and the overlap for the broad-niche organization is less than one. If the intensity of competition experienced by an organization is assumed to be a monotonic function of overlap (the standard assumption), then the narrow-niche organization faces more intense competition and presumably has lower viability. The problem with this line of argument is that it runs counter to the principle of allocation—the argument does not account for the tendency for the narrow-niche organization to have higher fitness in the region of overlap.

The fuzzy-niche construction solves this problem. Our proposed measure of overlap of fuzzy niches takes grades of membership in social positions into account and leads to the implication that broadening a niche normally increases levels of overlap.

Core Organizational Structure

Organizational ecology's original theory of structural inertia pertains to changes in the so-called core features of organizations. In developing this theory, Hannan and Freeman (1984) posited a core consisting of four features: (1) the organization's mission, (2) its form of authority (including the nature of the exchange between the organization and its members), (3) the basic technology used to transform inputs into outputs, and (4) the general marketing strategy. Limiting the scope of the theory in this way proved unwise because it has not constrained empirical research much or helped to sort out the occasionally inconsistent findings in a definitive way.

We developed an alternative structural way to specifying coreness. Specifically, we analyzed changes in an organization's architecture, defined as a code system associated with audiences. We traced the impact of architectural change in terms of the cascades of subsequent changes throughout the organization. We proposed that core changes are those that produce long cascades on average.

We followed the original theory in positing that architectural changes initiate reorganization periods. We characterized the time dimension of reorganization periods as (1) the total time spent reorganizing in all parts of the organization, even if some changes co-occur, and (2) the temporal span required to bring all the organization's feature values in line (no code inconsistencies) with the new architecture. We assumed that reconfiguring the architecture diminishes an organization's ability to take advantage of opportunities. As a result, we expect that organizations undergoing change miss more opportunities than those not undergoing change. Therefore, architectural reorganization causes resources to shrink and mortality hazards to rise.

14.4 THEORETICAL PROGRESS

Form Emergence

Although the form concept plays a major role in organizational ecology and many other theories of organization, little theory explains in any depth how a form might emerge. In this book, we considered the emergence of concepts from initially unstructured or minimally structured situations.

A first step in the form emergence process consists of identifying clusters of producer organizations or products that agents believe for some reason belong together in one sense or another. We considered clustering based on perceived similarity. Such clustering demands significant effort; at least some members of the audience must be energized for these processes to be completed. That is, some agents must gather information, compare producers and products, and propose and defend different ways of understanding the distinctions being made among organizations. These activities involve much more effort and engagement than is required of an audience member in a settled set of arrangements and distinctions. The agents in the audience who produce clusterings are called activists or enthusiasts.

In the second step in the process, activists associate labels with the clusters. When an audience obtains high consensus on the extension of a label (the objects to which the label applies), then we refer to the label as denoting a class. This analysis allows for partiality on both sides of the story: producers/products can be partial members of an audience member's extension of a label and audience members can share in an extensional consensus to varying degrees. The degrees of inclusion on both sides are therefore seen as vague or fuzzy and are indicated by grade of membership functions that vary from zero to one.

In the next step, audience members attempt to dimensionalize classes, elucidating abstractly the distinctions that establish who belongs to a class to one degree or another and who does not. That is, this stage involves a kind of (perhaps retrospective) sense making. We describe this activity as creating (private) schemata that specify the patterns of feature values that consistent with a high grade of membership in a label (from the perspectives of different audience members).

If the audience achieves strong consensus about the meaning of a label in the sense that their schemata for the label are similar, then a class becomes a category.

Finally, as we noted above, audience members might come to see a category as natural and treat as a default that objects that bear the category label will fit their schemata for the category. If a high fraction of the audience treats a category as natural and taken for granted in this sense, then the category is a form.

These developments led to a new way of defining an organizational population. The fuzzy construction allows for labels and category schemata to apply only partially to individual organizations. It also allows organizations to be members of more than one population. In this kind of construction, the density of a population is a sum of grades of membership of the producers/products in the meanings that the audience members associate with a label rather than a simple count of members.

Density and Contrast

We defined the density of a fuzzy set (e.g., a population) as the sum of the grades of membership in the set over the producers/products in the domain. Because populations can reach the same density by many different combinations, we also proposed the notion of contrast. Contrast tells the degree to which a set stands out from its domain. Specifically, the contrast of a population is the average grade of membership among those with nonzero grade of membership in the population.

We argue that an audience segment reaches a high level of intensional agreement most commonly when the producers/products in a class stand out sharply from the background for most audience members. When the average contrast of a class is high, it contains few marginal members, for whom disagreement about grades of membership is likely. Moreover, the members of a class will tend to have very similar feature values, ones that differ from those of the nonmembers of the class.

So not only will there be few marginal members when contrast is high, the members will generally share feature values. Both conditions make it likely that the members of an audience segment will attend to the same features and pick out the same feature value ranges as relevant. Therefore, we postulated that the expected level of intensional consensus about a label increases monotonically with the average contrast of the population.

We argued that the tendency to shift to defaults will be stronger when there is greater consensus in the audience about the meaning of a label. Why? When intensional consensus is high, an audience member will less likely be surprised at what she finds upon encountering a producer/product that another audience member claims is a typical member of the class. If, on the other hand, intensional consensus is low, then the picture will look confused; and the agents are unlikely to treat satisfaction of any given schema as a default for members of the class other than those for which they have direct evidence of fit. But, relying on direct evidence means *not* relying on defaults. Because we assume that the members of audience segments communicate with each other, the segment is the relevant unit for considering the effect of intensional consensus on legitimation. Therefore, we postulate that legitimation increases with the strength of the intensional consensus in a segment. It then follows that the expected level of legitimation of a label increases with the average (over audience members) of the contrast of a population.

This line of argument implies that a proliferation of marginal members of a population will impede legitimation, not enhance it. More specifically, suppose we take two identical populations with fairly high contrast and add some marginal members to one of them. Such an influx increases density but lowers contrast. According to the theorem, the level of legitimation of the population with an influx of marginal members falls below that of the unchanged population.

This distinction is possible only because we have allowed partial memberships. The original density-dependence theory, by not saying otherwise, followed the nearly universal convention in the social sciences of treating sets as crisp. In such a classical setup, there is no problem of marginal members and contrast is not relevant. The intuition that the legitimation of a population depends on its salience naturally focused on growth in density. The current approach emphasizes the state of the audience, especially its degree of consensus about meanings, which depends on contrast, not density.

Multiple Category Memberships

In defining populations based on categories, previous ecological research created classical sets in the sense that any given organization was defined as a member of the population or not. Researchers (or others who produce the records that researchers consult) usually construct hard-and-fast rules to make these assignments, typically by forcing individual cases into categories based on the preponderance of evidence.

The fuzzy construction that we developed in this book (partially) relieves theorists and empirical researchers of these often difficult, absolute classification decisions. It implies weighting cases comprising populations and associated constructs such as density by grades of membership.

This approach appears to have great potential value for ecological analysis: an organization can be a member of several populations in a nontrivial sense; forcing it one way or the other ran counter to the facts. An organization might contribute to the social reality of several categories, but less than more-typical members. This approach also provides a coherent treatment of conglomerates, something previously lacking in ecological research on organizations.

Engagement

In developing the theory of niche width, we dug deeper into the interface between the product that an organization offers and its appeal to an audience. We distinguished between the intrinsic appeal of the product and its actual appeal. We argued that converting intrinsic appeal into actual appeal depends on the actions taken by the organization that makes the offering. We refer to such activities as engagement. We define engagement by the attention that producers pay to different subaudiences that control parts of the resource distribution. We find it natural to think that engagement involves a tradeoff: paying attention to a broader—and thus more diverse—audience comes at the cost of less attention paid to each narrower subaudience.

Nonmetric Niche Theory

The entire line of work on organizational niches has treated the space within which a niche is defined as metric, as we noted above. We began our reformulation of niche theory along these lines, and we treated the space as a set of metric social positions. Once we had completed the formalization we found, to our surprise, that most of the central results did not depend upon the metric properties of the space. In particular, we could relax the constraint of a metric on the space and still obtain most results (while some still depend on the assumption of a metric). As a result, the theory is more general than we had envisioned initially. We doubt that we would have come to the realization that the key results do not depend on metric assumptions had we not formalized the theory.

Niche Convexity

Organizational niches in a metric space might contain gaps. In formal terms, niches with such gaps lack convexity. Put differently, the absence of gaps can be expressed as the property of convexity.

The lack of discussion in the literature about niche convexity suggests that organizational analysts have assumed implicitly that niches do not contain gaps. While this assumption might be well-founded, why this is the case is not obvious. Accordingly, we developed new theory about niche convexity.

We developed an argument that implies that an organization with a convex niche has higher fitness than a comparable organization with a concave niche. This is because the intrinsic appeal of an offer declines monotonically with the distance from the closest position in its region of peak appeal, which, in turn, implies that the intrinsic appeal cannot be concave—it is not possible that an offer has nonzero appeal at two positions but zero intrinsic appeal at some positions between these two positions. To display a concave fundamental niche, an organization must be engaged at a concave set of positions. Considering the "holes" in the engagement, the intrinsic appeal of the offer must be higher in the hole than it is on at least one side of the cavity. Organizations with concave niches engage positions where the intrinsic appeal of their offer is lower than in some positions that they do not engage. Had they engaged these positions, their actual appeal would have been higher at the positions where their intrinsic appeal is higher.

Given the principle of allocation, organizations with convex fundamental niches are more fit than those with concave niches. With some restrictions, we developed a theorem stating that an organization with a concave niche has higher hazard of mortality than one with a close convex alternative.

Cascades of Change

In extending the theory of cascades as core change, we developed arguments about how the total time spent reorganizing in response to an initial architectural change increases with four structural features of the organization. The first is intricacy, a strong and complex pattern of interconnections among the organization's component units. The second is viscosity, the typical time it takes for a unit to respond to changes and bring local architecture into conformity. The third is opacity, structural limits on the foresight of those initiating a change. And the fourth feature is asperity, narrow cultural bounds on acceptable architectural features.

The theory ties these four structural features to mortality hazards using the standard assumption that an organization's hazard of mortality is inversely proportional to its stock of resources. Reconfiguring an organization lessens its ability to recognize and benefit from opportunities. So a reorganizing organization misses more opportunities, yielding a lower resource base and a higher hazard of mortality. Because each factor lengthens the reorganization period, the elevation of the hazard heightens with the intricacy of an organization's design, with the viscosity of processes, with the opacity of its change initiators, and with the asperity of its culture.

Progress in Unification

Given our emphasis on unifying the fragments, it is worth noting some progress on this score.

In the reformulated theory, density dependence now sits more snugly on top of a model of perception and consensus in an audience. Previously, the macro changes in the environment that produce legitimation and result in institutionalized forms did not receive deep analysis. Our formulation proposes that they occur as a result of consensus among agents in an audience and their ambiguous perceptions about what is being observed. Moreover, both the degree of consensus and the level of ambiguity matter for the strength and speed of legitimation.

Categories and niches have also been at least partly unified. For instance, we have constructed a category niche and developed arguments about categorical constraints on niche expansion. Moreover, ecological process of resource partitioning sometimes creates discontinuities in previously coherent organizational populations. A discontinuity arises as organizations in the near-center of a market fall victim to the competitive pressures generated by the winners of the scale-based competitive struggle in the market center. That is, partitioning eliminates the near-center organizations that are responsible for the perceived unity of the population. It thus sets the stage for clustering, labeling, and codification of the set of producers in the periphery, much as with primitive form emergence. The rise of such peripheral categories can stabilize a partitioning.

Previously, theory about age dependence posited many different underlying processes, both structural and cultural. But these ideas were underdeveloped, and they have often been conflated in making predictions. The reformulated theory develops several of the processes in depth, including especially those about cultural severity, which we call asperity. The theory now links age to asperity and asperity to structural change and possible failure.

Recognizing that efforts at expanding niches generally entail architectural reorganization provided a natural point of departure for integrating niche theory and the theory of architectural change. According to the unified argument, intricate, opaque, and aspere organizational contexts likely make niche expansion more precarious.

14.5 EMPIRICAL IMPLICATIONS

Experienced researchers who read parts of this book prior to publication always wanted to discuss the fact that our new theories place new and challenging demands on empirical research. We agree with their assessment, and we need to point to nothing more than the fuzzy conception of forms and their associated grades of membership to illustrate the severity of the challenge. To think of collecting average GoMs by audience segment over long periods of a population's history is clearly mind boggling. Quite frankly, we do not yet know exactly the best way to do it at the moment, as we discuss below.

It might come as a surprise to learn that, nonetheless, we do not view this unsettled empirical research situation as troubling. In fact, we think that such situations often occur in science when theoretical progress has been made. For instance, at one time a simple microscope was enough to do "microbiology," but each new set of discoveries pushed empirical research to develop new kinds of instruments that provide more detailed information (or, to use the obvious example of high-energy physics, to build gigantic and incredibly expensive accelerators and colliders). So, if we are lucky, the fact that empirical research has to move beyond the old technology might be a sign of progress.

Perhaps it is informative to note that prior stages of organizational ecology regularly required shifting away from the easy and conventional ways of doing things. Initially, the ecological notion of population (and the understanding that population does not equal industry) meant that analysts could not rely on standard industry classifications and use data organized in this way. The theoretical centrality of organizations rather than establishments meant that ecologists could not use available census extracts for data. The focus on coherent populations meant that researchers could not rely on ad hoc but available groupings of firms, e.g., the Fortune 500. Then, the theories advanced regarding organizational evolution required full histories on all organizations in a population over its entire history. Later, making progress on understanding age dependence required obtaining (with great difficulty) regularly updated size data on all organizations in a population. Recently, the identity interpretation of partitioning in brewing and form emergence in health care implied that scientists could no longer rely so heavily on industry directories and the like.

Note that at each juncture, the new data demands appeared ominous; and it was not clear how they would be met. But innovative and energetic researchers found a way. Similarly, we have faith now that the challenges presented by the new integrated theory will be overcome. As an assist to this process, we end by noting some specific theory developed in the book that calls out for some innovative new empirical tests. We mention several of the more important ones here, organized by theory fragment.

Classification of Organizations

As just mentioned, the most central empirical challenge presented by the unified theory might be the fuzzy conception of categories and forms and their associated grades of membership. Clearly, the situation calls for the development of new empirical technology or protocols. Along these lines, we think that laboratory experimentation might be a useful tool, as the GoM classification problem is inherently cognitive in nature. We hope that the potential implications of form classification are compelling enough to prompt scientists from sister disciplines such as psychology, anthropology, and cognitive science to join the enterprise.

However useful it might prove to be, the lab will not solve the problem of estimating average GoMs by audience segment over long periods of a population's history. We hope that this issue too will command a great deal of attention by empiricists. We are encouraged by the potentially interesting ideas that we have already heard from Bogaert, Boone, and Carroll (2006) about using the distribution of professional association memberships and from Kovacs (2006) about using similarities calculated from links generated by Web pages on the Internet.

Form Emergence

In our theory of form emergence, we have posited many details that remain to be investigated empirically. In our view, almost any kind of study of the form emergence process would be informative. However, with respect to the proposed theory, we have special interest in those forms that apparently emerge from similarity clusters. We wonder how difficult it would be to identify a sample of similarity clusters prior to knowing whether a form will actually emerge. We are also eager to learn about cases that correspond (or not) with our proposed sequencing of developments: Does labeling occur as early we posit or later? At what stage does extensional consensus form? Intensional consensus? How do schema get initiated and accepted? What are the ways a schema becomes the default? The empirical agenda here is vast.

Codes

In the revised theory, the emergence and establishment of the codes shaping categories and forms play central roles. Yet most of our current understanding of codes, where they come from and how they develop, relies on social histories written for a more general audience. This leaves ample room, in our view, for more focused research, perhaps intensive case studies, on specific codes in particular industries and other settings. We believe that theoretical accounts of social codes might change significantly once more detailed empirical material becomes available. In particular, we are eager to learn the histories of competing codes and their outcomes, because we believe that casual retrospective accounts of such processes often make the outcomes appear inevitable. Our sense is that these processes are often fragile and contain large random components.

Age Dependence

Previous empirical studies supported three different types of theories of the age dependence of the mortality hazards: liability of newness, liability of adolescence, and liability of obsolescence. Unfortunately these theories are pairwise inconsistent in a classical logic. Our effort to integrate them into a coherent theory using nonmonotonic reasoning apparently does a good job of fitting the empirical patterns reported both for the specific arguments that apply to given phases of an organization's life course as well as for the global pattern.

But our logical formalization also presents a new challenge for empirical studies. The integrated theory introduces two parameters, the normal age of ending of endowment and the normal age of the beginning of obsolescence. In conjunction with population age, these two parameters make predictable what kind of age-dependence patterns should be observable in different populations. For example, if the population age at the time of a study is less than the age of end of endowment for a population, then the unified theory predicts that research will yield evidence of positive age dependence. If, on the other hand, the endowed period is very short or nonexistent and the observation window is such that no organization reached the age of obsolescence, then the theory predicts negative age dependence.

Now a different type of empirical study, a metastudy of sorts, would be useful. This study would look over all the well-done empirical studies, identify the two parameters as well as population age and the width of the observation window, thereby exposing the unified theory to systematic empirical challenge. In this way, we can find out how well the unified theory fits with the facts.

Finally, the age-dependence formalization also reveals the importance of exploring empirically several related issues. These include how aging relates to capability, how capability influences the mortality hazard, how aging relates to the level of an organization's endowment, and how the level of endowment influences the mortality hazard.

Asperity

We have theorized about asperity—cultural severity—based on anecdotes, cases and intuition. Insightful as these arguments might be, there are no substitutes for systematic empirical research. Asperity about organizational architecture is little studied; it deserves attention, if our arguments are right. Among the pertinent questions: Where does asperity arise? Why? How does it affect organizational behavior? Under what conditions do aspere organizations compete effectively?

Density Dependence and Contrast Dependence

In revisiting the ecological theory of legitimation and competition, we theorized that the expected level of legitimation of a class grows monotonically with the (average) contrast of the population rather than density. This altered empirical prediction requires empirical confirmation.

The theory also makes predictions about density and contrast dependence in an earlier phase of form emergence—the labeling of a cluster. It says that the chances of a cluster getting labeled by an agent increase with both density and contrast. To our knowledge, these propositions currently lack solid empirical support.

Architectural Reorganization and Cascades

Our reformulation of the theory of structural inertia also provides different, specific advice for conducting empirical research. Current studies examine only a single type of change in a population of organizations, yielding a commonly observed pattern suggesting that mortality hazards jump when changes get undertaken but that they then decline with the time elapsed from the change. The revised theory implies that it matters whether the studied structural change is the initiating change in a cascade or simply one episode in a longer sequence. It implies that a design that records the entire cascade of changes and measures better the temporal aspects of reorganizing might very well yield different findings. The theory also provides guidance on interpreting results based on an organization's intricacy, opacity, and asperity.

Principle of Allocation

As with much prior ecological theory, we have relied on the principle of allocation to obtain implications (and predictions). This principle, in our generalization, holds that organizations possess a finite budget of total engagement and total intrinsic appeal. According to the principle, expenditures of engagement in one part of the niche diminish the possibilities of engagement in other parts. Application of this principle led us to argue that multiple category membership diminishes competitive strength and viability. But does it really? Empirical demonstrations are needed to make the case compelling.[1]

Resource Partitioning

The revised theory of resource partitioning contains more detailed guidance for empirical testing. Rather than relying on concentration and a summary measure of niche width, empirical analysts now can base predictions on an organization's location vis-à-vis the center and the level of crowding it experiences. The revised theory also points to some new issues for empirical research, such as the predicted organizational limits on niche expansion from the center.

Niche Expansion

Recent research shows that niche shifts typically induce deleterious outcomes. That is, niche expansion typically raises the hazard of mortality in the period following the change. In developing theory about these effects, we argued that expanding the niche leads to higher mortality in the period following expansion for at least two general reasons: (1) it takes time to establish engagement at a new position, and (2) the architectural reorganization often associated with expansion. Both issues could benefit from empirical verification. So too could our additional predictions that niche expansion exerts stronger effects on mortality when occurring in organizations with high intricacy, opacity, and cultural asperity, when the expansion lies further from an organization's region of peak appeal, and when the expansion lies further from the support of an organization's fundamental niche.

Audience Structure and Dynamics

A relatively undeveloped part of the new theory concerns the structure and dynamics of the audience. Our neglect does not reflect a view that these issues are unimportant or uninteresting. Rather, we face a dearth of empirical knowledge about the structure and dynamics of audiences, as they concern organizations and their forms. At various points in the text, we have referred to ideas or insights that seem potentially useful; and we developed the implications of authority structures and social movement mobilization. Otherwise, we have refrained from developing a formal account of audience structure, because we think we need a better empirical foundation. Along these lines, it would be helpful to know how audience segments emerge and evolve, especially as organizational forms do. We are also interested to learn how audience structure might affect consensus formation and corresponding processes of identity formation and interaction. Again, the empirical agenda is vast and wide open.

A potentially valuable extension of our notion of audience segment would consider geography. We defined segments as subsets of an audience that are largely closed with respect to interaction and communication. Such closure often takes a spatial form: social networks tend toward spatial closure. Therefore, audience segments likely form in spatial patches. This would mean that agreement about labels

[1] Hsu (2006) provides a model for such analyses.

and their meanings might also vary over space. Such heterogeneity might contribute to the observed spatial agglomeration in many industries Sorenson (2003) and Sorenson and Audia (2000) attribute such clustering to (local) social networks as conduits of intangible knowledge required for starting an organization. Perhaps variation over local audience segments in the legitimation of categories also plays a role.[2]

Atypical Members of Populations

We consistently developed arguments for typical members of categories, forms, and populations on the grounds that the available intuitions come from considering such cases. But, we also argued that many cases of interest might not be typical. So it is unclear how much—if any—of the theory applies to atypical members of categories, forms, and populations. If researchers devise research designs that can produce information on grades of membership in categories, it will be possible to undertake analyses of the implications of atypicality. Such research will be extremely informative about the applicability of the new theory.

Finally, we conclude with a paraphrase of the aforementioned Dr. Seuss: we meant what we said and we said what we meant. In other words, language matters!

[2]Romanelli and Khessina (2005) and Khessina and Romanelli (2006) have initiated a move in this direction by advancing the notion of regional industrial identities.

Appendix A

Glossary of Theoretical Terms

This appendix provides brief descriptions of key theoretical terms. If the term has a formal label in our syntax, it follows the term in parentheses. (The Glossary of Symbols in the following appendix describes the full set of symbols used.)

Activist (ACT)	Agent in audience with an intense interest in the domain. Same as enthusiast.
Actual appeal (ap)	The relative attractiveness of a product offering to an audience member. Actual appeal grows with intrinsic appeal and engagement.
Age (a)	The time elapsed since an organization entered a population.
Architecture	The set of codes that distinguish between allowed and not-allowed values of organizational feature values.
Asperity (A)	The degree to which an organization's culture restricts its architectural choices.
Audience	Role in the domain composed of the agents who inspect, evaluate, and consume the output of the producers. Commonly used to refer to audience segment.
Audience segment member	A member of a part of the audience that is separated from other parts by type of interest and social structural boundaries.
Authoritative support (AUTH)	Process by which an agent with authority labels a producer, leading members of the audience to apply the label and to treat the fit of the producer to their schemata for the label as a default.
Authority	An agent has authority if other agents recognize and abide by the agent's claims, including especially the pronouncement of codes.

Cardinality, fuzzy set (card)	The sum over the objects in the universe of discourse of grades of membership in the set. Applies to clusters, types, and populations.
Cascade (**cas**)	Sequence of resolutions of induced violations of organizational architectural codes.
Category (CAT)	A category is a class about whose meaning an audience segment has reached a very high level of intensional semantic consensus.
Category niche (γ)	The fuzzy set of social positions with grade of membership given by the intrinsic appeal of a full-fledged member of the category to an audience member with the typical taste at a position.
Cavity (CAV)	A gap or hole in a niche (defined over a metric space).
Center position (CEN)	An organization occupies a center position in a market if its position of peak appeal lies in a market center.
Centrality (cen)	The position of a unit in a hierarchy of control relations.
Class (CLASS)	A label for which the level of extensional semantic consensus in an audience segment exceeds a threshold.
Cluster	See Similarity cluster.
Code	A set of interpretative signals (as in the "genetic code") and a set of rules of conduct (as in the "penal code"). A schema with a high level of taken-for-grantedness is a code.
Code clash (CLASH)	Two codes clash when the perception that a high degree of satisfaction of one code produces a perception of a low degree of satisfaction of the other.
Comembership (CM)	A pair of organizations are comembers if they have high grades of membership in a prominent (high-contrast) population.
Competitive pressure ($Comp$)	The extent to which a producer faces rivals in the market.

Concave niche	A niche (defined on a metric space) where some position that does not lie between two positions in the niche also belongs to the niche.
Concept (CONCEPT)	A type for which an agent treats as a default that the objects with the type label have feature values that satisfy the agent's schema for the type label.
Contrast of a fuzzy set (c)	The average grade of membership among those with nonzero grade of membership in the set (the set density divided by the cardinality of the support for the cluster). Applies to clusters, types, and populations.
Convex niche (CVX)	A niche in a metric space where every position that lies between two positions in the niche also belongs to the niche.
Crisp set	A collection of objects with a membership function that equals either zero or one.
Crowding (CROWD)	A market is crowded if the expected level of niche overlap thicknesses of center organizations on near-center organizations and of near-center organizations on peripheral organizations each exceed certain thresholds.
Cultural consensus (cul)	The degree of schematic consensus among the members of an organization about its architecture.
Default code violation (DCV)	An audience member detects a (new) violation of a default about code satisfaction.
Default status	Assumed fit to a schema. Default standing means that audience members fill in the feature values that fit their schemata unless they see evidence to the contrary.
Delegitimation	The process by which legitimation wanes.
Density [classical]	The cardinality of a crisp set.
Density, fuzzy set (card{})	See Cardinality, fuzzy set.
Density dependence	Relationship of the hazards of founding and mortality to density. Linked to legitimation and competition in a theory of organizational ecology.

Diffuse competition (DCOMP)	Competition among producers or products is diffuse if and only if each triplet of focal producer, rival producer, and audience member is equally likely to occur in a competitive encounter.
Domain	A culturally bounded slice of the social world composed formally of agents in audience roles and producer roles as well as a language.
Endowment (dow)	A stock of material and social resources at an organization's founding. Endowments depreciate unless replenished by continuing positive flows of material and social resources from the environment.
Engagement (en)	A diverse set of actions including (1) learning about the idiosyncrasies of the local subaudience, (2) designing features of the offering to make it attractive to that audience, and (3) trying to establish a favorable identity in the relevant subaudience.
Engagement niche (ϵ)	A producer's engagement niche with respect to a category is a fuzzy subset of the set of social positions with grade of membership in a position given by the producer's engagement devoted to the audience at a position.
Enthusiast	Same as activist.
Extension of a label	The set of objects to which an agent applies a label.
Extensional consensus (ec)	Strength of agreement among audience members about the extension of a label.
Expanded engagement (ϵ^+)	A set of positions at which a producer newly engages.
Fitness (ϕ, Φ)	An organization's relative fitness at a position is its share of the total appeal at the position. An organization's overall relative fitness is given by the sum over social positions of its relative fitness.
Form (FORM)	A category with a high (average) level of legitimation.

Fundamental niche (**f**)	A fuzzy set of social positions with grade of membership in a position is its expected actual appeal to agents with the typical taste for a category at the position.
Fuzzy set	A set of pairs consisting of objects in some universe and a function mapping to $[0, 1]$ that tells the object's grade of membership in the set.
Grade of membership (μ)	A function that maps from elements of the universe of discourse to the [0,1] interval. This function tells the degree to which an entity belongs to a fuzzy set.
Hazard of mortality (ω)	A producer's hazard of experiencing mortality.
Identity (**id**)	The composition of all the labels that an agent applies to an object and the feature values that the agent treats as conforming by default to her schemata for the labels.
Immunity (im)	A degree of protection from the hazard of mortality.
Induced code violation ($viol$)	A unit experiences induced violation of an architectural code if and only if an induced change in its architectural code causes its feature values to violate an architectural code when no violation existed prior to the change.
Induction from a test (INDUC)	An agent induces from the observation that a producer passes a test code that its unobserved feature values also fit the applicable schema.
Intension of a label	The meaning that an agent associates with a label.
Intensional consensus (ic)	The level of agreement among audience-segment members about the meaning of a label.
Intricacy (I)	A strong and complex pattern of interconnections among an organization's component units. Specifically, intricacy is the mean of the centralities of the units in the organization.
Intrinsic appeal ($\widehat{ap}$)	A complex assessment by an audience member of the degree to which an offer fits his tastes.

Label	A descriptive tag or name given to a set of objects.
Legitimation (L)	The average degree to which audience-segment members take for granted that producers to which they assign a label conform to the agents' schemata for the label, conditional on passing some minimal tests.
Liability of adolescence	Condition occurring when an endowed organization's hazard of mortality is constant during its period of immunity, jumps when its immunity ends, and decreases with further aging but remains above the level during the immunity period.
Liability of newness	Condition occurring when an unendowed organization's hazard of mortality declines monotonically with its age.
Liability of obsolescence	Condition occurring when an unendowed organization's hazard of mortality increases with age in a drifting environment.
Local intrinsic appeal (τ)	The intrinsic appeal of the offering to a prototypical member of the taste that prevails at a social position.
Market center ($\mathbf{ctr}$)	A market center for a population is a set of social positions at which the local audience controls a high level of population-relevant resources.
Market segment	A region of the market. See Center market position, Near-center market position, and Peripheral market position.
Metric audience space	A representation of the audience in which the set of social positions map to the natural numbers.
Minimal test (MTST)	A minimal test code—see Test code.
Near-center position (NC)	An organization occupies a near-center position in a market if its position of peak appeal does not lie in a market center but its fundamental niche does intersect a market center.
Niche	See Fundamental niche, Realized niche.
Niche overlap (ov)	The intersection of one producer's niche with another's.

Niche width (wd)	The evenness of a niche GoM over positions (where evenness is defined as one minus the diversity of the GoMs).
Nonmetric audience space	A representation of a set of social positions that lacks an ordering.
Obsolescence (ob)	Lack of fit to a drifting environment due to organizational inertia.
Opacity (O)	An incomplete view of the connections among units of an organization.
Peak appeal (**pk**)	A set of social positions in which a producer's offering has its maximal appeal.
Peripheral position (PER)	An organization occupies a peripheral position in a market if its fundamental niche does not intersect a market center.
Population (**pop**)	The organizational population associated with an audience segment's label or category is the fuzzy set of producers in the domain defined by their average grades of membership in the class or category.
Position ($z \in \mathbf{p}$)	A location in a sociodemographic space.
Principle of allocation	The "constant sum" constraint that increased width of a niche comes at the expense of lowered appeal at some positions.
Producer	An organization or individual who produces material products or services.
Prominent population (PR)	An organizational population with a high level of contrast.
Realized niche (**r**)	A fuzzy subset of the set of social positions with grade of membership given by the organization's fitness at a position.
Resistance (rst)	The occurrence of cultural resistance within an organization unit to imposed changes in architecture.
Rivalry ($rival$)	A pair of producers experience rivalry when both attempt to appeal to the same audience members at a time point.
Scale advantage (SA)	Condition in which the expected engagement of an organization in a class or category increases with its scale.

Schema (σ) — A kind of model (simplification of reality) that explains for a cluster, type, or category which entities are in, which are out, and the variations between these extremes. Formally, a schema is a subset of values of the features that the agent considers as relevant.

Schematization — The process by which a schema is developed.

Similarity (sim) — A judgment about the agreement/disagreement of feature values of a pair of objects.

Similarity cluster (CLUS) — A fuzzy set whose GoM tells the degree to which an object resembles the other members.

Social movement support (SM) — A social movement supports a label if all nonactivists apply the label to any object that the set of activists assign the label and each nonactivist treats as a default that the producer satisfies her schema for the label whenever the set of activists agree in assigning the label.

Support of a fuzzy set (supp) — The classical set that consists of the elements in a fuzzy set for which the grade of membership in the set is positive.

Taken-for-grantedness (g) — Broad and strong reliance on defaults. The use of defaults for the members of a category indicates the onlooker takes for granted the existence of the category.

Test code (TST) — A set of feature values that an agent checks to assess a producer's fit to his schema for a label such that observed fit on the test code leads the agent to treat as a default that the producer's feature values satisfy the rest of the schema.

Type ($\langle l, \sigma^l \rangle$) — An association of a label and a schema.

Unit centrality (cen) — A unit in an organization is central to the extent that it constrains units that are themselves central.

Viscosity (η) — The expected time it takes for an organizational unit to respond to induced architectural code violations and bring local architecture into code conformity.

Appendix B

Glossary of Symbols

Logical Constants

$\vee$	disjunction ("and/or")
$\wedge$	conjunction ("and")
$=$	identity
$\neg$	negation ("not")
$\rightarrow$	material implication ("if then")
$\leftrightarrow$	bi-implication ("if and only if")
$\Rightarrow$	logical implication
$\Leftrightarrow$	logical equivalence
$\exists$	existential quantifier
$\forall$	universal quantifier
$\mathfrak{N}$	nonmonotonic "normally" quantifier
$\mathfrak{A}$	nonmonotonic "assumedly" quantifier
$\mathfrak{P}$	nonmonotonic "presumedly" quantifier
$\boxed{\mathrm{D}}$	modal default operator
$\boxed{\mathrm{P}}$	modal perception operator

Meta Symbols

$\mathbb{N}$	the natural numbers
$\equiv$	equal by definition
$\longrightarrow$	(a function) maps to
$\hookrightarrow$	partial maps to
$\models$	provides a model for
$[\![\cdot]\!]$	denotation
$\sqsubset$	more specific than
$\sqsubseteq$	at least as specific as
U	universe of discourse
$\uparrow$	monotonic positive relationship
$\downarrow$	monotonic negative relationship
$\Uparrow$	delayed monotonic positive relationship
$\Downarrow$	delayed monotonic negative relationship
$\oplus$	composition operator for labels

Set-Theoretic Symbols

$\{.\}$	a (crisp or fuzzy) set
$\cup$	union
$\cap$	intersection
$\in$	classical set membership
$\subset$	proper subset relation
$\subseteq$	subset relation
$\setminus$	set subtraction
$\mid\cdot\mid$	cardinality of a crisp set
card	cardinality of a fuzzy set
$\langle.\rangle$	an ordered n-tuple
$\mathcal{P}(.)$	powerset (set of all subsets) of a crisp set
c	contrast of a fuzzy set
d(., .)	symmetric set difference for fuzzy sets
supp	support of a fuzzy set

Key Sets

$\mathbf{a}$	the set of members of the audience segment
$\mathbf{cas}(u, x, t)$	set of stages in a cascade initiated by unit u in organization x at time t
$\mathbf{ctr}(l, t)$	set of center positions of the market of population l at time t (partial function)
$\mathbf{f}(l, x, t)$	x's fundamental niche in l at time t
$\boldsymbol{\epsilon}^{+}(l, x, t)$	set of x's newly engaged positions with respect to class/category l at t
$\mathbf{id}(x, y, t)$	x's identity to y at t
$\mathbf{lab}(x, y, t)$	the set of labels that y applies to x at time t
$\mathbf{p}$	set of social positions
$\mathbf{o}$	the set of producers/products in the purview of the focal audience segment
$\mathbf{pk}(l, x, t)$	set of social positions at which x's offering has peak appeal in l (partial function)
$\mathbf{pop}(l, t)$	organizational population designated by a label l in an audience segment at time t
$\mathbf{r}(l, x, t)$	x's realized niche in l at t
$\mathbf{t}$	a set of time points
$\mathbf{z}^{+}(l, x, t)$	positions that organization x adds to its portfolio of engagement in l just after time point t

Key Predicates

AUTH(l, t)	the label l is authorized at time t
CAT(l, t)	l is the label of a category for the audience segment $\mathbf{a}$
CAV$(\mathbf{c}, \mathbf{f}(l, x, t))$	organization x's fundamental niche in l at t contains cavity $\mathbf{c}$
CCA$(\mathbf{f}(l, x, t), \mathbf{f}(l, x', t))$	the convex fundamental niche $\mathbf{f}(l, x', t)$ is a close convex alternative to the concave niche $\mathbf{f}(l, x, t)$
CENT(l, x, t)	organization x has a central-market position in market l at time t
CLASH(κ, κ', y)	code κ' is incompatible with code κ from y's perspective
CLASS(l, t)	audience segment $\mathbf{a}$ has reached agreement on the extension of the label l at t
CLUS(k, y, t)	k is a similarity cluster for the agent y at t
CM(l, x, x', t, t')	x and x' are full-fledged members of the prominent population labeled l at times t and t'
CROWD(l, t)	the market for population l is crowded at t
CVX$(\mathbf{f}(l, x, t))$	organization x's fundamental niche in l is convex at time t
DCOMP(l, t)	competition within population l is diffuse at t
DCV$(l, \mathbf{s}^l, x, y, t)$	y perceives that x violates the schema s^l associated with the label l at t
FORM(l, t)	l is the label of a form for the audience segment $\mathbf{a}$
INDUC$(\sigma(l, y, t), \mathbf{v}_i : \mathbf{w}_j)$	y induces satisfaction of $\sigma(l, y, t)$ from the replacement $\mathbf{v}_i : \mathbf{w}_j$ at t
M(l, x, t)	x is a full-fledge member of the population labeled l at t
MTST$(\sigma(l, y, t), \mathbf{w}_j)$	$\mathbf{w}_j$ is a minimal test for induction for y's schema $\sigma(l, y, t)$ at t
NC(l, x, t)	organization x has a near-center position in market facing population l at t
OPQ(u, u')	unit u' is opaque to u
PCAT(l, t)	l is the label of a positively valued category for the audience segment $\mathbf{a}$ at t
PER(l, x, t)	organization x has a peripheral position in market facing population l at t
PR(l, t)	the population labeled l is prominent (has high contrast) at t
RE(u, t)	unit u is reorganizing at t
SA(l)	the market for population l allows scale advantage
SM(l, t)	a social movement endorses the label l at t
TEST$(\sigma(l, y, t), \mathbf{w}_j)$	$\mathbf{w}_j$ is a test for induction for y's schema $\sigma(l, y, t)$ at t

$\text{U}(u, x)$	u is a unit in organization x
$\text{VET}(l, t)$	an authority vets the class l at time t

Probabilities and Hazards

$\delta(u, x, t)$	hazard of unit u in organization x initiating change at t
$\Delta(x, t)$	hazard of organization x initiating change at t
$\eta(x)$	viscosity: the expected duration of an induced violation of an architectural code for a unit in x
κ_x	probability that organization x misses an opportunity while not in reorganization
$\tilde{\kappa}_x$	excess probability that organization x misses an opportunity due to reorganization
$\lambda(l, t)$	hazard of entry or founding in l at t
π_x	probability that a change in a unit will trigger further changes in subordinate units
$\psi(u, x, t)$	hazard of the arrival of opportunities to unit u in x at t
$\Psi(x, t)$	hazard of the arrival of opportunities to organization x at t
$\omega(x, t)$	hazard of mortality of x at t
$\Omega(x, t, t')$	integrated hazard of mortality of x over the interval $[t, t')$

Grade-of-Membership Functions

$\gamma(l, z, t)$	GoM specifying the niche of category l
$\epsilon(l, x, z, t)$	relative engagement in l of organization x at position z at t
$\zeta(l, x, z, t)$	GoM specifying x's fundamental niche in l at t
$\mu_k(x, y, t)$	GoM of x in the cluster k assigned by agent y at t
$\mu_{e(l)}(x, y, t)$	GoM of x in the extension of the label l for the perspective of agent y at t
$\mu_{i(l)}(x, y, t)$	GoM of x in the intension of the label l from the perspective of agent y at t
$\bar{\mu}_{p(l)}(x, y, t)$	GoM of x in the population l as perceived by agent y at t
$\nu_{e(l)}(y, t)$	agent y's GoM in the extensional consensus about the label l
$\nu_{i(l)}(y, t)$	agent y's GoM in the intensional consensus about the label l at t

$\rho(l, y, z, t)$	GoM of y in the typical taste for l at a position z at t
$\tau(l, x, z, t)$	intrinsic local appeal in l of producer x at position z at t
$\phi(l, x, z, t)$	organization x's relative fitness in l at position z at t
$\Phi(l, x, t)$	organization x's overall fitness in l at t

Other Functions

$a(x, t)$	age of organization x at time t
$A(x)$	level of asperity of organization x
$ap(l, x, y, t)$	actual appeal of offering x to y in the market for l at t
$Ap(l, x, t)$	total actual appeal of the offering x in the market for l at t
$\widehat{ap}(l, x, y, t)$	intrinsic appeal of producer x's offering to y in the market for l at t
$asp(u, x)$	level of asperity of unit u in organization x
$\mathbf{B}(x)$	matrix of architectural relations in x
$\mathbf{B}_u^*(x)$	matrix of architectural relations from u's vantage point
β_j	expected duration of reorganization in a condition specified by j
$c_k(y, t)$	contrast of the fuzzy set k as perceived by agent y at t
$\bar{c}_{p(l)}(t)$	the average contrast of the population l to an audience segment at t
$cap(l, x, t)$	capability of x in population l at t
$cen(u, x)$	centrality of u in organization x
$cen^*(u, x)$	(partially) obscured centrality scores of u in organization x
$ch(u, x, t)$	unit u in organization x induces an architectural change at t (= 1; 0 otherwise)
$Ch(x, t)$	organization x experiences an architectural change at t (= 1; 0 otherwise)
$comp(l, x, x', y, t)$	competitive pressure exerted by x' on x for attention from y in the market for l at t
$Comp(l, x, t)$	competitive pressure experienced by x in the market for l at t
$cul(u, x, t)$	the level of cultural agreement about architecture among the members of unit u organization x at t
$d(u, x, t)$	duration of an uninterrupted spell of reorganization in u in x from a spell that started at t
$D(x, t)$	total amount of reorganization time in a cascade in x beginning at t
$D^*(u, x, t)$	foreseen length of the cascade beginning at t from the vantage of u in x

$d\_\mathbf{f}$	distance from the nearest position in the fundamental niche
$d\_\mathbf{pk}$	distance from the nearest position in a set of positions of peak appeal
$dcv(l, y, t, t')$	the number of violations of the default code associated with the label l that y perceives in the interval $[t, t']$
$dis(z_1, z_2)$	social distance between positions z_1 and z_2
$dow(l, x, t)$	the level of endowment of x in population l at t
$ec(l, t)$	the level of extensional consensus about the label l in the audience segment at t
$en(l, x, z, t)$	x's level of engagement at position z
$ex(l, y, y', t)$	the level of extensional agreement about the label l for a pair of agents y and y' at t
$g(l, x, y, t)$	the degree to which y takes for granted that x's feature values conform to y's schema for l at t
$G(l, y, t)$	the degree to which agent y takes for granted that bearers of the label l conform to his schema for l at t
$\theta(l, z, t)$	potential demand for the offerings of prototypical members of category l at position z at time t
$I(x)$	intricacy of x's design
$I^*(x)$	partially obscured intricacy of x's design
$ic(l, t)$	strength of the intensional consensus about the label l in the audience segment at t
$im(x, t)$	the level of immunity of x to mortality at time t
$is(\sigma, \sigma')$	the fraction of the patterns of feature values that satisfy the schema σ that also satisfy σ'
$L(l, t)$	legitimation of the label l to the audience segment **a** at t
$l\_ap(l, z, t)$	the share of total appeal to a full-fledged member of the class/category l at the position z at t
$M(x, s, t)$	number of opportunities missed by organization x during $[s, t)$
$miss(u, t)$	the unit u misses an opportunity at t ($\{0,1\}$)
$n_k(y, t)$	density of the fuzzy set k as perceived by agent y at t
$\bar{n}_{p(l)}(t)$	density of the population l to an audience segment at t
$O(x)$	opacity of organization x's
$ob(l, x, t)$	obsolescence of x in population l at t
$op(u, x)$	opacity of the organization x from unit u's perspective
$ov(l, x, x', t)$	thickness of the overlap of the niche with respect to the label l of x' on x at t
$Ov(l, x, t)$	total thickness of niche overlaps with respect to the label l for x
$pos(y)$	social position of audience member y
$miss(u, t)$	unit u misses an opportunity at t
$rival(l, x, x', y, t)$	x encounters x' as a rival for y in the category l at t (= 1; 0 otherwise)

$rst(u, t)$	cultural resistance to a change in unit u at t (= 1; 0 otherwise)
$s(l, x, t)$	scale of organization x in l at t
$\sigma(l, y, t)$	y's schema for the label l at t
$s\_ov(l, x, x', t)$	scale-weighted thickness of the overlap of the niche with respect to the label l of x' on x at t
$s\_Ov(l, x, t)$	total scale-weighted thickness of niche overlaps with respect to the label l for x
$\bar{s}^c(l, t)$	average scale of organizations in the center of the market for population l at t
$\bar{s}^{nc}(l, t)$	average scale of organizations in the near-center of the market for population l
$s\_Ov(l, x, t)$	x's scale-weighted total niche overlap in l at t
$sim(x, x', t)$	degree to which an agent perceives x as being similar to x' at t
$strict(u, y)$	probability that a random architectural change in the unit u violates the code of member y
$T(x, t)$	temporal span of a random cascade in organization x at t
U_x	number of units in organization x
$V(x, t)$	number of induced violations in a cascade with random origin in organization x at t
$V^*(u, x, t)$	number of induced violations in a cascade initiated by unit u in organization x that can be foreseen by the relevant actors u at t
$vl(u_i, u_j, x, t)$	unit u_j experiences a violation of new architectural code induced by unit u_i in x at t (= 1; 0 otherwise)
$w(l, x, z, t)$	maximal waiting time for gaining nonzero expected local appeal in class/category l at a newly engaged position z for organization x at t
$wd\{\cdot\}$	width of a set of positions in a niche

Appendix C

Some Elementary First-Order Logic

This appendix sketches some basic elements of classical first-order logic (FOL).[1] It is intended to provide some background for appreciating the formal arguments presented in the book.

BUILDING THE LANGUAGE

Standard definitions require that a logic system be coherent and systematic. For coherence, a suitable logic must respect the following consideration: the conclusion of a sound inference should not imply anything that the premises of the inference do not already imply. In other words, a logic should not generate information—its role is to make information explicit.

To be systematic, a logic should be based on a clearly defined set of grammatical categories; and a systematic account of sound argumentation should respect these grammatical categories. We add one requirement: a suitable logic has to be symbolic (formal). Whether or not the premises imply a conclusion should depend only on the formal structure of the premises (and the conclusion). In other words, it must be possible to assess the soundness of the argument independent of the substantive content of the premises and the conclusion.

What defines a suitable logic? Logicians argue that any specification of a logic should start with a definition of a formal language. A logic's intended task determines what kind of expressive power the language should possess as well as how the language expresses what it does.

This section sketches the language of first-order logic (FOL). Logicians customarily refer to the well-formed (declarative) sentences of a formal language as the *well-formed formulas*, wff, for short. So we describe the language of the logic by spelling out the properties of its wff.

Logical Equivalence

Languages generally allow alternative sentences to have identical meaning. In logic, this possibility is called logical equivalence. The formulas ϕ and ψ are logically equivalent, in formal terms $\phi \Leftrightarrow \psi$, if and only if (iff) they are true under exactly the same circumstances (and, therefore, false under the same circumstances).

[1] More expansive, accessible treatments of this subject can be found in Barwise and Etchemendy (1999) and Gamut (1991a).

Terms

First-order logic deals with a world that is called a universe of discourse, denoted by U. The universe is a nonempty set that contains the objects of interest. There are two ways to refer to the elements of the universe of discourse. Some of these elements have proper names. In the language of FOL these names are called individual constants. These expressions are called constants because they refer to the very same objects in all contexts. The set of individual constants is at most countable.

The other way to refer to the elements of the universe of discourse is to use variables. In logic, variables are the formal counterparts of pronouns. Their reference is context dependent (as opposed to the fixed reference of the individual constants). Variables are often used in contexts of quantified formulas. The reference of a variable is only fixed within the scope of a quantifier. For technical reasons it is important that the language of FOL contain countably infinitely many variables.[2] The individual constants and (individual) variables together are called terms.

Predicates

The language of FOL has expressions for properties and relations. On the level of the grammar, a property is a so-called functor, an operator that takes a name and gives a formula. Some of the properties should be given in the dictionary of this formal language, just as ordinary English provides a list of intransitive verbs, which includes expressions such as "runs" and "smiles."

Relational expressions have a common grammatical characteristic: they take names and produce properties or other relations. Think of the related category of transitive verbs in English and other natural languages. For example, "loves" is a transitive verb. Whenever we feed it a name (such as Romeo), it outputs an expression, e.g., "loves Romeo" (a property that was allegedly true of Juliet).

Logicians generalize over these considerations and use the term *predicate* to refer to both properties and relations. Different predicates accept different numbers of names as input. The number of terms that a predicate takes is called its arity; and the terms that a predicate takes are called its arguments. Now, provided that the dictionary of the language gives us some names (in the logical jargon, these are called individual constants), we can create formulæ. An n-argument predicate "filled" with n names is called a *formula.* $\text{UNIVERSITY}(Oxford)$ is a formula, for instance.

The language of FOL contains a special two-argument predicate, denoted by $=$, that expresses that two terms refer to the same object. This predicate is called the *identity relation.* A formula formed of two names and the $=$ symbol is true if and only if the terms on the two sides of $=$ refer to the very same entity.

[2]This might be surprising, since any formula contains only finitely many of the variables. Nonetheless, constraining the number of variables to any finite number actually yields a different logic.

Functions

Functions are ordered $n+1$-tuples. A function filled with an appropriate number of terms creates a complex name. (This is just as in ordinary arithmetic, $+$ is a two-place function, i.e., the three-tuple: $(3, 8, 11) \in +$ is often written as $3 + 8 = 11$. The interpretation of $3+8$ is as a complex name for 11.) In general we could define the function $sum(x, y)$ as the set of ordered triples such that the first element is x, the second is y, and the third is the sum of x and y (written in arithmetic as $x + y$).

Functions, like predicates, differ in the number of terms that they take. So arity applies to the function constants as well. We use of the three-place function $a(l, x, t)$ that tells the age of the entity x at time point t in the organizational population l. This function is a four-tuple and maps from ordered triplets of entities, $\langle l, x, t\rangle$, to the nonnegative real numbers. As in this example, we write functions as lowercase strings to help distinguish them from predicates.

Logical Constants

The language of the logic also contains expressions that have a fixed meaning over contexts (their meaning does not have to be interpreted). These expressions are called the logical constants. The language of FOL can be constructed with the following four logical constants.

Negation

The language expresses the fact that an entity does not possess a property or that a relation does not hold with a prefix symbol $\neg$, called negation.

Conjunction

The logical constant $\wedge$, called conjunction, expresses the fact that two formulas are true simultaneously.

Disjunction

The formula $(\phi \vee \psi)$, called the disjunction of ϕ and ψ, is true iff at least one of the terms is true, that is, $(\neg\phi \wedge \neg\psi)$ is false.

Material Implication

Things get more complicated when we consider conditionals. The most important condition is the material implication. We can define material implication in terms of negation and conjunction (or equivalently in terms of negation and disjunction) as follows:

$$(\phi \rightarrow \psi) \overset{def}{\Leftrightarrow} \neg(\phi \wedge \neg\psi) \Leftrightarrow (\neg\phi \vee \psi).$$

The definition given by the middle term has the advantage of using only the most basic operations: negation and conjunction. However, the definition on the right in the foregoing formula provides more intuition. It says that $\phi \rightarrow \psi$ is true iff either ψ is true or else ϕ is false, that is, if ϕ is true, then ψ is true.

Material implication captures the meaning of some conditional constructions in natural languages, and it provides a natural means for developing the simplest formal model of causal claims. A prototypical conditional construction has the form "If ... then ...." Other constructions can be a little harder to recognize. "... unless ...," "... provided, that ..." are also well translated as involving material implication. But what are the antecedents and the consequents in these implications? In the case of ϕ–unless–ψ, the formal counterpart is $\neg\psi \rightarrow \phi$; and ϕ-provided-that-ψ is normally translated as $\psi \rightarrow \phi$.

The symbol for the identity relation is often listed among the logical constants, because its meaning is always the same, it does not depend on the interpretation of the language. This is a property that the previously mentioned logical constants share with two more expressions of the language of FOL, the existential and the universal quantifiers, which we discuss below.

QUANTIFICATION

As we noted above, names are fixed labels for given objects. Variables merely point to objects in the universe. Therefore, they do not have a fixed reference. For instance, above we referred to the function for organizational age using $a(x, t)$. In this expression, x and t are variables, not names. There is no organization named x and no time point named t. The reference of these variables is not fixed by the interpretation of the language but rather by what is called valuation, meaning the assignments of these variables. Therefore the reference of $a(x, t)$ depends on the variable assignments.

When they need only a few variables, logicians customarily use x, y, z, etc. When they need more, they commonly use x', x'', etc. When they need a more systematic use, they conventionally use $x_0, x_1, x_2, \ldots$ as variables. The potentially infinite store of variables suffices to meet the requirement that a variable (in a given context) always refers to the very same entity.

In modeling substantive arguments, we use a somewhat different convention in labeling variables. We use an informal kind of "sorting" of variables such that the label of a variable tells what sort of variable it is. For instance, we consistently refer to time points with the variables t or t'. We refer to clusters using k, labels with l, organizations (and products) using x and x', and to audience members using y and y'. We introduce the various sorts as they become relevant. Use of this set of conventions allows us to simplify formulas, because we do not have to tell formally, for instance, that t in the expression $a(x, t)$ refers to a time point and that x refers to an organization.

The language of FOL contains an existential quantifier, $\exists$, which expresses that a certain type of object exists in the universe of discourse. This quantifier must be followed by a variable and a formula in brackets, $\exists x\, [\phi]$, to make a wff. (It is important for avoiding ambiguity to have a way to indicate the context boundaries for quantification. We follow the standard practice of using a pair of brackets [,] to indicate these context boundaries.)

The universal quantifier, whose symbol is $\forall$, can be defined in terms of the existential quantifier. The relation is that $\forall x[\phi]$ is true iff there is no object u in the universe of discourse that, according to the valuation v $v(x) = u$, makes ϕ false. . In other words, the relation between the existential and universal quantifiers is

$$\forall x[\phi] \Leftrightarrow \neg\exists x[\neg\phi].$$

THE WELL-FORMED FORMULAS

The official definition of a formal language tells what qualifies as a "grammatically correct" complex expressions, the wff. The language of classical FOL contains five linguistic categories:

1. logical constants,
2. nonlogical constants: individual constants, predicate constants, and function constants,
3. variables,
4. terms,
5. formulas.

Intuitively speaking, the logical constants are expressions that do not need to be interpreted. We opt for the following set as the (primitive) logical constants: $(,), [,], =, \neg, \wedge, \exists$.

Meaning (reference to the world) enters with the nonlogical constants. nonlogical constants (such as "age," "organization," and "large") require interpretation, because they might be interpreted differently in different contexts. The nonlogical constants fall in three important subcategories: individual constants (or proper names), predicate constants, and function constants. Individual constants (e.g. "Stanford University") are just like proper names: they always refer to the same entity.

The well-formed formulas (wff) can be characterized as the smallest set that satisfies the following conditions:

1. If a and b are terms, then $a = b$ is a wff.
2. If P is a predicate with arity n, and $a_1, \ldots, a_n$ are terms, then $P(a_1, \ldots, a_n)$ is a wff.
3. If ϕ is a wff, then $\neg\phi$ is a wff.
4. If ϕ and ψ are wff, then $(\phi \wedge \psi)$ is a wff.
5. If x is a variable and ϕ is a wff, then $\exists x[\phi]$ is a wff.

Note that this definition allows "official" contextual definitions of the other relevant logical constants as follows:

6. *disjunction:* $(\phi \vee \psi) \Leftrightarrow \neg(\neg\phi \wedge \neg\psi)$;
7. *material implication:* $\neg(\phi \wedge \neg\psi) \Leftrightarrow (\phi \rightarrow \psi)$;
8. *bi-implication:* $(\phi \leftrightarrow \psi) \Leftrightarrow ((\phi \rightarrow \psi) \wedge (\psi \rightarrow \phi))$;
9. *universal quantification:* $\forall x[\phi] \Leftrightarrow \neg(\exists x[\neg\phi])$.

The definition given above actually defines a *class* of languages, because the sets of individual constants, predicates, and functions generally differ from language to language (depending on the application). The user has to provide these sets of constants to get a language.

SEMANTICS

As we pointed out in the first chapter, FOL uses a *truth-functional* definition of the logical consequence relation. This section outlines the semantics of the language as a preparatory step. Although these abstract ideas are important in any attempt to use the language, they are not essential for understanding our substantive applications.

We want to formalize the idea that an implication is sound if there is no way that the premises can be true and the would-be conclusion is false. This task obviously requires a formal rendering of truth and falsity. The standard (Tarskian)interpretation of truth is the following: a sentence is true whenever the facts in the world are as the sentence asserts. Now this interpretation does not do much good for us unless we know, and formally represent, how things are in the world. Obviously this task that would require omniscience. Logicians have developed a less demanding, but still useful, approach to defining truth. The standard approach defines formal models of the language, i.e., (over)simplified versions of the world, and relativizes truth and falsity to such models.

Logical models of the language of classical FOL are *interpretations* of this language. This means that they contain just enough information to tell which wffs are true and which ones are false. Building an interpretation requires that one know what the individual constants denote and whether or not certain predicates are true of a (sequence of) individual constants. We achieve this later task by assigning sets of (n-long sequences of) individuals to the (n-argument) predicates, and we define the truth of the "$P(a)$" formula as follows: this formula is true in a model if the denotation of "a" is an element of the set that the model assigns to "P."

The standard formal model of meanings for this language contains just enough information to tell (1) the denotations (references) of terms, (2) what corresponds to function expressions in FOL, (3) which objects have given properties, and (4) which objects stand in given relations to one another. This information suffices to tell whether (or not) any wff is true in the world. [3]

---

[3]The definition of the formal semantics (the meanings expressed by the language) proceeds in four stages:

1. interpreting the nonlogical constants: individual constants, predicates, and functions,
2. assigning the variables,

Interpretation

If we wish to make claims about the objects in the universe of discourse (as any scientific theory must do), then the formal language must have a systematic way of connecting formal representations of these claims to the objects in the universe. The interpretation function plays this role.

The interpretation function of the language is an ordered pair: $\langle \mathrm{U}, \rho \rangle$, where ρ denotes the interpretation function. The interpretation function works as follows.

1. The interpretation of an individual constant points to an object in the universe of discourse, e.g., the interpretation of "Stanford University" is the object that bears that name constant.

2. The interpretation of an n-place predicate is a subset of the n-long sequences composed of the elements of the universe of discourse, called the extension of the predicate, e.g., the interpretation the one-place predicate UNIVERSITY(x) is the set of those objects in the universe of discourse that have the property "is a university."

3. The interpretation of an n-place function symbol is an ordered n-tuple of elements of the universe. For example, the interpretation of the "age" function $a(x, t)$ is the set of ordered triples in the universe of discourse such that first element is an organization, the second is a time point, and the third is the age of the organization at that time point. (Note that the universe of discourse has to be defined such that it contains the necessary time points and real numbers as entities, assuming that we treat time as real valued.)

Assignment

Interpretation connects the main vocabulary (individual constants, predicates, and functions) to the universe of discourse. But what about the variables? The so-called assignments give denotations to the variables. An assignment is a function, v, that maps the set of variables into the universe of discourse.

Denotations of Terms

FOL follows Frege's principle of compositionality, which requires that the denotation of a complex term depend only on the denotations of the components and how they are combined.

Truth-values of wff

The truth-values of wff are defined as follows:

---

3. telling (in general) what the terms denote, and
4. telling whether or not any wff of the language of FOL is true in a "model" (which depends upon the interpretation and valuation).

1. An identity statement is true if and only if the denotation of the two terms on the opposite side of the "=" symbol is the same.

2. An atomic formula is true in a model if its denotation is an element of the interpretation of P.

3. A negated formula is true just in case its not-negated version is false.

4. The conjunction of two formulas is true iff both conjuncts are true.

5. An existentially quantified formula is true iff there is an object in the universe that makes the nonquantified version of the formula true.

In applications, we must designate the universe of discourse, U. The universe is a nonempty set that contains the objects of interest.

LOGICAL CONSEQUENCE

The construction of the representation of logical consequence proceeds in two steps. The first defines the satisfiability of a set of well-formed formulas. A set of formulas, Φ, is satisfiable iff there exists an interpretation and an assignment that makes each $\phi \in \Phi$ true. The (ordered) pair consisting of an interpretation function and a valuation is called a *model* of Φ. (This property is expressed using the "models" relation: $\models$.)

The second step works as follows. The set of formulas Φ logically implies the formula ψ (in notation, $\Phi \Rightarrow \psi$) iff $\Phi \cup (\neg\psi)$ is not *satisfiable* (meaning that it does not have a model). In other words, ψ is a logical consequence of Φ iff any interpretation of the language and any assignment of the variables that make all of the elements of Φ true also make ψ true. That is, there is no way that all of the premises can be true and the *negated* conclusion also be true (given the interpretation and assignment).

Note that there is a logical connection between the logical consequence relation and logical equivalence:

$$\phi \Leftrightarrow \psi \text{ iff } \{\phi\} \Rightarrow \psi \text{ and } \{\psi\} \Rightarrow \phi.$$

PROOF METHODS

It is impossible to check all of the potential interpretations and assignments to learn whether one makes the premises true but the conclusion false. Modern logic features a more feasible task. Suppose, as above, that the proposed consequence relation links the premises Φ and the consequent ψ. Take the conjunction of Φ and the *negation* of the conclusion, that is, $\Phi \wedge \neg\psi$, and check whether any model makes this conjunction true. The inference fails if there is such a model; otherwise, the inference "goes through": ψ is a logical consequence of Φ (alternatively Φ logically entails ψ).

Of course, this procedure depends on the existence of methods for constructing systematically the relevant interpretations and assignments. Formal proof methods developed by logicians have the needed properties. Modern logic has developed a variety of proof methods, including the use of Venn diagrams, Beth tableaux, and machine proof. Standard texts introduce these methods.

The approach to proving proposed consequence relations has a very important implication. If a set of premises contains an inconsistency, then the combination of these premises with a proposed consequence (or its negation) is guaranteed to be inconsistent (unsatisfiable). In this sense, anything and everything is a consequence of a set of unsatisfiable premises, because the conjunction of the premises and the negation of the putative consequence will not have a model (but merely because the inconsistent premises alone do not have a model). Therefore, the consistency of the premises must be checked before attempts at proving theorems.

SIMPLE INFERENCE PATTERNS

Since at least Aristotle, the validity of arguments is often demonstrated by breaking the argument up to sound argumentation patterns, which logicians often call *argument schemata.* These frequently used argumentation patterns are also known as syllogisms. Here we mention only four of them and introduce their broadly used names.

1. *Modus ponens:* $\{A, A \rightarrow B\} \Rightarrow B$.

   To show that this schema is valid, we only have to show that there is no model that makes A true, B false, and, at the same time, $A \rightarrow B$ true. Now the only models that make $A \rightarrow B$ false are exactly the ones that make A true and B false, so none of them would make $A \rightarrow B$ true.

2. *Cut rule (or chain rule):* $\{A \rightarrow B, B \rightarrow C\} \Rightarrow A \rightarrow C$.

   To see the validity of this inference schema, we have to exclude the possibility of a model that makes both premises true but the conclusion false. If the conclusion is false, then A must be true and C must be false. However, if C is false, $B \rightarrow C$ is true only if B is false. Now from a similar argument we get that if B is false, $A \rightarrow B$ is true only if A is false, but that cannot be the case, because A must be true (if the first premise is true).

3. *Contraposition:* $\{A \rightarrow B\} \Rightarrow (\neg B \rightarrow \neg A)$.

   An easy way to see that $A \rightarrow B$ and $\neg B \rightarrow \neg A$ are, in fact, logically equivalent in classical FOL is to consider the circumstances under which both are false: just in case A is true and B is false. If they are false under the same circumstances, they also must be true (in a classical setup) under the same circumstances, so they must be logically equivalent.

4. *Modus tollens:* $\{A \rightarrow B, \neg B\} \Rightarrow \neg A$.

   Any monotonic logic warranting contraposition and modus ponens must support modus tollens as well. According to contraposition $\{A \rightarrow B\} \Rightarrow (\neg B \rightarrow \neg A)$, and modus ponens gives us $\{\neg B \rightarrow (\neg A, \neg B \Rightarrow \neg A\}$. The monotonicity of the logic allows us to combine the two arguments; and we get modus tollens $\{A \rightarrow B, \neg B\} \Rightarrow \neg A$.

We think that contraposition and modus tollens are intuitively problematic for scientific applications, as we explain in Chapter 6.

Appendix D

Notation for Monotonic Functions

Many of the assumptions and theorems in our formulations involve monotonicity statements. We simplify presentation of formulas stating such relations by adopting a notational shorthand. Suppose ϕ and ψ are functions defined for a label, an organization, and a time point. We can denote such a function in the following format: $\phi(l, x, t)$, where l is the label that identifies a population, x refers to a producer/product, and t is a time point. We will often want to compare the values of these functions for different organizations and time points but the same label (or for other sets of variables such as audience members, units of an organization, or social positions). We use the expression $\phi \uparrow \psi$ to indicate a monotonic positive relationship between the two functions, and we use $\phi \downarrow \psi$ to indicate a monotonic negative relationship.

More precisely, we use the following shorthand:

$$\delta^+(\phi) \leftrightarrow \phi(l, x, t) > \phi(l, x', t');$$
$$\delta^-(\phi) \leftrightarrow \phi(l, x, t) < \phi(l, x', t');$$
$$\delta^0(\phi) \leftrightarrow \phi(l, x, t) = \phi(l, x', t');$$

and

$$\phi \uparrow \psi \leftrightarrow (\delta^+(\phi) \rightarrow \delta^+(\psi)) \wedge (\delta^0(\phi) \rightarrow \delta^0(\psi));$$
$$\phi \downarrow \psi \leftrightarrow (\delta^+(\phi) \rightarrow \delta^-(\psi)) \wedge (\delta^0(\phi) \rightarrow \delta^0(\psi)).$$

The functions we introduce come with a sequence of sorted variables. We use the following informal sorting:

Variable	Sort
l	label
t	time point
x	producer or product
y	member of the audience
z	social position

Across all the applications the number of arguments of the function (its arity), the order of the variables, and the sorts of the variables remain constant. To take advantage of this consistency, we introduce the following notational convention to simplify the representation of the variables of quantification. Let f be a function with the appropriate sequence of sorted variables. (The letter we use to indicate the variable displays the sort.) Instead of spelling out all the variables we just use $\mathbf{q}$ to indicate the appropriate sequence of variables and use $\mathbf{q}'$ for the sequence of the "primed" versions of the variables. For example, if f requires l, t, x, y, z, then $f(\mathbf{q}) = f(l, t, x, y, z)$ and $f(\mathbf{q}') = f(l, t', x', y', z')$. Note that the variable l remains the same in $\mathbf{q}'$ in this example.

Many of our substantive claims express monotonicity claims about the relationship between different functions. To express these claims in a convenient manner first we establish the following convention. Let $\underline{f}$ be a function that works as follows

$$\underline{f}(\mathbf{q}, \mathbf{q}') = \begin{cases} 1 & \text{if } f(\mathbf{q}) > f(\mathbf{q}') \\ 0 & \text{otherwise.} \end{cases}$$

Definition D.1 (Notation for monotonic relations). *With $\underline{f}(\mathbf{q}, \mathbf{q}')$ given as above, the monotonic positive relationship, $f \uparrow g$, is defined as follows:*

$$(f \uparrow g)(\mathbf{q}, \mathbf{q}') \leftrightarrow \underline{f}(\mathbf{q}, \mathbf{q}') = \underline{g}(\mathbf{q}, \mathbf{q}').$$

The monotonic negative relationship, $f \downarrow g$, is defined as follows:

$$(f \downarrow g)(\mathbf{q}, \mathbf{q}') \leftrightarrow (1 - \underline{g}(\mathbf{q}, \mathbf{q}')) = \underline{f}(\mathbf{q}, \mathbf{q}').$$

These sort of functional relations usually appear in formulas quantified over the variables that appear in $\mathbf{q}$ and $\mathbf{q}'$. For instance, most premises contain, in the antecedent, the comembership relation in a prominent population: $\text{CM}(l, x, x', t, t')$. If $\mathbf{q} = \langle l, t, x \rangle$ and $\mathbf{q}' = \langle l, t', x' \rangle$, then we drop the variables in CM when it appears within the scope of quantification of $\mathbf{q}, \mathbf{q}'$. For instance, we write

$$\mathfrak{N}\, \mathbf{q}, \mathbf{q}' \, [\text{CM}(l, x, x', t, t') \rightarrow (f \uparrow g)(\mathbf{q}, \mathbf{q}')]$$

as

$$\mathfrak{N}\, \mathbf{q}, \mathbf{q}' \, [\text{CM} \rightarrow (f \uparrow g)(\mathbf{q}, \mathbf{q}')]$$

in such a case. We follow this procedure for other predicates and functions when it does not cause confusion.

We sometimes also consider monotonic relationships with some delay. We use the following notation. The delayed monotonic positive relationship $f \Uparrow g$ holds if and only if any difference between the f values of two organizations that is sustained for a long enough period results in a similar difference between their g values (provided that their g values were equal at the beginning of the period in consideration. To make exactly the comparisons we want to make it is important to introduce variants of variable sequences. The idea here is (just as in the definition of the formal semantics of classical first-order logic) that we keep the sequence of variables but change them at one place. A notational shorthand is useful: If $\mathbf{q} = \langle t, x, y, z \ldots \rangle$ is a sequence of variables and v is a variable, then $\mathbf{q}_y^v$ is the sequence of variables we get by substituting all occurrences of y in $\mathbf{q}$ with v: $\mathbf{q}_y^v = \langle t, x, v, z, \ldots \rangle$. In case of sorted variables, we assume that both the new (incoming) variable and the old (outgoing) variable belong to the same sort, so the replacement operation keeps the argument structure of predicates and functions intact.

Definition D.2 (Notation for monotonic relations with delay). The delayed monotonic positive relationship, $f \Uparrow g$, is defined as follows:

$$(f \Uparrow g)(\mathbf{q}, \mathbf{q}') \leftrightarrow \forall \mathbf{q}, \mathbf{q}' \, \exists s \, \forall t'' \, [(0 \leq t'' < s) \wedge (f(\mathbf{q})_t^{t+t''} > f(\mathbf{q}')_{t'}^{t'+t''}) \wedge (g(\mathbf{q}) = g(\mathbf{q}')_{t'}^{t}) \rightarrow (g(\mathbf{q})_t^{t+s} > g(\mathbf{q}')_{t'}^{t'+s})].$$

Similarly, the delayed monotonic negative relationship, $f \Downarrow g$, is defined as follows:

$$(f \Downarrow g)(\mathbf{q}, \mathbf{q}') \leftrightarrow \forall \mathbf{q}, \mathbf{q}' \, \exists s \, \forall t'' \, [(0 \leq t'' < s) \wedge (f(\mathbf{q})_t^{t+t''} > f(\mathbf{q}')_{t'}^{t'+t''}) \wedge (g(\mathbf{q}) = g(\mathbf{q}')_{t'}^{t}) \rightarrow (g(\mathbf{q})_t^{t+s} < g(\mathbf{q}')_{t'}^{t'+s})].$$

Appendix E

The Modal Language of Codes

In this appendix we provide a technical specification of the perception and default modalities. We provide the full technical details because, unlike the language of the nonmonotonic logic, this material has not yet been published.

We recap some standard models for modalities due to Saul Kripke (1959, 1963).[1] We spell out how our two modalities (perception and default) show up in this framework. Modalities come in pairs. (The paradigmatic example is "necessity" and "possibility.") It is always possible to define the dual of a modal operator as follows: If $\Box$ is a modal operator, then its dual $\Diamond$ is defined contextually as follows. If ϕ is an arbitrary formula, then

$$\Diamond\phi \Leftrightarrow \neg\Box\neg\phi.$$

If $\Box$ is the necessity modal operator and $\Diamond$ is the possibility modal operator, then this formula reads as "ϕ is possible just in case it is not necessarily the case that ϕ does not hold." It is obvious that

$$\Box\phi \Leftrightarrow \neg\Diamond\neg\phi.$$

(That is, "ϕ is necessary just in case it is not possible that ϕ does not hold.")

Kripke models of modalities use a set of possible worlds, W, and a binary accessibility relation R defined on W. We explain these constructions below.[2]

The formula $\Box\phi$ is true in the possible world w provided that ϕ is true in all of the possible worlds that are accessible from w. In formal terms,

$$([\![\Box\phi]\!]_{\mathrm{w}} = 1) \Leftrightarrow \forall \mathrm{w}' \, [(\mathrm{w}' \in \mathrm{W}) \wedge \mathrm{R}(\mathrm{w}, \mathrm{w}') \rightarrow ([\![\phi]\!]_{\mathrm{w}'} = 1)].$$

PERCEPTION AND POSSIBLE WORLDS

We use a version of modal logic to express formally the difference between facts and perceptions. A modality is an intensional construct. Representations of intensional constructs build on the notion of possible worlds. Although some extreme

[1]Gamut (1991b, Chapters 2 and 3) provides a very clear overview of these models and methods.

[2]When we talk about semantic values, components of a formal model (of a language), we actually use two languages: the object language, whose properties are discussed, and its metalanguage, which allows us to name both expressions in the object language and components of its models. Of course a full-fledged formal semantics establishes a homomorphism between the syntactic realm (expressions of the object language) and the semantic realm (the components of formal models). Here we try to reduce some of the complexity by using the following convention: we refer to variables belonging to the object language with italic letters; and we refer to the corresponding semantic objects with normal (Roman) fonts.

realists,[3] might argue that there is only one world—the actual one—it is easy to see that ideas about perception depend on ideas about possible worlds.

The social and behavioral sciences routinely assume that agents base their behaviors on their perceptions. This assumption matters only if perception and the actual world can differ in some way. There are (at least) two ways in which perception tends to differ from reality: partiality and inaccuracy.

Perception is partial *per definitionem,* as Tversky's similarity formulation assumes (Chapter 2). Partiality means that only some features of reality are observed. While any well-formed proposition must be either true or false in reality (the real world), the best one can say of perception is that it makes some propositions true, others false, and leaves open whether others are true or false. Therefore, perception leaves a number of options open. This kind of partiality means that perception cannot identify exactly what the actual world looks like. Even if everything that is perceived is true, certain facts might not be observed. The best that perception can achieve is an accurate circumscription of the world. Such a circumscription provides a set of possible worlds that contains the actual world; however, perception cannot tell which of the worlds in this set of possible worlds is the actual (real) world. The less partial is the perception, the smaller is the size of the set of (still) possible worlds. If perception were complete (and accurate), then the set of possible worlds shrinks to the real world as described by classical logics (and the sciences that depend upon them).

It would be overly optimistic to postulate that perception is always accurate. Sometimes perception might be mistaken, either because imperfect instruments are used or because of unavoidable distortions. If perception were total (not partial), then mistakes of perception would mean that whatever is perceived is not the actual world but a different possible world, which would be the case if the perception were accurate. In other words, perception paints a picture of a world, but it is not the real world—just a different possible world.

That the problems of partiality and mistakes get combined in any realistic account of perception provides an even stronger motivation for using the formal machinery of possible worlds in representing perception. Perception provides a set of possible worlds; and the real world might even be absent from the set. These arguments lead to the conclusion that if perception-based behavior differs from fact-based behavior, then constructing different possible worlds and specifying the relations among them is a useful exercise.

It will prove helpful to have a way of marking the distinction between facts and perceptions formally. The modal logic that we define below specifies that $\boxed{\mathrm{P}}_y\phi$ tells that "y perceives that ϕ (a statement in the factual language) is the case." What does this notation represent, some peculiar sort of higher-order formula? It is a *modal operator,* a special kind of a sentential operator. A sentential operator transforms sentences to other sentences. The special property is that the results of

[3]Leibniz first introduced the possible worlds in serious philosophical debates and got severely criticized for this by Voltaire in *Candide.*

the operation are closed under logical deduction.[4]

The modal operator $\boxed{\mathrm{P}}_y$ can be used to form expressions as follows:

$\boxed{\mathrm{P}}_y\,\phi$ "the agent y perceives that ϕ is the case";

$\boxed{\mathrm{P}}_{y},\neg\phi$ "the agent y perceives that ϕ is not the case";

$\neg\boxed{\mathrm{P}}_y\,\phi$ "the agent y does not perceive that ϕ is the case";

$\neg\boxed{\mathrm{P}}_y\,\neg\phi$ "the agent y does not perceive that ϕ is not the case".

The language of perception allows the audience to make and share similarity judgments on the basis of perceived properties. Such communication provides a potential basis for clustering within the domain. It is very important to note that clusters produced in this way are extensional. Any time that an organization first passes a similarity threshold and then enters the set, the composition of the set changes. The same thing happens when an existing member of the set no longer passes the threshold. In other words, contemporaneous membership defines clusters.

What an agent perceives obviously depends upon the context. Had the actual world been different, so too could be the perceptions. As we pointed out above, such dependence is represented with an *accessibility relation* in Kripke semantics. We model the perception modality by defining the accessibility relation R^{P}. The world w' is *perception-accessible* from the world w if the "real world" can be w' according to the agent's perception as represented by w. In this case, w' incorporates all of the agent's perceptions as facts and assigns truth values to all the propositions whose truth values are not determined by the perception. These perception-accessible worlds are the worlds that are still possible, given the perceptions (as accurate). In terms of the foregoing discussion, these worlds are those that lie within the circumscription marked out by perception.

What do we gain by interpreting operators as modalities? We see two advantages. First, we can use these techniques to build a theory of social codes, in large part because Kripke (1959, 1963) developed now-standard modeling techniques to describe the behavior of (most) modal operators. Kripke's approach works in terms of possible worlds and certain properties of the accessibility relations among possible worlds.

The second advantage is more technical. Modal logics typically are the well-behaved parts of otherwise very complicated logics. It is clear that we need a fairly complicated logic to represent facets of perception (as well as applicability and taken-for-grantedness, which we discuss below). Using modal operators, instead of general operators of the same class, allows us to avoid some undesirable (meta)properties in the logic.

---

[4]Formally, $\boxed{\mathrm{P}}_y\phi$ is a modal operator over the logic language L iff

$$\boxed{\mathrm{P}}_y\phi \wedge (\phi(x,t) \overset{L}{\Rightarrow} \phi'(x,t)) \rightarrow \boxed{\mathrm{P}}_y\phi'(x,t),$$

where $\phi \overset{L}{\Rightarrow} \phi'$ denotes that the fact that ϕ logically implies ϕ' according to the logic L. (For most cases this L is either classical propositional logic or first-order logic; but, in general, one can define modalities over any logic.)

ACCESSIBILITY RELATIONS

Above we introduced an accessibility relation: R^P. To model the defaults as a (□ type) modality we need another accessibility relation: R^D. First we discuss some of the formal properties these relations should satisfy. Later we show how these properties turn out to be helpful in demonstrating some of the formal properties of our models.

There are two properties that these relations must share to provide a realistic model. First, we want to rule out worlds that are isolated in the sense that no other worlds are accessible to them (in terms of the two accessibility relations). Therefore, we impose the following restriction on the class of acceptable accessibility relations.

Postulate E.1. *Worlds are not isolated.*

$$\forall R, w\,[(R \in \{R^P, R^D\}) \wedge (w \in W) \rightarrow \exists w'[(w' \in W) \wedge R(w, w')]].$$

A second important general consideration is that we do not want reflexive accessibility relations for either modality. If the accessibility relationship for perception is reflexive, then whatever is perceived is true. We pointed out above that this would be a ludicrous constraint on perception. The damage of allowing reflexivity in for the default modality would also be considerable; it would imply that taken-for-grantedness yields satisfaction. To avoid these highly undesirable consequences we postulate that both accessibility relations are irreflexive.

Postulate E.2. *The accessibility relations are irreflexive.*

$$\forall R, w\,[(R \in \{R^P, R^D\}) \wedge (w \in W) \rightarrow \neg R(w, w)].$$

THE DEFAULT MODALITY

We want to define the modalities such that whenever a member of the audience y holds as a default for an entity that a certain formula is true (e.g., that its feature values satisfy a schema) and has not perceived that this formula is false since it became a default, then it perceives that the sentence continues to be true. What assumptions do we have to introduce to ensure that this relation holds? To answer this question we have to define the time point that marks the beginning of (the most recent period) in which the audience member takes for granted that the sentence is true. A small complication is that there might be several occasions when the truth of a formula gains the default status, and perceptions that the sentence is false at some time point might take away the default status. Periods of perceived satisfaction of the formula might restore the status again.

Definition E.1 (The (most recent) beginning of a period of the default that a formula is true). *Let w and t be a possible world and a time point, respectively, and assume that y refers to an element of the universe of discourse such that*

$$\forall w'\,[R^D_y(w, w') \rightarrow [\![\phi(x, t)]\!]_{w'} = 1].$$

$$since_s(\boxed{\text{D}}_y \phi(x,t)) = \min_{w}\{s : \forall w', z\,[R^{\text{D}}_a(w,w') \wedge (s \leq z \leq t) \rightarrow [\![\phi(x,z)]\!]_{w'} = 1]\}.$$

Now we can state the formal assumption our model should satisfy to obtain the desired relationship between the default and perception modalities.

Postulate E.3. *Let w and t be a possible world and a time point as above:*

$$\forall \text{w}'\,[\text{R}^{\text{D}}_a(\text{w},\text{w}') \rightarrow [\![\phi(x,t)]\!]_{\text{w}'} = 1].$$

$$\forall x, y\,[\forall s[(since_w(\boxed{\text{D}}_y(\phi(x,t)) \leq \text{s} < \text{t})) \rightarrow \exists \text{w}'[\text{R}^{\text{P}}_a(\text{w},\text{w}') \wedge [\![\phi(x,s)]\!]_{\text{w}'} = 1]] \rightarrow \forall \text{w}'\,[\text{R}^{\text{P}}_a(\text{w},\text{w}') \rightarrow [\![\phi(x,s)]\!]_{\text{w}'} = 1].$$

Finally, we define the semantics for the two modalities as follows.

Definition E.2 (Semantics for the modalities: code frames). *Let $\langle U, W, R^{\text{P}}, R^{\text{D}}, \rho, v\rangle$ be a 7-tuple such that*

1. *$\text{U} \neq \emptyset$ is a universe of discourse;*
2. *W is a (nonempty) set of possible worlds;*
3. *$R^{\text{P}}, R^{\text{D}}$ are binary relations on W satisfying Postulates E.1–E.3;*
4. *ρ is an interpretation function from the set of nonlogical constants of the language of codes to $\langle U, W\rangle$ such that ρ assigns entities (elements of U) to individual constants in general and to y in particular, and assigns intensions to predicates, that is, if P is an n-place predicate, then*

   $$\rho(P) : W \longrightarrow \mathcal{P}(W^n),$$

   where $\mathcal{P}(W^n)$ is the powerset (set of all subsets) of W^n;
5. *v is a variable assignment, that is, $v : VAR \longrightarrow U$.*

We call this 7-tuple a code frame.

Now again it is instructive to show that this assumption guarantees that defaults really work as defaults in (say) computer science: in the absence of (specific) evidence to the contrary compliance is perceived. Another way of phrasing this is to say that defaults eliminate (perceptual) contingencies. This is indeed the case, because the following theorems hold in a code frame.

Theorem E.1. *Defaults eliminate perceptual contingencies: if an audience member holds a code as a default for an organization and has not perceived a violation of this code since the compliance with this code is taken for granted, then the audience member perceives compliance.*

$$(\boxed{\text{D}}_y \phi(x,t) \wedge \forall s\,[(since(\boxed{\text{D}}_y(\phi(x,t)) \leq s < t) \rightarrow \neg \boxed{\text{P}}_y \neg\phi(x,s))]) \Rightarrow \boxed{\text{P}}_y\, \phi(x,t).$$

Bibliography

Allmendinger, J. and J. R. Hackman. 1995. The more the better? A four-nation study of the inclusion of women in symphony orchestras. *Social Forces* 74:423–50.

Amburgey, T. L., D. Kelly, and W. P. Barnett. 1993. Resetting the clock: The dynamics of organizational change and failure. *Admin. Sci. Quart.* 38:51–73.

Amelio, G. 1998. *On the firing line: My 500 days at Apple.* New York: HarperBusiness.

Anderson, J. R. 1991. The adaptive nature of human categorization. *Psych. Rev.* 98:409–29.

Barnett, W. P. 1997. The dynamics of competitive intensity. *Admin. Sci. Quart.* 42:128–60.

Barnett, W. P. and G. R. Carroll. 1995. Modeling internal organizational change. *Ann. Rev. Soc.* 21:217–36.

Barnett, W. P. and M. Woywode. 2004. From Red Vienna to the *Anschluss:* Ideological competition among Viennese newspapers during the rise of National Socialism. *Am. J. Soc.* 109:1452–99.

Baron, J. N. 2004. Employing identities in organizational ecology. *Indust. Corp. Change* 13:3–32.

Baron, J. N., M. T. Hannan, and M. D. Burton. 2001. Labor pains: Organizational change and employee turnover in young, high-tech firms. *Am. J. Soc.* 105:960–1012.

Barron, D. N. 1998. Pathways to legitimacy among consumer loan providers in New York City, 1914–1934. *Org. Studies* 19:207–33.

____. 1999. The structuring of organizational populations. *Am. Soc. Rev.* 64:421–45.

Barron, D. N., E. West, and M. T. Hannan. 1994. A time to grow and a time to die: Growth and mortality of credit unions in New York, 1914–1990. *Am. J. Soc.* 100:381–421.

Barth, F. 1987. *Cosmologies in the making: A generative approach to cultural variation in New Guinea.* Cambridge: Cambridge Univ. Press.

——. 1993. *Balinese worlds.* Chicago: Univ. of Chicago Press.

Barwise, J. and J. Etchemendy. 1999. *Language, proof, and logic.* Stanford: CSLI Publications.

Baum, J. A. C. and J. V. Singh. 1994. Organizational niches and the dynamics of organizational mortality. *Am. J. Soc.* 100:346–80.

Becker, H. S. 1982. *Art worlds.* Berkeley and Los Angeles: Univ. of California Press.

Berger, P. L. and T. Luckmann. 1966. *The social construction of reality.* Garden City, N.Y.: Doubleday.

Black, M. 1937. Vagueness: An exercise in logical analysis. *Phil. Science* 4:427–55.

Blau, J. R. 1995. Art museums. Pp. 87–120 in G. R. Carroll and M. T. Hannan (eds.), *Organizations in industry.* Oxford Univ. Press.

Bogaert, S., C. Boone, and G. R. Carroll. 2006. Contentious legitimacy: Professional associations and density dependence in the Dutch audit industry 1884–1939. Presented at the Organizational Ecology Conference, Sintra, Portugal.

Boisard, P. 2003. *Camembert: A French national myth.* Berkeley and Los Angeles: Univ. of California Press.

Bonacich, P. 1987. Power and centrality: A family of measures. *Am. J. Soc.* 92:1170–82.

Boone, C., V. Bröcheler, and G. R. Carroll. 2000. Custom service: Application and tests of resource partitioning among Dutch auditing firms from 1880 to 1982. *Org. Studies* 21:355–81.

Boone, C., G. R. Carroll, and A. van Witteloostuijn. 2002. Environmental resource distributions and market partitioning: Dutch daily newspaper organizations from 1968 to 1994. *Am. Soc. Rev.* 67:408–31.

Bourdieu, P. 1984. *Distinction.* Trans. R. Nice. Cambridge: Harvard Univ. Press.

Brewka, G., J. Dix, and K. Konolige. 1997. *Nonmonotonic reasoning: An overview.* CSLI Lecture Notes. Chicago: Univ. of Chicago Press.

Brüderl, J., P. Preisendörfer, and R. Ziegler. 1996. *Der Erfolg neugegründeter Betriebe.* Berlin: Duncker & Humbolt.

Brüderl, J. and R. Schüssler. 1990. Organizational mortality: The liabilities of newness and adolescence. *Admin. Sci. Quart.* 35:530–37.

Bryk, A. S., V. E. Lee, and P. B. Holland. 1993. *Catholic schools and the common good.* Cambridge: Harvard Univ. Press.

Carlson, G. N. 1980. *References to kinds in English.* New York: Garland.

_____. 1995. Truth-conditions of generic sentences: Two contrasting views. Pp. 224–37 in G. N. Carlson and F. J. Pelletier (eds.), *The generic book.* Chicago: Univ. of Chicago Press.

Carroll, G. R. 1983. A stochastic model of organizational mortality: Review and reanalysis. *Social Sci. Res.* 12:303–29.

_____. 1985. Concentration and specialization: Dynamics of niche width in populations of organizations. *Am. J. Soc.* 90:1262–83.

_____. 1987. *Publish and perish: The organizational ecology of newspaper industries.* Greenwich, Conn.: JAI Press.

Carroll, G. R., S. D. Dobrev, and A. Swaminathan. 2002. Organizational processes of resource partitioning. *Res. Org. Behavior* 24:1–40.

Carroll, G. R. and M. T. Hannan. 1989. Density delay in the evolution of organizational populations: A model and five empirical tests. *Admin. Sci. Quart.* 34:411–30.

_____. 2000. *The demography of corporations and industries.* Princeton: Princeton Univ. Press.

Carroll, G. R., H. A. Haveman, and A. Swaminathan. 1990. Karrieren in Organizationen: Eine ökologische Perspektive. *Kölner Zeitschrift für Soziologie und Sozialpsychologie* (Sonderheft) 31:146–78.

Carroll, G. R. and Y.-P. Huo. 1988. Organizational and electoral paradoxes of the Knights of Labor. Pp. 175–193 in G. R. Carroll (ed.), *Ecological models of organizations*. Cambridge, Mass: Ballinger.

Carroll, G. R. and A. Swaminathan. 1991. Density dependent organizational evolution in the American brewing industry from 1633 to 1988. *Acta Sociologica* 34:155–75.

_____. 2000. Why the microbrewery movement? Organizational dynamics of resource partitioning in the U.S. brewing industry. *Am. J. Soc.* 106:715–62.

Carroll, G. R. and A. C. Teo. 1996. Creative self-destruction among organizations: An empirical study of technical innovation and organizational failure in the American automobile industry, 1885–1981. *Indust. Corp. Change* 5:619–44.

Carroll, G. R., H. Xu, and Ö. Koçak. 2005. Diverse organizational identities of newspapers: An empirical study of election turnout in American local communities, 1870–1972. Annual Meetings of the Academy of Management, Honolulu.

Chang, V., W. P. Barnett, and G. R. Carroll. 2001. Agilent Technologies: Organizational change (A). Stanford Graduate School of Business (Case OD–1A).

Chang, V., J. Chatman, and G. R. Carroll. 2001. Dreyer's Grand Ice Cream (A) and (B). Stanford Graduate School of Business (Case OB–35).

Cole, S. 2001. Why sociology doesn't make progress like the natural sciences. Pp. 37–60 in S. Cole (ed.), *What's wrong with sociology?* London: Transaction Publishers.

Coleman, J. S. 1964. *Introduction to mathematical sociology*. New York: Free Press.

Costello, F. J. and M. T. Keane. 2000. Efficient creativity: Constraint-guided conceptual combination. *Cognitive Sci.* 24:299–349.

Cyert, R. M. and J. G. March. 1963. *A behavioral theory of the firm.* Upper Saddle River, N.J.: Prentice Hall.

D'Andrade, R. G. 1995. *The development of cultural anthropology.* Cambridge: Cambridge Univ. Press.

Diesing, M. 1995. Bare plural subjects and the stage/individual contrast. Pp. 107–54 in G. N. Carlson and F. J. Pelletier (eds.), *The generic book.* Chicago: Univ. of Chicago Press.

DiMaggio, P. J. 1986. Structural analysis of organizational fields: A blockmodel approach. *Res. Org. Behavior.* 8:335–70.

——. 1987. Classification in art. *Ann. Rev. Soc.* 52:440–55.

——. 1997. Culture and cognition. *Ann. Rev. Soc.* 23:263–87.

DiMaggio, P. J. and W. W. Powell. 1983. The iron cage revisited: Institutional isomorphism and collective rationality in organizational fields. *Am. Soc. Rev.* 48:147–60.

Dobrev, S. D. 2001. Revisiting organizational legitimation: Cognitive diffusion and sociopolitical factors in the evolution of Bulgarian newspaper enterprises, 1846–1992. *Org. Studies* 22:419–44.

Dobrev, S. D., T.-Y. Kim, and G. R. Carroll. 2003. Shifting gears, shifting niches: Organizational inertia and change in the evolution of the U.S. automobile industry, 1885–1987. *Org. Sci.* 14:264–82.

Dobrev, S. D., T-Y. Kim, and M. T. Hannan. 2001. Dynamics of niche width and resource partitioning. *Am. J. Soc.* 106:1299–1337.

Dowty, D. R., R. E. Wall, and S. Peters. 1980. *Introduction to Montague semantics.* Dordrecht: Kluwer Academic.

Duhem, P. 1991. *The aim and structure of physical theory.* Princeton: Princeton Univ. Press. [originally published in 1906]

Dwyer, J. 2005. Once mighty, Catholic schools find status is diminished. *New York Times,* February 13, 37, 43.

Edelman, L. B. 1992. Legal ambiguity and symbolic structures: Organizational mediation of civil rights law. *Am. J. Soc.* 97:1531–76.

Edelman, L. B., C. Uggen, and H. S. Erlanger. 1999. The endogeneity of legal regulation: Grievance procedures as rational myth. *Am. J. Soc.* 105:406–54.

Fatsis, S. 2005. Sports Illustrated loses a key ruling. *Wall Street Journal,* July 18, B2.

Fichman, M. and D. A. Levinthal. 1991. Honeymoons and the liability of adolescence: A new perspective on duration dependence in social and organizational relationships. *Acad. Management Rev.* 16:442–68.

Fine, G. A. 2004. *Everyday genius: Self-taught-art and the culture of authenticity.* Chicago: Univ. of Chicago Press.

Fiske, S. T. and S. E. Taylor. 1991. *Social cognition.* Second ed. New York: McGraw-Hill.

Freeman, J., G. R. Carroll, and M. T. Hannan. 1983. The liability of newness: Age dependence in organizational death rates. *Am. Soc. Rev.* 48:692–710.

Freeman, J. and M. T. Hannan. 1983. Niche width and the dynamics of organizational populations. *Am. J. Soc.* 88:1116–45.

Frege, G. 1892. Über Sinn und Bedeutung. *Zeitschrift für Philosophie und philosophische Kritik* 100:25–50.

_____. 1893. *Grundgesetze der Arithmetik.* Jena: Verlag Hermann Pohle, Band I. Partial translation as *The basic laws of arithmetic,* by M. Furth, Berkeley: Univ. of California Press, 1964.

_____. 1903. *Grundgesetze der Arithmetik.* Jena: Verlag Hermann Pohle, Band II.

Fujiwara-Greve, T. and H. R. Greve. 2000. Organizational ecology and job mobility. *Social Forces* 79:547–68.

Gamut, L. T. F. 1991a. *Logic, language, and meaning,* Volume 1: *Introduction to logic.* Chicago: Univ. of Chicago Press. [L. T. F. Gamut is the collective pseudonym for J. F. A. K. van Benthem, J. A. G. Groenendijk, D. H. J. de Jong, M. J. B. Stockhof, and H. J. Verkuyl.]

_____. 1991b. *Logic, language, and meaning,* Volume 2: *Intensional logic and intensional grammar.* Chicago: Univ. of Chicago Press.

Goffman, E. 1963. *Stigma: Notes on the management of spoiled identity.* Englewood Cliffs, N.J.: Prentice-Hall.

Goldsmith, C. 1999. Investors are split over Reuters' identity. *Wall Street Journal,* December 20.

Greve, H. R. 1994. Industry diversity effects on job mobility. *Acta Sociologica,* Series A, 37:119–39.

Greve, H. R., J.-E. Posner, and H. Rao. 2006. Vox populi: Identity and resource in the resurgent micro-radio movement. *Am. J. Soc.* 112:802–37.

Guy, K. M. 2003.*When champagne became French: Wine and the making of a national identity.* Baltimore: Johns Hopkins Univ. Press.

Hampton, J. A. 1998. Similarity-based categorization and fuzziness of natural categories. *Cognition* 65:137–65.

——. 2006. Typicality, graded membership, and vagueness. *Cognitive Sci.* in press.

Hannan, M. T. 1988. Social change, organizational diversity, and individual careers. Pp. 161–74 in M. Riley (ed.), *Social structures and human lives.* Newbury Park, Calif.: Sage.

——. 1979. The dynamics of ethnic boundaries in modern states. Pp. 253–75 in J. W. Meyer and M. T. Hannan (eds.),*National development and the world system.* Chicago: Univ. of Chicago Press.

——. 1997a. On logical formalization of theories from organizational ecology. *Soc. Methodology* 27:145–50.

——. 1997b. Inertia, density, and the structure of organizational populations: Entries in European automobile industries, 1886–1981. *Org. Studies* 18:193–228.

——. 1998. Rethinking age dependence in organizational mortality: Logical formalizations. *Am. J. Soc.* 104:85–123.

——. 2005. Ecologies of organizations: Diversity and identity. *J. Econ. Perspectives* 19:51–70.

Hannan, M. T., J. N. Baron, G. Hsu, and Ö. Koçak. 2006. Organizational identities and the hazard of change. *Indust. Corp. Change* 15:755–84.

Hannan, M. T. and G. R. Carroll. 1992. *The dynamics of organizational populations: Density, legitimation, and competition.* New York: Oxford Univ. Press.

Hannan, M. T., G. R. Carroll, E. A. Dundon, and J. C. Torres. 1995. Organizational evolution in multinational context: Entries of automobile manufacturers in Belgium, Britain, France, Germany, and Italy. *Am. Soc. Rev.* 60:509–28.

Hannan, M. T., G. R. Carroll, and L. Pólos. 2003a. The organizational niche. *Soc. Theory* 21:309–40.

———. 2003b. A formal theory of resource partitioning. Research paper 1763. Graduate School of Business, Stanford University.

Hannan, M. T. and J. Freeman. 1977. The population ecology of organizations. *Am. J. Soc.* 82:929–64.

———. 1984. Structural inertia and organizational change. *Am. Soc. Rev.* 49:149–64.

———. 1986. Where do organizational forms come from? *Soc. Forum* 1:50–57.

———. 1987. The ecology of organizational founding: American labor unions, 1836–1985. *Am. J. Soc.* 92:910–43.

———. 1988. The ecology of organizational mortality: American labor unions, 1836–1985. *Am. J. Soc.* 94:25–52.

———. 1989. *Organizational ecology.* Cambridge: Harvard Univ. Press.

Hannan, M. T., L. Pólos, and G. R. Carroll. 2003a. Cascading organizational change. *Org. Sci.* 14:463–82.

———. 2003b. The fog of change: Opacity and asperity in organizations. *Admin. Sci. Quart.* 48:399–432.

———. 2004. The evolution of organizational inertia. *Indust. Corp. Change* 13:213–42.

Harrison, J. R. and G. R. Carroll. 2006. *Culture and demography in organizations.* Princeton: Princeton Univ. Press.

Haveman, H. A. 1992. Between a rock and a hard place: Organizational change and performance under conditions of fundamental environmental transformation. *Admin. Sci. Quart.* 37:48–75.

Haveman, H. A. and L. E. Cohen. 1994. The ecological dynamics of careers: The impact of organization founding, dissolution, and merger on job mobility. *Am. J. Soc.* 100:104–52.

Hawley, A. H. 1968. Human ecology. Pp. 328–37 in D. L. Sills (ed.), *International encyclopedia of the social sciences.* New York: Macmillan.

Hechinger, J. 2005. Battle over academic standards weighs on for-profit colleges. *Wall Street Journal,* September 30, A1, A6.

Hsu, G. 2006. Jacks of all trades and masters of none: Audiences' reactions to spanning genres in feature film production. *Admin. Sci. Quart.* 51:420–50.

Hsu, G. and M. T. Hannan. 2005. Identities, genres, and organizational forms. *Org. Sci.* 16:474–90.

Hsu, G., M. T. Hannan , and Ö. Koçak. 2007. Multiple category memberships in markets: A formal theory and two empirical tests. Unpublished ms.

Hutchinson, G. E. 1957. Some concluding remarks. *Cold Spring Harbor Symposium on Quantitative Biol.* 22:415–27.

——. 1959.Homage to Santa Rosalina or why are there so many kinds of animals? *Am. Naturalist* 93:145–59.

Ingram, P. and T. Simons. 2000. State formation, ideological competition, and the ecology of Israeli workers' cooperatives, 1920–1992. *Admin. Sci. Quart.* 45:25–53.

Jepperson, R. L. 1991. Institutions, institutional effects, and institutionalism. Pp. 143–63 in W. W. Powell and P. J. DiMaggio (eds.), *The new institutionalism in organizational analysis.* Chicago: Univ. of Chicago Press.

Kalleberg, A., D. Knoke, P. V. Marsden, and J. L. Spaeth. 1996. *Organizations in America: Analyzing their structures and human resource practices*. Thousand Oaks, Calif.: Sage.

Khessina, O. M. and E. Romanelli. 2006. Regional industrial identity and spatial arrangements in the U.S. biotherapeutics industry, 1976–2004. Presented at the Organizational Ecology Conference, Sintra, Portugal.

King, B., E. S. Clemens, and M. Fry. 2004. Learning to do education: The emergence of form in Arizona's charter schools. Unpublished manuscript.

Klir, G. J. and T. A. Folger. 1988. *Fuzzy sets, uncertainty, and information.* Englewood Cliffs, N.J.: Prentice Hall.

Koçak, Ö. and G. R. Carroll. 2006. Growing church organizations in diverse U.S. communities 1890–1906. Annual Meetings of the Am. Sociological Ass., Montreal.

Koopmans, R. and S. Olzak. 2004. Discursive opportunities and the evolution of right-wing violence in Germany. *Am. J. Soc.* 110:198–230.

Kovacs, B. 2006. Measuring grade-of-membership of organizations. Presented at the Organizational Ecology Conference, Sintra, Portugal.

Kratzer, A. 1995. Stage level and individual level predicates. Pp. 125–75 in G. N. Carlsson and F. J. Pelletier (eds.), *The generic book.* Chicago: Univ. of Chicago Press.

Krifka, M., F. J. Pelletier, G. N. Carlson, A. ter Meulen, G. Chierchia, and G. Link. 1995. Genericity: An introduction. Pp. 1–124 in G. N. Carlson and F. J. Pelletier (eds.), *The generic book.* Chicago: Univ. of Chicago Press.

Kripke, S. A. 1959. A completeness theorem in modal logic. *J. Symbolic Logic* 24:1–14.

——. 1963. Semantical considerations on modal and intuitionistic logic. *Acta Phil. Fennica* 16:83–94.

Kuhn, T. S. 1962. *The structure of scientific revolutions.* Chicago: Univ. of Chicago Press.

Kuilman, J. and J. T. Li. 2006. The organizers' ecology: An empirical study of foreign banks in Shanghai. *Org. Sci.* 17:385–401.

Lager, F. 1994. *Ben & Jerry's: The inside scoop.* New York: Crown Trade.

Lakatos, I. 1976. *Proofs and refutations: The logic of mathematical discovery.* Cambridge: Cambridge Univ. Press.

——. 1994. *The methodology of scientific research programmes: Philosophical papers.* Vol. 1. Cambridge: Cambridge Univ. Press.

Land, K. C., W. R. Davis, and J. R. Blau. 1994. Organizing the boys of summer: The evolution of U.S. minor league baseball, 1883–1990. *Am. J. Soc.* 100:781–813.

Laurence, S. and E. Margolis. 1999. Concepts and cognitive science. Pp. 3–81 in E. Margolis and S. Laurence (eds.), *Concepts: Core readings.* Cambridge: MIT Press.

Levins, R. 1968. *Evolution in changing environments.* Princeton: Princeton Univ. Press.

Levinthal, D. A. 1991. Random walks and organizational mortality. *Admin. Sci. Quart.* 36:397–420.

Lewis, D. 1973. *Counterfactuals.* London: Blackwell.

Loken, B. and J. Ward. 1987. Measures of attribute structure and underlying product typicality. *Advances in Consumer Res.* 14:22-6.

MacArthur, R. H. 1972. *Geographical ecology: Patterns in the distribution of species.* Princeton: Princeton Univ. Press.

Makinson, D. 1994. General nonmonotonic logic. Pp. 35–110 in D. M. Gabbay, C. J. Hogg, and J. A. Robinson (eds.), *Handbook of logic in artificial intelligence and logic programming: Nonmonotonic reasoning and uncertain reasoning.* Vol. III. Oxford: Oxford Univ. Press.

March, J. G. and H. A. Simon. 1958. *Organizations.* New York: Wiley.

Mark, N. 1998. Birds of a feather sing together. *Social Forces* 77:453–86.

McCarty, J. 1980. Circumscription—a form of nonmonotonic reasoning. *Artificial Intelligence and Logic Programming* 13:27–39.

McKendrick, D. G. and G. R. Carroll. 2001. On the genesis of organizational forms: Evidence from the market for disk drive arrays. *Org. Sci.* 12:661–83.

McKendrick, D. G., J. Jaffee, G. R. Carroll, and O. M. Khessina. 2003. In the bud? Analysis of disk array producers as a (possibly) emergent organizational form. *Admin. Sci. Quart.* 48:60–94.

McPherson, J. M. 1983. An ecology of affiliation. *Am. Soc. Rev.* 48:519–35.

——. 2004. A Blau space primer: Prolegomenon to an ecology of affiliation. *Indust. Corp. Change* 13:263–80.

McPherson, J. M., P. Popielarz, and S. Drobnič. 1992. Social networks and organizational dynamics. *Am. Soc. Rev.* 57:153–70.

McPherson, J. M. and J. Ranger-Moore. 1991. Evolution on a dancing landscape: Organizations and networks in dynamic Blau space. *Social Forces* 70:19–42.

Menzies, P. 2001. Counterfactual theories of causation. *The Stanford encyclopedia of philosophy* (Spring 2001 Edition), E. N. Zalta (ed.), URL = http://plato.stanford.edu/archives/spr2001/entries/causation-counterfactual/.

Merton, R. K. 1968. *Social theory and social structure.* Enlarged edition. Glencoe, Ill.: Free Press.

Meyer, J. W. and B. Rowan. 1977. Institutionalized organizations: Formal structure as myth and ceremony. *Am. J. Soc.* 83:340–63.

Meyer, J. W. and W. R. Scott. 1992. *Organizational environments: Ritual and rationality.* Updated edition. Newbury Park, Calif.: Sage.

Minkoff, D. C. 1999. Bending with the wind: Change and adaptation for women's and racial minority organizations. *Am. J. Soc.* 104:1666–1703.

Montgomery, J. D. 2000. The self as a fuzzy set of roles, role theory as a fuzzy system. *Soc. Methodology* 30:261–314.

Murphy, G. L. 2002. *The big book of concepts.* Cambridge: MIT Press.

Murphy, G. L. and B. H. Ross. 2005. The two faces of typicality in category-based induction. *Cognition* 95:175–200.

Negro, G., M. T. Hannan, H. Rao, and M. D. Leung. 2006. No barrique, no Berlusconi: Conflict and terroir among Italian wine producers. Presented at the Organizational Ecology Conference, Sintra, Portugal.

Olzak, S. and S. C. N. Uhrig. 2001. The ecology of tactical overlap. *Am. Soc. Rev.* 66:694–717.

Olzak, S. and E. West. 1991. Ethnic conflicts and the rise and fall of ethnic newspapers. *Am. Soc. Rev.* 56:458–74.

Osherson, D. N. and E. E. Smith. 1981. On the adequacy of prototype theory as a theory of concepts. *Cognition* 9:35–58.

_____. 1982. Gradedness and conceptual combination. *Cognition* 12:299–318.

_____. 1997. On typicality and vagueness. *Cognition* 64:189–206.

Park, B. and R. Hastie. 1987. Perception of variability in category development: Instance- versus abstraction-based stereotypes. *J. Personality and Social Psych.* 53:621–36.

Park, D. and J. M. Podolny. 2000. The competitive dynamics of status and niche width: U.S. investment banking, 1920–1950. *Indust. Corp. Change* 9:377–414.

Péli, G. 1997. The niche hiker's guide to population ecology: A reconstruction of niche theory using logic. *Soc. Methodology* 27:1–46.

Péli, G., J. Bruggeman, M. Mausch, and B. O'Nualláin. 1994. A logical approach to organizational ecology: Formalizing the inertia fragment in first-order logic. *Am. Soc. Rev.* 59:571–93.

Péli, G. and M. Masuch. 1997. The logic of propagation strategies: Axiomatizing a fragment of organizational ecology in first-order logic. *Org. Sci.* 8:310–31.

Péli, G. and B. Nooteboom. 1999. Market partitioning and the geometry of resource space. *Am. J. Soc.* 104:1132–53.

Péli, G., L. Pólos, and M. T. Hannan. 2000. Back to inertia: Theoretical implications of alternative styles of logical formalization. *Soc. Theory* 18:193–213.

Periera, J. and A. Klein. 2000. Returned Xerox chief cites more woes, including bad debts, hotter competition. *Wall Street Journal,* June 19, A3.

Peterson, R. A. 1997. *Creating country music: Fabricating authenticity.* Chicago: Univ. of Chicago Press.

Phillips, D. J. 2001. The promotion paradox: The relationship between organizational mortality and employee promotion chances in Silicon Valley law firms, 1946–1996. *Am. J. Soc.* 106:1058–98.

Phillips, D. J. and D. A. Owens. 2004. Incumbents, innovation, and competence: The emergence of recorded jazz, 1920 to 1929. *Poetics* 32:281–95.

Phillips, D. J. and E. W. Zuckerman. 2001. Middle-status conformity: Theoretical restatement and empirical demonstration in two markets. *Am. J. Soc.* 107:379–429.

Podolny, J. M. 1993. A status-based model of market competition. *Am. J. Soc.* 98:829–72.

Podolny, J. M. and M. Hill-Popper. 2004. Hedonic and transcendent conceptions of value. *Indust. Corp. Change* 13:91–116.

Podolny, J. M., T. E. Stuart, and M. T. Hannan. 1996. Networks, knowledge, and niches: Competition in the worldwide semiconductor industry, 1984–1991. *Am. J. Soc.* 102:659–89.

Pólos, L. and M. T. Hannan. 2002. Reasoning with partial knowledge. *Soc. Methodology* 32:133–81.

——. 2004. A logic for theories in flux: A model-theoretic approach. *Logique et Analyse* 47:85–121.

Pólos, L., M. T. Hannan, and G. R. Carroll. 2002. Foundations of a theory of social forms. *Indust. Corp. Change* 11:85–115.

Popper, K. 1959. *The logic of scientific discovery.* New York: Basic Books.

——. 1963. *Conjectures and refutations.* London: Routledge & Kegan Paul.

Porac, J. F. and H. Thomas. 1990. Taxonomic mental models in competitor definition. *Acad. Management Rev.* 15:224–40.

Porac, J. F., H. Thomas, F. Wilson, D. Paton, and A. Kanfer. 1995. Rivalry and the industry model of Scottish knitwear producers. *Admin. Sci. Quart.* 40:203–27.

Ragin, C. C. 2000. *Fuzzy-set social science.* Chicago: Univ. of Chicago Press.

Ranger-Moore, J., J. Banaszak-Holl, and M. T. Hannan. 1991. Density dependence in regulated industries: Founding rates of banks and life insurance companies. *Admin. Sci. Quart.* 36:36–65.

Rao, H., P. Monin, and R. Durand. 2003. Institutional change in toque ville: Nouvelle cuisine as an identity movement in French gastronomy. *Am. J. Soc.* 108:795–843.

——. 2005. Border crossing: Bricolage and the erosion of categorical boundaries in French gastronomy. *Am. Soc. Rev.* 70:968–91.

Romanelli, E. 1991. The evolution of new organizational forms. *Ann. Rev. Soc.* 17:79–103.

Romanelli, E. and O. M. Khessina. 2005. Regional industrial identity: Cluster configurations and economic development. *Org. Sci.* 16:344–58.

Rosa, J. A., K. M. Judson, and J. F. Porac. 2005. On the sociocognitive dynamics between categories and product models in mature markets. *J. Business Research* 58:62–9.

Rosa, J. A., J. F. Porac, J. Runser-Spanjol, and M. S. Saxon. 1999. Sociocognitive dynamics in a product market. *J. Marketing* 63:64–77.

Rosch, E. 1973. Natural categories. *Cognitive Psych.* 4:328–50.

____. 1975. Cognitive representations of semantic categories. *J. Exp. Psych.* 104:192–223.

Rosch, E. and C. B. Mervis. 1975. Family resemblances: Studies in the internal structure of categories. *Cognitive Psych.* 5:573–605.

Rosch, E., C. B. Mervis, W. D. Gray, D. M. Johnson, and P. Boyes-Braem. 1976. Basic objects in natural categories. *Cognitive Psych.* 8:382–439.

Ruef, M. 2000. The emergence of organizational forms: A community ecology approach. *Am. J. Soc.* 106:658–714.

____. 2004a. The demise of an organizational form: Emancipation and plantation agriculture in the American South, 1860–1880. *Am. J. Soc.* 109:1365–1410.

____. 2004b. For whom the bell tolls: Ecological perspectives on industrial decline and resurgence. *Ind. Corp. Change* 13:61–90.

Russell, R. 1995. *Utopia in Zion*. Albany: State Univ. of New York Press.

Sandell, R. 2001. Organizational growth and ecological constraints: The growth of social movements in Sweden, 1881 to 1940. *Am. Soc. Rev.* 66:672–94.

Sander, W. 2001. *Catholic schools: Private and social effects.* Boston: Kluwer Academic.

Schubert, L. K. and F. J. Pelletier. 1988. An outlook on generic sentences. Pp. 357–72 in M. Krifka (ed.), *Genericity in natural language.* Tübingen: Universität Tübingen.

Scott, W. R. 1981. *Organizations: Rational, natural, and open systems.* Englewood Cliffs, N. J.: Prentice-Hall.

Scott, W. R. and J. W. Meyer. 1991. The organization of societal sectors: Propositions and early evidence. Pp. 108–40 in W. W. Powell and P. J. DiMaggio (eds.), *The new institutionalism in organizational analysis.* Chicago: Univ. of Chicago Press.

Selznick, P. 1957. *Leadership in administration.* New York: Row, Peterson.

Simon, H. A. 1962. The architecture of complexity. *Proceedings Am. Phil. Soc.* 106:467–82.

Simpson, E. H. 1949. Measurement of diversity. *Nature* 163:688.

Sloan, A. P., Jr. 1963. *My years with General Motors.* New York: Currency Doubleday.

Sloutsky, V. M., Y.-F. Lo, and A. Fisher. 2001. How much does a shared name make things similar? Linguistic labels, similarity, and the development of inductive inference. *Child Development* 72:1695–1709.

Smith, E. E. and D. L. Medin. 1981. *Categories and concepts.* Cambridge: Harvard Univ. Press.

Smith, E. E. and S. A. Sloman. 1994. Similarity- versus rule-based categorization. *Memory and Cognition* 22:377–86.

Snow, D., S. A. Soule, and H. Kriesi (eds.) 2004. *The Blackwell companion to social movements.* Oxford: Blackwell.

Sørensen, J. B. 2000. The ecology of organizational demography: Tenure distributions and organizational competition. *Indust. Corp. Change* 8:713–44.

——. 2002. The strength of corporate culture and the reliability of firm performance. *Admin. Sci. Quart.* 47:70–91.

Sørensen, J. B. and O. Sorenson. 2007. Corporate demography and wage inequality: Vertical and horizontal sorting as sources of regional wage dispersion. *Am. Soc. Rev.* forthcoming.

Sørensen, J. B. and T. E. Stuart. 2000. Aging, obsolescence, and organizational innovation. *Admin. Sci. Quart.* 45:81–112.

Sorenson, O. 2003. Social networks and industrial geography. *J. Evolutionary Econ.* 13:513–27.

Sorenson, O. and P. G. Audia. 2000. The social structure of entrepreneurial activity: Geographic concentration of footwear production in the United States, 1940–1989. *Am. J. Soc.* 106:424–61.

Stinchcombe, A. L. 1965. Social structure and organizations. Pp. 142–93 in J. G. March (ed.), *Handbook of organizations.* Chicago: Rand McNally.

——. 1968. *Constructing social theories.* New York: Harcourt Brace.

——. 1990. *Information and organizations.* Berkeley and Los Angeles: Univ. of California Press.

——. 2005. *The logic of social research.* Chicago: Univ. of Chicago Press.

Strang, D. 1995. Health maintenance organizations. Pp. 163–82 in G. R. Carroll and M. T. Hannan (eds.), *Organizations in industry.* New York: Oxford Univ. Press.

Strauss, C. and N. Quinn. 1997. *A cognitive theory of cultural meaning.* Cambridge: Cambridge Univ. Press.

Swaminathan, A. 1995. The proliferation of specialist organizations in the American wine industry, 1941–1990. *Admin. Sci. Quart.* 40:653–80.

——. 2001. Resource-partitioning and the evolution of specialist organizations: The role of location and identity in the U.S. wine industry. *Acad. Management J.* 44:1169–85.

Swaminathan, A. and J. B. Wade. 2001. Social movement theory and the evolution of new organizational forms. Pp. 286–313 in C. B. Schoonhoven and E. Romanelli (eds.), *The entrepreneurship dynamic.* Stanford: Stanford Univ. Press.

Swift, J. 1906. *Gulliver's travels, and other works.* Exactly reprinted from the 1st ed., and edited with some account of Cyrano de Bergerac and of his Voyages to the sun and moon, by the late Henry Morley, L.L.D. New York: E. P. Dutton. [Originally published in 1726.]

Thompson, J. D. 1967. *Organizations in action.* New York: McGraw-Hill.

Tilly, C. 1986. *The contentious French.* Cambridge: Harvard Univ. Press.

Tversky, A. 1977. Features of similarity. *Psych. Rev.* 84:327–52.

Uzzi, B. and J. Spiro. 2005. Collaboration and creativity: The small world problem. *Am. J. Soc.* 11:447–504

van Benthem, J. F. A. K. 1996. Logic and argumentation theory. Pp. 18–31 in F. H. van Eemeren, R. Grootendorst, J. A. Blair, and C. A. Willard (eds.), *Perspectives and approaches: Proceedings of the third ISSA Conference on Argumentation, Vol. 1.* Amsterdam: International Center for the Study of Argumentation.

Veltman, F. 1991. Defaults in update semantics. Technical Report LP 91–02. ILLC, Universiteit van Amsterdam

_____. 1996. Defaults in update semantics. *J. Phil. Logic* 25:221–61.

Verde, M. F., G. L. Murphy, and B. H. Ross. 2005. Influence of multiple categories on property prediction. *Memory and Cognition* 33:479–87.

Viswanathan, M. and T. L. Childers. 1999. Understanding how product attributes influence product categorization: Development and validation of fuzzy set based measures of gradedness in product categories. *J. Marketing Research* 36:75–94.

Wasserman, S. and K. Faust. 1994. *Social network analysis: Methods and applications.* Cambridge: Cambridge Univ. Press.

Watson, J. L. 1997. Introduction: Transnationalism, localization, and fast foods in East Asia, Pp. 1–38 in J.Ł. Waston (ed.) *Golden arches East: McDonald's in East Asia.* Stanford: Stanford Univ. Press.

Weber, M. 1968. *Economy and society: An outline of interpretive sociology.* New York: Bedmeister. 3 vols. [Originally published in 1924.]

Werning, M., E. Machery, and G. Schurz (eds.) 2005a. *The compositionality of meaning and content. Volume I: Foundational issues.* Frankfurt: Ontos.

_____. 2005b. *The compositionality of meaning and content. Volume II: Applications to linguistics, psychology and neuroscience.* Frankfurt: Ontos.

White, H. C. 2001. *Markets from networks: Socioeconomic models of production.* Princeton: Princeton Univ. Press.

Williamson, O. E. 1975. *Markets and hierarchies.* New York: Free Press.

Wittgenstein, L. 1961. *Tractatus logico-philosophicus.* translated by D. F. Pears and B. F. McGuinness. London: Routledge and Kegan Paul. [Originally published in 1921.]

——. 1953. *Philosophical investigations.* Translated by G. E. M. Anscombe. New York: Macmillan.

Zadeh, L. 1965. Fuzzy sets. *Information and Control* 8:338–53.

——. 1983. A computational approach to fuzzy quantifiers in natural languages. *Computing and Mathematics with Applications* 9:149–84.

Zelizer, V. A. 1978. Human values and the market: The case of life insurance and death in 19th-century America. *Am. J. Soc.* 84:591–610.

Zerubavel, E. 1997. *Social mindscapes: An invitation to cognitive sociology.* Cambridge: Harvard Univ. Press.

Zuckerman, E. W. 1999. The categorical imperative: Securities analysts and the legitimacy discount. *Am. J. Soc.* 104:1398–1438.

Zuckerman, E. W. and T.-Y. Kim. 2003. The critical trade-off: Identity assignment and box-office success in the feature film industry. *Indust. Corp. Change* 12:27–66.

Zuckerman, E. W., T.-Y. Kim, K. Ukanwa, and J. von Rittman. 2003. Robust identities or non-entities? Typecasting in the feature film labor market. *Am. J. Soc.* 108:1018–74.

Index